Fiscal and Monetary Policies in Developing Countries

The COVID-19 crisis has fractured the pre-existing structural rigidities and institutional fragilities in the economies of developing countries more than ever, necessitating a rethinking of fiscal and monetary policies, the main vehicles for relief, recovery and reconstruction.

This book examines the barriers to transformation in developing countries in the wake of the pandemic and analyses the paths to recovery based on an economic policymaking agenda. It juxtaposes fiscal and monetary policies and state-building from pre- and post-colonial periods to the present-day context. It employs an interdisciplinary approach and ventures beyond the well-rehearsed tendency to explain the state of developing countries by considering the experiences of advanced economies. The book utilises data on three levels: the aggregate level using world data, the single-country context with case studies and a cross-country assessment for comparative analysis. Further, the book critically assesses the relevance of different schools of thought and provides nuanced, thought-provoking theoretical apparatuses applicable to developing countries, as well as allowing the reader to undertake a country-specific analysis through the detailed historical country case studies undertaken in each chapter. Each chapter has a detailed and separate theoretical and empirical section for the ease of understanding of the key propositions in the book.

The book will find an audience among scholars and researchers alike, who wish to gain a deeper understanding of the formulation of fiscal and monetary policies, specifically in developing countries. For policymakers and policy advocates, the book will serve as the groundwork for monetary and fiscal policies in the context of developing countries, providing more relevant instruments for transformational pathways.

Rashed Al Mahmud Titumir is a professor in the Department ofDevelopment Studies, Faculty of Social Sciences, at the University of Dhaka, Bangladesh.

Routledge Studies in Development Economics

154 Gender, Poverty and Access to Justice
Policy Implementation in Sub-Saharan Africa
Edited by David Lawson, Adam Dubin and Lea Mwambene

155 Energy Sustainability and Development in ASEAN and East Asia
Edited by Han Phoumin, Farhad Taghizadeh-Hesary and Fukunari Kimura

156 A Quantitative Analysis of Regional Well-Being
Identity and Gender in India, South Africa, the USA and the UK
Vani Kant Borooah

157 Economic Liberalisation in Latin America
Gerardo Angeles-Castro

158 Migration, Remittances and Sustainable Development in Africa
Maty Konte, Linguère Mously Mbaye and Valentina Mazzucato

159 Developmental State of Africa in Practice
Looking East with Focus on South Korea
Edited by Steve Kayizzi-Mugerwa and Charles Leyeka Lufumpa

160 The Evolution of Economic Development in Africa
African Trade, 1948–2017
Francis K. Mbroh

161 Trade Liberalisation and Economic Development in Africa
Gift Mugano
Edited by Michael Brookes

162 Fiscal and Monetary Policies in Developing Countries
State, Citizenship and Transformation
Rashed Al Mahmud Titumir

163 Law and Development
Theory and Practice (Second Edition)
Yong-Shik Lee

For more information about this series, please visit: www.routledge.com/series/SE0266

Fiscal and Monetary Policies in Developing Countries

State, Citizenship and Transformation

Rashed Al Mahmud Titumir

Routledge
Taylor & Francis Group
LONDON AND NEW YORK

First published 2022
by Routledge
2 Park Square, Milton Park, Abingdon, Oxon OX14 4RN

and by Routledge
605 Third Avenue, New York, NY 10158

Routledge is an imprint of the Taylor & Francis Group, an informa business

British Library Cataloguing-in-Publication Data
A catalogue record for this book is available from the British Library

Library of Congress Cataloging-in-Publication Data
Names: Al Mahmud Titumir, Rashed, author.
Title: Fiscal and monetary policies in developing countries: state, citizenship and transformation/Rashed Al Mahmud Titumir.
Description: 1 Edition. | New York, NY: Routledge, 2021. |
Series: Routledge studies in development economics |
Includes bibliographical references and index.
Identifiers: LCCN 2021036356 (print) | LCCN 2021036357 (ebook) |
ISBN 9781032063461 (hardback) | ISBN 9781032063485 (paperback) |
ISBN 9781003201847 (ebook)
Subjects: LCSH: Fiscal policy–Developing countries. |
Monetary policy–Developing countries. | Developing countries–Economic policy. | COVID-19 (Disease)–Economic aspects.
Classification: LCC HJ1620 .A5 2021 (print) | LCC HJ1620 (ebook) |
DDC 336.09172/4–dc23
LC record available at https://lccn.loc.gov/2021036356
LC ebook record available at https://lccn.loc.gov/2021036357

ISBN: [9781032063461] (hbk)
ISBN: [9781032063485] (pbk)
ISBN: [9781003201847] (ebk)

DOI: 10.4324/9781003201847

Typeset in Bembo
by Deanta Global Publishing Services, Chennai, India

To my wife

Munira Nasreen Khan

Contents

Figures

Tables

Preface and acknowledgements

This book is about three variables: state, citizen and transformation in developing countries. It investigates the dynamics of economic policies, state and institutions and suggests necessary, sufficient and transformation conditions in developing countries, particularly post-colonial states in Africa and Asia. The book presents these variables and their analysis in relation to the necessary and sufficient conditions in a manner that is not ridden with numbers and mathematics but provides sufficient empirical evidence to support its claims to the inquisitive reader. It complements the ease of understanding by using summary matrices of the key points in the chapter, wherever necessary, to provide quick access for the policymaker.

The book takes a new approach to study economic policymaking through the use of institutions—formal and informal, past and present—to theorise the politico-economic structures in developing countries to comprehend the problems. It is based on the premise that transformation is rooted in the cooperation and collaboration of the state and the citizenry. The institutions form the sufficient conditions which are linked with the circular flow in the economy—stocks and flows of households and firms. The cause-and-effect relationships and directionalities between the variables will allow the drivers and triggers for transformational pathways to be determined.

In doing so, the book employs the notion of formal and informal institutions as sufficient conditions for transformation, and also the countervailing power in opposition to the dominant forces of collusion among self-interested, resource-dependent networks. Primarily, the discussion pertains to two main spheres: the production and distribution of rents and resources. Along the lines of these spheres, the book puts forth key hypotheses for growth and development in post-colonial states, using an amalgamation of old and new economic theories to uncover novel, innovative strides in the research on the economic policies and growth of developing countries.

The role of the state is envisaged as one that is primarily associated with the protection of three core values—liberty, equality and social justice. The state should therefore not be extractive in terms of resources and economic decisions concerning households and firms. In addition, the state should assume the key responsibility of strengthening formal institutions, allowing the economy to embark on a transformational trajectory.

Citizens form the basis of informal institutions in terms of the norms and values upheld in the economic behaviour of the citizenry. Informal institutions in developing countries are largely reflective of the power and political settlement status quo and hence determine the strength of the countervailing power against a coercive state that catalyses a concentration of capital. The rent-seeking nature of the political settlement has dismantled the formal institutions supposed to uphold the rule of law and property rights. The norms and values in society over the years have made citizens subject to discrimination, widening the alienation from the state while allowing clientelist networks to accumulate power and capital.

In addition, the pandemic has fractured the pre-existing structural rigidities in these economies more than ever, necessitating a rethinking of fiscal and monetary policies, the main vehicles for relief, recovery and reconstruction. The economic downturn warrants the need for deliberately targeted interventions in the form of fiscal and monetary stimulus to resuscitate a withering economy. Broken and incoherent parts of the broader system have been left exposed—the fractures have revealed the pre- and post-COVID-19 fault lines by exhibiting the efficacy of the state in combating a crisis and the role of citizenship in tending to the shortcomings in society.

The introductory chapter unearths the relationship between the nature of the state and consequential economic policies in developing countries, laying a suitable groundwork for the chapters to follow. The historical institutional analysis of pre- and post-colonial epochs, including the COVID-19 period, grids the transmission mechanisms of the realities between economic policy making and concentration of wealth and power and the differential access to markets and resources. State formation in developing economies has inherently led to the creation of rentier classes, whose primary goal is the accumulation of the factors of production.

The second chapter makes an attempt to understand the cause-and-effect relationships as well as the transformational conditions of economic policies and the alienated citizen–state relationship. The discussion posits that transformational institutions are key to a functioning market and state. It also questions the so-called apolitical approach of new consensus, neoclassical/monetarists and public choice theorists and establishes that fiscal policy is an overtly political process by demonstrating how decisions of state–citizens–firms are shaped by formal institutions, contingent upon informal institutions of norms (informal codes) and values (reproduced by society).

The third chapter argues for the importance of fiscal policy in under-developed countries, delineating a different objective than that of advanced countries. It suggests that, to achieve transformation, fiscal policy has to accelerate the rate of physical and human capital formation by expanding investments in public and private enterprises and by diverting resources from socially less desirable sectors to achieve full employment and the equitable distribution of income and wealth. During the COVID-19 crisis, the state–citizen relationship has been analysed by following state directives and the distribution process of fiscal stimulus to the productive sectors in the economy.

The fourth chapter demonstrates how productivity can be influenced by existing power relations, discussing the role political settlement plays in this regard and how the endogeneity of politics affects the advancement of the whole process. This chapter exhibits that productivity in factors of production—labour, capital and technology—are brought about through the endogeneity of political settlement or social property relationships and informal institutions, as understood in terms of the nature and distribution of power in a given society. In the context of COVID-19, developing countries may choose to use these instruments to boost productive economic sectors and induce an effective policy response to improve productivity.

The fifth chapter provides a new framework for understanding inequality while being mindful of the systemic escalation of inequality arising out of low returns on labour vis-à-vis capital (permanent systemic inequality). This chapter also demonstrates the factors needed for a welfare state in the trajectories of debates on the necessary and sufficient conditions for sustained and rapid improvements in living standards, exacerbated by the COVID-19 crisis. This chapter looks into people's struggles and aspirations for equality, human dignity and social justice and proposes a wide range of redistributive fiscal tools for translating those normative principles as a part of developmental needs and state-building.

The sixth chapter challenges the mainstream consensus concerning the money–inflation trade-off and the neutrality of money to present ways through which monetary policy exerts real effects on growth and employment in the long term. It then establishes additional channels through which monetary policy augurs credit to sectors that are crucial for long-term growth, employment creation and productivity growth. In order to recover from the economic slowdown due to the COVID-19 crisis, the chapter determines that monetary policy should seek to ensure that financial conditions are sufficiently accommodative to incentivise high-capital investments and deficit-financed spending. The transmissions under such a context are driven by variations in wages and employment outcomes in the real economy.

The penultimate chapter focuses primarily on the transmission mechanism of a sound monetary policy. The chapter argues that the dominant theories fail to clarify the inflation experience of developing states. It points out that structural and institutional weaknesses provide widespread opportunities for rent seeking in the production and distribution process, leading to higher prices for consumers. For this purpose, it exhibits how structural and institutional factors, both formal and informal, are linked to the inflationary process and how different objectives and instruments for monetary policies affect the situation.

The concluding chapter lays out the various aspects of monetary and fiscal policies in developing countries by conflating the outcomes of each chapter. The chapter integrates the propositions laid out in each chapter and summarises the relevant implications in constructing fiscal and monetary policies suited to the context of developing countries for their transformation, including those required for recovery and reconstruction from downturns induced by the COVID-19 pandemic, thus laying out an agenda for transformation to serve as a roadmap for the post-pandemic world.

I am thankful to the anonymous referees at Routledge for their insightful observations for the development of the book.

I wish to express my gratitude to my team of researchers at the Unnayan Onneshan—Wahid Haider, Adrina Ibnat Jamilee Adiba, Md. Shah Paran and Mustafa Kamal—who assisted me in research with unwavering dedication.

I have drawn inspiration from my mother—Rawshan Ara Begum—a teacher, a guide and a tireless beacon of light, hope and sustenance. My father—Prof. Dr. M Arshad Ali—has always been the first reader and critique of the manuscript. Gratitude to my youngest brother—Rashed Al Ahmad Tarique—for taking the trouble of copyediting the manuscript, despite his tiresome schedule in his busy life in South Australia. Three brothers, one sister and their families have been there for me through sickness and good health, laughter and sorrow, applause and empathy. My son, Muharrir Munir Arshad Titumir, wants to take it forward!

The book is a transient study of debates that are changing and evolving as we speak. This is but a humble contribution with hopes to inspire further discussions in the future. Meanwhile, I shall remain liable for any errors, shortcomings and inadvertences in the book.

Rashed Al Mahmud Titumir,
Dhaka

Abbreviations

ADB	Asian Development Bank
BB	Bangladesh Bank
BBS	Bangladesh Bureau of Statistics
BC	before Christ
BDT	Bangladeshi Taka
BEAC	Bank of Central African States
BOE	Bank of England
CEMAC	Central African Economic and Monetary Community
CMC	circulation of commodities
CMT	Consumer Monetary Theory
CPD	Centre for Policy Dialogue
CPI	Consumer Price Index
CRI	Commitment to Reduce Inequality
ECB	European Central Bank
EU	European Union
FDI	foreign direct investment
FPI	foreign private investment
GDP	gross domestic product
GED	general economic division
GFI	global financial integrity
GOB	Government of Bangladesh
HIES	household income and expenditure surveys
ICP	Investment Corporation of Pakistan
ICT	information and communication technology
IDBP	Industrial Development Bank of Pakistan
ILO	International Labour Organisation
IMF	International Monetary Fund
JDB	Japan Development Bank
MDG	millennium development goals
MITI	Ministry of International Trade and Industry
MNC	multi-national corporations
MP	Members of Parliament
NAIRU	non-accelerated inflationary rate of unemployment

NBR	National Board of Revenue
NGO	non-governmental organisation
NPL	non-performing loan
OECD	Organisation for Economic Co-operation and Development
OOP	out of pocket expenditure
PICIC	Pakistan Industrial Credit and Investment Corporation
PRSP	Poverty Reduction Strategy Papers
RBI	Reserve Bank of India
R&D	research and development
REHAB	Real Estate & Housing Association of Bangladesh
RET	Ricardian equivalence theory
RMG	ready-made garments
SDG	sustainable development goals
SEA	South East Asia
SME	micro, small, medium enterprises
SOE	state-owned enterprise
SSNP	social safety net programmes
TFP	total factor productivity
USD	United States dollars
VAT	value added tax
WHO	World Health Organisation

1 State-building and economic policymaking

Introduction

The book deals with the role of state in economic policymaking, particularly in developing countries. To understand the mechanisms and rationale behind policymaking, this book delves into a historical analysis of state formation and subsequent policymaking in developing nations. Economic policymaking, in the form of monetary and fiscal policy, is an indispensable part of the state organ. The effect of these policies is not just limited to traditional activities that shape an economy. The outcome of economic policies has influenced public choice in electing governments and political leaders as well.

The foundation of economics is still based upon the interaction between the agents of "production, distribution and consumption" as per the words of Jean Baptiste Say (1836), though economics has gone through various phases over the years as new ideas have been brought in to overcome any challenges. The basic idea of economics can be understood as the circular flow between agents, i.e., households and firms. As a concept, circular flow is not new; rather, it has been around for more than 200 years. The foundation of the concept was laid by John Law, and later works by Richard Cantillon and Francois Quesnay established the model in mainstream economics. John Law first devised the model based on an island economy. Paper money was circulated among three agents in the economy: landlords, manufacturing workers and farmers. Landlords used paper money to buy commodities from manufacturing workers (Murphy, 2009). The workers then used that money for buying food from the farmers, and later the farmers paid the landlords rent in money earned from selling the food. Later on, Richard Cantillon in his book *Essay on the Nature of Trade in General*, published in 1755, developed the model based on both the agrarian and the urban economy. Economic agents in his model were property owners, farmers, entrepreneurs, labourers and artisans. Circulation of money in the rural areas was very rare due to the barter system between farmers and property owners. Hence, Cantillon included the urban economy and incorporated labours and artisans to allow a circular flow of income and expenditure (Murphy, 2009).

DOI: 10.4324/9781003201847-1

Francois Quesnay has been credited with the idea of the circular flow of income, even though much of his model was influenced by Cantillon. Quesnay was the first to visualise the flow of economy among three agents: the proprietary class, the productive class and the sterile class (Murphy, 2009; Parto, 2005). A modern economy with more agents and intricate transactions can be explained by adopting the circular flow model. The circular flow model adopted in this book has three major agents: households, firms and government. Households provide the factors of production and receive returns on those factors from firms. This transaction occurs within a market. All the debates surrounding economics revolve around this transaction and the nature of the agents. For example, the classical school of economics hailed the idea of a free market, which was later adopted and modified by the neoclassical school. The neoclassical school believed that the market would determine the equilibrium from demand and supply and that there is no transaction cost. However, the failure of the neoclassical approach to take property rights and transaction costs into account resulted in the debate shifting towards institutions, both formal and informal, to explain market failure. The complex nature of interaction between the economic agents requires an understanding of the entailed institutions like rules, regulations, norms and values.

Institutions are an inherent part of market exchange. It is now an established fact that a market cannot function in the absence of institutions, and nowadays, institutions are entrenched in the economic system more than ever. For instance, it is an institution in the form of government regulation that prohibits the sale of narcotics or restricts child labour. Institutions have been categorised into two groups: formal and informal institutions. Formal institutions are the ones established by formal rules through government regulation, the constitution, formal laws and the legal system. The culture, norms and values of a society are considered informal institutions (North, 1990; Boettke & Coyne, 2009). Formal institutions are deeply embedded in the economic policies we see today. They set policies and regulations in the market so that one group cannot accumulate at the cost of others. Again, when someone or some group breaches the policies, formal institutions punish them through the legal system of the state. Formal institutions hence create an enabling environment for maintaining an equal and just economic system within society. Informal institutions, on the other hand, have often been left out of mainstream economic theories. While formal institutions restrict certain businesses and market exchange, it is the informal institutions, or the societal culture and norms, which shape the boundaries. Formal rules and laws can only work in a system when it is based upon the culture and societal norms (Posner, 1998; North, 1990; Hodgson, 2006).

The study of institutions became of particular interest in terms of economic policies when African and Asian countries that had been under European colonial power failed in their quest for economic development. Policies that powered the European states were implemented in these nations, yet they crumbled and only aggravated the situation over the years. The very transformational path that had worked for the colonial powers failed miserably in the countries they had ruled for hundreds of years. The failure of both the market and the government called for a retrospection of the policies. This failure in the South reinforced the idea that economic policies cannot work under the impression of a "rational economic being and society". Different societies take different paths in forming states, and hence indigenous solutions are required. State formation is important in this regard. Europe saw a rapid transformation from a communal state to a feudal state and finally a feudal state to a capitalist one. This transformation was reflected in its economic prosperity. On the other hand, the countries colonised by the Europeans took another path towards the formation of their present state, and this was strikingly different from the European one.

State formation depends on people's capacity to articulate and exercise power, which requires the existence of a vibrant civil society and strong democratic political culture (Haque, 1997). The colonial legacy of discouraging the burgeoning of a strong civil society is still prevalent in developing countries. As a result, accountable and transparent government has not been established yet. Rather there exist feudalistic social relations that perpetuate patron–client relations, creating barriers to the development of societal relations irrespective of family, race and class, which ultimately impede the formation of strong civil society. Thus, the common feature of feudalistic class and caste based social structures in developing countries prevents people from having a "social contract" that binds its citizens with the state. During the colonial period, the institutions of developing countries were established by the colonisers in order to extract resources. The politics, economy and administration of post-colonial countries are influenced by the colonial legacy. Most of the colonial arrangements are still in functioning that are extractive in nature. Colonisers were the exploiter. They created an intermediate class to perpetuate their rule over and exploitation of the colonies. The later politicians, administrators and policymakers in post-colonial countries have come from this intermediate class. Political regime is associated with a host of conflicts and confrontations amongst these classes. The rise of a new intermediate class during the post-colonial period has fuelled this conflict. The winning class always tries to suppress the other. The perverted competition of the intermediate class in terms of gaining economic and political power has left little room for the citizenry. The state fails to become a citizen state in the true sense. This absence of a strong state creates a despotic form of government whereby the state becomes omnipotent. This is one of the main reasons for the deep-rooted undemocratic political culture in most developing nations—in Asia, West Africa, Latin America and the Middle East (Haque, 1997). As a result, the state has become unresponsive to the public's demands and safeguards the interest of the ruling class. This ruling coalition is comprised of politico-bureaucratic-military oligarchy keeping the branches of the state—legislature, judiciary and executive—unrepresentative. As a result, a centralised government with bureaucratic authoritarianism and undemocratic culture is prevalent where the general populace remains excluded but the executive enjoys absolute power.

The economic policies have followed the extractive nature of the state–citizen relationship in developing countries. Ordinary people have no participation in policymaking. The policies are chosen by the political leadership since, in most cases, they enjoy absolute power. Often this leadership acts as benevolent guardians and make the policies based on their beliefs, leaving no room for ordinary citizens' participation (Krueger, 1994). As a result, the extractive nature of colonial structure has endured and society is still far from being a public society. The nature of both political and economic institutions in developing countries is extractive (Acemoglu & Robinson, 2012).

This extractive nature of institutions leads to policies that are also extractive and serves the interests of the powerful ruling class. As a result, ordinary people have remained excluded from the policies and the state, whereas the powerful group has become tantamount to the state itself. The economic features of developing countries include a larger informal economy, a widespread primitive accumulation process and the use of state power to create and dissipate rent amongst the powerful factions (Khan, 2005). The informal channel of transactions and the primitive accumulation process have created an environment of economic activities based on patron–client relations. A powerful group maintains and controls the economy. This network has a kind of absolute power in policy formulation, with citizens outside this group being excluded. This clientelist group uses the state's monopoly power to meet their vested interests. They formulate and reform the policies that fulfil their interests. Thus, the developing state apparatus has little connection with the citizenry.

Since the relations between state and citizen have not been based on equal power structures, undemocratic, authoritarian and despotic governments make the state policies that safeguard their regime. It is observed that the economically and politically powerful class supports the governments that set lower taxes but provide rents to them (Acemoglu, Ticchi & Vindigni, 2011). As a result, the tax regime in most developing countries remains regressive; ordinary people bear the major share of the tax burden, but upper-class, powerful people enjoy tax evasion and tax exemption as the norm. Besides, a major portion of government expenditure goes to unproductive sectors— such as salaries and allowances for public servants, which are unnecessarily large. Furthermore, in most developing countries, the tax–GDP (gross domestic product) ratio as well as the amount of income tax is very low. The government, in most of these countries, has failed to impose income taxes on high-income people. The powerful coalitions always want a state that provides all facilities to their establishment.

The COVID-19 pandemic has changed the world of economic policymaking to the extent that it will never be the same, far beyond any typical economic recession. This pandemic has caused a major disruption in the demand–supply value chain along with a closure of economic activities—mobility of factors from, and return to, households and firms—by governments. Moreover, the pandemic is a public bad, and the free-market system is yet to come to terms with such public bads. Employment has shrunk significantly because of the pandemic. As a result, income has been eroded, which damages the purchasing power of the population. Mass hoarding of essential products by the higher income population has created a shortfall and increased the prices of those goods. The healthcare sector in developing countries were already in a poor shape, lacking modern technologies and equipment. COVID-19 shows the potential for global poverty to rise further to the highest rate in comparison to the other recent global pandemics. To be exact, the number of people living in poverty may increase by 420–580 million (Sumner, Ortiz-Juarez & Hoy, 2020). On the other hand, the World Bank (WB) estimates that the population living in extreme poverty (income less than $1.90 per day) will rise by 40–60 million by the end of 2020. In addition, global poverty could increase by 8.23 percent to 9.18 percent. The World Bank predictions suggested that a global recession, triggered by COVID-19, might cost 70 percent of the employment in emerging and developing economies. The World Bank's prediction about global poverty states that 88–115 million will be added to the existing number of poor people (World Bank, 2020). Besides, the coronavirus fallout is predicted to be distressing and diversified. It has had a more significant impact on global poverty, unemployment, labour income, inflation and food security than any other pandemics in several decades. For instance, the International Labour Organisation (ILO) (2020a) estimated an overall loss in labour income between 860 and 3,440 billion USD and a rise in unemployment of between 5.3 and 24.7 million.

In light of these figures, the orthodox solutions will not work. With providence and prudence, the governments of developing states need to lead the response to this unmatched catastrophe since these states are suffering the most. The lives and livelihoods of citizens have been affected due to the pandemic and they are in need of government assistance. It is now a big challenge to trigger a new monetary and fiscal policy framework focusing on the citizens of the country. In light of the crisis, a new indigenous paradigm has to replace the existing one to overcome a "once in a generation" crisis. It would be unwise to assume that developing countries are facing such a mammoth task only because of the pandemic. The structural rigidity of developing countries was weak even before the pandemic arrived. Hence, the pandemic has only aggravated an existing structural problem, both in the economic and the political spheres. While citizens required government intervention to mitigate the losses from the pandemic and ultimately for recovery, governments failed to do so due to limited institutional capacity.

Extraction, alienation and transformation in developing countries

The state by itself is coercive in nature. Max Weber (1946) defined the state as the authority that has a monopoly on the legitimate use of power and coercion. The state apparatus includes the judiciary, parliamentary and executive branches, which all work in tandem to make a functioning state. Yet this only works when the citizenship remains strong with norms and values. A state can only function when the branches of the state and citizenship go hand in hand. A strong citizenship culture can hold the branches accountable and will not allow the state to become an extractive one. A weak citizenship only works as a catalyst to an extractive state. Hence, any destabilising force can be tackled with strong citizenship (Figure 1.1).

State formation plays an important role in shaping the type of institutions in a country. Informal institutions, including norms and values, are the outcome of the historical experience of countries. The norms and values, through the constitution, create a social contract that eventually forms formal institutions. Hence, informal institutions constitute a large part of state functions. The historical journeys of developing countries can be categorised into three different eras: the pre-colonial period, the colonial period and the post-colonial period. Pre-colonial and colonial regimes have played a key role in defining the state formation in developing countries.

During pre-colonial rule, citizens provided taxes directly to the rulers. These rulers ruled under a territory. The territory was not fixed, and rulers could gain new territory through warfare. The introduction of colonial rulers brought an end to territorial rule. Citizens were now providing taxes to feudal lords, who provided rents to the colonists. This allowed the colonial regimes to extract resources with the help of intermediate classes. These intermediate classes, after the end of colonial rule, gained significant power in the newly formed states. The clientelist groups now exchange rents with the governments (Figure 1.2).

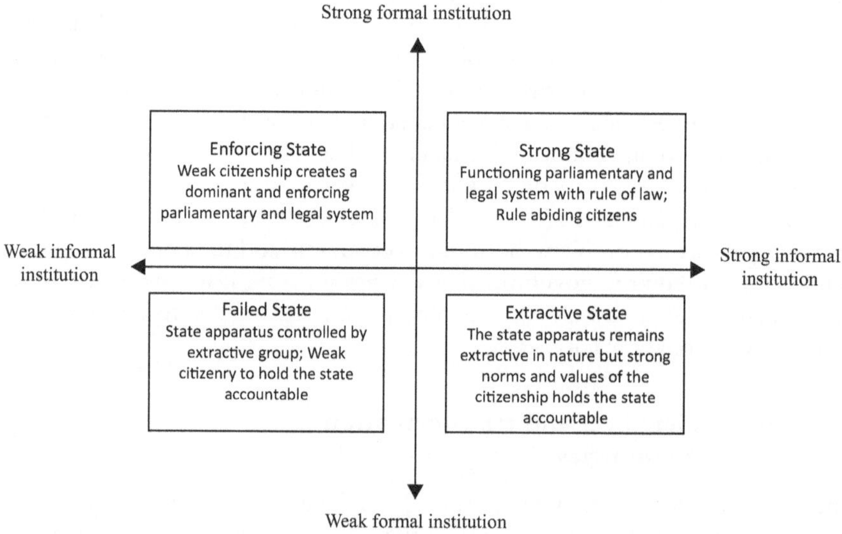

Figure 1.1 Outcome of institutions. Source: Prepared by the author

Alienation between the state and citizens also took shape during the colonial regimes. In both Asia and Africa, this alienation has resulted in rent-seeking institutions and policies. The extractive nature of present states is the result of century-long colonisation in the continents. This extraction from the citizens took many forms, such as taxation. First comes the pre-colonial period where the rulers were very firm in tax collection, yet sometimes acted as benevolent rulers. As they were mostly from the indigenous region, arguably the trickle down of wealth from them helped the common people to some extent. The colonial rulers were mainly interested in rent collection for their respective countries. The trickle down of wealth that was present in the previous period subsided under colonial rule. They, however, undertook certain initiatives and reform measures to ensure the continuation of revenue collection and made certain alterations in response to the changing global landscape. Finally, a different political settlement emerged in the post-colonial states left by the colonial powers, and the ensuing neoliberal policies had a strong influence in shaping the lives of the masses (Figure 1.3).

The notion of a "social contract" results in a nation state. However, the similarity in the nature of the relationship between the state and its citizens in developing countries in all periods is quite stark. Citizens have been providing taxes but receiving very few benefits. On top of this, the use of power and force by the state has made the citizens less connected to the state. The alienation between the state and its citizens has turned into a norm over the years. People now feel alienated from the state apparatus, which further emboldens those in power. This very nature of extraction and alienation will be discussed in this section, drawing examples mostly from the Indian subcontinent and Africa.

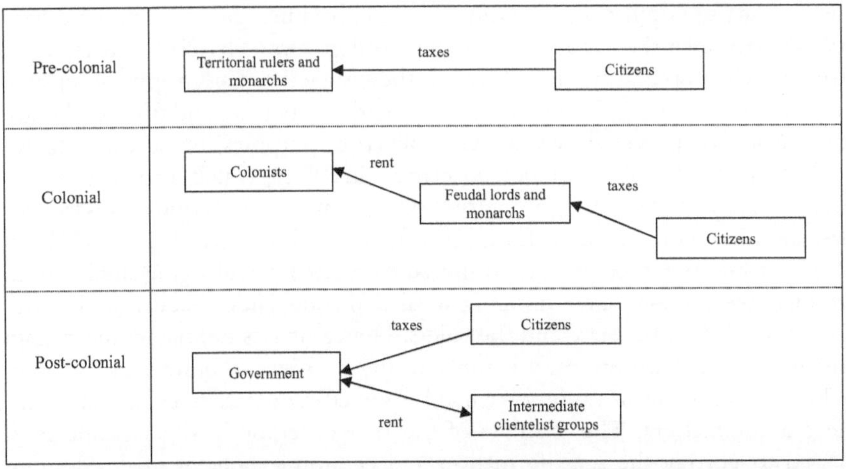

Figure 1.2 Tax and rent distribution in different regimes. Source: Prepared by the author

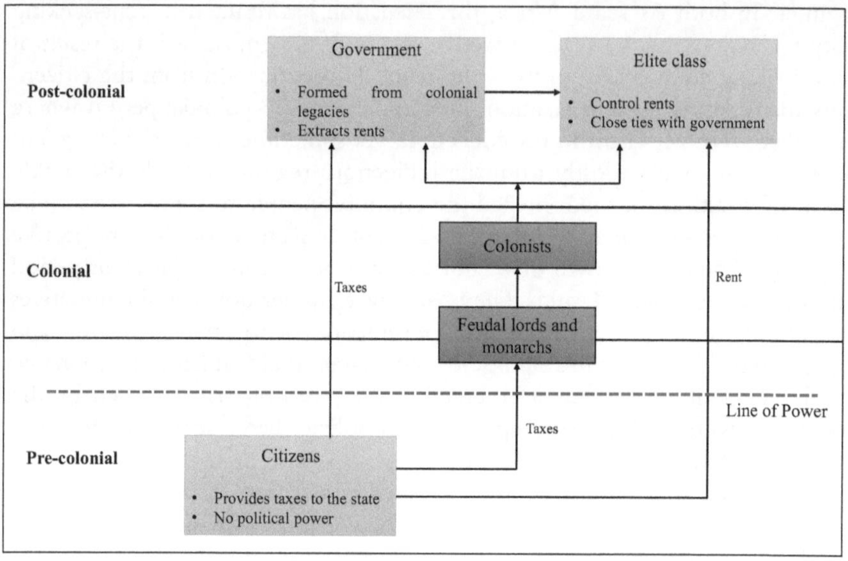

Figure 1.3 Extraction and alienation in different areas. Source: Prepared by the author

Pre-colonial period

Communalism and feudalism had been present in Africa and Asia even before the colonists arrived on their shores. State formation in Africa, for example, came into being on the basis of the transition to feudalism from communalism. Prior to colonisation, states in Africa used to be weak and had a territorial border. The shadow of communalism remained in political sphere, however, due to a sparse population according to the communal groups. The state had little control over the groups as they were still governed by clan leaders. This changed when taxes were introduced in these societies. Early forms of repression and power emerged when citizens refused to pay taxes and tributes. States attained formal power slowly for tax collection purposes in the early states. Sophisticated political areas emerged sparsely in Africa, which formed a labour class. People started breaking away from the communal restrictions. This labour class soon joined the manufacturing sector. It was the ruling classes, and their desire for luxury goods, which prompted early manufacturing. Manufactured products were traded after fulfilling local demand. These trade routes were also controlled by the state and the rulers. Hence, it was ultimately the ruling class who benefited from early manufacturing in Africa (Rodney, 1973). The Indian subcontinent, on the other hand, showed moderate state formation in the pre-colonial era. The example of the Bengal region in the subcontinent is used to portray the state formation and economic policies of developing countries.

A useful starting point for the discussion is the *Mauryan* empire (321–181 BC), which was the first notable indigenous empire in the Indian subcontinent and was regarded a prosperous period (Eaton, 1993). As far as is known now, taxes existed in various forms in the *pre-Mauryan* period, such as taxes on cultivated land, taxes on produce from land, collective tax levied on an entire village, labour tax and livestock tax. Such taxes mostly contributed to the wealth of the elites. In addition, artisans had to serve the state, and the state charged private owners for services like irrigation canals and dams. The Mauryan rulers were also able to collect the assigned revenue from every population and every class. The majority of this revenue went to the maintenance of the royal family and military and administrative services (Avari, 2007). Thus, ordinary people enjoyed no or negligible benefits from their taxes. The ruling classes controlled all state affairs. The differentiation between the ruling class and the ordinary citizens was based upon caste. The lower-caste ordinary people outside the ruling group were bound to obey the orders of the rulers. This type of separated relations between the rulers and the ruled favoured policies that benefited the rulers (Avari, 2007).

Serfdom in this region appeared during this period. This resulted in the bondage of the peasantry. Alongside the landlords and peasants, caste stratification gave rise to bias in law and justice in favour of the higher castes and landlords (Jha, 2009). As far as the ordinary people were concerned, the reality was harsher. The vast majority of them lived a short life, one that was economically precarious and disadvantaged by social, cultural and gender inequalities (Avari, 2007). The empires were safeguarding the interests of the ruling and powerful class, whereas ordinary people faced oppression. The dynasty's king and his allies were the state. Little is known about the people's struggle to achieve their rights as citizens. What is known about the political developments are the wars among the competing empires and kings to expand their empire. These were the affairs of the kings. Ordinary people had no relations with them, though they were exposed to any changes. The conquering empire continued with similar oppression over their new subjects. The former or newly more extractive and oppressive policies followed, uninfluenced by any relations with or views of the ruled. Since political affairs were closed to the ruling class and ordinary people had no participation in the decision-making process, policies were the business of kings. This alienation of common people from state affairs was followed by the policies that alienated them from their rights.

The Mughal era in the Indian subcontinent started in the early sixteenth century. The term *Mughal* came from the origin of the rulers who belonged to the Mongols. Their rule can be divided into two distinct periods. In the first period, from 1576 to 1616, the land was under the direct control of Delhi. In the second period, Bengal was ruled by leaders commonly known as Nawabs, who were nominally under the rule of Delhi and in practice were independent. Despite the Mughal conquest of Bengal in 1576, their authority over the region was limited to the capital Rajmahal and several other regions, and it took until 1613 to establish effective Mughal control over the entire region (Sarkar, 1972).

The prosperity of Bengal during the Mughal period has frequently been described in various documents. Bernier (1891), who travelled across Moghul India during 1656–1668 AD, compared the fertility of the soil of Bengal to that of Egypt. Bengal was especially affluent in agricultural products. Its prosperity, however, was not only restricted to food grains; it included such products as cotton, silks, salt and a variety of animal products as well.

The formation of large *zamindaris* was encouraged during this period. Zamindars were the feudal landlords who collected land revenue. The larger *zamindars* could effectively maintain internal peace and security and had the means to do so, and they could and did organise local police. They furnished merchants and travellers with escorts wherever necessary. The larger zamindars could afford to advance agricultural loans—*takavai*—to their tenants in case of droughts and flooding. Zamindars were also in charge of the preservation of the embankments of rivers. As a result of this encouragement, it was possible to end disputes over revenue collection since the larger zamindars introduced severe punishments for disorder (Sinha, 1967).

Rulers were entitled to state authority as a hereditary gift. As in other periods before the Mughal, ordinary citizens had no political rights as local elites had been accumulating rents with the help of the administration (Guha, 2020). They were subjects, who were bound to pay taxes and obey the rules and regulations imposed. The lives of the general people were better during this era compared to previous reigns, but the state still remained alienated from ordinary citizens. State decisions were made by the emperor and his ministries, which were dominated by the emperor's closest allies. Staying shut off from state affairs made citizens indifferent about political development. Their narrow scope for political participation and decision-making made them disinterested in whatever occurred in the royal palace. The people, as a result, did not participate in protecting Bengal from the British occupation. It was as if a changing regime and political power were solely a matter for the rulers. It seemed that the battle was between the Nawab and the British. The allies of both parties took the sides of the respective wing, but ordinary people were reluctant to get involved with the crisis brewing in the political spheres of Bengal. The battle was for control over the politics, economy and culture of Bengal, and ultimately the victims were the ordinary people. This case illustrates that the alienation of general citizens from state affairs made them indifferent, even when they were colonised.

Colonial rules

Colonial regimes all over the world demonstrated a uniform ruling ideology, which was one of extracting resources from colonised countries and transferring these for the development of the colonist country. Colonists formulated and controlled the economic policies of colonised countries in two ways.

Firstly, colonists used excessive power to control the production of goods in colonised countries. They determined what products should be grown, and their choice was firmly based on the market scenario in their own countries. They immediately banned the production of any product grown in African or Asian countries that might be a competition to the British. They also forced the production of primary goods for use in factories in the United Kingdom (Tadei, 2014). Secondly, colonists controlled the trade of goods. For example, France enacted trade barriers and created monopsonies, which forced producers to sell products at a much lower price and thus give the colonial traders a higher margin (Tadei, 2014).

Colonial rule thrived largely because of the existing alienation of citizens from the state apparatus. It becomes clear from the example of Africa, where the transition from communalism to mature feudalism was slower and at an immature stage. Existing ethnic groups in African society created a vertical political division within a state, which made the conquest easy (Englebert, 2000). In South Asia, there were far fewer political divisions than in Africa. In particular, a well-disciplined Mughal empire made it difficult for the colonial powers to reign in this subcontinent. It took some time and warfare for the British to gain a foothold in India.

The political structure in India came as a blessing for the British in disguise after capturing the state. This allowed the colonists to deal directly with the existing rulers and not to deal with general citizens, which would have cost more in terms of both time and money. The British could use the rulers to extract rent, which the rulers were already doing. This caused immense problems for the citizens, however. The case of Bengal can be used as an example to illustrate the process of colonial rule.

Bengal fell into the hands of the British East India Company after the Battle of Plassey, which took place at Palashi (Anglicised version: *Plassey*), south of the then capital Murshidabad. Bengal's economy, however, was still in good shape when the British East India Company came to power, and, although it gradually deteriorated over the period, it was still in a better position than many other parts of the Indian subcontinent. In the British period, Bengal enjoyed practically a monopoly in jute cultivation. It was also the largest producer of rice and a fair producer of sugar and oil-seeds (Sarkar, 1917). Agriculture in that period did not see any technological advancement. The introduction of the iron mill for crushing sugarcane can be said to be the only notable change in the techniques of production. The new mills were three times more productive in sugarcane crushing and 25 percent more productive in sugar yield compared to the old ones. They were also safer and labour saving. After the government assumed a direct role, especially in the form of the provision of loans for the construction of new wells and the undertaking of some irrigation projects, some improvement was seen in artificial irrigation as well. However, such assistance was often inadequate and lasted only for short periods (Chowdhury, 1967).

Bengal was a major source of resources for the colonial rulers and was ruthlessly exploited in the first two decades after the Battle of Plassey. The plunder was not to the level of Nader Shah, the Iranian ruler who invaded India in 1739, who took almost the same amount of wealth from India that the British took in two decades from Bengal. The reason is that the British understood better that the destruction of the country would be counterproductive to their long-term interests (Maddison, 1970; Riddick, 2006; Vohra, 1997). Despite this, the dual rule of the Nawab and the East India Company took a heavy toll on the people, and Bengal saw a fall in revenue. There was also a famine in 1770 that killed one-third of its population. Between 1766 and 1768, the country exported ten times more than it imported, and such means of transfer was used by the European powers to appropriate surplus from the colonies, which was termed as *drain of wealth* by Dutt (1902). The revenues collected from Bengal can be regarded as a large financial prize for the rulers; they were estimated to produce an annual income of between £2 million and £4 million a year and enabled the East India Company to grow its army and strengthen its control over the territory (Bowen, 1991).

Bengal's role as a revenue source continued through the middle of the nineteenth century as it continued to produce large amounts of revenue compared to its expenditure. This surplus was used in other regions and areas. Even though the British followed the taxation system of the previous Mughal rulers, they did a better job in raising revenue. The last Muslim ruler of Bengal realised a land revenue of £817,553 in the last year of his administration in 1764; the British rulers, within 30 years, were able to collect a land revenue of £2,680,000 annually from the same province (Dutt, 1902).

The discussion of changes to the revenue system in British India indicates that the exploitation of revenue played a major role in British policy in India. The British East India Company soon took over the administration of Bengal in 1772 with the intention of expanding revenues. The British East India Company took direct control over revenue, unlike the Dutch rulers of Java, who continued with the indigenous system. The British objective was to eliminate the intermediary class (Stokes, 1978). As intermediate collectors were siphoning off a large part of the revenue, the British administration organised bids in 1772 to make a 5-year arrangement with the highest bidders. A decennial settlement was made in 1789–1790 with the zamindars of Bihar and Bengal, which was declared permanent by Cornwallis in 1793, as a long-term revenue settlement was preferred; the net sum of this settlement amounted to Rs. 26,800,989 payable to the government. This act was known commonly as the Permanent Settlement Act (Hardy, 1972).

This Act was supposed to be one that reduced the burden on people (Dutt, 1902; Naoroji, 1901). Even then, the amount collected cannot be underestimated. During the eighteenth century, the land tax in England was mostly set at between 5 and 20 percent. In contrast, the land tax in Bengal was set at over 90 percent of the rental between 1793 and 1822, and at over 80 percent in Northern India over the same period (Dutt, 1902).

Furthermore, the property rights arrangement in Bengal lowered agricultural productivity and led to lower investment in health and education compared to other areas of India. Areas where property rights were in the hands of landlords were less productive than the areas where property rights belonged to the cultivators (Banerjee & Iyer, 2005). In Bengal, since the landlord was the owner of the land and the peasants had no rights over the land, productivity in the agricultural sector was low, whereas the tax rate was higher than in any other region. The system of property rights delineates that where ordinary people are given the entitlement to property—in other words, where general people are given their due rights—their productivity increases and the policies favour them. Bengal's property rights structure was such that it perpetuated exploitation by the arbitrary powerful class of the ordinary people (Banerjee & Iyer, 2005).

England banned all imports of cotton or calicoes from India in 1700, although India was the leading producer of cotton cloth at that time (Dowd, 2000). The tariff system introduced in 1810, for example, reduced the cost of overseas trade while increasing the cost of local trade. A consequence was that domestic producers found it more difficult to compete with imports. A heavy burden of taxation was placed on India's exports to China and to other places eastward of the Cape of Good Hope, the southern tip of Africa. In 1819, the Indian cotton export to Britain was as high as 67.5 percent, while a number of Indian goods such as embroidered shawls, handkerchiefs, silks and coloured muslins were totally prohibited from being imported (Banerjea, 1922). In Africa, colonists had forced farmers to grow raw materials for the industrial revolution. In return, they paid very little to the farmers and, with economies of scale, industries in colonist countries like Great Britain made fortunes from the finished product. On top of it, they sold that very product in the colonised countries at high prices. As trade was captured by the British, African countries were forced to buy those products at that price. Moreover, the East India company through creating a monopoly in trade in India, bought products with the money they collected from tax and then those products were re-exported to other destinations at almost double the original prices. It is estimated that the British Empire siphoned out approximately USD 45 trillion through this trade practice. This largely contributed to industrialisation in Great Britain (Chakrabarti & Patnaik, 2017).

In the name of relief to commerce, the Bank of Bengal and Bengal Chamber of Commerce, an organisation established to promote trade and commerce in India, pressured the government to act on the question of the paper currency reserve as quickly as possible and pass a Bill for the purpose, which actually made it possible for the European merchants, bankers, etc. to have Indian taxes at their disposal—the resulting profits could be repatriated more conveniently. The wretched taxpayers not only had to find the money for an unrighteous system of government expenditure, but also supply capital to exploit their own resources (Naoroji, 1901). Central to this effort of the British Empire in Bengal regarding its business with Canton, present-day China, was to ensure a method of payment for products purchased from China, such as tea. Since the Chinese had little demand for Bengal exports, the British Empire used the transfer of the revenue surplus to Canton to continue their trade with China, because few of the goods that the Company exported from Bengal were in sufficient demand in China to allow any profit to be made from their sale to be used for the purchase of large amounts of tea. This carried the risk of exacerbating existing currency problems in Bengal as large amounts of bullion were shifted to China (Bowen, 1991).

These extractive policies were reflected in the nature of the relations between the state and its citizens. The ordinary citizens saw segregated relations with the state. Thus, whatever policies the state formulated were to favour the powerful class and exploit the general citizens. The political and economic settlement was such that it created opportunity for the rulers, their allies, the *zamindars* and the moneylenders to earn rent, whereas the burden fell on the tenants. The landlord and the tenants were seen to become friendly when the land was owned by the same family for years. The Permanent Settlement made it possible to dislodge such landlords and replace them with a new class of owners who considered the land mainly as a source of income (Sarkar, 1917).

Thus, it becomes clear that during the British era, political and economic settlement was in favour of the *zamindars*. In this circumstance, the ordinary people gradually began to fight back against this oppression. The East India Company rule faced opposition for the first time in 1857 in the form of "sepoy mutiny". This mutiny was run by the agitated classes who had lost their political and economic resources due to the British occupation. This mutiny led to the fall of company rule in India and brought it under the direct rule of Britain. Under British Empire, the potential for ordinary people to engage in politics started to open up, although the policies were still extractive. Despite segregated relations between the state and the citizen, the new rising intermediate classes was struggling for equal rights (Khan, 2010a). The British also progressively allowed room for political activism by the Indians, which ultimately led to the independence of India, creating two separate states—India and Pakistan. Unfortunately, the intermediate classes who were representing the people in politics did not represent the peasants and ordinary people in any true sense. The Muslim intermediate class was mainly comprised of *jotedar*, or the wealthy peasant class, who were actually trying to replace the Hindu elites (Khan, 2010a). Thus, peasants and ordinary people remained excluded from state affairs. After the partition of Bengal, Bengali Muslims became disenchanted and they started facing a new type of oppression, which is discussed in the following section.

Post-colonial state

As decolonisation started after World War II, a massive question was left to the colonists. What happens to these states now? How do they run? Knowing very well the consequences of leaving these countries without any leadership, colonist powers installed Western ideologies and prescribed policies for development, which failed miserably (Furnivall, 2014). Many theorists have blamed the colonial legacy for the underdevelopment of the colonies. At the same time, theorists have tried to associate the failure of post-colonial states with patrimonialism. The roots of patrimonialism go back to the pre-colonial past of Africa, where the states were rulers that appropriated rents (Médard, 2014). Patrimonialism exists in a society when a political leader diverts rents in a way that maximises the benefit for people close to him (Booth & Golooba-Mutebi, 2012). On the other hand, theorists now believe that it is neopatrimonialism that retards economic development in Africa. Patrimonialism is not limited to the close allies of the ruler; instead, rents are now distributed across a broader spectrum involving bureaucracy and political leaderships (Médard, 2014). This characteristic of rent extraction has its roots in the colonial past, where rent distribution had spread to the bureaucracy.

This extractive nature of institutions during colonial regimes has prevailed in the post-colonial state in a new dimension. Rent extraction has now spread beyond patrimonialism and neopatrimonialism. Rent distribution now prevails across a wider section of the population. Weaker property rights and institutions have resulted in rent extraction not just by those in power but also by the elite class in society. This extraction of rents at the expense of the general populace has continued throughout the developing world. As a result, the alienation of citizens from the state has persisted. The elite class that was created during colonial rule took control of businesses and remained at the top of hierarchies in the newly formed state. Very little changed for the citizens as political power was focused on a limited few who had the blessing of the colonist rulers.

Post-colonial state of Bangladesh

The desire for a better life on the part of the working and the middle classes led to the emergence of Pakistan in 1947. The ruling class, comprised of big landlords and capitalists, however, suppressed the aspiration of the masses with their own interests. Hindu *zamindars*, who were numerous in Bangladesh, migrated to West Bengal after partition (Riaz, 2005). They were replaced by the large Muslim *jotedars*, who expropriated much of the land left behind by the Hindu *zamindars*. Over time, big landlords and migrated capitalists became influential in Pakistani parliament. It was in the interests of the landed class that much of the political changes and corruption in the 1950s took place. After 1958, the power of these landed elites was curtailed, but only in favour of the rising capitalist class. Ultimately, 22 capitalist families were able to increase their personal wealth to such an extent that at one time they owned 66 percent of industry, 97 percent of insurance and 80 percent of banking (Farooqi, 1972).

Pakistan's economic and nation-building policy had a negative impact on its eastern region. For example, even after independence, East Pakistan could trade with Calcutta through mechanisms such as a modified customs union. Lack of trust with India influenced its economic policies, and the circumstances of Pakistan's creation and these unfriendly relations with India were important determinants of the economic policies adopted by Pakistan. The country also believed economic dependence on India to be problematic for its economy and nation-building. It also decided to increase the trading relations between the two parts which had virtually no trade before partition (Bose, 1989).

The simple revenue and government expenditure data fails to reveal the source of the exploitation of the East. East Pakistan's share in the country's total revenue did not increase. In better years, it reached about one-third of the total revenue of the whole of Pakistan, despite showing gradual improvement over time. Comparatively, the province received a higher share of development expenditure and an even higher portion of the total government expenditure.

The profit earned from the selling of jute exports was appropriated by the capitalist class in West Pakistan. First, the decision of the Pakistani government not to devalue its currency in 1949 was beneficial to its Import Substitute Industrialisation (ISI) strategy. The policy, however, created a problem for the export sector, especially the jute industry of East Pakistan; jute exports fell from 1.22 million tons in 1947–1948 to 600,000 tons in 1949–1950 (Bose, 1989). Second, the eastern province was required to buy over-priced industrial products from West Pakistan, although the same product was available on the global market at lower prices. According to one estimate, a total transfer of about Rs. 2,500 million took place between the two provinces for 14 years (about Rs. 180 million per year), which was more than two percent of East Pakistan's annual income for the period (Power, 1963).

Because of exploitative policies, Bengal saw little or no improvement in living standards during the 24 years (1947–1971) of its existence as East Pakistan, a World Bank report evaluates (World Bank, 1974). Despite the issue of the reliability of the quantitative data, it seems reasonable for the report to conclude that per capita income between 1947 and 1971 just kept pace with the growth rate of population, and in rural areas, it may have actually fallen to some extent (World Bank, 1974). The level of average income in East Pakistan seemed to be lower during the Pakistan rule than it was in 1757, as Dhaka's status was relegated from being the capital of Bengal and the great centre of the luxury handicraft industry of Mughal India to a different position (Maddison, 2006). While income increased slowly in East Pakistan, it rose rapidly in West Pakistan, which aggravated regional disparity between the two provinces.

The amount of private investment was meagre in East Pakistan compared to West Pakistan. Moreover, most of these investments in East Pakistan were made by West Pakistani entrepreneurs. As estimated, 47 percent of fixed assets and 72 percent of industrial assets were controlled by non-Bengali business houses (Sobhan & Ahmad, 1980). On the other hand, 45.1 percent of the privately controlled firms in Bangladesh were held by 43 families, only one of which was Bengali (Riaz, 2005).

Little is known about the fiscal and monetary policies of pre-colonial Bengal, but it is clear that economic policies were in favour of the ruling class. The ruling class was comprised of the elite section of society. In most cases, the general populace were alienated from political activities. State apparatus was run by the elite. The nature of relations between state and citizen was segregated and extractive. State policies followed this since the nature of policies is determined by the nature of the relations between state and citizen. As a result, monetary and fiscal policies were designed mainly to fulfil the demands of the ruling class and the empire, but very little was done, as was the case in different regimes, for the welfare of the masses. The economy was agriculture-based. Lack of innovation in the productive sectors led to low productivity along with lower levels of labour skills. The organization of land favoured the peasants. Though land grants were made to the officers of the king, which was the beginning of feudalism in India, policy favoured agriculture. Despite these issues, Bengal did trade its agricultural products— mainly rice and jute—with the world and with other parts of India (Khan, 1999).

The colonial era mostly saw resource extraction by the British. Colonial economic and political institutions were extractive in nature. The British arranged the land and other property rights in a way that gave stability to their rule so that they could perpetuate the extraction. They kept the *zamindars* and elite class satisfied by providing facilities on the basis of different economic arrangements, preventing any political upheaval. Although some infrastructural development did occur—especially rail—this was done to make revenue collection easier. A shortage of capital and low levels of investment in human capital generation did not help productivity expansion. In lieu of creating skilled labour, this system created a salary class. Furthermore, deindustrialisation occurred during the British era. Hence, citizens received little benefit from economic policies in this period.

During the period of the establishment of Pakistan, the aspirations of the Bengali people, for which they struggled against the British and formed a new state—Pakistan—were ruined. There were huge differences both in the economic and the political arenas of East and West Pakistan. A new Muslim elite was ruling Pakistan, where rights of the masses were being ignored. A "civil–military–bureaucratic" trio alliance was controlling both the political and the economic power of the Pakistani state (Alavi, 1990). East Pakistan lagged behind because of its exploitation by West Pakistan. Major industrialisation was occurring in West Pakistan, whereas East Pakistan was agriculture-based. A lack of capital and skilled labour as well as a dearth of technological advancement kept the agricultural sector of East Pakistan lagging behind (Khan, 1999). East Pakistani Muslims soon got agitated with Pakistan, and a new struggle started between the intermediate classes in the provinces of Bengal and Punjab. This struggle for equality, human dignity and social justice ultimately led to independent Bangladesh. Despite this struggle for political and economic rights from Bengali intermediate classes, the voice of the ordinary people and subordinate class remained unheard.

Pre-independent Bangladesh was a highly stratified society where ordinary people were excluded from almost all kinds of economic and political facilities, although they had to bear the burden of tax. Since the nature of the state was extractive and the relationship between the state and general citizens was a distant one, favouring the ruling elites, the fiscal and monetary policies took on the extractive and alienated nature of the state (Table 1.1). Thus, productive capacity did not expand.

Independent Bangladesh

Economic policy in independent Bangladesh represented a different type of crisis. The people's say in policymaking significantly increased in comparison to earlier regimes. The ruling class belonged to the land. The nature of capital flight therefore changed dramatically. The problem of policy choice, however, did not change. The ruling elite very often accepted policies that benefitted them and their allies. They never considered variations within the school or the context. The result could be seen in a comparatively slower growth regime that also failed to achieve better results in terms of human development.

When Bangladesh achieved independence from Pakistan on December 16, 1971, not only was the per capita income of the country low, but it was also suffering from the stagnation of the past 20 years. The country was overcrowded, as population density was almost 1,400 per square mile, with a growth rate of 3 percent per year. A short life expectancy at birth was observed—under 50 years. The unemployment rate was unusually high, in many cases 25–30 percent, and people were largely illiterate as the literacy rate was under 20 percent (World Bank, 1972).

After independence, there were hardly any entrepreneurs in independent Bangladesh who could take control of the industry units abandoned by the Pakistanis. Bangladesh Bank nationalised 12 banks, except for the foreign ones, and consolidated them into six nationalised commercial banks. It also nationalised 64 insurance companies, of which 12 were Bangladeshi-owned, and then converted them into four holding companies. In 1972, the government took control of 92 percent of industrial assets, 90 percent of bank activities and 90 percent of foreign trade (Chowdhury, 1990).

> Ideology had very little to do with the growth in the size of the state sector in the economy during 1972. Where ideology did come into play, was in the takeover of Bengali owned enterprises in jute and textile as well as in banking and insurance as a result of a policy decision to nationalise these sectors, taken in March 1972 and formalised under Presidential Order (PO) no. 27. It is however evident that the major contribution to the growth of the SOE sector originated in historical circumstances created by the liberation of Bangladesh.
>
> (Sobhan, 2002)

The war-torn country faced serious challenges, both from economic and political perspectives. The rulers during this period failed to establish a pluralistic democratic society. Bangladesh became an authoritarian state after just 4 years of independence. There was no opposition in the parliament. The ruling party changed the constitution and started a one party–led government.

Table 1.1 Summary of different regimes

Regime	*Societal configurations*			*Political formations*		*Economic arrangement*	
	Stratification	*Mobility*	*Patronage distribution*	*Principal contradictions*	*Countervailing forces*	*Drivers*	*Outcomes*
Pre-colonial Bengal	Stratified society based on caste and class	Society was stagnant—less mobile	Elites were the main beneficiary	Politics was controlled by the elites; little sign of mass movement against establishment	Different dynasties were competing and fighting	Agriculture-based economy, drivers were the peasants	Unequal wealth distribution
British era	Stratified, where zamindars were exploiting peasants	Struggle was evident for social change	Elite zamindars and the collaborators with colonial rule were the beneficiaries	Controlled by Calcutta-based zamindars	New rising middle class	Agriculture-based economy, peasants were the drivers	Resources extraction both by the colonial rulers and the zamindars
Pakistan period	Elite vs. masses	Struggle for equal, just and democratic society	Powerful Punjabi elites were the beneficiaries	Controlled by West Pakistan	Rise of Bengali new middle class	Agriculture-based economy; Jute was the major source of income, peasants were the drivers of the economy	Wealth drained from East to West Pakistan

Source: Prepared by the author

Thus, the political space became narrow. There was no room for dissent. The state failed to become a public society. It failed to nurture the spirit of the war of liberation. A group of people started extracting resources using state power. Looting became rampant. Minimum standards of law and order were absent. Such irregularities in state affairs led to the famine, which took a heavy toll on the masses and paved the way for foreign dominance in the state. Thus, the aspirations of the people were dashed just after independence (Titumir, 2019)

The core hypothesis is where Bangladesh stands in terms of the three pillars of independence— equality, human dignity and social justice— pronounced in the country's proclamation of independence, and how the fiscal and monetary policies have been pursued during different regimes to attain the aspiration of independence. Despite Bangladesh moving forward after independence, the three pillars of independence are yet to be realised. It is claimed that GDP growth is increasing; however, its benefit is going to a particular portion of society. Thus, inequality is rising tremendously. Despite some significant improvements, questions have emerged about its sustainability. The economic outcome is benefiting the ruling powerful class.

The state is run by the ruling elites in a way that meets their demands. As a result, Bangladesh has failed to become a public society where people irrespective of class and caste benefit from the policies the state implements. Furthermore, the democratic journey started to be shattered by the ruling elites as soon as its journey as an independent state had begun. Despite people's struggles for democracy and for a just society where they have representation in the ruling process, their aspirations have been dashed.

The ruling elites formulate the policies that favour their interests. On the other hand, the general populace suffer since the nature of those policies is still extractive. The uneven distribution of power has failed to make the state a democratic one; rather, a confrontational politics has emerged. Since the political arrangement failed to make the society a public one, the economic benefits are concentrated in the hands of the powerful class whereas the general citizen enjoys little rights. Thus, society is divided between the powerful elite and powerless masses (Khan, 2010a). Bangladesh has fallen behind in terms of democracy as seen from different indices. Bangladesh ranked 154th in the Liberal Democracy Index 2021 by Varieties of Democracy (V-dem). This necessarily means that the country is heading towards autocracy (Coppedge et al., 2021).

Policy and outcomes in post-colonial states

The outcomes of century-long colonial rule has shaped the post-colonial states of Africa and Asia. These outcomes are also dependent on the nature and length of colonisation. The different colonial experiences of Asia and Africa are evident from their present state. South Korea, for instance, lived under colonisation by Japan until the Second World War and then later suffered from civil war, which divided Korea into two and gave birth to South Korea and North Korea. Yet South Korea has surpassed many developed countries in terms of economic development. A combination of an active state and civil society made this development possible. The state actively espoused industrial policies, which have transformed the economy from an agrarian one to an industrial one. In forming the present South Korean state, the government was centralised and remained engaged in policymaking. As a result, the government aggressively pursued industrialisation while leaving social policies in the hands of society.

On the other hand, the economic woes of African countries are often linked to their weak political institutions. Weak political infrastructure has diminished the developmental nature of the state. Many attribute the nature of political institutions in Africa to its colonial past. Politicians resorted to neopatrimonial policies to exert their power over citizens. They have used state resources to strengthen their rule in the region. Such policies significantly crippled the developmental capacity of the state (Englebert, 2000). Undemocratic and politically powerful classes have been involved in decision-making processes. Rent distribution among the powerful classes exacerbated the economy and created fiscal pressure. As a result, many of these nations turned to the International Monetary Fund and international donor agencies as a last resort to ease the pressure. Conditional lending by the donor agencies did very little to boost the economies of African nations, which were yet to recover from their colonial history.

The debt crisis in Africa took place due to the existing political infrastructure. Firstly, the public investment barely created any industries. The political ruling classes gained their power because of their ties with the colonists. Most of the industries and plantations were controlled by Western countries and the rentier class. The nature of resource extraction by these classes did not benefit the economy. Excessive government intervention in the countries resulted in the accumulation of capital, as after independence from the colonists, most of these countries were governed by military and authoritarian regimes. Poorer countries relied on private investment, debt relief and new aid to finance their public expenditure.

Secondly, African countries predominantly relied on agriculture and primary commodity production due to the low cost of labour. European countries became the major export destination for commodities after colonisation. Central Africa and parts of Southern Africa were dominated by companies backed by the European states, and soon they were involved with the economic structure of the countries. Public works, communication and even taxation was controlled by colonists. A vicious cycle was created with countries being producers of primary commodities and agricultural goods like coffee and cocoa. Powerful elitist groups grabbed power in most African countries after decolonisation at the end of the Second World War. The fragile and fragmented political leadership left by the colonists only exacerbated the situation because of their rent seeking nature. The African debt crisis spiralled in the 1970s. The oil crisis and the drop in price of commodities like coffee and cocoa resulted in low earnings. This led to higher capital inflows from abroad in the form of aid and loans to finance spending. The crisis continued sporadically over the next two decades. Once government expenditure increased, the government could not reduce it even after commodity prices started going up. Hence, the gap between expenditure and revenue never closed up.

East Asian countries in general had a very low spending on social sectors. Confucian teaching, which puts a focus on family, allowed the governments in these countries to leave much of the duties to the families. Industrial policy focused on only specific sectors. Less important sectors were not prioritised in the policy. Sector specific industrial policy allowed economic growth as well as employment for the population. Economic development later allowed states to increase spending in social sectors. The centralisation of state power inherited from colonial legacies allowed the East Asian tiger economies, especially South Korea, to become developmental states. It is important to distinguish between a developmental state and a welfare state. South Korea in its early days was certainly a developmental state that had focused on economic growth, but it was not a welfare state, as the policies were skewed towards a certain group. However, as the developmental state had control over the policies that accounted for the growth, very soon they transformed into a welfare state. The norms and values instilled in the societies from the Confucian ideology also benefited state formation in these countries.

Compared to East Asian countries, private investment in the African region is miniscule. Foreign investment by the United Kingdom increased manifold in the beginning of the twenty-first century, but only a small portion reached Africa. Africa received only 2 percent of the book value level of FDI by British companies by the end of 2006. South Africa has gained the most FDI among African nations, and Sub-Saharan countries received only a tiny amount (Bracking, 2009). African countries relied greatly on foreign aid to finance consumption. As a result, the debt owed to bilateral and multilateral sources increased over time. Low investment coupled with lower revenue due to the crisis led to absolute dependence on foreign borrowing. Hence, the ratio of debt to GDP started increasing, and it was proving extremely difficult for African nations to service the debt as well as initiate poverty alleviation programs. Countries like Nigeria, Ghana, Malawi, Zambia and Kenya saw a rise in the debt-to-GDP ratio. The external debt of the African countries had risen to 350 billion USD in the year 2000 from 5 billion USD in 1970. Capital inflows from external resources in the 1980s were almost 43 percent for the African countries. The number was two times higher for poorer nations like Mauritania (Obasanjo, 1988). The external debt of Nigeria stood at more than 35 billion USD by 2008.

The staggering debt of the African countries showed no sign of improvement due to poor debt management. Poor exchange-rate policies and currency devaluation also worked against the nations. The debt crisis was crippling an already poor region tackling widespread poverty and hunger. In 2005, developed countries adopted the Multilateral Debt Relief Initiative (MDRI) in order to write off the unsustainable debt of 36 low-income countries, of which 29 were African states. Major creditors, also known as the "Paris Club", and multilateral financing institutes like the IMF and the World Bank initiated debt relief programmes and at the same time created new plans for the development of the region. The debt relief programme wrote off a significant chunk of external debt held by the countries. As a result, the debt-to-GDP ratio came down to 35 percent in 2012 from 110 percent in 2001 (Coulibaly, Gandhi & Senbet, 2019). The debt relief programme was followed by a "Big Push" by the developed countries. The Group of Eight (G8) countries doubled the development assistance to African nations. The massive debt relief had reduced the burden on the nations and as a result increased public spending. The outcome was short lived, however, as the world plunged into recession in 2008 and the lending by the African countries started increasing again; as a result, the debt burden has again started inflating.

COVID-19 challenges for developing countries

The coronavirus disease (COVID-19) is a highly transmittable and pathogenic viral infection, which emerged in Wuhan, China. It spread worldwide within a short period. The virus infected the whole world quickly and aggravated economies' pre-existing limitations and pitfalls. The COVID-19 pandemic is arguably the most significant challenge to humanity since the Second World War. The pandemic has spread at an alarming rate, causing infections and a large death toll, and has disturbed global economic stability. Since the COVID-19 outbreak started, the economic damage has already become evident and represents the most massive economic shock the world has experienced in decades. For example, the Asian Development Bank (2020) predicts that the global economy might lose between $5.8 trillion to $8.8 trillion due to the pandemic, which is equivalent to 6.4 percent–9.7 percent of the global gross domestic product (GDP).

The economy of the developing states is the most affected by this pandemic since they already had pre-existing economic discrepancies. The pandemic has had a severe impact on both the national economy and the household economy of the developing states. Demand–supply disruption is the most catastrophic impact of the pandemic in the developing states. The national economy has faced a demand shock in both external and domestic markets as well as a supply shock. The export-oriented industries faced a decline in external demand, and a huge amount of economic output deteriorated because countries all over the world declared a lockdown as an essential tool for fighting the pandemic. Remittances are one of the major sources of income for developing countries like Bangladesh, since they have a comparative advantage in productivity because of the utilisation of cheap labour. The lockdown has put a stress on the consumer and business environment since both entrepreneurs and consumers have been forced to stay at home as per the priority of the health issue. As a result, inequality started to deepen because of the job losses faced by workers in the informal sector. Moreover, the pandemic has caused social and economic

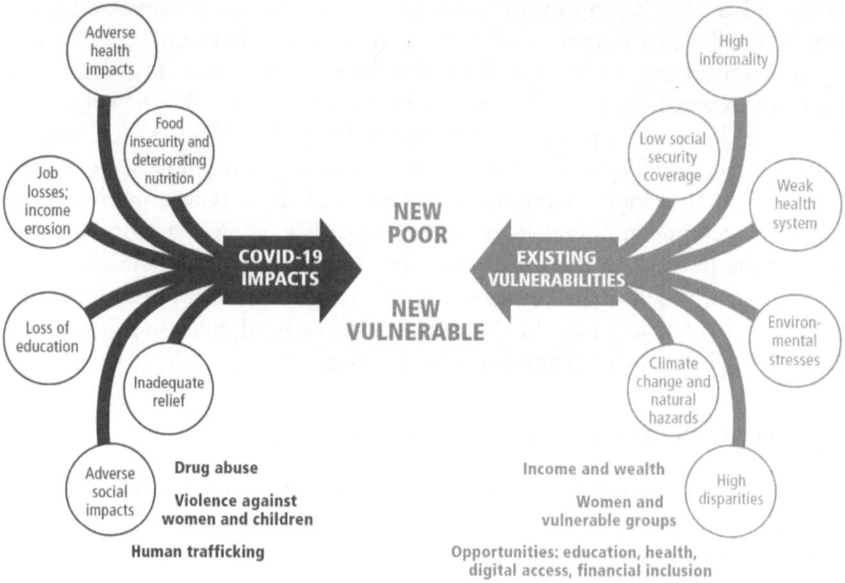

Figure 1.4 COVID-19 and pre-existing vulnerabilities. Source: Adapted from Titumir (2020). Which recovery path may we pursue? New Age, 15 October. Available from www.newagebd.net/article/118990/which-recovery-path-may-we-pursue in United Nations, Asian Development Bank & United Nations Development Programme, 2021

uncertainties in the states as governments have been forced to enforce lockdown measures for an indefinite time (Figure 1.4).

The household economy, on the other hand, faced massive unemployment, increases in poverty and loss of income due to the pandemic. Daily labourers suffered all the more since they had lost their only source of income and, as a result, massive food insecurity struck in these households. Small and medium enterprises (SMEs) suffered a huge loss under the lockdown. Many SMEs were forced to shut down since they were unable to generate any revenue and had already invested all the capital they had.

Key challenges for transformation

The discussion in this chapter suggests following stylised facts, which can also be found in other post-colonial developing countries.

The challenges lie in the harmonisation of formal and informal institutions in developing countries where both the government and citizens remain in an extractive relationship. The lack of accountability on the part of government stems from the capacity of the citizens. This affects market exchange in developing countries, as factors of production remain under-utilised and are often accumulated (Figure 1.5).

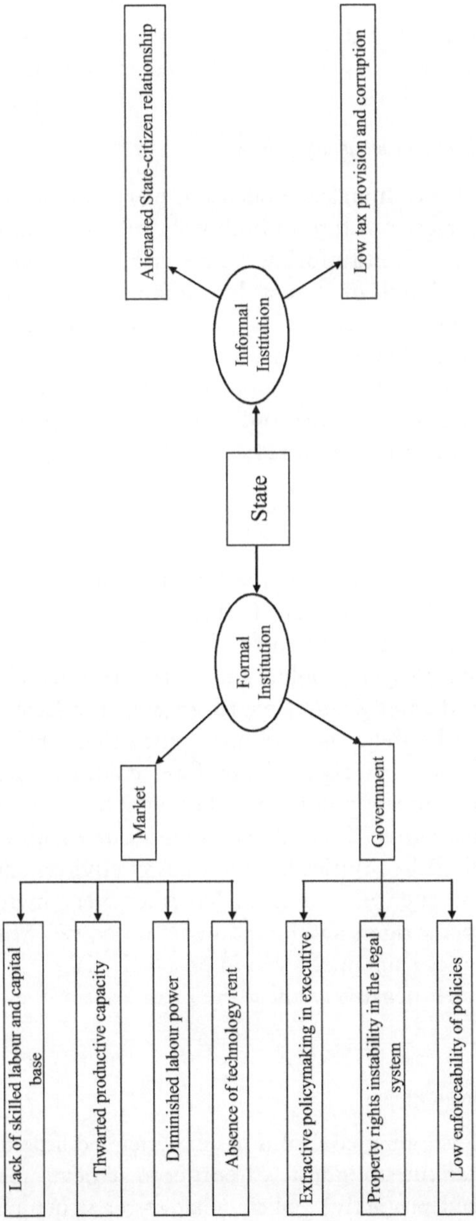

Figure 1.5 Challenges for transformation. Source: Prepared by the author

Formal institutions

The main challenges for the developing state lie in formal institutions. The extractive nature of government has resulted in absence of rule of law in the state. The implementation of the laws and policies have allowed certain political and elite groups to accumulate more resources while ordinary citizens have suffered. Policy orientation in such countries is skewed towards fulfilling the wishes of the elites in society. While government was brought in the economy to create an environment to stop monopolisation, political settlement has only created an oligarchy in society that has increased extraction.

Extractive nature of fiscal and monetary policies

The nature of fiscal and monetary policies in post-colonial developing countries follows the extractive nature of both political and economic institutions. The extractive nature of institutions was a result of the colonial legacy, though it was prevalent to a significant extent during the pre-colonial period too, and it has been further perpetuated during the post-colonial period. The extractive (both economic and political) institutions (Acemoglu & Robinson, 2012) retard the growth and development process of post-colonial states. Thus, policies favour the ruling class, whereas ordinary people are exploited. As a result, inequality is rising at a tremendous rate.

Property rights instability and the legal system

Conflicts arise when state dictates ownership of property, which basically benefits the ruling class. Since the state is run by the powerful elite who have bargaining power over ordinary people, the new structure of property rights goes in their favour. Property rights, therefore, are established in ways that do not enhance productivity rather retard growth. Furthermore, the colonial rulers sought political stability for resource extraction, which was guaranteed by certain form of property rights. Therefore, colonial rulers created many conflicting rights to maintain political stability, which was more damaging than destabilised property rights (Khan, 2009). Besides, the nature of political settlement in post-colonial countries creates a costly environment for economic activities. As a consequence, transaction costs are very high in these countries. Unstable property rights and high transaction costs—which are inherited from colonial rule and maintained even in post-colonial periods in most of the developing countries—negatively affect the prosperity of these states.

Thwarted productive capacity

The economy of developing countries has experienced little transformation in the move from agriculture to industry. In order to achieve rapid growth developing countries need pro-active policies that foster structural transformation and spawn new industries—the kind of policies that today's advanced economies employed themselves on the way to becoming rich (Rodrik, 2011). Extraordinarily high growth rates are almost always the result of rapid structural transformation—particularly industrialisation, with the only exception of natural-resource bonanzas (Rodrik, 2014). Economic growth in developing countries has not been complemented by accompanying growth in productive employment in the industrial sector, with the exception of labour-intensive manufacturing. This is unlike the spectacular growth and economic transformation experienced by the East Asian countries, which enabled them to capitalise on the demographic dividend (Titumir & Rahman, 2017).

Absence of technology rent for offsetting loss

Technological backwardness in developing countries is one of the most significant bottlenecks preventing rapid growth. It can be seen that manufacturing growth in the least developed countries during the 1980s was accelerated due to incentives created by fortuitous rents, which allowed capability development and investments in new sectors (Khan, 2010b). Growth convergence depends on a variety of arrangements that allowed countries to address market failures that were constraining technology acquisition to varying extents (Khan, 2010b). Technology acquisition, therefore, is necessary for growth in developing countries. Catching up in terms of technology requires organisational and institutional capabilities as well as political conditions. Moreover, productivity depends not only on the formal education and training of workers and managers but also on the tacit knowledge that is acquired in the actual process of production (Dosi, 1988). It is, therefore, observed that tacit knowledge is an important part of the skills and organisational capabilities that are necessary for the success of firms (Nelson & Winter, 1982; Dosi, 1988; Pelikan, 1988; cited in Khan, 2010b).

Tacit knowledge can be acquired through a learning-by-doing process, which can explain why developing countries can initially only achieve a level of labour and input productivity that is significantly lower than in more advanced countries (Khan, 2010b). Entrepreneurs in developing countries face certain current losses during their initial investment, while the learning-by-doing process may yield higher returns in the future than the present. A variety of loss financing schemes, therefore, may enable learning-by-doing to commence (Khan, 2000), which means providing technological rents to the entrepreneurs since these rents can reduce or prevent the financial losses they face. Firms suffer losses since the current levels of technological capabilities of workers and managers operating in the current infrastructural context implies production costs that are higher than the globally competitive level (Khan, 2010b). Providing technological rents, therefore, enables producers to invest in new sectors despite incurring higher costs, because it increases firms' knowledge gain through learning by doing, which may make them competitive in the future. Technological acquisition is required along with growth, but it is further observed that without aggressive technological development, faster growth cannot be realised. For instance, China is flourishing tremendously in terms of technological development, which can be seen as one of the main factors behind its robust growth.

Lack of skilled labour and capital base

The post-colonial state maintains the colonial legacy in most cases where public investment in health and education is meagre. The education system has been proven to fail to generate a skilled labour force on one hand and a sense of citizenship on the other. Since colonisers extracted resources and deindustrialisation occurred, productive sectors did not flourish. Therefore, capital creation failed. On the other hand, the share of revenue collection by the government is still small, making the capital base rickety. If a large and growing proportion of the population in their prime working ages cannot be employed fully in high-productivity sectors during the structural transformation, the demographic dividend cannot be realised. This only happens when rapid economic growth coalesces with high employment growth along with growth in productivity and real wages (Titumir & Rahman, 2017). When "job-rich" economic growth absorbs the growing labour force into productive employment and creates a virtuous cycle, economic development grows faster. Generally, the ration of tax revenue to GDP in most developing countries like Bangladesh is two to four times lower than that of developed countries. Mobilising tax revenue by at least 25 percent of the GDP is decisive for strengthening the government's capacity to engineer development by undertaking comprehensive interventions and considerable investments in the economy (Titumir & Rahman, 2017). Coupled with domestic resource mobilisation, attracting more foreign direct investment (FDI) can boost economic growth and add dynamism to the economy.

Diminished labour power

Developing countries in Asia and Africa have been facing a declining real-wage growth rate. African countries have seen a growth rate of real wages in the negative. The growth rate has been fluctuating in Asia and the Pacific in the last decade and is on the decline. The rate is much lower when China is excluded (ILO, 2020b). Bangladesh experienced little growth in real wages with low returns on labour and rising inequality in labour income. In fact, real wages are declining alongside an alarming rise in inequality and unemployment. Recently the rate of poverty reduction has also decreased (Unnayan Onneshan, 2019).

A comparative trend analysis of labour productivity in Bangladesh, India and China shows that Bangladesh's gain in labour productivity growth is substantially lower than those of China and India, both of which have experienced rapid growth in productivity since the year 2000. Expanding the productive capacity of an economy requires that an increasing number of resources will be mobilised and invested in infrastructure, human capital development and productive employment creation. First and foremost, the rate of economic growth and productive capacity of an economy cannot be expanded without mobilising increased domestic savings and investment in a country (Titumir & Rahman, 2017).

Poverty and inequality

Policies in post-colonial states have perpetuated inequality in developing countries. Developing countries in particular face an absence of rights-based universal social security, which exacerbates inequality (Titumir, 2021). On top of this, primitive accumulation by political elites widens the gap. This has resulted in a higher rate of poverty and inequality in Africa. Inequality in Bangladesh has been worsening as well over the years. The growth rate in poverty reduction has also declined. Fiscal measures including low expenditure in social sectors like health and education widens inequality. Better education facilities can generate a skilled labour force that can reduce the inequality gap through better wages (Titumir, 2021). On the other hand, developing countries have among the highest levels of out of pocket expenditure for securing healthcare. High out-of-pocket expenditure can be linked to rising inequality as citizens have to bear the burden.

Informal institutions

Informal institutions have gained little importance in policymaking in developing countries. Financial illiteracy and tax evasion by citizens has more to do with norms and values than implementation of laws. Social norms dictate tax compliance as well as tax evasion. This is the reason why tax compliance and tax evasion differs in many countries. Societies which have higher social cohesion see relatively more tax compliance and less tax evasion (Torgler, 2003a). Tax compliance is also dependent upon the nature of the government and people's trust in it. The quality of institutions determines the level of tax compliance in a country. A higher quality of institutions tends to result in higher tax compliance (Torgler & Schneider, 2009; Bethencourt & Kunze, 2019). When institutions in a country respect the rights of the citizens, trust increases and citizens are more compliant in terms of taxes (Torgler, 2003b). Hence, the roots of higher tax evasion in developing countries lies in the lower quality of institutions and social cohesion. Citizens have an alienated relation with the state and often fail to hold the state accountable for its policies. This has resulted in a social norm of self-entitlement in developing countries. Active citizenship can make the state more responsible in policy formulation.

Alienated relations between state and citizen

The aspiration and struggle of the people for equality, human dignity and social justice in post-colonial countries guarantee a public society. Aspiration and struggle has been observed in developing countries throughout history, but these have failed to become a public society where people irrespective of class, caste or creed are entitled to equal rights, human dignity and social justice. Instead of safeguarding the people's aspirations, the state acts in favour of the powerful ruling class. The policies, therefore, are formulated to serve the interests of the powerful clientelist network. The policies are established on the premise that economic rent can be dissipated amongst the clientelist powerful networks. This clientelist class uses the monopoly power of the state in their favour, which makes the state extremely coercive. As a result, the state gets alienated from its citizens and fails to become a citizen state. The powerful class does not pay heed to ordinary people's needs and opinions. Instead, the ruling class appropriates "the 'spontaneous' consent given by the masses imposed on social life by the dominant fundamental group" (Gramsci, 1971). The ruling class, therefore, becomes hegemonic by establishing both material dominance and intellectual and moral leadership over society and by succeeding in persuading the lower classes that their relative positions of subordination and superordination are just, proper and legitimate. In post-colonial countries it can also be seen from various struggles that the common feeling of the people— particularly the aspiration for a public society—can be operationalised against the establishment of a powerful elite. Since political elites do not hear the voices of the masses, elite ideological projects would likely flounder against daily practices of resistance. The common feeling of the masses has been an obstacle to elite hegemonic projects (Hopf, 2013).

Low enforceability of policies

A lack of enforcement of policies causes the failure of economic policies—which is prevalent in developing countries. Low institutional quality causes economic policies like inflation targeting and exchange-rate regimes to fail in developing countries (Huang & Wei, 2006). Under limited enforcement, there does not exist a policy rule that implements a unique outcome (Barthelemy & Mengus, 2019). Enforcement mechanisms, therefore, should be the main instrument of monetary policy established by central banks. An emphasis on monetary policy in the short term has to be on understating the level of price, the sources of inflation and relationships with other complementary policies affecting growth and employment, as opposed to the inflation targeting approach (Titumir & Hossain, 2014). These activities require an enforcement targeting approach so that the financial sector can be an effective source of capital formation without any fear of losses from capital market distortions.

Culture of tax evasion and corruption

Developing countries have consistently shown lower tax-to-GDP ratios than developed ones. While the government is often to blame for lower tax collection, citizens in developing countries show a tendency to evade taxes and duties. Only a small percentage of the population pays taxes even though the taxable population is much higher in these countries. Lower revenue collection hinders government activities and the provision of public goods. Active citizenship requires that citizens pay their due taxes. At the same time, corruption is as much a result of slipping societal norms as it is the result of poor governance. Rampant corruption can be attributable to all the population rather than only to a group in developing countries.

Conclusion

This chapter laid out a historical analysis of state formation and outcomes in developing countries. While doing so, it concludes that state formation in developing countries, more precisely the post-colonial states in Africa and Asia, has been shaped by colonial rule. The colonial regime gave rise to a political class that is extractive in nature. This extractive class has dominated economic policymaking in developing countries and has used the machines of policymaking for its own benefit. The continuation of such extraction has led to weaker institutions, both formal and informal. State formation in developing countries has been demonstrated by focusing on the case of Bangladesh. The analysis includes pre-colonial, colonial and post-colonial experience in understanding state formation in Bangladesh. For instance, emerging stylised facts delineate the economic institutions of the Indian subcontinent, particularly the province of Bengal, of which Bangladesh was a part. The institutions were extractive in nature, and politics was reserved for the elite class. As a result, the relation between state and citizen was segregated and exploitative. Since the nature of policies depends on the relationship between state and citizen, this distorted relation led to policies that often favoured the ruling elite class and their allies. This relation of state and citizenship includes both a state's formal and informal institutional setting. The institutional setting was historically extractive in Bengal. It was in favour of the ruling elite. Such an exploitative and extractive type of citizen–state relationship has perpetuated an extractive policy regime that alienates people from their states. As a result, Bengal failed to become a public society that safeguards the rights and welfare of the people irrespective of class. The people of Bengal struggled for a long time to have a society free from exploitation and oppression, but the people's aspiration was thwarted repeatedly.

In comparison with pre-independence Bangladesh, independent Bangladesh has managed notable achievements in all respects. In spite of these achievements, the real aspirations of the people—equality, human dignity and social justice—are yet to be realised. Over the years, the country's productive capacity did not expand as expected, the labour force remain poorly skilled, capital formation is weak and technological backwardness is rampant; in addition, the enforcement of policies is very poor, which ultimately results in a vulnerable economy. Since the nature of the state–citizen relationship is yet to break with the colonial legacy that is extractive and repressive, the policies determined by this relation fail to achieve the core aspiration of the people. As a consequence, many aspects of the political and economic affairs of the state of Bangladesh have remained similar to the colonial pre-independent situation. This failure of the state to become a public society is perpetuating the suffering of the people.

Developing countries are now facing one of the most critical periods in their economic history. It became a challenging job for the policymaker to keep a balance between life and livelihood. To eliminate the spread of the contagious COVID-19 virus and save lives, the government announced a prolonged lockdown. The shutdown has caused some inevitable consequences, such as a drop in consumption, income erosion, aggravated poverty, increased unemployment, reduced export demand, remittance shortfall, a sharp decrease in GDP growth, etc. There has been a diversified impact on every sector of the economy, and almost every sector has experienced lower profits, income erosion, a fall in demand, job losses, etc.

Further complicating matters, unemployment and inequality are going to be very salient during and after the COVID-19 pandemic, as estimates suggest that the numbers of those living in extreme poverty will increase by tens of millions. Fiscal policies should take into account, on the spending side, that investing in people is the solution to this crisis. In this context, providing a universal basic income, giving access to education, ensuring access to health and entitling people to access new job opportunities should be the immediate response.

To help sustain economies during the pandemic and revive them after the pandemic is over, governments in developing countries must take multidimensional initiatives. That is, they should react immediately with proper strategies to tackle the economic crisis; they not only need to act immediately, but they also need to be visionary and proactive in setting up strategies to revive the economy when the pandemic spread lessens and there is a return to normalcy. Specifically, some long-term measures are necessary to make economic improvement sustainable and durable. In the developed and developing world, several countries have considered such aspects of strategic planning and policy implementation and have established social security schemes. The evidence indicates that these have played an essential role in keeping people out of extreme poverty and helping them to sustain themselves in the long run. The institutional mechanisms of these countries can be contextualised to enact laws, create organisations, devise policies and design an operational system for social security schemes. Such exercises are not a far-fetched task, given that the leadership is visionary and considers both short-term and long-term economic solutions.

References

Acemoglu, D., & Robinson, J. A. (2012). *Why Nations Fail: The Origins of Power, Prosperity and Poverty*. New York: Crown.

Acemoglu, D., Ticchi, D., & Vindigni, A. (2011). Emergence and persistence of inefficient states. *Journal of the European Economic Association*, 9(2), 177–208.

Asian Development Bank. (2020). *An Updated Assessment of the Economic Impact of COVID-19*. Manilla, Philippines: Asian Development Bank.

Alavi, H. (1990). Authoritarianism and legitimation of state power in Pakistan. In S. K. Mitra (Ed.), *The Post-Colonial State in Asia: Dialectics of Politics and Culture*. New York: Harvester Wheatsheaf.

Avari, B. (2007). *India: The Ancient Past*. New York: Routledge.

Banerjee, A., & Iyer, L. (2005). History, institutions and economic performance: The legacy of colonial land tenure systems in India. *American Economic Review*, 95(4), 1190–1213. doi:10.1257/0002828054825574

Banerjea, P. (1922). *Fiscal Policy in India*. London: Macmillan and Co.

Barthelemy, J., & Mengus, E. (2019). Monetary rules, determinacy and limited enforcement. HEC Paris Research Paper No. ECO/SCD-2017-1202. Retrieved from SSRN https://ssrn.com/abstract=2962259 or doi:10.2139/ssrn.2962259

Bernier, F. (1891). *Travels in the Mogul Empire, A.D. 1656–68. A Revised and Improved Edition Based upon Irving Brock's Translation by Archibald Constable (With Maps and Illustrations, Chronicle of Events, and Bibliography)*. London: Archibald Constable.

Bethencourt, C., & Kunze, L. (2019). Tax evasion, social norms, and economic growth. *Journal of Public Economic Theory*, 21(2), 332–346.

Boettke, P. J., & Coyne, C. J. (2009). An entrepreneurial theory of social and cultural change. *Markets and Civil Society: The European Experience in Comparative Perspective*, 5, 77.

Booth, D., & Golooba-Mutebi, F. (2012). Developmental patrimonialism? The case of Rwanda. *African Affairs*, 111(444), 379–403.

Bose, S. R. (1989). The Pakistan economy since Independence (1947–70). In D. Kumar & T. Raychaudhuri (Eds.), *The Cambridge Economic History of India* (Vol. 2: c. 1757-c. 1970, pp. 995–1026). New York: Cambridge University Press.

Bowen, H. V. (1991). *Revenue and Reform: The Indian Problem in British Politics 1757–1773*. New York: Cambridge University Press.

Bracking, S. (2009). *Money and Power: Great Predators in the Political Economy of Development*. The Third World in Global Politics Series, London: Pluto Press.

Chakrabarti, S., & Patnaik, U. (Eds.) (2017). *Agrarian and Other Histories: Essays for Binay Bhushan Chaudhuri*. Tulika Books: New Delhi.

Chowdhury, B. K. (1967). Agrarian economy and agrarian relations in Bengal 1859–1885. In N. K. Sinha (Ed.), *The History of Bengal (1757–1905)* (pp. 237–336). Calcutta: Calcutta University Press.

Chowdhury, J. A. (1990). Privatization in Bangladesh. Working Paper No. 92. International Institute of Social Studies of Erasmus University (ISS).

Chowdhury, A. A. (2020). *Growth and Structural Transformation in African LDCs (2000–2020)*.

Coppedge, M., Gerring, J., Knutsen, C. H., Lindberg, S. I., Teorell, J., Alizada, N., Altman, D., Bernhard, M., Cornell, A., Fish, M. S., Gastaldi, L., Gjerløw, H., Glynn, A., Hicken, A., Hindle, G., Ilchenko, N., Krusell, J., Lührmann, A., Maerz, S. F., Marquardt, K. L., McMann, K., Mechkova, V., Medzihorsky, J., Paxton, P., Pemstein, D., Pernes, J., von Römer, J., Seim, B., Sigman, R., Skaaning, S.-E., Staton, J., Sundström, A., Tzelg ov, E., Wang, Y.-T., Wig, T., Wilson, S., & Ziblatt, D. (2021). V-Dem Country–Year Dataset v11. Varieties of Democracy (V-Dem) Project.

Coulibaly, B. S., Gandhi, D., & Senbet, L. W. (2019). Is sub-Saharan Africa facing another systemic sovereign debt crisis? New Delhi: Brookings India.

Dowd, D. (2000). *Capitalism and Its Economics: A Critical History*. London: Pluto Press.

Dosi, G. (1988). The nature of the innovative process. In G. Dosi, C. Freeman, R. R. Nelson, G. Silverberg, & L. Soete (Eds.), *Technical Change and Economic Theory*. London: Pinter Publishers.

Dutt, R. (1902). *The Economic History of India Under Early British Rule* (Vol. 1). Triibner, Great Britain: Kegan Paul.

Eaton, R. M. (1993). *The Rise of Islam and the Bengal Frontier, 1204–1760*. California: University of California Press.

Englebert, P. (2000). Pre-colonial institutions, post-colonial states, and economic development in tropical Africa. *Political Research Quarterly*, 53(1), 7–36.

Farooqi, M. (1972). *Pakistan: Polices that Led to Break-up*. New Delhi: New Age Printing Press.

Furnivall, J. S. (2014). *Colonial Policy and Practice*. Cambridge: Cambridge University Press.

Gramsci, A. (1971). *Hegemony*. na.

Guha, S. (2020). Mughal India: Economy, resources, and governance. In *The Oxford Handbook of the Mughal World*. In R. M. Eaton, & R. Sreenivasan (Eds.), Oxford: Oxford University Press.

Haque, M. S. (1997). Local Governance in developing Nations: Reexamine the question of accountability. *Regional Development Dialogue*, 18(2), ii–xxiii.

Hardy, P. (1972). *The Muslims of British India*. New York: Cambridge University Press.

Hodgson, G. M. (2006). What are institutions? *Journal of Economic Issues*, 40(1), 1–25.

Hopf, T. (2013). Common-sense constructivism and hegemony in world politics. *International Organization*, 67(2), 317–354.

Huang, H., & Wei, S. J. (2006). Monetary policies for developing countries: The role of institutional quality. *Journal of International Economics*, 70(1), 239–252.

ILO. (2020a). *COVID-19 and the World of Work: Impact and Policy Responses*. Geneva: International Labour Organization.

ILO. (2020b). *Global Wage Report 2020–21. Wages and Minimum Wages in the Time of COVID-19*. International Labour Organization

Jha, D. N. (2009). *Ancient India in Historical Outline*. New Delhi: Manohar.

Khan, M. (1999). *The Political Economy of Industrial Policy in Pakistan 1947–1971*.

Khan, M. H. (2000). The Political Economy of Industrial Policy in Pakistan 1947–1971. Working Papers 98, Department of Economics, SOAS, University of London, London.

Khan, M. H. (2005). Markets, states and democracy: Patron–client networks and the case for democracy in developing countries. *Democratization*, (12) 5, 704–724.

Khan, M. H. (2009). *Governance Capabilities and the Property Rights Transition in Developing Countries*. Department of Economics, SOAS, University of London.

Khan, M. (2010a). *Bangladesh: Partitions, Nationalisms and Legacies for State-Building*. Department of Economics, SOAS, University of London.

Khan, M. H. (2010b). *Learning, Technology Acquisition and Governance Challenges in Developing Countries*. Department of Economics, SOAS, University of London.

Krueger, A. O. (1994). Lessons from developing countries about economic policy. *The American Economist*, 38(1), 3–9.

Maddison, A. (1970). The historical origins of Indian poverty. *PSL Quarterly Review/Banca Nazionale del Lavoro*, 23(92), 31–81.

Maddison, A. (2006). *Class Structure and Economic Growth: India and Pakistan since the Moghuls*. New York: Routledge.

Médard, J. F. (2014). Patrimonialism, neo-patrimonialism and the study of the post-colonial state in Sub-Saharan Africa. *Occasional Paper*, (17), 76–97.

Murphy, A. E. (2009). *The Genesis of Macroeconomics: New Ideas from Sir William Petty to Henry Thornton*. Oxford: Oxford University Press.

Naoroji, D. (1901). *Poverty and Un-British Rule in India*. London: Swan Sonnenschein.
Nelson, R. R., & Winter, S. G. (1982). The Schumpeterian tradeoff revisited. *The American Economic Review*, 72(1), 114–132.
North, D. C. (1990). *Institutions, Institutional Change and Economic Performance*. Cambridge: Cambridge University Press.
Obasanjo, O. (1988). *Africa Embattled: Selected Essays on Contemporary African Development*. Ibadan: Fountain Publications.
Parto, S. (2005) Economic activity and Institutions: Taking stock. *Journal of Economic Issues*, 39(1), 21–52, doi:10.1080/00213624.2005.11506779
Pelikan, P. (1988). Can the Imperfect Innovation System of capitalism be Outperformed?. *Technical change and Economic Theory/ed. by G. Dosi et al.*—London: Pinter Publishers.
Power, J. H. (1963). Industrialization in Pakistan: A case of frustrated take-off? *The Pakistan Development Review*, 3(2), 191–207.
Posner, R. A. (1998). Creating a legal framework for economic development. *The World Bank Research Observer*, 13(1), 1–11.
Riaz, A. (2005). *Unfolding State: The Transformation of Bangladesh*. Canada: de Sitter.
Riddick, J. F. (2006). *The History of British India: A Chronology*. Westport, Connecticut: Praeger Publishers.
Rodney, W. (1973). *How Europe Underdeveloped Africa*. London: Bogle-L'Ouverture Publications.
Rodrik, D. (2011). The Future of Economic Convergence. NBER Working Paper No. 17400. National Bureau of Economic Research, Massachusetts, Cambridge.
Rodrik, D. (2014). The past, present, and future of economic growth. *Challenge*, 57(3), 5–39.
Sarkar, J. (1917). *Economics of British India* (4th ed.). London: Longmans, Green & Co.
Sarkar, J. N. (1972). *Islam in Bengal*. Calcutta: Ratna Prakashan.
Say, J. B. (1836). *A Treatise on Political Economy: Or the Production, Distribution, and Consumption of Wealth*. Philadelphia: Grigg & Elliot.
Sinha, N. K. (1967). Introduction. In N. K. Sinha (Ed.), *The History of Bengal (1757–1905)* (pp. 5–21). Calcutta: Calcutta University Press.
Sobhan, R., & Ahmad, M. (1980). *Public Enterprise in an Intermediate Regime, A Study in the Political Economy of Bangladesh*. Dhaka: Bangladesh Institute of Development Studies.
Sobhan, R. (2002). *Privatization in Bangladesh: An Agenda in Search of a Policy CPD Occasional Paper Series* (Paper 16). Dhaka: Centre for Policy Dialogue.
Stokes, E. (1978). *The Peasant and the Raj: Studies in Agrarian Society and Peasant Rebellion in Colonial India* (No. 23). *CUP Archive*.
Sumner, A., Ortiz-Juarez, E., & Hoy, C. (2020). *Precarity and the Pandemic: COVID-19 and Poverty Incidence, Intensity, and Severity in Developing Countries* (No. 2020/77). WIDER Working Paper.
Tadei, F. (2014). *Extractive Institutions and Gains From Trade: Evidence from Colonial Africa*. Working Papers 536, IGIER (Innocenzo Gasparini Institute for Economic Research), Bocconi University).
Titumir, R. A. M., & Hossain, A. M. (2014). Inflation and growth: An empirical analysis of Bangladesh. *The Jahangirnagar Economic Review*, 25, 1–12.
Titumir, R. A. M., & Rahman, M. Z. (2017). Demographic transition and its implications for productive absorption of labour force: The case of Bangladesh. *Dhaka University Journal of Development Studies*, 2(1), 123–146.
Titumir, R. A. M. (2019). *Political Settlement and Economic Outcome*, (in Bangla). Dhaka: Samhati Publications.

Titumir, R. A. M. (2020). Which recovery path may we pursue? *New Age*, 15 October. Retrieved from www.newagebd.net/article/118990/which-recovery-path-may-we-pursue

Titumir, R. A. M. (2021). *Numbers and Narratives in Bangladesh's Economic Development*. Singapore: Palgrave Macmillan.

Torgler, B. (2003a). *Tax Morale: Theory and Empirical Analysis of Tax Compliance* (Doctoral dissertation), University of Basel.

Torgler, B. (2003b). Tax morale and institutions. Retrieved from SSRN 663686.

Torgler, B., & Schneider, F. (2009). The impact of tax morale and institutional quality on the shadow economy. *Journal of Economic Psychology*, 30(2), 228–245.

United Nations, Asian Development Bank, and United Nations Development Programme. (2021). *Responding to the COVID-19 Pandemic: Leaving No Country Behind*. Bangkok, Thailand: United Nations.

Unnayan Onneshan. (2019). Bangladesh Economic Update (Vol. 10, No. 07). Dhaka: Unnayan Onneshan.

Vohra, R. (1997). *The Making of India: A Historical Survey*. New York: ME Sharpe.

Weber, M. (1946). Politics as a vocation. In *From Max Weber: Essays in Sociology*, translated by H. H. Gerth and C. W. Mills. Oxford University Press.

World Bank. (1972). *Reconstructing the Economy of Bangladesh* (Vol. 1). Washington DC: The World Bank.

World Bank. (1974). *Bangladesh: Development in a Rural Economy* (Vol. 1). Washington, DC: The World Bank.

World Bank. (2020). COVID-19 to add as many as 150 million extreme poor by 2021. Press Release. Washington, DC: The World Bank.

2 Framing fiscal and monetary policies for developing countries

Introduction

The chapter makes an attempt to understand the cause-and-effect relations among economic policies, citizen and state. The discussion posits that transformational institutions are key to a functioning market and state. Against the backdrop of different schools of thought, the chapter comes up with an alternative diagnostic framework. It questions the so-called apolitical approach of "new consensus", neoclassical/monetarists and public choice theorists and establishes that economic policymaking is an overtly political process by demonstrating how decisions of state-citizens-firms are shaped by formal institutions, contingent upon informal institutions such as norms (informal codes) and values (reproduced by society).

Throughout the chapter, the analysis pertains to the linkages between the formal and informal institutions and the circular flow in the economy, which associate factors of production with labour and capital returns and the expansion of productive capacity. Subsequently, formal and informal institutions contribute to power relations and resulting political settlement, which affects economic policies that are directed to yield a certain outcome. Moreover, the analysis sheds light on the postulations of the diverse schools of economic thought, while surpassing the confines of new institutional economics, which has solely focused on property rights, information asymmetry and transaction costs. In doing so, it bolsters the role of the informal codes and values reproduced by society and their impact on the trajectory of economic policies in developing countries.

The current debates on development investigate the most rapidly growing countries of the world, transitional states and the so-called "failed states" to find out the determinants of the acceleration or deceleration of the transition from low-to-middle-income to high-income status. Yet these debates miss major political economy questions as regards the crisis in the formation of the postcolonial independent state. Thanks to the erroneous intellectual basis and consequential policymaking, the crises in postcolonial states have continued unabated and some have descended into failed states in Asia, Africa and Latin

DOI: 10.4324/9781003201847-2

America, though taxpayers continue to pump resources due to "the white man's burden" (Easterly, 2006).

It is also important to understand that although the original writings of past economists on a number of subjects have been examined differently in later periods, it is however the later interpretation that is widely accepted in today's academia and in common understanding, and the appropriate role of the state is one such area. Hence, the evolution and reservations of the different schools of thoughts and the ideas of influential figures regarding the role of the state need to be re-examined. Any school of thought should be evaluated based primarily on the original texts and their internal logical criteria, and only later should empirical and ideological issues be considered (Tsoulfidis, 2010). Accordingly, this chapter deals with present interpretations as well as original texts. Moreover, it is often argued that identifying similarities instead of differences can be more effective in the investigation and synthesis of knowledge (Shionoya & Nishizawa, 2008). This chapter, therefore, understanding the above issue, treats the relevant economic literature based on what has been said and what has remained relevant to understanding the economic issues of developing countries in today's world.

On the basis of its criticism of the different schools of thought regarding the state in the economic arena, this chapter undertakes three tasks. First, it reveals that there exist significant variations within different schools about how the state is relevant for the economy, which often have been neglected in favour of a single dominant view. Nonetheless, the role of the state has always been important in the economic arena irrespective of the school of thought. Thus, the importance of a proactive state and activist economic policy cannot be ignored. Second, the role of the accumulation of capital, power and class has been missing in the major theories; it can explain the relationship between the state and citizen in a capitalist developing country to promote state-building and maximise public choice and development. Finally, the chapter presents an alternative framework that demonstrates how the understanding of the role of the state through its use of policy tools is required to comprehend state-building and development performance in a developing country like Bangladesh.

Economic policy: A review

This section ascertains that markets cannot provide solutions to all economic problems. As a theoretical construct, when the circular flow of income in the economy leads to a virtuous cycle among households, firms and institutions, a functioning state is activated. A functioning state in turn results in a functional market, for which the main sufficient condition is the presence of transformational institutions. Transformational institutions refer to the countervailing power against the extractive nature of the state and the capital accumulation motives of the ruling elites. Although most neoclassical and monetarist economics take such a radical view of markets, it represents only a special case, as this section would argue. In particular, markets may be the best mechanism in the case of macroeconomic decisions, but they have to be complemented by the state. Hence institutions (both formal and informal), political settlement and class have a crucial role to play in policy decisions.

The main objective is to ensure aggregate demand, full employment and price stability in the state with the help of the fiscal policy, and the central bank helps the government to fulfil it with the help of the monetary policy.

Fiscal policy will have implications both at the household and firm levels. At the household level, fiscal policy will have ramifications primarily through employment generation, social security provision and inequality reduction. Productive employment is a credible form of poverty reduction with accelerated growth. This can be achieved by combining both the demand and supply sides of labour market policies, which are mainly economic growth–driven and quality-adjusted labour force growth, respectively. Fiscal policies and institutions execute the strategies to accelerate growth, expand the formal sector and thereby create new jobs. Fiscal policies are also associated with the provision of a fully-fledged social security programme suitable to the life cycle of the public—children, mothers, youth and the elderly. Social security directly impacts the well-being of the people and is crucial for the large populations living below the poverty line in developing countries. In addition, the structure of the fiscal policy determines the degree to which it acts as a key instrument in the redistribution of income, mainly by taxing higher levels of income heavily and spending proportionally on providing benefits to the low-income population.

At the firm level, fiscal policy is useful in the expansion of productive capacity in the economy. Fiscal policy may be used to provide financial incentives to key strategic industries in the economy, support small business and cottage industries and provide greater public investment in human capital and technology in order to enhance productivity. Increased fiscal stimulus and productivity will help augment productive capacity in an economy, ensuring a transformative pattern of growth that will in turn support employment creation for households. Simultaneously, a productive expansion will enable diversification to take place, as the productive real sectors are rendered conducive to supporting the emergence and development of new industries and innovation.

Fiscal policy is a government's decisions regarding spending and taxing. If a government wants to stimulate growth in the economy, it will increase spending for goods and services. This will increase demand for goods and services. As demand goes up, production goes up. If production goes up, firms may need to hire more households. Households that were once unemployed may now have jobs and money to spend on goods and services. If the government thinks the economy is overheating—or growing too fast—the government may decrease spending. A decrease in government spending will decrease overall demand in the economy. The other side of fiscal policy is taxes. If the government does not have enough revenue to support spending, it will have to borrow money.

Managing the money supply is the main purpose of the central bank, using the monetary policy. The money supply includes forms of credit, cash, cheques and money market mutual funds. The most important of these forms of money is credit. Credit includes loans, bonds and mortgages. Monetary policy increases liquidity, or the presence of money or financial assets available to households and firms to facilitate investment and consumption, in order to create economic growth. Monetary policy is used to reduce liquidity to prevent inflation as well. Central banks use interest rates, bank reserve requirements and the amount of government bonds that banks must hold. All these tools affect how much banks can lend. The volume of loans affects the money supply. Monetary policy and fiscal policy should work hand-in-glove. It rarely works this way.

At the household level, monetary policy is directly associated with prices and inflation, which impact the consumption expenditure and saving patterns of households. Households are interested in a rise in wages and prices in the flexible price markets. Their behaviour contributes to the money supply through savings and deposits made from labour returns and changes in price. Households are also a major contributor to demand-side pulls on inflation, when purchasing power originating in wage increases is not aligned with a proportionate expansion in productive capacity.

At the firm level, monetary policy evidently relates to the nature of capital accumulation carried out by capitalists. The neoclassical growth theory emphasises the accumulation of capital as the source of productivity and assumes diminishing returns in production. In contrast, the literature on endogenous growth theory shifted attention to human capital accumulation and assumed that diminishing returns to investment in education, training and research may not be inevitable.

The functioning of the economy

Classical authors like Smith, Ricardo, Say and John Stuart Mill gave a role to the state in their economic theories. Through a simple representation of Say's Law that "supply creates its own demand", such a role has been relegated to obscurity in the mainstream representation of the classical school (Kates, 2005). The classical school actually believes in the supremacy of the market in economic decision-making to a great extent, but not altogether. Their idea is that a market is the best mechanism for producing the optimum amount of goods according to public choice as reflected through the market mechanism.

Adam Smith is credited with many of the ideas that provided the cradle for the classical school. Smith is the one who developed the most comprehensive argument against the mercantile ideology, which was an obstacle to industrial capitalism, and argued in favour of a free-market economy as a means to enhance the wealth of nations (Dowd, 2000). He emphasised the role of the invisible hand in bringing the best outcomes in production and employment decisions and identified how the self-interest of human beings directs their actions. According to Smith, this self-interest of human beings brings the best material benefit for humankind when operated through the mechanism of a free-market economy.

Smith, however, did not hold human motives upon all questions and seemed to be well aware of the limitations of the free-market system and its pro-capital bias that works against the workers. Adam Smith advocated the public provision of education with partial contributions from the enrolled students (Thomas, 2017). He called for education for all, believing that it would offset the harmful effects of the division of labour on the workers, and therefore, education had to be accessible to the workers (Thomas, 2017). In short, Smith supported the enhancement of human ability through the public provision that promotes prosperity.

Later, French economist Jean-Baptiste Say (1767–1832) developed the principle known as Say's Law, which strengthened the background of classical economic theory to affirm the supremacy of the market in maintaining full employment. Say's Law is generally taken in mainstream economics to mean "supply creates its own demand"—when a producer produces a product of a certain value, he or she produces a demand of equal value. Moreover, the classical school holds that wages and prices are flexible enough to adjust quickly. As a result, it rules out overproduction as well as prolonged unemployment and recession. Another assumption that is linked to classical economists is that they did not make any fundamental difference between a barter economy and a monetary one (Samuelson & Nordhaus, 2010).

It is, therefore, argued that there is no scope for recession in classical economics. A policy conclusion is that government spending can only increase price levels, and does not have any effect on employment and output. However, it is obviously true that not all products are consumed; a certain portion is saved. Classical economists believe that such savings are not a problem as they are channelled into investment through movement in interest rates.

Say's Law as depicted in the mainstream explanation, however, is a deviation from what Say actually meant. Say did not rule out the possibility of the overproduction of certain goods and the underproduction of certain others or the existence of involuntary unemployment. He was well aware of those limitations of a free market and attempted to explain them within the structure of production—it is that the producers produce the wrong combination of goods, not that purchasing power is insufficient (Kates, 2009).

Say, however, seems to be only of the opinion that what a society observes is an excess demand of a certain commodity, but it cannot observe an excess of aggregate demand over aggregate supply. If production is small and limited to a small number of products, there is a high chance that certain products may fail to find a market, although there remains unmet demand for other products (Say, 1821). In case of the respective importance of consumption and investment, which later became a major issue of debate between classical economists like David Ricardo and John Stuart Mill on the one hand and Malthus on the other, Say clearly favoured investment over consumption (Kates, 2009).

Adding supply-side explanations

It was Thomas Robert Malthus (1766–1834), David Ricardo (1772–1823) and Robert Torrens (1780–1864) who expanded the supply-side explanation for economic downturn and added the concept of money to the equation. In his

Essay on the Production of Wealth, Torrens (1821) more clearly linked the overproduction of particular commodities to a more general economic downturn or recession. If several producers produce commodities for which there is no demand in the market, they would not be able to receive money for their goods. As a result, their ability to purchase commodities from other producers would be compromised, and consequently, those producers would also fail to sell theirs as well. The process could continue to include the whole economy, and thus the particular overproduction of certain commodities could result in a general downturn (Kates, 2009).

Ricardo (1821) was another classical economist who followed Say in arguing that goods are produced to buy other goods and that the overproduction of certain commodities is possible, but not general overproduction. Additionally, Ricardo was of the opinion that money's role in the whole process is only to facilitate exchange and nothing more. Ricardo's belief that it is the tendency of the people to expend money, however, immediately comes in contrast to the belief that the demand for money could change at times.

The final figure to discuss in this regard is John Stuart Mill (1806–1873). The idea of demand deficiency has been addressed in several of Mill's books, and it is his version of Say's Law that has prominently appeared in Keynes. Mill's interpretation of Say's Law was later taken as the standard classical understanding, especially by English economists, for almost a century (Kates, 2009). Mill believes that any increase in productivity along with a similar increase in the money supply would increase the purchasing power by the same proportion, but this would still not result in demand deficiency. The desire to purchase less on the part of the masses is a more logical possibility as a reason for a demand deficiency than a deficiency occurring from any increase in money supply (Mill, 1965).

Mill also included in his analysis the desire to hold money. He seems to agree that any increase in the desire to hold money from sources such as commercial crisis could result in deficiency of demand. Thus, the possibility of hoarding is accepted by Mill. However, he believes such an outcome is temporary. As he stated:

> But it is a great error to suppose, with Sismondi, that a commercial crisis is the effect of a general excess of production. It is simply the consequence of an excess of speculative purchases. It is not a gradual advent of low prices, but a sudden recoil from prices extravagantly high: its immediate cause is a contraction of credit, and the remedy is, not a diminution of supply, but the restoration of confidence. It is also evident that this temporary derangement of markets is an evil only because it is temporary.
>
> (Mill, 1965)

Based on the supply-side theory, the policies of cutting taxes on the rich intend to unleash new investment that spurs economic growth and boosts job creation, leading to economic improvements for everyone, have been proved ineffective since supply-side policies did not deliver as promised (Ettlinger & Linden, 2012). The economic performance of the USA after the tax increases of 1993 significantly outpaced that of the periods following the tax cuts of the early 1980s and the early 2000s (Ettlinger & Linden, 2012). Supply-side economics' foundation that supply creates its own demand does not work as follows:

> 1) Say's Law denies a problem of unemployment, as in recessions. Recessions, however, do occur, 2) Say's Law holds that aggregate supply and demand are equal. If people collectively decide to increase their cash balances, thereby reducing demand and not supply, 3) Say's Law holds money as a veil, making the economy essentially equivalent to a barter economy, making monetary theory impossible. Monetary theory is possible.
>
> (Combs, 2016)

Adding demand-side explanations

As opposed to the supply-side emphasis of Say, it was first Spence (1808) and later Malthus (1836) who channelled their arguments to consumption and thus to the demand side, by arguing in favour of promoting consumption to address the problem of deficient demand.

Spence's opinion regarding the importance of consumption was such:

> not only does the production of national wealth depend upon the expenditure of the class of land proprietors, but, for the due increase of this wealth, and for the constantly progressive maintenance of the prosperity of the community, it is absolutely requisite, that this class should go on progressively increasing its expenditure.
>
> (Spence, 1808)

Similarly, Malthus, who was a contemporary of Ricardo, differed with his fellow classical economists. Malthus not only emphasised consumption but also was sceptical about the increase of saving to promote production:

> It is therefore obvious that without an expenditure which will encourage commerce, manufactures, and personal services, the possessors of land would have no sufficient stimulus to cultivate well; and a country … with too parsimonious habits, infallibly become poor and comparatively unpeopled.
>
> (Malthus, 1836)

Even if consumption was unproductive, Malthus firmly argued that it had a beneficial role in the economy. In correspondence with Ricardo, Malthus argued that rapid investment in productive activities would permanently increase the demand for factors of production in comparison to the products produced by the employment of those factors. If such accumulation of labour into the productive sector continues without reaching any limit from the lack of land or meeting further demand from unproductive consumption demand, the desire for further accumulation would ultimately come to a halt. It is therefore vital for any country to have a destination for the produce of their unproductive production, i.e., consumers that are more and more willing to buy consumer goods (Malthus, 1836). Malthus also provided a persuasive argument about the two components of demand, the ability to purchase and the will to purchase, and argued that having purchasing power does not mean having the will to spend money (Kates, 2009).

In short, demand-driven growth models state that investment decisions are made based on expected future demand (Nell, 2012). It means slow growth indicates lower expectations for future demand and suppresses investment below the rate required to achieve the natural or optimum growth rate (Nell, 2012). Thus, increased growth requires an expenditure-led policy. Despite acknowledging the necessity of an expenditure-led policy for increased aggregate demand through increased investment, demand-driven growth models do not provide any explanation of the role of politics in policymaking.

Ricardo was interested in taxation on the unearned increment of factors of production since it creates inequality. Basically, this idea is centred on his idea of economic rent, which is the income received by the owner of a factor of production that exceeds the amount which is economically or socially necessary. Thus, economic rent is unearned income to the owner of a factor of production as any payment over and above the minimum payment needed to bring a factor of production into productive use. As a result, owners of factors of production extract the major pie from their production. Since they are the powerful group, they try to influence the rules that keep them enjoying their economic rent. Rents create inequality, and it is necessary to shield the economy against rents (Piketty, 2014). Piketty's analysis was based on the neoclassical assumption; he assumes that increase in inequality is due to too much real investment and too much production flexibility (Palma, 2016, Rowthorn, 2014; Taylor, 2014 cited in Palma, 2018). Thus, in this neoclassical logic, if one has too much of a good thing, one unfortunately ends up with higher inequality (Palma, 2018). Piketty, however, acknowledges that institutional changes and political shocks, which he rightly views as endogenous to the inequality and development processes, themselves played a major role in the past, and it will probably be the same in the future (Palma, 2018).

Markets and double function

John Maynard Keynes (1883–1946) rejected the classical perspectives. His rejection of the classical view came from the fact that the doctrine of total withdrawal of the state from the market involves the possibility of the collapse of the capitalist system itself (Beaud, 1997). To Keynes, capitalism had no conceivable alternative, but his emphasis on government action in correcting the market economy made him the focus of much hatred within the capitalist community (Dowd, 2000). In his book *The General Theory of Employment, Interest and Money*, Keynes did accept the role of free markets, but he departed from the classical school's view that markets ensure full employment by matching aggregate demand with aggregate supply (Matyas, 1985). Government plays a greater role in Keynes' own analysis than has been ascribed to him by later scholars.

Keynes' criticism regarding the classical school mainly involves the latter's acceptance of the assumption that supply creates its own demand. He pointed out three specific faults with the classical school in this regard. First, Keynes challenged the consensus of flexible wages. Keynes argued that although the classical school's acceptance of "frictional" and "voluntary" unemployment is consistent with the basic principles of the school, he departed from the classical economists over the presence of a third category of unemployment, which he termed as "involuntary".

Keynes (1936) linked the concepts of money wage and real wage to elaborate his point: although the money wage is inflexible, the real wage and therefore the marginal disutility of labour tend to move downwards, but still unemployment exists. Thus, the real wage could go down because of rising prices, which although the classical school supposes of little importance, actually is not that unimportant. Thus, although workers do not attempt to repel any fall in nominal wages, such practice is not observed in any rise in prices.

Second, Keynes (1936) argued that the modern economy is a monetary economy, and the rules that hold for a monetary economy are different from a barter economy. When money enters into the economy, the relationship that was predicted by Say's Law seems to fail.

Third, and most importantly, Keynes questions the concept of equality between the aggregate demand and aggregate supply since the factors that determine the decision to abstain from present consumption are not related to the factors that determine the decision to provide for future consumption. As aptly expressed by Dowd: "Keynes argued, savings are instead a function of the level of income—Say's Law collapses, as does a major pillar of the edifice of *laissez-faire* capitalism" (Dowd, 2000). As appropriately summarised by Blaug (1990):

> In a monetary economy, therefore, savings and investment cannot be always and necessarily equal to the supply and demand for loans. But in equilibrium this will be true because equilibrium is given by the condition that people are satisfied with their cash holdings … Since the classical economists held Say's equality rather than Say's identity, they must have allowed for the Keynesian possibility that intended saving may not be realised … Clearly, if intended saving exceeds intended investment, the rate of interest will fall and the price level will rise, working to restore equilibrium. The only difference between this kind of argument and the

> Keynesian one is that saving according to Keynes is a function of income, whereas in classical analysis saving is a complicated function of the interest rate and the level of prices via the character of investment opportunities. Income variations produce equilibrium in Keynes; price and interest variations produce equilibrium in classical theory.
>
> (Blaug, 1990)

What Keynes did was to provide a system that explains how aggregate demand could fall below the aggregate supply, leading to a fall in employment. Despite this view not being unique to Keynes, as previously Malthus had expressed a similar view, what Keynes did was to develop the elaborate mechanism that explained the economy.

According to Keynes, entrepreneurs would employ labour only to the extent that would maximise their profits by selling the output produced by the labour and no more than that, and thus it is the profit that determines employment not only for individual firms but also for the industry and the economy. When income increases, the demand for consumption also increases, but not by as much as income. The more people are employed, the more will be the supply price for producers, which in turn would increase the gap between the supply price for producers and the amount that the community is expected to spend on consumption. If therefore there is no change in people's desire to consume, employment would not increase, as this would kill the profit. The only way to counter this is to increase new investment.

The propensity to consume, according to Keynes, is greater for a poor economy, which means a moderate boost in investment would be enough to provide full employment. Conversely, as the economy becomes richer, because of the falling tendency of the propensity to consume with income, the economy would have to find much greater opportunities to invest if it wants to remain at full employment level.

As opposed to his classical colleagues, Keynes thus was not optimistic about the ability of the laissez-faire economy to provide full employment. Finally, not only did he believe that the state has an important role to play in reducing the fluctuations of the economy and full employment, but he was also concerned about the distributional aspect of wealth. Despite its acknowledgement of the role of the state in the economy, Keynesianism provides no clear roadmap on how to enforce the role of the state and to what extent the state can intervene in the economy. It thus fails to incorporate politics and class as well as power relations into its analysis, which are the precursors in state policy formulation.

New consensus economics

Keynes himself was at times critical of the deviations. For example, in his correspondence with Hicks in 1937, Keynes criticised Hicks for making investment dependent on current income rather than on expected future income (Dimand, 1999). Among the various lines of such interpretation, three distinct lines are noteworthy. They are neo-Keynesians, new Keynesians and post-Keynesians. The neo-Keynesian perspective is also known as the Neoclassical Keynesian Synthesis. As the name suggests, neo-Keynesians attempt to integrate Keynesian models into traditional or neoclassical economics, such as the Keynesian Cross model of Paul Samuelson and the IS–LM framework of John Hicks and Alvin Hansen. These models emphasise overall demand for goods and services in the economy as the determinant of the economy's performance (Dolenc, 2004). In contrast, the fiscal policy view of the new Keynesians, now called "new consensus" economics, can be considered "a significant advance when compared to the older neoclassical perspectives that reject fiscal deficits altogether", i.e., any effect altogether (Seccareccia, 2011). Nonetheless, this new consensus macroeconomics and fiscal policy, which was the result of a major shift within macroeconomic policy over the last two decades or so of the twentieth century, opposes "the use of discretionary fiscal policy and of long-term budget deficits" (Arestis & Sawyer, 2004a). As the reason behind such a move, the cases of crowding out and of the Ricardian Equivalence Theorem (RET) are widely put forward (Arestis & Sawyer, 2004a).

Again, the category of "crowding out" can be divided into four different lines of argument. The first line of argument in favour of crowding out comes in the context of the IS–LM model, when a fiscal expansion is supposed to give rise to interest rates (Arestis & Sawyer, 2004a). The counterargument here is that whether the crowding out would happen in this case depends on the corresponding changes in monetary policy tools, and not because of how a self-functioning market responds.

The second source of the crowding-out argument is connected to the role savings play in fiscal policy, where a rise in government deficit works as a sign of a fall in government saving and gives rise to domestic crowding out or international crowding out or both (Cunningham & Vilasuso, 1994). This need not be the case, as domestic savings are considered to be exogenous in this line of argument (Arestis & Sawyer, 2004a). The treatment of domestic savings can be ruled out to be exogenous "in that its size responds to changes in, inter alia, government expenditure" (Arestis & Sawyer, 2004a). On the other hand, international crowding may not also "materialise" as a number of forces can cancel each other out under certain conditions.

The third source of the crowding-out argument can be linked to the notion of supply-side equilibrium and the adjustment of aggregate demand to the supply-side equilibrium. In this case, it is believed that supply-side equilibrium must be achieved. However,

> in the absence of some powerful automatic market forces or a potent monetary policy, which can ensure that the level of aggregate demand moves quickly to be consistent with the supply-side equilibrium, fiscal policy has a clear role to play. The path of aggregate demand can itself influence the supply-side equilibrium.
>
> (Arestis & Sawyer, 2004a)

Finally, the RET can be treated as the fourth source of crowding out in an economy (Arestis & Sawyer, 2004a). Ricardo in 1877 proposed two ways in which war can be better financed: either "through new government debts, or through a temporary tax" (Belingher & Moroianu, 2015). Ricardo viewed no difference between these ways, as he said, "debt is nothing else than postponed taxes" (Belingher & Moroianu, 2015). Later, it was Barro and Buchanan whose contemplation led to the revival, revision and birth of Ricardian equivalence (Belingher & Moroianu, 2015; Dow & Saville, 2001).

There are however some assumptions behind the Ricardian equivalence hypothesis: "economic agents will foresee this inevitability, will perceive no change in their permanent income, and thus will make no change in their current spending". It further assumes that agents are perfectly 'altruistic', and treat as equivalent to their own welfare that of their heirs – and (their heirs also being held to be altruistic) by implication the welfare of the heirs of their heirs" (Dow & Saville, 2001). Ricardian equivalence can be critiqued on the basis that "the consequences of the government's intertemporal budget constraint are far less obvious to average citizens than to economists". Moreover, even if an individual is aware of the connection between government bonds and future taxes, "there are profound difficulties in making even an approximately Ricardian consumption choice in a modern mixed economy" (Gruen, 1997).

> Finally, "however, when fiscal policy is approached in 'functional finance' terms that is the government runs a budget deficit because there is a difference between savings and investment at the desired income level, then the Ricardian equivalence approach is scarcely relevant. In the absence of a budget deficit, the excess of savings over investment cannot occur"
>
> (Arestis & Sawyer, 2004b).

Empirical estimates are also not very convincing of the Ricardian equivalence hypothesis. Historically, conflict with France led the size of British government debt to rise about twice its national income by the 1820s, which was probably a record. From the estimates of the return on a variety of private assets such as land and houses in England between 1725 and 1839, at most, debt and deficits had "a very modest impact on private rates of return" and evidence of "little crowding out" (Clark, 2001). In the developed United States, "the cost to an immortal intertemporally-optimising consumer of being ignorant of the link between bonds and future taxes", who was "exposed to the changing level of US Federal government debt over the 30-year period 1961–90", was estimated to "range from about $1 to $10 per annum." The author therefore concluded that

> provided governments do not use bond-financing too aggressively, the utility gains from making approximately Ricardian consumption choices may not outweigh the utility cost of collecting, understanding and analysing the information necessary to make such choices. Ignoring the link between bonds and future taxes may be privately optimal. Then bond-financed

> fiscal policy has significant systematic effects on aggregate demand and national savings
>
> (Gruen, 1997).

Similarly, the empirical results from India on annual data for 1950–1951 to 2009–2010 did not provide any proof of a "long-run relationship between public saving and private saving and invalidated Ricardian equivalence in India (Singh, 2017). "Despite a huge body of both theoretical and empirical work, Ricardian equivalence remains a hypothesis about which there is remarkably little professional agreement" (Gruen, 1997).

Like the neo-Keynesians, new Keynesians also follow the equilibrium approach to macroeconomic analysis. Unlike their neo-Keynesian counterparts, they adopt the rational expectations hypothesis and the natural rate hypothesis of Milton Friedman. Therefore, new Keynesians are not overly enthusiastic about the ability of fiscal policy to counter negative business cycles. Moreover, their explanation of market failure stood on the modelling of wages and price stickiness (Dolenc, 2004). New Keynesians like Janet Yellen advocate the use of monetary policy in stabilising economic activity over the business cycle and observe the inverse relationship between unemployment and inflation as the Phillips curve does. New Keynesians also put an emphasis on the efficiency wage model to explain involuntary unemployment. Worker's productivity depends on the real wage as Yellen (1984) argued:

> Any reduction in the wage paid would lower the productivity of all employees already on the job. Thus, the efficiency wage hypothesis explains involuntary unemployment.
>
> (Yellen, 1984)

During a recession, wages do not fall to the level such that every job seeker can find a job, which would lower unemployment. If the demand for labour falls, this lowers wages. But because wages have fallen, the probability of "shirking" (workers not exerting effort) will have risen. If wages fall, this will lower the workers' productivity. As a result, wages do not fall enough to maintain employment at the previous level, because firms want to avoid excessive shirking by their workers (Shapiro & Stiglitz, 1984). Hence, unemployment rises due to high wages during a recession. Shapiro and Stiglitz (1984) also observe the information structure of the market that affects unemployment.

Post-Keynesians mostly disagree with neoclassical economics and rational expectations and emphasise the non-neutrality of money, in contrast to the neo-Keynesians and the new Keynesians who believe the classical notion that money is "neutral", especially in the long term (Dolenc, 2004). Later post-Keynesians, however, have crossed the works of Keynes to borrow ideas from economists such as Roy Harrod, Joan Robinson, Nicholas Kaldor, Michal Kalecki and Piero Sraffa (Lavoie, 2006). Post-Keynesians have rejected the three axioms that Keynes suggested rejecting in *The General Theory*. These are the ergodic axiom, the gross-substitution axiom and the neutral-money axiom.

The orthodox theory assumes that all income is immediately spent on produce. As a result, there is always effective demand for the goods and services that an economy can produce in full employment. Post-Keynesians reject this ergodic axiom by recognising that the future is uncertain (nonergodic) and cannot be reliably predicted. Rather, people decide on how much can be consumed or not be consumed on the basis of their income and they instead save a certain amount of the income for future consumption (Syll, 2013).

Post Keynesians reject the gross substitution axiom as applicable to assets that savers use to store their savings. Consequently, higher liquid asset prices do not divert this savings demand for liquid assets to a demand for producibles whose relative price has declined (Syll, 2013). Likewise, post-Keynesians also reject the classical neutral-money axiom by asserting that changes in the money supply due to borrowing from banks in order to finance investment affect the level of employment and output both in the short term and the long term.

Post-Keynesians differ from the proponents of the new classical school, who argue that capital can be seen as a completely mobile factor of production which can be moved from one production technique to another and opine that economic techniques are defined and chosen in advance. Thus, a decision-maker does not face mobile and competitive markets for factor inputs but has to choose between predetermined techniques (Tcherneva, 2011). There is a trade-off between wages and profits (Dray & Thirlwall, 2010). In the 1950s, this led to the Cambridge Capital Controversy, the debate between Cambridge University in the United Kingdom and the Massachusetts Institute of Technology in Cambridge, the United States, that implied a fallacy of composition in the neoclassical theory, such that microeconomic concepts cannot be aggregated to reflect the economy as a whole. While neoclassical economists consider utility-maximising consumption decisions of individuals as the driving force of economic activity, with the allocation of given, scarce resources as the fundamental economic problem, the school of Cambridge University argues for a return to a classical political economy vision (Cohen & Harcourt, 2003). Therefore, the profit-making decisions of capitalist firms are the driving force, with the fundamental economic problem being the allocation of surplus output to ensure reproduction and growth (Walsh, Walsh & Gram, 1980, cited in Cohen & Harcourt, 2003). Analysis of social class, therefore, becomes relevant since individuals depend on the market for their livelihoods.

Differing from new classical economics, post-Keynesians argued that state intervention is needed since the so-called free-market economy can hardly handle the swings, boom and busts in business cycles. Thus, Minsky calls for government steps to control these through regulation, central bank action and other tools (Minsky, 1974). Though they ask for the analysis of class and power relations of society and the role of the state in effective economic policies, they seldom explain the political settlement of postcolonial countries. It is, furthermore, argued that post-Keynesianism and eco-development share the same position regarding economic growth through the concept of radical uncertainty, and the importance of the precautionary principle (Berr, 2015). Despite its focus on intergenerational and intragenerational perspectives of development, again post-Keynesianism provides no clear-cut road map on how such decisions are to be made based on the political and class reality.

Savings and investment

The new classical school of economics considers that actors have rational expectations. This school argues that individual rationality will lead to the maximisation of utility or profit through a mechanism of supply and demand. As opposed to Keynesian economics, it states that savings determine investment. This approach was developed in the nineteenth century, mainly from the writings of William Stanley Jevons, Carl Menger and Léon Walras, which became popular in the early 20th century and remained dominant in economic policymaking. Since individuals take rational decisions, as this school assumes, economy reaches an equilibrium through its pricing mechanism. Thus, the state is pushed out of economic activities. The free market emerges as the means to efficient and optimal allocation of the resources in the economy.

Monetarism believes that the total amount of money in an economy is the primary determinant of economic growth. Based on the quantity theory of money, monetarists argue that government should keep the money supply steady for economic growth. Monetarists argue that fiscal policy as an instrument of controlling an economy hinders growth. To them, the market becomes distorted when government intervenes. Thus, the government is seen as detrimental to the economy. They further believe that, like the new classical school, government intervention in the market could lead to large deficits, increased debt and higher interest rates, which would eventually force the economy into a state of destabilisation.

Monetarist economists, of which the most notable of course is Milton Friedman, used the concept of the natural rate of unemployment hypothesis to argue that economies are more stable than previously thought. Friedman (1977) argued that the permanent trade-off between inflation and employment as expressed by the Phillips curve does not hold. Rather, each economy has a specific rate of employment called "non-accelerating inflation rate of unemployment" (NAIRU).

The consequence is that beyond that natural level, monetary and fiscal policies are ineffective in the long run in reducing the level of unemployment, and would only produce rising inflation. This happens because agents adjust their behaviour to the observed trend in the inflation rate, and rising prices do not mean higher demand and thus better business opportunities. Monetary policy seeking to stimulate effective demand in the economy can therefore produce a real effect only in the short term at a cost of higher inflation. In the long run, agents adapt, and the natural rate of unemployment prevails. Thus, monetarists believe that the free market is enough to ensure the optimal use of resources (Beaud, 1997).

> Friedman firmly denied, however, that the government could speed up this process using macroeconomic tools. Activist policies, if unanticipated, could have a short-run effect on output and employment, Friedman argued. But he denied their effectiveness Keynes and the classics over a longer time span. Even worse, Friedman claimed that such policies could actually destabilise the economy.
>
> (Drobny, 1988)

The new classical school, which has close connections with the Monetarist school and which is often stricter than the monetarists in rejecting the imperfections of the market, alleged that it was in part developed to counter the influence of Marxian ideology and to meet the demands of the business community (Dowd, 2000). What the new classical school did was to develop the monetarist analysis by adding the concept of rational expectations to natural rate models. Thus, a stronger impetus of new classical economists has been established in favour of the argument that output and employment always remain at a natural rate and that both product and labour market always stay in equilibrium (Beaud, 1997; Drobny, 1988).

Furthermore, when new modes of production are introduced, deploying new resources, rents emerge as the addition of value that results from entrepreneurship, which is known as Schumpeterian rent (Sautet, 2014). This rent is transient since, as Schumpeter explains, it does not persist in equilibrium. It emerges during the creative destruction of the market when new combinations of resources are deployed by the entrepreneurs. The creative destruction initiates new modes of production, with new knowledge and technology destroying the old modes of production. Thus, Schumpeter emphasises entrepreneurship through new knowledge and technological advancement that replaces the old. While new classical economics considers technological change as an exogenous factor and argues that the critical element for growth is the rate of savings and investment compared to the rate of depreciation and population growth (Dornbusch, Fischer & Startz, 2007), new growth theory considers technological change as an endogenous factor.

New growth theory calls for investment in ideas and technological advancement. The proponents of this theory observe that the twentieth century's robust growth performance is mainly attributed to international free trade, technological change and the easy flow of technology and high levels of investment in human capital generation (Romer, 1990). Hence, they argue that due to low investment in human capital and a large population, underdeveloped countries lagged behind, but that they can overcome the problem by introducing high engagement in international free trade and acquiring technological and ideological advancement from abroad. For this, state investment in human capital generation and innovation is necessary, since human capital and innovation are potential determinants of high growth performance (Barro, 1991). As endogenous growth theory predicts, on the one hand, government expenditure could distort incentives, and on the other, the same could solve the problem of externalities; such a mixed result cannot be ruled out. Understandably, on the empirical side, the effect of government expenditure and taxes on the economic growth of a country has been found to be mixed (Angelopoulos & Philippopoulos, 2007). Moreover, some empirical evidence shows that although a significant increase in government expenditure does produce strong growth effects in developing countries, such effects vary substantially across the nations (Gregoriou & Ghosh, 2009). A particular reason could be how different classes interact and how the available policy space contains them.

As argued, the new classical approach holds that people have rational expectations; they contend that with such rationality and flexible prices and wages, any anticipated monetary policy will have no effect on output and employment in the short term. For them, it is only an unanticipated increase in the money supply that will affect output and employment. They further argue that any changes in aggregate demand will have no effect on output and employment even in the short term by pursuing a systematic monetary policy. Since wages and prices are flexible, buyers and sellers adjust their economic activities, anticipating an increase in the money supply. Therefore, the new classical school calls for clear monetary rules instead of discretionary monetary policy to prevent unanticipated changes in aggregate demand and unemployment deviating from its natural level. This school opposed the evaluation of economic policies based on econometric macroeconomic models, since such models are based on parameters derived from past data collected under particular policies. Thus, attempts to use those macroeconomic models based on past data to predict the consequences of alternative policies may be wrong, since economic agents change their behaviour, which may change the parameters of the models too (Hoover, 1992).

According to this school, changes in output and employment are based on the equilibrium supply decisions of firms and workers, based on their perceptions of relative prices. Thus, an increased aggregate supply of output and labour comes from the appropriate policy measures to increase output and reduce unemployment.

On the other hand, the public choice school uses economic tools to deal with the traditional problems of political science. It takes the same principles that economists use to analyse people's actions in the marketplace and applies them to people's actions in collective decision-making. This theory believes that although people acting in the political marketplace have some concern for others, whether they are voters, politicians, lobbyists or bureaucrats, they are self-interested. Like market failures, this theory argues that there is government failure, and that is why government intervention in many cases does not attain the desired goals. It states that voters have a lack of incentive to monitor the government. It analyses the role of voters, politicians and bureaucrats in government. Since these actors are self-interested, they become rent seekers for safeguarding their interests. But this falls short to explain why people vote, assuming individuals as self-interested beings instead of assuming a purposive one (Pressman, 2004).

Public choice theory criticises Keynesian and post-Keynesian fiscal policy, arguing that politicians will make policies that will benefit them. Keynes and post-Keynesians failed to incorporate politics and political processes into their analysis (Buchanan, 1986). Since politicians seek to benefit themselves rather than the whole nation or national economy through fiscal and monetary policies, this theory argues that it creates a worse economic performance than occurs under a free market. Thus, it advocates the free-market approaches of new classical economics over interventionist policies by the government.

The constitutional model of economics raised a question: Even if the citizens prefer a government to prevent anarchy, would citizens like their government to exercise absolute power over them, or would they restrict the power of the government? They affirm that the traditional approach to public finance depends on the view that the government is a benevolent entity, yet it imposes restrictions on government activities through the constitution. On the one hand, such a view believes the government is benevolent and is working to promote their interests; on the other, constitutional constraints are put on the government. They also point out that modern public choice theory puts forward the claim that the officials making decisions on behalf of the public behave in the same way as the people they represent, i.e., they have the same choices, motivations and preferences (Brennan & Buchanan, 2000).

This raises questions about the means which the citizens hope to use in such a setting to restrict the power of government to coerce and argues that the constitution is not enough to act as a protection. But why do restrictions imposed on certain governments in providing services differ from one another (Brennan & Buchanan, 2000)? Moreover, Brennan & Buchanan believe that:

> It is clear intuitively that the choice among alternative strategies that a player might make in the course of a game is categorically quite distinct from his prior choice among alternative sets of rules. A tennis player after hitting a particular shot may reasonably wish that the net was lower, yet prior to the game he may have agreed to a set of rules in which the height of the net was specified.
>
> (Brennan & Buchanan, 2000)

Having the power to tax does not mean that the government would use this power in a certain manner (Brennan & Buchanan, 2000). As a result, fiscal constraints can be used to restrict the government's power to tax, which can act as a more effective form of electoral constraint. Later they again emphasise:

> As we have noted earlier, current public-choice theory, as well as the prevailing political ethos or public philosophy, has concentrated its attention largely on voting rules and arrangements as the primary means of constraining governmental behaviour. Our analysis shifts emphasis to non-electoral means of achieving these ends. Our object is, of course, not to deny that electoral processes may constrain in some cases over some range, any more than we would seek to deny that dictatorial governments may exercise their discretionary power benevolently in some cases over some range.
>
> (Brennan & Buchanan, 2000)

In this model, the government is not benevolent. Rather, it can be described as having a character of indifference, or even malevolence, which is a major modification of the benevolence principle of the orthodox school. The model also assumes that although citizens could predict the level and distribution pattern of income and consumption in a post-constitutional period, they do not possess any knowledge about their own place and taste in that future society (Brennan & Buchanan, 2000). In a class society, even if a person does not have an idea about his ultimate position in the distribution of income, he could still form a fairly accurate prediction falling within a certain range.

In another book, Buchanan and Wagner (1978) were especially critical of Keynes. According to them, Keynes seemed to free the government from any leash. Before Keynes, the prevailing ideology was that of the classical economists, who believed in a self-correcting market where government policy was nothing more than a source of the disturbance. As a result, there was a strong inclination to limit the size of government, and a balanced budget was the preferred option. The Keynesian vision, however, made the expansive fiscal policy a requirement in the face of a falling economy, as monetary policy is unsuccessful in promoting a self-correcting economy and thus nullified the principle of a balanced budget in the conduct of fiscal policy. What happened as a result was that the government no longer thought it necessary to remain dependent on taxes alone, and their plan to expend more on various programmes than the revenue could afford generally resulted in budget deficits (Buchanan & Wagner, 1978). Buchanan and Wagner (1978), therefore, believed that Keynesian policy is suitable in a limited setting, not in a democracy. But the assumptions made about voters, politicians, bureaucrats and their behaviours by this school have serious shortfalls. As Pressman (2004) puts it:

> The public choice approach fails to help us understand what it was designed to explain—political behaviour. It has problems explaining why anyone would vote, it cannot explain a good deal of behaviour by politicians and bureaucrats, and it fails to explain changes in government spending and taxes over the past half century.

Furthermore, it is argued that neoliberal theories like public choice are not based on empirical research but rather derive from older philosophies that regarded humans in rather simplistic terms (Hodge et al., 2018). Public choice thus denies state intervention and is fundamentally founded on a neoclassical free-market approach. Decades after the initiation of the neoliberal market-based approach, however, there is little evidence that reforms have resulted in efficiency or that new policies lead to strong sustained growth, while under-development has not vanished in any of the reformed economies (Reyes & Galarza, 2018).

New classical economics assumes hyperrationality and ignores most of the hazards related to opportunism. It is based on the assumption of perfect information and defined property rights, which is flawed. Furthermore, the role of the state has been ignored and belittled in this analysis. The rational expectations hypothesis, which is the backbone of the new classical approach, has four main objections. First, it costs a lot to acquire, process and disseminate publicly available information. Therefore, the majority of economic agents cannot act on the basis of rational expectations. Rather, all markets do not continuously clear, and prices and wages are not flexible. There is collective bargaining in the labour market, which leads to wage contracts, leading to the stickiness of money wages. Instead of an aggregate supply hypothesis, aggregate demand is announced by the monetary authority that influences output and employment both in the short and long term.

Since new classical economics and its derivatives consider human beings to be "self-interested" rational agents who only want to maximise their profits, the policies based on this theoretical ground follow this assumption, which means self-interested policies must not have any cooperative, mutual or sharing orientations. The new classical school, therefore, ignores human sociality and fails to see human beings as cooperative and creative agents within society. As a result, policies become alienated from the masses and society.

Neoclassical economists deliberately imposed ideas on Smith which he had never said and/or meant. Despite Smith being an advocate of public investment in health and education for enhancing individuals' abilities, the new classical school often goes against Smith. They, therefore, mistakenly understood the classical school and made misleading assumptions about human nature and economy in certain ways: 1) to establish a liberal economy, the new classical school established an authoritarian market system based on a demand–supply mechanism; 2) instead of seeing humans as purposive beings, the new classical school considered them to be self-interested agents; and 3) as a result, new classical economics overrides human creativity, solidarity and any possible cooperation among human beings. Neoclassical economics diverted this "purposiveness" to self-interest. While making the economy liberal was supposed to be their prime objective, it has been proved gradually that acute demand–supplier authoritarianism originated in lieu of liberalisation.

Neoclassical economics disregards noneconomic motivations that guide human beings, and it also fails to take into account the extent to which humans are susceptible to become irrational or misguided. It ignores the "animal spirits" (Akerlof & Shiller, 2010).

Marxism

On the one hand, Marx considers humans to be purposive beings. He sees human beings as creative, conscious and purposive entities who form a free association of producers. According to Marx, human nature is that quality that is distinctly human. Distinctly human qualities are qualities that separate humans from nonhuman species or animals (Byron, 2016).

On the other hand, a profound difference that, according to Joan Robinson, differentiates Marxian economics from traditional orthodox economics is the fact that "the orthodox economists accept the capitalist system as part of the eternal order of Nature, while Marx regards it as a passing phase in the transition from a feudal economy of the past to the socialist economy of the future" (Robinson, 1974). As described by Roncaglia (2005):

> In his [Marx's] opinion, capitalism is not the final stage in the history of human societies, but only an intermediate stage. Indeed, as it was preceded in the history of human societies by other forms of organisation of society (serfdom, feudalism), so capitalism will give way to new forms of social organisation (socialism first, then communism). Therefore we should study the laws of motion underlying capitalism, to understand how it came into being, how it has changed in the course of its evolution, and the reasons why it will have to give way to a new form of social organisation, namely socialism.
>
> (Roncaglia, 2005)

The opening line of *Capital* consists of three key intertwined themes; these are mainly analytical, sociohistorical and experiential, and appear throughout Marx's study of capitalism (Shapiro, 2008). Firstly, Marx indicated that it is the structure of the capital society and its processes that generate profit, and not the relationship between the nation-state and market (Shapiro, 2008). He pointed out that the creative capabilities of human beings are diminished by structures of capitalism, as the goods they produce dominate them, in turn diminishing their purposeful nature through the capitalist alienation production process (Yuill, 2005). Secondly, Marx focused on writing specifically about societies in which capitalist ideals dominate, i.e., capitalist societies. In these discussions, Marx focuses on the specific features of capitalism that render it new and distinguishable from earlier practices (Shapiro, 2008). Finally, Marx posits in *Capital* that different economic practices should be defined in terms of the processes of how and why they produce goods in the economy, instead of how and why people choose to consume the goods, which is where Marx and Smith differ in their perspective. While Smith (1776) assumes the market to represent consume choices as its most important economic function, Marx insists that the sphere of production is the actual location that is significant (Shapiro, 2008).

Marx's theory about capitalism on the one hand helps to explain why demand may remain low at the worker's side, and why profits, and hence incentive to invest, may fall to the other side. Thus, the demand-side explanation is strengthened as well as the supply-side explanation being added to the theory. What today's economies do is expand consumer demand through debt promotion and consumerism, while increasing profits.

Marx questions what it is in commodities that equates the value of one with that of another. His answer is "labour". Marx then explains the rule of exchange based on labour:

> Let us now take two commodities, for example corn and iron. Whatever their exchange relation may be, it can always be represented by an equation in which a given quantity of corn is equated to some quantity of iron, for instance 1 quarter of corn = x cwt of iron … Each of them, so far as it is exchange-value, must therefore be reducible to this third thing … If then we disregard the use-value of commodities, only one property remains, that of being products of labour … How, then, is the magnitude of this value to be measured? By means of the quantity of the "value-forming substance", the labour, contained in the article … What exclusively determines the magnitude of the value of any article is therefore the amount of labour socially necessary, or the labour-time socially necessary for its production.
>
> (Marx, 1982)

According to Marx, the exchange of commodities in a capitalist society takes the form of commodity to money and then again to commodity, and as a result of the whole process, someone who starts with a commodity ends with another commodity, and the process is complete. At this point comes what seems the first criticism of Say's Law:

> Nothing could be more foolish than the dogma that because every sale is a purchase, and every purchase a sale, the circulation of commodities necessarily implies an equilibrium between sales and purchases. If this means that the number of actual sales accomplished is equal to the number of purchases, it is a flat tautology. But its real intention is to show that every seller brings his own buyer to market with him.
>
> (Marx, 1982)

Marx then turns to another concept, capital. In the direct form of circulation of commodities, or C–M–C, a person starts with a commodity, then exchanges it for money and later again exchanges the money obtained from the first transaction for some other commodity he or she desires, which is selling in order to buy. There is, however, another form of circulation along with this first type, where an individual starts with money, then converts it into commodities and at the end re-converts the commodities into money, taking the form M–C–M, i.e., buying in order to sell. According to Marx, "Money which describes the latter course in its movement is transformed into capital, becomes capital, and, from the point of view of its function, already is capital" (Marx, 1982).

Marx believes that the key to explaining this additional value is labour-power:

> the use of labour-power is labour itself. The purchaser of labour-power consumes it by setting the seller of it to work. By working, the latter becomes in actuality what previously he only was potentially, namely labour-power in action, a worker.
>
> (Marx, 1982)

Marx then describes the value creation process:

> Our capitalist has two objectives: in the first place, he wants to produce a use-value which has exchange-value … and secondly he wants to produce a commodity greater in value than the sum of the values of the commodities used to produce it, namely the means of production and the labour-power he purchased with his good money on the open market … In fact, the seller of labour-power, like the seller of any other commodity, realises its exchange-value, and alienates its use-value. He cannot take the one without giving the other.
>
> (Marx, 1982)

Then comes Marx's famous assertion: the tendency of profit to fall. He also describes the functioning of business cycles. To do so, he divides the part of capital into two portions, one of which is spent on labour and the other on the other means of production. Marx identified six ways in which a capitalist economy could counter the general law of the falling rate of profit. One of these actually involves the calculation procedure of the rate of profit. The other five may be classified into two broad categories: one class is concerned with keeping down the organic composition of capital, which is the cheapening of the elements of constant capital. The other is involved with raising the rate of surplus value, such as raising the intensity of exploitation, the depression of wages below their value and relative overpopulation. One strategy, which is foreign trade, falls under both categories (Sweezy, 1962).

However, if a comparison is made between Marx and Keynes regarding the solution to the capitalist economic crisis, although the crises in capitalist society were not portrayed in terms of class conflict by Keynes, his solution to the crises was still considered by the capitalist class. Thus, Keynes provided an alternative interpretation of the conflict between capital and class. Importantly, Keynes also argued that the interests and policy preference of finance capital was damaging not only for labour but also for the economy. Finally, the most substantial difference between Keynes and Marx emerges from their proposed solution to the class struggle. Whereas Keynes was in favour of repositioning the financial sector to serve the interests of industry and labour, Marx was in favour of the abolition of the market system or private property through the Communist Revolution (Tily, 2010).

The accumulation of capital for any sort of production is a must. Therefore, it is necessary to have a prehistorical presupposition for some original or primitive capital accumulation preceding the capitalist mode of production. This primitive accumulation was defined as previous accumulation by Adam Smith, "an accumulation not the result of the capitalistic mode of production, but its starting point" (Marx, 1982).

Though Marx characterises the modern state as an agent of primitive accumulation with arms and dominance to champion capitalism, Roberts (2017) finds that:

> Marx mistakenly portrays primitive accumulation as a bloody moment in the past, since replaced by the relatively bloodless workings of the mature capitalist system. Second, as much as Marx condemns the violent expropriation of the peasantry, he also justifies it as a necessary step on the way to the communist future.

Thus, there is agreement that primitive accumulation is rampant, fostered by the powerful class of the society. The classes who are close to state power extract the resources by using the monopoly power of the state, where ordinary people become exploited. But Marxian analysis provides little explanation as to how power and political settlement set production decisions and corresponding distribution.

Historical and neo-institutionalism and its derivatives

For the old institutional school of economic thought, institutions were more than just imperatives on individual action but encapsulated for the most part acknowledged ways of thinking and behaving. Hence, institutions worked to form the preferences and values of people brought up under their influence. Within this system, Veblen created his examinations of "conspicuous consumption" and consumption norms; the impact of corporate finance on the possession and control of firms; trade and budgetary methodologies for profit-making, charismatic skill and publicising; the development of a specialist administrative class; business fluctuations; and numerous other subjects (Veblen, 1899; Veblen, 1904).

Although new institutional economics recognises the role of institutions in the marketplace, it is silent about the role of the state. North (1991) defines institutions as "humanly devised constraints that structure political, economic and social interactions". These constraints are devised as formal rules (constitutions, laws, property rights) and informal restraints (sanctions, taboos, customs, traditions, codes of conduct), which usually contribute to the perpetuation of order and safety within a market or society. North (1984) argues that neoclassical economic theory overlooks the institutions required to create efficient markets with low monitoring and transaction costs. This school also recognises that all transaction costs are rooted in information asymmetries between the parties to an exchange. Thus, according to this school, the set of rules in a society is key to the determination of transaction costs. In this sense, institutions that facilitate low transaction costs boost economic growth (North, 1984). Transaction cost economics differs significantly from new classical economics, as Williamson (1996) argues—transaction cost economics is grounded on bounded rationality and imperfect markets, unlike the new classical school, but it ultimately advocates for markets. Thus, state, politics and class have remained outside their analysis. New institutional economics, furthermore, describes the accumulation process of developing countries as crony capitalism. But this process of accumulation in developing countries can better be explained as primitive accumulation. The foundation of new institutional theory is new classical economics (Agboola, 2015); thus, it excludes the state from its analysis.

The new institutionalism has worked to fortify critical dialog not about formal rules and governance structures, but of informal norms and social networks and of the connections between them. There has also been an expanded interest in the part played by shared values and the sociological literary works encompassing such concepts as social capital, trust, community and respectful society (Knight, 1998), and in the endogeneity of preferences to forms of institutional change (Bowles, 1998). In spite of the fact that the new institutionalism centres on structures and associations instead of on "individual behaviour", the concern with hypothesis and explanatory strategies is shared with behavioural approaches to politics. While the more seasoned form of institutionalism was substituted to depict institutions, the more current adaptation looks to clarify them as a "dependent variable" and, more critically, to clarify other questions about institutions as the "independent variables" forming policy and administrative behaviour.

The approach adopted in this book combines the postulations of historical and new institutionalism in a manner which prioritises the existence of both formal and informal institutions in the politico-economic sphere. Informal institutions in developing countries are largely the drivers of the nature of the political settlement that evolves depending on the networks of power in the economy. Political settlements are a significant determinant of the direction of fiscal and monetary policies, distorting the linkages between factors of production and labour vis-à-vis capital returns in the circular flow. This chapter proceeds towards constructing a new transformational pathway that caters to the association between political settlement, institutions and economic policies, and resulting vicious or virtuous cycles.

Property rights and class

Adam Smith believed in a minimalist state where interventions are limited to upholding property rights, establishing justice and contributing to education and health. The principle that was upheld by Smith was individual freedom and liberty. Smith's

> recommendations with regard to the functions of government are designed to ensure the freedom of the individual to pursue his own (socially beneficial) ends and merely require that the state should provide such services as facilitate the working of the system, while conforming to the constraints of human nature and the market mechanism.
>
> (Campbell & Skinner, 2014)

As argued earlier, Smith has been interpreted mistakenly by mainstream economics.

The corresponding figure of Smith in the philosophical arena is Locke. Locke's importance can be understood from the fact that the United States of America, which is one of the most powerful industrialised nations in history and one of the prime examples of a laissez-faire economy, is also said to be the most Lockean of nations. The appeal to the concept of freedom was not only made in historic America but has also been made from time to time by US presidents in defending recent American foreign policy in the post 9/11 world. Moreover, through the influence of Locke's ideas on the British Empire and thus on its colonies, especially the United States, Locke's ideas have had a profound impact on the history of the last three centuries, the most important of which is Locke's account of the rights to private property—which alternatively can be argued as one's right to the fruits of one's labour. Thus, Locke's idea of rights has always acted as the defence of the modern free-market economy, as one implication of Lockean rights are the concepts of limited government and religious liberty (Feser, 2007). And why would a person want to live under a government? Locke's answer is simple, which is to protect property, despite him sometimes using the term "property" in a rather broader sense than the standard meaning (Harrison, 2003). It is, however, observed that governments in many countries have been proved inefficient in providing secured property rights.

It is Hume's (1711–1776) contribution regarding politics and government that roughly became part of the intellectual developments of the late twentieth century and even the current century (Hardin, 2007). Hardin also argues that the main contribution of Hume's theory is to show how coordination produces mutually beneficial benefits even for people with different and widely varied values. Thus, Hume eliminates the necessity of an all-powerful sovereign by showing that even without such a body, social order can be established as a convention that is commonly beneficial. Moreover, social norms and conventions, according to Hume, can be enough to maintain order in small societies. In a precise manner, Humean convention is a general sense of common interests, a sense which all the members of the society express to one another and which induces them to regulate their conduct according to certain rules (Hume, 1739 cited in Latsis, 2009). According to Hume, self-interest or avidity of acquiring goods and possessions for members of the society and their kith and kin is insatiable, perpetual, universal and directly destructive for society.

Mainstream economics does not take class and accumulation into consideration. It does not provide any links about how economy and economic policy changes and thereby transforms the nature of accumulation and vice versa. Moreover, the ruling-class elite does not often comprise a homogenous group. On the other hand, in developing economies like Bangladesh, primitive accumulation is seen even in the later stages of development, and primitive accumulation is also present in advanced economies, although in subtler forms. There is a Marxian explanation that includes class. In such economies, however, the market does not have much of a role to play. A market economy therefore needs an idea of the state that uses the power of the market but that also understands the limitations placed on it by power, accumulation and class.

Citizenship, rights and welfare

Citizenship is defined as the ongoing contribution of citizens to solving community and public problems and creating the world around us (Boyte & Skelton, 1998). Learning and citizenship are lifelong activities that extend far beyond the formal educational setting (Battistoni, 1997). Democracy relies on strong, active citizenship within and outside government. Moreover, the economy depends on strong, active consumption behaviour. Both of these, democracy and the economy, are dependent on institutions. The resounding response to the failure of these institutions to deal with common social problems and living conditions has been to restructure or reinvent the institutions. In the real world, the idea of liberal democracy complements the market economy. Despite the concept of citizenship being understood from a number of angles, there is a discrepancy between the idea of the "independent" citizen and of the "consumer" citizen because of their relation to liberal democracy and the consequences for state-building. As will be argued here, this type of citizen has a negative implication for state-building. The idea of citizenship and citizens' rights therefore needs to be modified in the context of state-building to meet the developmental needs of growing economies; what is required is a tool to make citizens obedient to the state and its development process.

The independent citizen is taken to be a rational and competent individual. Their rationality means the person makes decisions to maximise their well-being. On the other hand, technical competence implies the ability to acquire and accumulate information. Subsequently,

> The preference independent citizen prefers to live with the injustice of the market rather than the injustice of the political process … The independent citizen discourse is about less government–less intervention and more reliance on markets and competition.
>
> (Mullard, 1999)

The idea of independent and consumer citizenship often has negative implications for state-building. According to Bauman (2003):

> More and more the culture of consumer society was subordinated to the function of producing and reproducing skilful and eager consumers, rather than obedient and willing subjects of the state; in its new role, it had to conform to needs and rules as defined, in practice if not in theory, by the consumer market.
>
> (Bauman, 2003)

A consumer society provides identity to individuals based on what products they possess (Mullard, 1999). Consuming native products and supporting local sports teams no longer unites people as in earlier periods. Moreover, the process of strengthening the rights of individuals has further contributed to the creation of the above kind of citizens, which has important implications for welfare. The introduction of individualised rights has often led to the strengthening of the process of individualisation in redistributive welfare states like the Nordic ones, undermining the social solidarity on which the very basis of those welfare states has been formed (Hvinden & Johansson, 2007). The problem with the frequent search for legitimacy in the case of state-building arises from the fact that long-term objectives, which are often important for state-building, are often overlooked.

Moreover, the rights and obligations of citizens taken for granted in a liberal economy may not be applicable to all societies. The concept of rights is different between societies, which in some respects can be broader and, in some other respects, narrower. For example, "the main hallmarks of liberal democracy—human rights, democracy, and capitalism—have been substantially modified during the course of transmission to East Asian societies that have not been shaped by liberalism to nearly the same extent" (Bell, 2006).

It is thus important to shift the preference of citizens to the state-building process and the welfare of the masses. Mainstream efforts to explain national economic and political performance are abstract in their nature. They also do not consider countries' historical and contextual settings. For example, both Hume and Hobbs share "the view that universal egoism, which is merely welfarism at the individual level, can be channelled by government to produce universal welfare and that egoists, for their own benefit, would therefore want government" (Hardin, 2007).

Some abstract values, however, cannot of course automatically provide the foundation for the type of state and economy as is described as ideal in liberal economy or politics. Three important criticisms were put forward by Marx about such individualistic nonhistoric approaches. First, for Marx, the idea of individualism in social contract theory was a tool to universalise and dehistoricise the nature of the human being, which is in fact a product of the market society and is produced to justify the same society. Marx also considers the concept of cooperative and harmonious individuals coming into the marketplace as contracting agents to be an ideological pretension. Second, Marx was critical of the type of freedom fancied in a liberal economy, because the majority of the people in such a society, especially the workers who only bring their own labour to the market, do not have much substantive freedom. Finally, as opposed to abstract theory building, Marx favoured the road of empirically grounded research. For writers like Locke, property was a natural right, and for Rousseau, who was knowledgeable of the havoc that a capitalist system could wreak on society, capitalist society was the only way to achieve human emancipation; however, Marx insisted that the destruction of capitalism was necessary for a new society (Wilde, 2005).

The identification of common interests and forms of cooperation and distribution for the pursuit of those interests can be used as powerful state-building motives. Accordingly, economic policy has to change citizens' allegiance back to the state through an inclusive state-building process. Thus, the role of the state in citizens' welfare and development has been recognised throughout the ages. Even in capitalist transition, though the role of the private sector was dominant in early developed countries, the role of the state along with the private sector has been observed across the late capitalists. As Khan (2005) puts it:

> The capitalist late developers were different in many respects from the early developers, but they are recognisably capitalist given the important role of private sector capitalists in these transitions. But in late developers, states played a bigger role in ensuring and maintaining high rates of investment and the shift to higher productivity technologies.

The state has patronised private sectors, maintained the required law and order and formulated policies that have helped capitalism thrive. It is argued that stable property rights and a well-functioning market were behind the capitalist transformation in earlier capitalist countries. However, in developing countries, these features are commonly absent. Here is where the role of the state comes in to ensure these stable and favourable conditions. The state in developing countries frequently fails to do so. Thus, if it can run properly where state and civil society are more evenly matched, an inclusive government will result (Acemoglu & Robinson, 2017). This inclusive government is supposed to make the state a citizen state that guarantees all the conditions for capitalist transformation.

A transformational pathway

The understanding of the state-building process should emerge from the fundamental debate about the nature of the relationship between human action

Table 2.1 Summary of major schools of thought

School of thought	*Main contributions*	*Understanding on the state*	*Understanding on the citizens/agents*	*Fiscal Instruments*	*Monetary instruments*	*Appropriateness in understanding postcolonial developmental transformation*
Classical School	Advocates free market, believes in invisible hand and calls for division of labour	Minimalist state, public provision on education and health	Rational self-interested individual	Government expenditure and taxes (balanced budget)	Quantity theory of money	Based on early capitalist country experience; society and state remained out of scope
Keynesianism and its derivatives	State intervention for increasing aggregate demand through increased investment	Acknowledges the ability of state to ensure economic efficiency	Self-interested individual, state	Government expenditure and taxes (functional budget)	Functional financing, interest rate, debt management, regulation	Acknowledgement of state's role in gaining economic efficiency but fails to analyse politics, power, class and institutions, and provides no roadmap for enforcement of policies

Neoclassical school and its derivatives	Calls for free market, getting prices right, individual rationality, utility maximisation	No state intervention; state is exogenous factor	Hyperrational individuals who are self-interested	Government expenditure and taxes (balanced budget); the flexible adjustment of prices and wages, which serve to keep the economy at or near the natural level of real GDP at all times	Quantity theory of money, inflation-targeted approach; open market operations; changes in reserve requirements, and changes in the discount rate	Ignores the role of the state, politics, power and class, based on early capitalist experience and based on the hyperrational, self-interested individual
New institutional school—historical institutionalism	Acknowledges the role of both formal and informal institutions, property rights, transaction cost	Follows the methodology of neoclassical school, thus state remained excluded	Rejects hyperrationality of individual but still believes in self-interested individual	Includes role of institutions in neoclassical thought	Includes role of institutions in neoclassical thought	Ignores the political settlement, class and accumulation process
Marxian School	Class, labour and labour-power, historical interpretation	Role of state is acknowledged	Capitalists and working class	Monopolistic nature of capitalism, nationalised economy, creative labour	Monopolistic nature of capitalism, nationalised economy, relations between money and commodity	Explains the historical class relations of society, production relations of society, fails to underscore power and political settlement

Source: Prepared by the author

and agency. According to Marx, "Men make their own history, but they do not make it just as they please in circumstances they choose for themselves; rather they make it in present circumstances, given and inherited" (Marx, 2002). The decision of agents brings about physical changes in the world. The agents, however, have to act under social contexts and structural conditions, such as kinship patterns, culture, law, the political system and distribution of wealth, which are beyond their control. The fundamental question that arises then involves the relationship between the agents and structures: Do agents create social structures? Or it is the social structures that shape the identities and interests of agents? (Burch, 2001).

Two polar cases are found as answers. Mainstream economics, or more specifically, neoclassical economics, takes the methodological individualist perspective, assuming that all action comes from the choices of individuals. It is also argued that choices arise out of something else, such as desires or opportunities. Thus the neoclassical school conforms to the standard cause-and-effect model; it does not provide an account of human action and agency (Davis, 2001). On the other hand, Marx suggests that a society is built on an economic foundation, understood in terms of the forces and relations of production, on which stands the more visible structure of the social and political system. Since from the economic structure of society rises the social and political superstructure, centred on which are the prevailing forms of social consciousness, it can be argued that it is not the consciousness of humans that determines their existence; rather it is their social existence that determines their consciousness. At a certain stage, the development of the material forces of production in society comes in conflict with the existing relations, and as a consequence, social revolutions occur (Sweezy, 1962). It is argued that in a capitalist economy, the working class in and of itself does not possess any relationship to either capitalism or class society. Moreover, the labour class has the ability to step outside of the causal framework of the capitalist system and act as an agent of historical change (Davis, 2001).

Elements of the model

Monetary and fiscal policy in the capitalist economic system is used to nurture existing social relations. Therefore, limitations in the policy arena affect state-building efforts as they fall short of including different views, classes, accumulation and power. Thus, state-building depends on the Marxist tradition on following spontaneous development in the economic arena and corresponding movements and actions from the working class. On the other hand, the mainstream economic theory does not have a theory for it. The framework that is required to understand the process of state-building thus needs both necessary and sufficient conditions, which include stability, transformation and sustainability of growth (Figure 2.1). It requires, therefore, the identification and understanding of different drivers of stability, transformation and sustainability of growth. This framework underscores that fulfilling the necessary conditions,

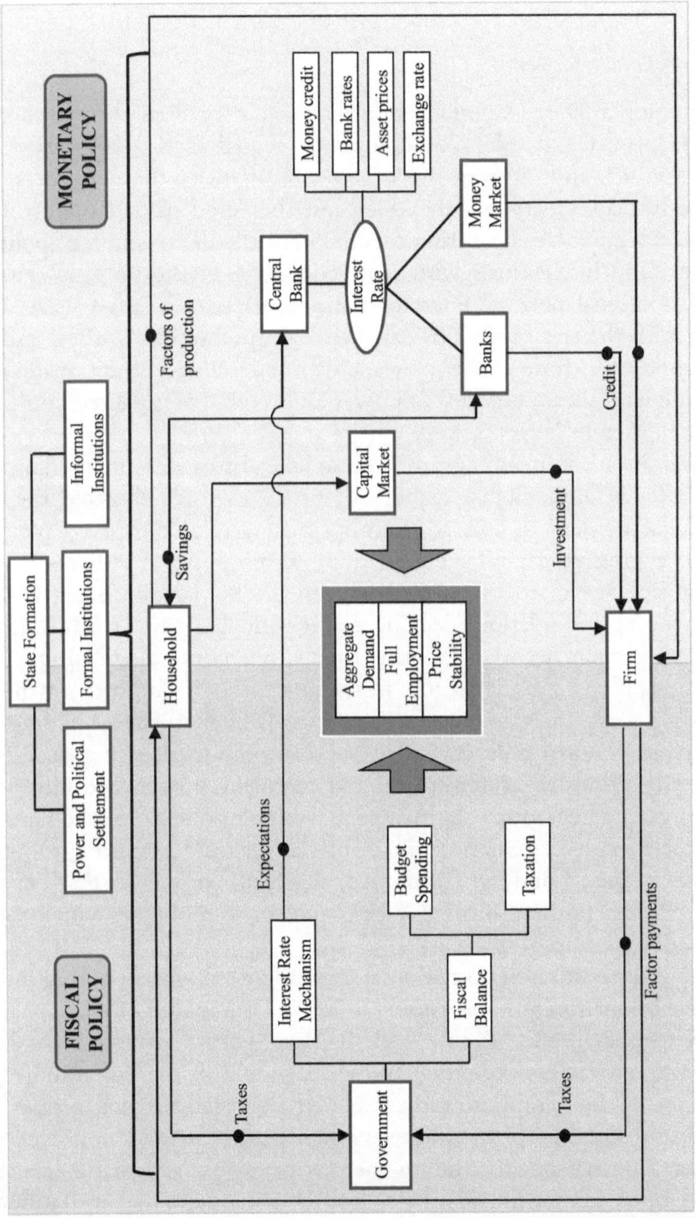

Figure 2.1 Circular flow of an economy. Source: Prepared by the author

or solving the problems related to land, labour, capital, technology, etc., will stabilise the economy, but for the economy to be welfare maximising and efficient, the state must be made a citizen state where equality, human dignity and social justice, irrespective of class, caste and creed, is ensured, which thus guarantees a public society that is efficient and equitable. Furthermore, in order to achieve a sustainable economy, it is argued that the fulfilment of sufficient conditions related to institutions, power, political settlement and class is a must.

Power and political settlement

The postcolonial state experienced a new wave of class formation due to changes in power and rule. The colonisers created a class that was obedient to the colonisers and enjoyed the facilities brought by the colonisers. These intermediate classes between the ruler and the ruled gained opportunity to bargain to have policies favouring them. These classes consisted of politicians, bureaucrats and intellectuals who assumed power in the political settlement in the postcolonial period. Therefore, the intermediate classes were directly involved with the state apparatus that allowed the interests of these groups to be prioritised over those of the masses. Given the multiple stratification among the intermediate classes in terms of power and wealth, it triggered competition among the different layers as well.

The aspirations of the emerging intermediate classes were focused on capital accumulation in any suitable manner or process, which directed the nature of political settlement to consist of groups that were able to exert power as a means for aggressive capital accumulation. When political settlement is unable to transfer power to the median citizen, capital accumulation is skewed based on the power relations, leaving out the median citizen. Thus, the state in developing countries like Bangladesh fails to become a citizen state. Since class relations play a significant role in shaping the state and society, the agent of analysis is class. In terms of contemporary failings in state-building, there are four main cohorts: politics, policy, state and the market (Figure 2.2). The tendencies of primitive accumulation and capturing power feed into politics, leading to policy hegemony during agenda-setting policies. At the same time, it leads to class non-cooperation and poor class consciousness, contributing to the failings of state-building. Combined, this leads to policies that encourage rent-seeking and nontransformative class and social mobility, which together alter market outcomes (Figure 2.2).

The state apparatuses of postcolonial states were established during the colonial regime by the foreign bourgeoisie following the nature of state apparatuses of the metropolitan state (Table 2.2). In fact, those apparatuses were being formed with a view to exploiting the local people of the colonised regions. For instance, police administration was being formed in such a way that it could help the colonial powers to exert their power in the colonised regions. Apparatuses that may be identified as coercive or extractive in nature are termed "overdeveloped". After independence from colonial rule, the apparatuses were

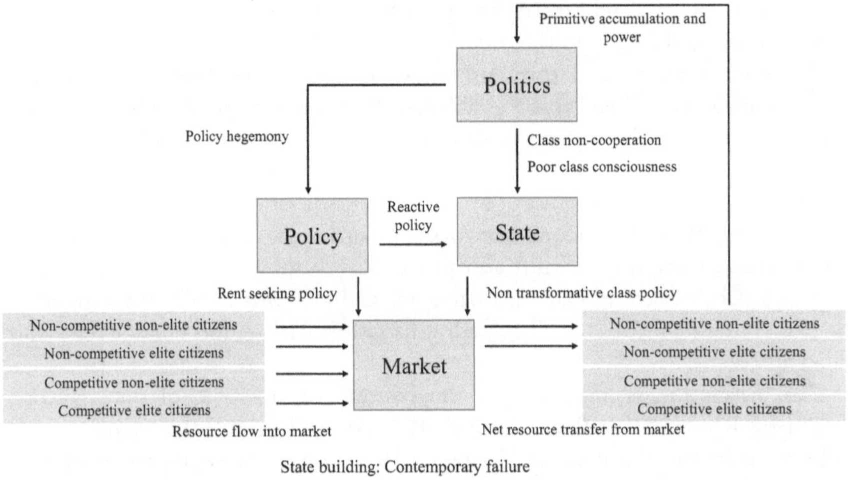

Figure 2.2 State-building: Contemporary failings. Source: Prepared by the author

Table 2.2 Nature of state apparatuses and agents' behaviours

		Nature of state apparatuses	
		Favourable	*Coercive*
Agents	Bureaucrats	Ideal type bureaucracy	Patrimonial bureaucracy
	Politicians	Have to remain accountable about their activities	Utilise the apparatuses to gain personal interests by means of political power
	Business elite	Have to perform business activity under effective rules and regulations	Can exercise their power (power acquired from ownership of property or wealth) to extract more resources

Source: Prepared by the author

not being reformed in many states (Alavi, 1972). The ruling-class relies on these state apparatuses to rule the masses. And, by exercising their power, they will be able to accumulate capital in their hands. The distinction between two types of state apparatuses is visible in developed and developing countries: favourable and coercive (Table 2.2). In developed states, or in postcolonial states where apparatuses are being reformed after independence, bureaucracy is found to be of an ideal type and the politicians are also needed to be accountable for their actions (Alavi, 1972). On the other hand, in those states where the apparatuses are found to be extractive in nature, as was the case in colonial regimes, bureaucracy is proved to be patrimonial in nature, which implies that all power flows directly from the bureaucrats. This constitutes essentially the blending of the public and private sectors, which results in an unequal distribution of resources and retards the growth of the economy. Business elites perform quite differently in these two contexts. Therefore, existing state apparatuses are extractive in nature and therefore should be abolished, and new forms of apparatuses need to be established that suit the specific characteristics of postcolonial developing states. The particular form of materialist incentives of primitive accumulation of resources through the use of power and coercion has led to a system of clientelist political networks in developing countries. The clientelist resource-dependent networks, in order to perpetuate their objective of accumulation of wealth and power, are symbiotically connected at a vertical level (local, regional, and national) and are intrinsically interlinked at the horizontal level with business, administration, law-enforcing agencies and judicial systems.

Class formation is important in the context of any type of state (as also argued by Khan, 2010; Riaz, 2005 & Kalecki, 1971), and this is also found to be true in the postcolonial context. The simple reason is that primitive accumulation on the part of the intermediate class hampers the transition and development process of the states.

The class composition is complex in postcolonial states, such that it depends on power relations between groups, and the intermediate classes have a relatively dominant role in this context owing to their aspiration of capital accumulation. Through the process of primitive accumulation, the wealth and surplus are appropriated by the intermediate classes, and the surplus value that they have been accumulating is not diverted towards productive sectors. In most cases, they come together to secure their wealth by using or abusing their power. There exist personal ties and influence between members of state government and the ruling-class elites—a "patron–client" relation. Thus, rent is abused or remains underused. This slows down the productivity of these rents in bringing technology acquisition or capital formation for industries and therefore retards the growth of the economy as well as the eventually successful transition of the state.

The relation between the different groups of the intermediate class in the process of primitive accumulation is also a very complex one. These groups are driven by the need to maximise their personal interests, but at the same time, their actions are influenced by the decisions of other groups. As a result, the relations between the classes may either be collusive or competitive, comparable to an oligopoly (Table 2.3). For instance, in order to optimise the receipt of benefits, bureaucrats and politicians may choose to form a coalition through which they can undertake complementary decisions that benefit both parties. These benefits, however, often come at the expense of other groups, such as the median citizen and the economy as a whole. Capital accumulation by the intermediate classes for the purpose of the concentration of wealth diverts investment and productive rents from technology and industry and leads to the creation of more unproductive rent by the state and political settlement. As a result, technology acquisition slows down the economy, hampering productive capacity. On the other hand, this class exploits the working class, not

Table 2.3 Politicians and bureaucrats in the process of primitive accumulation

		Politicians	
		Gain	*Loss*
Bureaucrats	Gain	Cooperation (Complementary relation)	Conflict (Competitive relation) [politicians attempt to influence the career of the bureaucrats]
	Loss	Conflict (Competitive relation) [bureaucrats attempt to down the image of the political parties to the masses]	Cooperation (Complementary relation) [jointly try to avoid loss and find out how to gain]

Source: Prepared by the author

Table 2.4 Unequal distribution and power

	Dimensions of power		
	Economic	*Political*	*Hegemonic*
Powerful group	Holds power based on ownership of wealth and income; induce to adopt rent-seeking behaviour	Holds power based on engagement with or within and political parties	Establishes both material dominance and intellectual and moral leadership over society
General people	Being exploited by the powerful class, neither have private property nor have proper access to public goods and common goods		

Source: Prepared by the author

through its direct ownership of the means of production, but through its control of the state, which owns the means of production.

The intermediate class is engaged in the process of primitive accumulation, and in this case, the most important factor is the holding of power of various dimensions (Table 2.4). By using various types of power, the powerful group can acquire more wealth and income in various ways. On the other hand, the general people are being deprived of having access to both private and public goods. It is evident that by exercising power, the powerful groups have been converting public goods into private property. This gives them more scope to generate profit. Moreover, they avoid paying taxes mainly by using political power. Thus, what has undermined the state-led accumulation process is the inability to impose direct taxes on property owners. As a result, on the one hand, the general people have limited access to public goods, and on the other hand, economic development is being retarded due to inefficient revenue collection.

Table 2.5 Political settlement and agents' behaviours

	Types of political settlement	
	Clientelist	*Capitalist*
Powerful group	Hold organisational power	Hold economic power
General people	Exploited by the powerful group and experience injustice in every sector (as rules and regulations don't work in this settlement)	Formal institutions work smoothly; people don't have to experience inequality

Source: Prepared by the author

This implies that where there is a clientelist type of political settlement, the powerful agents usually hold organisational power, which adversely affects the efficacy of rule of law and other formal institutions (Table 2.5). As a result, the power holders have the scope to accumulate wealth in unfair ways. They do not have any incentive to use those resources in the productive sector as they know that in this type of political settlement, holding organisational power is more important than having economic power. On the contrary, in the capitalist political settlement, the powerful class has economic power. But they acquire wealth by investing the economic resources in the productive sectors.

While discussing the key features of the colonial regime, it can be seen that an important attribute of that regime was that the colonial powers were successful in spreading the hegemonic view among the agents of the colonised area that the colonial powers are always superior. It is argued that such type of hegemonic ideology still presents in postcolonial states, making the economy dependent on the motives of international agencies. In this case, the international agents are being served by different national agents (again of the intermediate class) who actually can benefit by engaging in this process. It can be found that by influencing the policy measures of international organisations, the national agents promote the view that economic development is more important than political democracy (Table 2.6). This argument is totally fallacious. Economic growth cannot be regarded as the only indicator of development. Without the development of the social and political arena, development is found to be inefficient and unsustainable. Moreover, in this process, multinational corporations extract surplus from the national economy, which is being absorbed ultimately by the developed countries. In line with that, state agencies over the years have been depending on the aid or monetary support of donor agencies by arguing that there is always a budget deficit. Such a dependency only traps the national economy in the vicious circle of debt. Thus, the economy cannot flourish. The industries also have been largely dependent on foreign capital. This dependence is expressed in the need for foreign finances, technology, know-how, machinery and servicing for their

Table 2.6 Interplay between national and international agents

	International agents	
	International organisations	*Donor agencies*
National agents (politicians, bureaucrats, businessmen)	Promoting the view that Economic development is more important than political democracy	Falling into the vicious circle of the debt trap

Source: Prepared by the author

very functioning. Moreover, foreign capital investment is now disguised in the form of national investment.

Factors of production

The concept of class is based on the understanding that in a given society at a given time, some classes have a disproportionate share of assets (ranging from income to wealth and social status) than other social classes, and there exists a hierarchy among these classes. In the previous section, we discussed different agents and have found that the intermediate class is a prominent agent. Bureaucrats, political leaders, businessmen and the military mainly emerge from this class. So now it is necessary to discuss the means these intermediate classes have controlled and used to fulfil their choices.

Economic resources (labour, capital) can be regarded as key components through which agents can exercise or fulfil their choices. As discussed already, the intermediate class always tries to accumulate rent and thereby have captured significant amounts of capital. Moreover, this class has also the ability to use their own labour to generate income or wealth. Thus, in the postcolonial state, this group is significantly different from the bourgeoisie class of the developed states, who own only capital. However, that bourgeoisie class is found to have control over the working class (as found in Marxist theory), but in the postcolonial context, the intermediate class also can exert their control over the working class, albeit indirectly rather than directly.

These means of production (capital, labour etc.) have often being regarded in the economic models, but in addition to that, we want to argue that "power" can be an important variable which can influence the behaviour and choices of the agents and thereby the whole economy (Table 2.7). The intermediate class has a disproportionate share of economic and political power and has much freer access to the state and an ability to direct the rules of the power game in its favour. This power dimension is also related to the agents outside of the state, through the creation of a "hegemonic ideology" by the national agents.

The term *hegemony* is used according to its Gramscian connotations. As defined by Gramsci (1971), it is characterised by "the 'spontaneous' consent given by the great masses of the population to the general direction imposed

Table 2.7 Social division of labour in postcolonial states

Social class	*Control over own labour*	*Control over labour of others*
Top bureaucrats	Yes	Yes
Middle bureaucrats and intellectuals	Yes	No
Petty bureaucrats, foremen etc.	No	Yes
Workers and peasants	No	No

Source: Prepared by the author

on social life by the dominant fundamental group". From this point of view, a ruling class is hegemonic when it establishes both material dominance and intellectual and moral leadership over society and when it succeeds in persuading lower classes that positions of subordination and superordination are just, proper and legitimate.

The book argues that in postcolonial societies, the powerful class can easily produce this type of hegemonic ideology. In the first chapter, it has been seen that a common feature of colonial rule was that the metropolitan powers created hegemony among the local people of the colonial states and therefore could sustain their rule in those regions over a long period of time. After the end of the colonial regime, this attribute did not vanish; rather it has taken on a new form. It can be noted that the ruling class or the agents of the intermediate class often try to fulfil their personal interests and in doing so they are often being influenced by agents outside of the state, and they spread the message of developmental hegemony among the people as suggested by the international authorities. Thus, the developed states, in the name of development aid and support, always have tried to prove that they are superior.

Institutions—formal and informal

Even industrialisation may set the economy up for an eventual downfall if the requisite skills and institutions are not built up over time (Rodrik, 2014). Rodrik (2014) acknowledges the role of the state in enhancing skills and abilities and setting up well-functioning institutions; otherwise economic growth will not last long. As already stated, it is admitted that institutions matter in making the development process a successful one, as argued by NIE scholars. They were only concerned with the market-centric institutions and specifically put emphasis on the "property rights" issue. In postcolonial developing countries, there is instability in terms of property rights, which ultimately has a negative impact on the economy. There are extractive (both economic and political) institutions (Acemoglu & Robinson, 2012) that retard the growth and development process of those states (Table 2.8).

The key attributes in this regard can be identified as a lack of law and order, insecure property rights and regulations preventing the functioning of markets

Table 2.8 Institutional arrangements

		Economic institutions	
		Inclusive	*Extractive*
Political Institutions	Inclusive	Developed states (USA)	-
	Extractive	China	Developing or postcolonial states

Source: Adapted from Acemoglu and Robinson (2012)

and the creation of a nonlevel playing field. Thus, the institutional arrangement in these states is often designed by and for the benefit of the elite group. The recent literature on the impact of institutions on development has largely concentrated on the impact that institutions—generally understood as formal and informal rules and regulations governing economic activity, including tax laws, legal regulations, political freedoms, ethnolinguistic fractionalisation, religion, and infrastructure (democracy, authoritarianism, etc.)—have on economic growth (Acemoglu & Johnson, 2005; Acemoglu, Johnson, & Robinson, 2001; Aghion, Howitt, & Mayer-Foulkes, 2005; Hall & Jones, 1999; Knack & Keefer, 1997; Miguel, Gertler, & Levine, 2006).

A development-orientated institutional perspective also needs to emphasise more explicitly the role of informal institutions in shaping formal ones. It therefore needs to analyse the ways in which informal institutions—norms and values—gradually change the actions and interactions of agents in all sorts of social organisations (households, groups and villages, as well as firms and governments). It has long been clear that the evolution of institutions is driven by social institutions like gender, class, caste and social capital. Pateman (1988), for instance, explains how, within the social contract as normally described, a contract that validates gender inequality is hidden. Moral and ethical behavioural norms are often embodied in informal institutions like religion and caste that determine the quality and sustainability of formal institutions like schools, labour markets and the rules and regulations governing economic activity.

There are some other political dimensions of institutions that need to be considered in the context of postcolonial societies. The issues of "political settlement" and "primitive accumulation" are considered here. These issues are important because they can explain the factors that are beyond the analysis of market transaction or transaction cost analysis. However, the power dimension in transaction costs analysis has been brought up by Bowles and Gintis (1993). By critically discussing the propositions regarding transaction costs by previous economists, Bowles and Gintis argued that in the process of transaction, price and other terms of exchange often include a payment excess of at least one agent's next-best alternatives. The excess payments arise from a term of transaction called enforcement rent. Enforcement rent arises because the market is engaged in "contested nature of exchange" not in "voluntary exchange". As there remains an unequal sharing of information, the principal-agent problem arises in the exchange. Thus, the distribution of power is important and, in this case, it is related to the issue of political settlement. Before going to elaborate on this aspect, firstly primitive accumulation should be briefly defined. By *primitive accumulation* we are referring to the idea that was explained by Marx in the discussion of political economy. According to Marx, the whole purpose of primitive accumulation is to privatise the means of production, so that the exploiting owners can make money from the surplus labour of those who, lacking other means, must work for them. As found from the discussion of the characteristics of the agents, the intermediate class, through a patron–client network, in the same way is always trying to accumulate capital and thereby tries to privatise the means of production.

In the context of this study, the political settlement has been defined specifically as the distribution of power between social groups and classes (Khan, 2018). And, in postcolonial developing states, the existing type of political settlement clarifies that power is being concentrated in the hands of authoritative entities. The motive of the ruling elite is simply to have a state with a concentration of power. This results in the coercive power of the state.

Basically, power can be divided into two types: a) organisational and b) economic. Holding power measures the ability of a group to hold out against other groups in conflicts over distribution. The relationship between institutions and the distribution of power arises because adhering to any rule implies a specific distribution of benefits for the different parties that are subject to the rule (Khan, 2010). If a rule implies a distribution of benefits that powerful groups do not accept, enforcing that rule results in resistance and contestation. As a result, the final distribution corresponds more closely to the distribution of power. Thus, even where formal institutions exist in developing countries, their operation has significant elements of "informality", which is another way of describing partial enforcement. In developed states, there exists capitalist political settlement (based on income), whereas in postcolonial developing states the nature of the political settlement is clientelist. This can be defined as one where significant holding power is based on sources outside the incomes generated by formal institutions. The intermediate class of the developing states has this kind of power. This explains why informal organisations based on patron–client networks have been important and they set critical limits on the operation of evolving formal institutions.

In addition, the political settlement aspect on the global level (as described earlier about aid dependency of the developing states) has also affected the economic and political arena of concerned states. Thus, rent flows or primitive accumulation and international influences have been jointly creating distorted institutional arrangements, which ultimately create obstacles to productivity, which would enhance the transition of postcolonial developing states.

However, it has been found that the NIE approach is concerned with the transaction costs, and in terms of differences in types of political settlement, it seems relevant to bring the issue of "transition cost" to bear in the case of building models for particular types of the state as well. Thus, strategies for reducing growth-constraining transaction costs face political contestation and transition costs (Figure 2.3). This can be defined as the collective social costs of creating new rights or altering or destroying existing rights (Khan, 2009). Specifically, it places an emphasis on political contestation costs among different parties. Contestants typically impose costs on each other, on the state and often on broader society to signal that they will not give up their claim to the rights in question. However, the ability of one group to impose costs on competitors is indeterminate in reality, as it depends not just on the economic base but also on their political and organisational ability to form alliances. In developing countries, this is particularly important because of the factional organisation of politics.

Point *P1* represents the initial level of *GTC*; the higher the point, the lower the growth within the existing structure of rights (Figure 2.3). From this point, by reducing the transaction costs and thereby changing the existing structure of rights, growth can be achieved, but this has to face *TSC* as well. The slope of this "trade-off" curve tells us how steeply transition costs increase for this strategy of improving growth. The more vertical the curve is, the bigger the improvement in growth that is likely to be achieved for any given increase in transition costs. The flatter it is, the higher the price in terms of the transition costs that have to be "paid" for any given improvement in growth. We should obviously look for the strategy that achieves the greatest growth effect at the lowest social cost (at point *P2*). The point to be noted is that there can be several pathways (e.g. pathways 1 and 2, having different slopes) starting from the

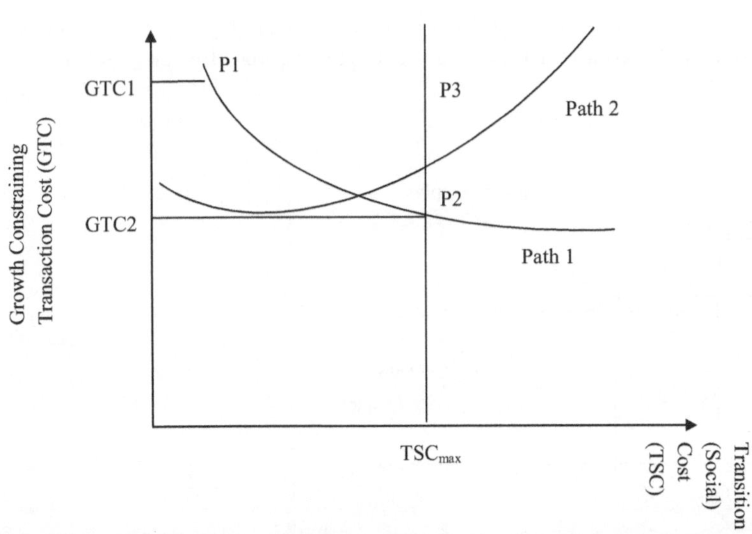

Figure 2.3 Trade-off between GTC and TSC. Source: Prepared by the author

P1 point, which represent different degrees of trade-off in particular societies. Here, *path 2* shows the trade-off in the context of the developing economy of the postcolonial state, where both higher *TSC* and *GTC* actually implies the state's slower transition.

Outcome

By having two components to our model, now we can scrutinise in which ways the product market is being affected, or what the effects are on the economy. This is very crucial and relevant in the context of our study as we have been trying to understand the theory of state from the viewpoint of economics. In the context of the postcolonial developing country, it can be said that we are trying to depict the ways in which the politico-economic behaviour of the agents of the states have been influencing (positively or negatively) the formation and transition process of the states.

Mainly, the state is being linked to the economy through the processes of rent creation, distribution and primitive accumulation. The role of the state is basically to provide freedom, civil rights and justice for the citizens. But in postcolonial states, due to unproductive rent creation and accumulation, the general populace is being deprived of the basic necessities of life, and power and wealth are being accumulated by a particular segment of people.

For the economist, rents refer to "excess incomes" which, in a simplistic neoclassical model, should not exist in efficient markets. Rent results in a significant amount of welfare costs (deadweight loss). Monopoly rent reduces the surplus of the economy (Figure 2.4). Restriction on supply (reducing supply from *Q1* to *Q2*) raises the price level from point *P1* to point *P2*, while the marginal cost of producing the smaller output is *OB*. Due to the rise in price, now the firm can earn a higher profit—*CD*. Total rent is shown by the area *P2BCD*. It is worth stating that the rent itself is not

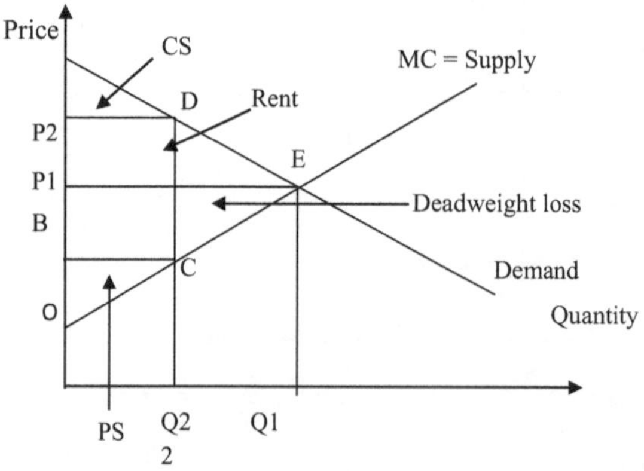

Figure 2.4 Monopoly rent. Source: Prepared by the author

a loss as far as society is concerned. It is notionally a transfer from consumers and factor suppliers to the owners of the firm, since it is composed of what was previously part of the consumer and producer surplus. The social cost of the monopoly is the net social benefit, which is lost as a result of the monopoly. In the figure, the lost net social benefit (known as the *deadweight welfare loss*) is measured by the little triangle *CDE*. This is an illustration of rent in the case of a single firm. This can be related to the context of developing states as well.

In these states, businessmen often influence the government authority or bureaucrats and politicians to permit them to earn rents in different ways. This instigates the process of the emergence of rent-seeking behaviour in the economic arena. The agents of the intermediate class become involved in corruption and other illegal means of rent-seeking. Simply, by exercising power, this class has succeeded in managing rent through a state-created monopoly.

Rent is not always inefficient. There are different ways in which rent can be used in productive ways which can help to have a positive impact on economies. In fact, by opposing the neoclassical economists' arguments in the later period, it has been claimed that in order to continue sustaining and increasing productivity in the economy, the creation of rent is essential. It needs to be ensured that the created rent is in turn going to the productive sector. In other words, in order to maintain economic growth, it is necessary to ensure that productive rent is not being hampered. Rents can sometimes be efficient, and in other cases they may be essential for promoting growth and development (Khan, 2000). This isn't happening in the postcolonial states. Through the primitive accumulation process, the capital earned through rent is being concentrated in the hands of few. This process is retarding the growth of the economy and as a result, the successful transition of the states isn't being experienced. In Piketty's (2014) words, it can be said that the state is moving towards a "rentier society".

It should be noted that public choice theorists argue that rent-seeking behaviour results in a significant amount of costs, which have a negative impact on the economy (Table 2.9). In cases where rent can be productive, it needs to be ensured that the rent-seeking process involves a lower amount of costs. But in developing states, rent-seeking costs are also high. Thus, high rent-seeking costs, along with unproductive rent, result in a negative effect on the economy as a whole. The picture is quite different in the context of developed states, as easily can be depicted in Table 2.9.

In developing countries, a significant part of the rent-seeking costs is spent within patron–client networks, and the rents produced as a result are also often distributed within these networks. There is likely to be a "circular flow" whereby part of the income from rents created for patrons as rent outcomes in one period provide the resources for the inputs of rent-seeking expenditures on clients in the next period. This sustains their organisational power and allows further rounds of rent-seeking.

Table 2.9 Rent-seeking costs, rent outcomes and the net effects of rent-seeking

		Social value of rent outcome	
		Negative	*Positive*
Rent-seeking costs	High	Net effect very negative (postcolonial developing states)	Net effect intermediate because of high rent-seeking costs
	Low	Net effect negative because of negatively valued rents	Net effect very positive (developmental states)

Source: Adapted from Khan (2000)

There are different types of goods or properties in the economy, and generally the state has the sole responsibility to provide public goods to its citizens. It is a concern that the state is also responsible for creating a congenial environment so that the provision of private property is also maintained in the economy. The crucial point is that the focus is on the intermediate class which has found out that they can accumulate capital by owning private property. Thus, private entities capture public goods by claiming that the state is not efficient enough to provide the goods.

Overall, the contested interplay of the agents of postcolonial states, the ownership of resources in the hands of a few and a lack of pluralism and creativity all have been retarding the growth or transition process of the postcolonial states. Though some states have been recorded as having a significant amount of GDP growth, the growth isn't actually sustainable. This is because the workers are contributing to the GDP but they have to remain in a vulnerable position, whereas the asset or capital owners are the gainers in every sector. This induces the workers not to use their labour and merit in the productive sector. The counter coalition of bureaucracy and military make authoritarianism the dominant mode of articulating power.

The above analysis, therefore, suggests that along with land, labour, capital, functional policies, productivity and innovations, institutions, political settlement, class and the accumulation process are important factors for securing growth. On the other hand, public provisions made through a citizen state are required to create stable, transformational and sustainable growth. This growth, therefore, can be realised through fulfilling both the necessary conditions and the sufficient conditions. By fulfilling the necessary conditions, a stable outcome can be realised, but for the transformation of the economy, a public society is a must, ensuring equality, human dignity and social justice. In the end, without the successful attainment of sufficient conditions, economic outcome and the transition of the economy cannot be sustained.

Conclusion

A circular flow in an economy results in a virtuous cycle among households, firms and government when transformational institutions are at work, leading to a functioning state and market. In broad terms, this chapter highlighted the processes of capital accumulation through factors of production in the economy, and how noneconomic factors influence economic outcomes. The discussion has laid out the linkages between the formal and informal institutions and the circular flow in the economy, which connect factors of production to labour and capital returns and the expansion of productive capacity. Formal and informal institutions in turn contribute to power relations and the resulting political settlement, which influences economic policies towards a certain outcome. In addition, the analysis has highlighted the postulations of the different schools of thought, while transcending the bounds of new institutional economics, which has only concentrated on property rights, information asymmetry and transaction costs. It does so by including the historical institutional school of thought, which emboldens the role of informal codes and values reproduced by society. Following this notion, the following chapters relate the circular flow in particular contexts to explain state formation, productive capacity expansion, inequality and welfare, prices and inflation, employment and growth.

Mainstream economics ignores the role of the state and citizens, emphasising the power of the free market. Markets are not perfect, particularly in resource allocation and coordination. For example, the prevalence of externality and moral hazard problems are admitted even in mainstream economics textbooks. Besides, human beings are not self-interested, hyperrational agents, as mainstream economics sees them; rather they are purposive beings. Moreover, the nature of state-building as the very determinant of relations between state and citizen is crucial when examining whether the state is a citizen state or not. Since states are important in both economic and political arenas, which group decides the policies, as well as how it communicates with the other groups, matters very much. Therefore, the distribution of power—the political settlement, accumulation of capital and class structure—come into the equation. The ideas of citizenship and order need to be considered for the purpose of state-building. The ideas of rights and social contracts need to be modified in the pursuit of the transformation of the state.

Mainstream economics, or more specifically, neoclassical economics, takes the methodological individualist perspective, assuming that all action comes from the choices of individuals. It is also argued that choices arise out of something else, such as desires or opportunities. Thus, the neoclassical school conforms to the standard cause-and-effect model, and it does not provide an account of human action and agency. On the other hand, Karl Marx suggests that a society is built on an economic foundation, understood in terms of the forces and relations of production, on which stands the more visible structure of social and political systems. Since from the economic structure of society arises the social and political superstructures on which stand the prevailing forms of social consciousness, it can be argued that it is not the consciousness of humans that determines their existence; rather it is their social existence which determines their consciousness.

At a certain stage, the development of the material forces of production in society comes into conflict with existing relations, and as a consequence, social revolutions occur. It is argued that in a capitalist economy, the working class in and of itself does not possess any relationship to either capitalism or class society. Monetary and fiscal policy in the capitalist economic system is used to nurture existing social relations. Therefore, limitations in the policy arena affect state-building efforts as they fall short of including different views, class, accumulation and power. Thus, state-building depends on the Marxist tradition and follows spontaneous development in the economic arena and corresponding movements and actions from the working class. On the other hand, mainstream economic theory does not have a theory for it.

The recent pandemic hit the healthcare sector severely. Mismanagement, insufficient resources, a shortage of skilled personnel across the health system, poor infrastructure, weak monitoring and governance and inadequate coordination among key stakeholders and worker shortage were revealed. The ongoing shortage of resources has put the whole world in a vulnerable position. The health sector requires a substantial amount of additional funding to respond to the pandemic, but this additional funding must not come at the expense of other critical health services.

It can be concluded that governments seem to have overlooked the public healthcare dimension of the crisis, despite the increasing number of affected people. A few factors have deteriorated the situation further, for instance, the government's late acknowledgement of the gravity of the situation, limited testing facilities, the absence of an effective mechanism to enforce social distancing in the overcrowded country, the lack of awareness among citizens, not enough safety equipment for healthcare professionals and religious leaders' unwillingness to discourage congregations. Moreover, affected citizens hide their travel history and affected symptoms from doctors and have infected doctors and nurses, which has burdened the healthcare sector further. More allocation for this sector could change the situation in the nation's favour.

To build a strong emergency response for COVID-19, protecting frontline workers is one of the essential tasks. The role of state policies in tackling the effects of the economic shutdown depends on the capabilities and responsive measures of the governments in developing states. The state-building situation of the developing countries is so vulnerable that the shocks of this pandemic are mostly affecting the economy of these countries in a way that can force economic growth into reverse. Thus, policymaking and implementation of emergency state policies to keep the economy stable are the need of the hour for developing countries.

The nature and effectiveness of the state is reflected in the effectiveness of its monetary and fiscal policy. The present chapter has developed a framework that includes distribution of power, class structure and the accumulation process as an analytical tool to understand the policies taken in a state. This framework underscores that necessary conditions need to be met for stable growth, and unless these sufficient conditions are met, the transformation of the economy to a citizen state cannot be achieved. Both the necessary and sufficient conditions shown in the framework are needed for sustained growth.

References

Acemoglu, D., Johnson, S., & Robinson, J. A. (2001). The colonial origins of comparative development: An empirical investigation. *American Economic Review*, 91(5), 1369–1401.

Acemoglu, D., & Johnson, S. (2005). Unbundling institutions. *Journal of political Economy*, 113(5), 949–995.

Acemoglu, D., & Robinson, J. A. (2012). *Why Nations Fail: The Origins Of Power, Prosperity, and Poverty*. Currency. New York: Crown

Acemoglu, D., & Robinson, J. A. (2017). *The Emergence of Weak, Despotic and Inclusive States*. NBER Working Paper Series 23657. National Bureau of Economic Research. Massachusetts, Cambridge.

Agboola, A. O. (2015). Neoclassical economics and new institutional economics. *Property Management*, 33(5), 412–429.

Aghion, P., Howitt, P., & Mayer-Foulkes, D. (2005). The effect of financial development on convergence: Theory and evidence. *The Quarterly Journal of Economics*, 120(1), 173–222.

Akerlof, G. A., & Shiller, R. J. (2010). *Animal Spirits: How Human Psychology Drives the Economy, and Why It Matters For Global Capitalism*. Princeton, New Jersey: Princeton University Press.

Alavi, H. (1972). The state in post-colonial societies Pakistan and Bangladesh. *New Left Review*, (74), 59.

Angelopoulos, K., & Philippopoulos, A. (2007). The growth effects of fiscal policy in Greece 1960–2000. *Public Choice*, 131(1/2), 157–175.

Arestis, P., & Sawyer, M. (2004a). *Re-examining Monetary and Fiscal Policy for the 21st Century*. Cheltenham, UK: Edward Elgar.

Arestis, P., & Sawyer, M. (2004b). On the effectiveness of monetary policy and of fiscal policy. *Review of Social Economy*, 62(4), 441–463.

Barro, R. J. (1991). Economic growth in a cross section of countries. *The Quarterly Journal of Economics*, 106(2), 407–443.

Battistoni, R. M. (1997). Service learning and democratic citizenship. *Theory into Practice*, 36(3), 150–156.

Bauman, Z. (2003). *Intimations of Postmodernity*. London: Routledge.

Beaud, M. (1997). *Economic Thought Since Keynes: A History and Dictionary of Major Economists*. New York: Routledge.

Bell, D. A. (2006). *Beyond Liberal Democracy: Political Thinking for an East Asian Context*. Princeton: Princeton University Press.

Belingher, D., & Moroianu, N. (2015). Empirical evidence on the Ricardian equivalence in Romania. *Theoretical and Applied Economics*, 22(2 (603)), 163–170.

Berr, E. (2015). Sustainable development in a post Keynesian perspective: Why eco-development is relevant to post Keynesian economics. *Journal of Post Keynesian Economics*, 37(3), 459–480.

Blaug, M. (1990). *Economic Theory in Retrospect*. New York: Cambridge University Press.

Bowles, S. (1998). Endogenous preferences: The cultural consequences of markets and other economic institutions. *Journal of Economic Literature*, 36(1), 75–111.

Bowles, S., & Gintis, H. (1993). The revenge of homo economicus: Contested exchange and the revival of political economy. *Journal of Economic Perspectives*, 7(1), 83–102.

Boyte, H., & Skelton, N. (1998). Reinventing citizenship. *Kettering Review* (Winter 1994), 7887.

Brennan, G., & Buchanan, J. M. (2000). *The Power to Tax: Analytical Foundations of a Fiscal Constitution*. Cambridge: Cambridge University Press.

Buchanan, J. M., & Wagner, R. E. (1978). The political biases of Keynesian economics. In J. M. Buchanan & R. E. Wagner (Eds.), *Fiscal Responsibility in Constitutional Democracy*. Boston: Martinus Nijhoff.

Buchanan, J. (1986). Budgetary bias in post-Keynesian politics: The erosion and potential replacement of fiscal norms. In J. Buchanan, C. Rowley, & R. Tollison (Eds.), *Deficits* (pp. 180–195). Oxford and New York: Basil Blackwell.

Burch, K. (Ed.) (2001). *Routledge Encyclopedia of International Political Economy* (Vols. 1). London: Routledge.

Byron, C. (2016). Essence and Alienation: Marx's theory of human nature. *Science & Society*, 80(3), 375–394.

Campbell, R. H., & Skinner, A. S. (2014). *Adam Smith*. London: Routledge.

Clark, G. (2001). Debt, deficits, and crowding out: England, 1725–1840. *European Review of Economic History*, 5(3), 403–436.

Combs, C. (2016). Say's Law: Criticisms, Responses, and Restatement. Retrieved from http://austrianstudentconference.com/wp-content/uploads/2017/02/ASSC-2017-Colin-Combs.pdf

Cohen, A. J., & Harcourt, G. C. (2003). Retrospectives: Whatever happened to the Cambridge capital theory controversies? *Journal of Economic Perspective*, 17(1), 199–214.

Cunningham, S. R., & Vilasuso, J. (1994). Is Keynesian demand management policy still viable? *Journal of Post Keynesian Economics*, 17(2), 187–210.

Davis, J. B. (2001). Human action and agency. In P. A. O'Hara (Ed.), *Encyclopedia of Political Economy* (Vol. 1). London: Routledge.

Dimand, R. W. (1999). Keynes and the classics debate. In P. A. O'Hara (Ed.), *Encyclopedia of Political Economy* (Vol. 1). London: Routledge.

Dolenc, P. (2004). Keynesian economics. In S. B. Hussain (Ed.), *Encyclopedia of Capitalism* (Vol. 1). New York: Facts On File, Inc.

Dornbusch, R., Fischer, S., & Stratz, R. (2007). *Macroeconomics* (9th ed.). New York: McGraw-Hill.

Dow, J. C. R., & Saville, I. D. (2001). *A Critique of Monetary Policy: Theory and British Experience*. New York: Oxford University Press.

Dowd, D. (2000). *Capitalism and Its Economics: A Critical History*. London: Pluto Press.

Dray, M. & Thirlwall, A. P. (2010). *The Endogeneity of the Natural Rate of Growth for a Selection of Asian Countries*. School of Economics Discussion Papers, No. 10,06. University of Kent, School of Economics, Canterbury.

Drobny, A. (1988). *Real Wages and Employment London and New York Keynes, Monetarism and the Labour Market*. London: Routledge.

Easterly, W. (2006). The white man's burden. *The Lancet*, 367(9528), 2060.

Ettlinger, M., & Linden, M. (2012). *The Failure of Supply-side Economics*. Center for American Progress.

Feser, E. (2007). *Locke*. Oxford: Oneworld Publications.

Friedman, M. (1977). Nobel lecture: Inflation and unemployment. *Journal of Political Economy*, 85(3), 451–472.

Gramsci, A. (1971). The philosophy of praxis. *Selections from the prison notebooks* (pp. 159–179). Duke University Press, Durham.

Gregoriou, A., & Ghosh, S. (2009). The impact of government expenditure on growth: Empirical evidence from a heterogenous panel. *Bulletin of Economic Research*, 61(1), 95–102.

Gruen, D. (1997). Ignorance and Ricardian equivalence. *The Economic Record*, 73(220), 35–44.

Hall, R. E., & Jones, C. I. (1999). Why do some countries produce so much more output per worker than others? *The Quarterly Journal of Economics*, 114(1), 83–116.

Hardin, R. (2007). *David Hume: Moral and Political Theorist*. New York: Oxford University Press.

Harrison, R. (2003). *Hobbes, Locke, and Confusion's Masterpiece*. New York: Cambridge University Press.

Hodge, S., Holford, J., Milana, M., Waller, R. & Webb, S. (2018). Economic theory, neoliberalism and the interests of educators. *International Journal of Lifelong Education*, 37(3), 279–282. doi:10.1080/02601370.2018.1484009

Hoover, K. (1992). *The New Classical Macroeconomics*. Cheltenham: Edward Elgar Publishing.

Hume, D. (1739). *A Tretise on Human Nature*. Oxford: Clarendon Press.

Hvinden, B., & Johansson, H. (2007). *Citizenship in Nordic welfare states: Dynamics of choice, duties and participation in a changing Europe*. London and New York: Routledge.

Kalecki, M. (1971). Class struggle and the distribution of national income. *Kyklos*, Wiley Blackwell, 24(1), 1–9.

Kates, S. (2005). 'Supply Creates its Own Demand': A discussion of the origins of the phrase and of its adequacy as an interpretation of Say's law of markets. *History of Economics Review*, 41(1), 49–60.

Kates, S. (2009). *Say's Law and the Keynesian Revolution: How Macroeconomic Theory Lost its Way*. Cheltenham, UK: Edward Elgar Publishing.

Khan, M. (2000). Rents, efficiency and growth. Eds. Khan, M.H. and Jomo K.S. ed. Rents, *Rent-Seeking and Economic Development: Theory and Evidence in Asia*. Cambridge University Press, Cambridge.

Khan, M. H. (2005). The capitalist transformation. In K. S. Jomo & E. S. Reinert (Eds.), *The Origins of Development Economics: How Schools of Economic Thought Have Addressed Development* (pp. 69–80). London: Zed Press.

Khan, M. H. (2009). *Learning, Technology Acquisition and Governance Challenges in Developing Countries* (DFID Research Paper Series on Governance for Growth). DFID. UK.

Khan, M. H. (2010). *Bangladesh: Partitions, Nationalisms and Legacies for State-Building*. SOAS, University of London.

Khan, M. H. (2018). Political settlements and the analysis of institutions. *African Affairs*, 117(469), 636–655.

Keynes, J.M. (1936). *The General Theory of Employment, Interest and Money*. London: Macmillan.

Knack, S., & Keefer, P. (1997). Does social capital have an economic payoff? A cross-country investigation. *The Quarterly Journal of Economics*, 112(4), 1251–1288.

Knight, J. (1998). The bases of cooperation: Social norms and the rule of law. *Journal of Institutional and Theoretical Economics (JITE)/ Zeitschrift Für Die Gesamte Staatswissenschaft*, 154(4), 754–763.

Latsis, J. (2009). Hume and the concept of convention. *Recherches sur la Philosophie et le Langage*, 26, 217–234.

Lavoie, M. (2006). *Introduction to Post-Keynesian Economics*. Hampshire: Palgrave Macmillan.

Malthus, T. R. (1836). *Principles of Political Economy*. London: William Pickering.

Marx, K. (1982). *Capital: A Critique of Political Economy* (Vol. 1). Middlesex, England: Penguin Books.

Marx, K. (2002). The Eighteenth Brumaire of Louis Bonaparte (Trans. T. Carver). In M. C. a. J. Martin (Ed.), *Marx's Eighteenth Brumaire: (Post)modern Interpretations*. London: Pluto Press.

Matyas, A. (1985). *History of Modern Non-Marxian Economics*. New York: St. Martin's Press.

Miguel, E., Gertler, P., & Levine, D. I. (2006). Does industrialization build or destroy social networks? *Economic Development and Cultural Change*, 54(2), 287–317.

Mill, J. S. (1965). *Collected Works of John Stuart Mill; Principles of Political Economy with Some of Their Applications to Social Philosophy Canada*. University of Toronto.

Minsky, H. (1974). Op-Ed Piece. Hyman P. Minsky Archive. 275. Retrieved from https://digitalcommons.bard.edu/hm_archive/275

Mullard, M. (1999). Discourses on citizenship: The challenge to contemporary citizenship. In J. Bussemaker (Ed.), *Citizenship and Welfare State Reform in Europe*. London: Routledge.

Nell, K. S. (2012). Demand-led versus supply-led growth transitions. *Journal of Post Keynesian Economics*, 34(4), 713–748.

North, D. C. (1984). Transaction costs, institutions, and economic history. *Journal of Institutional and Theoretical Economics*, 140(1), 7–17.

North, D. C. (1991). Institutions. *Journal of Economic Perspectives*, 5(1), 97–112.

Palma, J. G. (2016). Do nations just get the inequality they deserve? The "Palma Ratio" re-examined. In *Inequality and Growth: Patterns and Policy* (pp. 35–97). Edited by Basu, K., & Stiglitz, J. E. London: Palgrave Macmillan.

Palma, G. J. (2018). Behind the Seven Veils of inequality. What if it's all about the struggle within just one half of the population over just one half of the national income? *Development and Change* 50(5), 1–81. doi:10.1111/dech.12505

Pateman, C. (1988). The patriarchal welfare state. *The Welfare State Reader*, 2, 134–150.

Piketty, T. (2014). *Capital in the Twenty-first Century*. Cambridge, Massachusetts: Harvard University Press.

Pressman, S. (2004). What is wrong with public choice. *Journal of Post Keynesian Economics*, 27(1), 3–18.

Reyes, F. A., & Galarza, O. U. (2018). The death of development theory: From Friedrich von Hayek to the Washington consensus. *Journal of Post Keynesian Economics*, 41(4), 509–525. doi:10.1080/01603477.2018.1486210

Riaz, A. (2005). *Unfolding State: The Transformation of Bangladesh*. Canada: de Sitter.

Ricardo, D. (1821). *On the Principles of Political Economy and Taxation*. Kitchener, Ontario: Batoche Books.

Roberts, W. C. (2017). What was primitive accumulation? Reconstructing the origin of a critical concept. *European Journal of Political Theory*, 19(4), 1–21.

Robinson, J. (1974). *An Essay on Marxian Economics*. London: The Macmillan Press Ltd.

Rodrik, D. (2014). The past, present, and future of economic growth. *Challenge*, 57(3), 5–39. doi:10.2753/0577-5132570301

Romer, P. M. (1990). Endogenous technological change. *Journal of Political Economy*, 98(5), S71–S102.

Roncaglia, A. (2005). *The Wealth of Ideas*. New York: Cambridge University Press.

Rowthorn, R. (2014). A note on Piketty's *Capital* in the twenty-first century. *Cambridge Journal of Economics*, 38(5), 1275–1284.

Samuelson, P. A., & Nordhaus, W. D. (2010). *Economics*. New York: McGraw-Hill Irwin.

Sautet, F. (2014). *Schumpeterian Rents. The Palgrave Encyclopedia of Strategic Management*. London: Palgrave Macmillan. doi:10.1057/9781137294678.0611

Say, J.-B. (1821). *A Treatise on Political Economy, or the Production, Distribution and Consumption of Wealth*. New York: Sentry Press.

Seccareccia, M. (2011). The role of public investment as principal macroeconomic tool to promote long-term growth: Keynes's legacy. *International Journal of Political Economy*, 40(4), 62–82.

Shapiro, S. (2008). *How to Read Marx's* Capital. London: Pluto Press.

Shapiro, C., & Stiglitz, J. E. (1984). Equilibrium unemployment as a worker discipline device. *The American Economic Review*, 74(3), 433–444.

Shionoya, Y., & Nishizawa, T. (2008). *Marshall and Schumpeter on Evolution Economic Sociology of Capitalist Development*. Cheltenham, UK: Edward Elgar.

Singh, T. (2017). Ricardian equivalence and the public and private saving nexus in India. *Applied Economics*, 49(36), 3579–3598.

Smith, A. (1776). *An Inquiry into the Nature and Causes of the Wealth of Nations*. Indianapolis, Indiana: Liberty Classics.

Spence, W. (1808). *Britain Independent of Commerce, or, Proofs, Deduced from an Investigation into the True Causes of the Wealth of Nations, that Our Riches, Prosperity, and Power, and Derived from Sources Inherent in Ourselves, and Would Not Be Affected, even though Our Commerce Were Annihilated*. London: W. Savage, Bedford Bury.

Sweezy, P. M. (1962). *The Theory of Capitalist Development: Principles of Marxian Political Economy*. London: Dennis Dobson.

Syll, L. (2013). What is post-Keynesian economics? Real-World Economics Review Blog. Retrieved 26 June, 2019 from https://rwer.wordpress.com/2013/12/12/what-is-post-keynesian-economics/

Taylor, L. (2014). The Triumph of the Rentier? Thomas Piketty vs. Luigi Pasinetti and John Maynard Keynes. *International Journal of Political Economy*, 43(3), 4–17.

Tcherneva, P. R. (2011). Bernanke's paradox: Can he reconcile his position on the federal budget with his recent charge to prevent deflation? *Journal of Post Keynesian Economics*, 33(3), 411–433.

Thomas, A. M. (2017). Adam Smith on the Philosophy and Provision of Education. *Journal of Interdisciplinary Economics*, 30(1), 1–12.

Tily, G. (2010). *Keynes Betrayed*. Hampshire: Palgrave Macmillan.

Torrens, R. (1821). *An Essay on the Production of Wealth*. London: Longman, Hurst, Rees, Orme, and Brown Paternoster Row.

Tsoulfidis, L. (2010). *Competing Schools of Economic Thought*. New York: Springer.

Veblen, T. (1899). The barbarian status of women. *American Journal of Sociology*, 4(4), 503–514.

Veblen, T. (1904). *The Theory of Business Enterprise*. New York: Charles Scribners Sons.

Walsh, P. C., Walsh, V. C., & Gram, H. (1980). *Classical and Neoclassical Theories Of General Equilibrium: Historical Origins and Mathematical Structure*. New York: Oxford University Press.

Wilde, L. (2005). Marx against the social contract. In D. Boucher & P. Kelly (Eds.), *The Social Contract from Hobbes to Rawls*. New York: Routledge.

Williamson, O. E. (1996). *The Mechanisms of Governance*. New York: Oxford University Press.

Yellen, J. (1984). Efficiency wage models of unemployment. *The American Economic Review*, 74(2), 200–205.

Yuill, C. (2005). Marx: Capitalism, alienation and health. *Social Theory & Health*, 3(2), 126–143.

3 Fiscal policy and the state–citizen relationship

Introduction

In May of 2019, the government of Brazil passed a bill to cut education spending, leading to a nationwide protest. Prior to that, Brazil had been under severe recession for two years. The financial crisis had resulted in unprecedented unemployment, giving rise to unrest. This led to a conservative party coming to power with a mandate of economic recovery and reduction of public debt. As a result, the government went for a massive spending cut in education as well as pensions, angering the mass population. Such austerity measures, however, have become a standard measure after any economic downturn. In the United Kingdom, the Conservative Party initiated austerity measures to tackle a debt crisis, fully knowing that unemployment would rise. A Greek economic crisis led to a 40 percent cut in funding to the health system in the country, which caused a health crisis, not to mention the fact that half of the population remained unemployed (Stuckler & Basu, 2013). A similar course of action is now being seen amidst the pandemic, as governments have scrambled for emergency financial packages to tackle economic losses. The United States introduced a relief package of 1.9 trillion USD, aiming to provide a one-time payment of 1,400 USD to citizens. However, this stimulus too was met with political backlash from the Republican Party, a party known for its conservative ideas of less government intervention and low public debts. The stimulus bill was voted on along party lines, with the Democratic Party, having the majority in the house, narrowly passing the bill. Prior to the election, when the Republican Party constituted a majority in both the upper house and lower house, a similar bill had been rejected.

The instruments of fiscal policy remain in control of the government. Hence, fiscal policy is necessarily a function of politics. For instance, national budgeting is done by the executive branch of the government, held by the political party in power. The views and ideologies of political parties shape the outcome of the budget. In the United States, two dominant political groups exist. On one side is the Republican Party, which believes in conservative ideas, including that of a small government. Their economic viewpoint is that of little government spending in social sectors like education and health and

DOI: 10.4324/9781003201847-3

to limit government debts. On the other side is the Democratic Party, which believes in a bigger role for government. They promote healthcare for all and free education as well as minimum wage structures. The parties differ on tax structure as well. While the Democrats are more for taxing the richest population groups, the Republicans support tax cuts. Such political differentiation exists all over the world. The impact of political orientation on economic policy has become more visible since the financial crisis, which sent government debts through the roof. The fiscal policy of governments hence is motivated largely by the political philosophy of the ruling class. At the same time, political parties use fiscal policy to deliver benefits to the groups supporting the regime. These policies include tax cuts, subsidies and tax holidays. Therefore, the discussion on fiscal policy has to run parallel with the political process of a country.

The debate about fiscal policy can be categorised into two groups. The first one involves the extent of the public sector and the growth of taxes. The second one deals with how to raise and spend this sum to achieve state-building goals. Government has a variety of drivers at hand to devise fiscal policy. The most influential driver of fiscal policy is tax revenue. The structure of tax not only determines the level of government earning but also defines the social structure. Tax in any form has a redistributive effect. Raising income tax for the richest population can redistribute wealth to the poorest population. The redistribution is completed with the help of the next driver, that is, government spending. Government expenditure in social sectors, particularly in social sectors like education and health, can promote the human capital of the citizens. With skills and good health, citizens can raise their living standards. However, the choice of the driver largely depends on the ability to generate employment.

Since fiscal policy involves a political process, the process of state-building in developing countries needs to be critically understood. The process of state-building largely depends on the capacity of the government to raise sufficient revenues and then to utilise them in an efficient manner. The ability of governments to interact with society by means of fiscal policy to provide public goods and meet basic and other development needs are important components of state-building. Taxation is supposed to be an important tool for the purpose. The story of state-building through taxation starts with war. The rising cost of war led European monarchs to raise the level of direct taxation, for which they had to come to an agreement with the elite class. The story, however, does not end there. The process ultimately led to the establishment of parliaments and qualified bureaucracy (Bräutigam, 2008). How taxation can be used to promote state-building has remained an under-studied area in the academic arena.

Another working of fiscal policy is to divert socially less desirable resources to more desirable sectors. This is done in the form of full employment, price stability, equity in the distribution of income and wealth, stability in the economy, capital formation and growth, generation of investment etc. It also questions the apolitical approach of new consensus, neoclassical/monetarists and public choice theorists and establishes that fiscal policy is an overtly political process.

Moreover, in today's world, the market economy along with its political counterpart, liberal democracy, has established itself in a supreme position in the allocation of resources. Most of the world has now pledged its allegiance to this kind of economic and political system (Besley, 2006). The process of state-building now has to be carried out within the system of representative democracies. This creates a different background for newly independent countries to use taxation for state-building than what was possible for the now advanced economies. Macroeconomic policies have gone through a major change from the 1980s in terms of the relative importance of fiscal policy with respect to monetary policy.

While the position of monetary policy has gained prominence both in terms of policy and theory, fiscal policy has rarely earned any attention (Arestis & Sawyer, 2004a). The role of fiscal policy, therefore, has become limited in the neoliberal economic system. The Washington Consensus agenda further strengthened the negative view of fiscal deficits. As a consequence, the world has seen frequent international financial crises because of uncertainty created by unregulated capital flows and flexible exchange rates, requiring perpetual fiscal adjustment (Neto & Vernengo, 2004). Moreover, tax reform agendas have so far mainly been concerned about raising tax revenue in an economically efficient manner, without considering how such revenue enhancement is linked with broader governance objectives (Prichard, 2010).

The present chapter first shows how mainstream economic policy is unable to answer them in the context of a developing country and then attempts to develop appropriate policy tools for the purpose. This chapter, therefore, attempts to present an alternative theoretical framework against the backdrop of existing theories, which is followed by particular propositions. Each of the propositions has been tested with empirics.

Fiscal policy and state-citizens: A critical assessment

This section briefly reviews the position of traditional, Wicksellian and constitutional views of fiscal policy regarding how its objectives stand in connection with the needs of a developing country. Liberal public expenditure theorists tend to advance an apolitical technocratic view of the state and state finances. These models allow only a narrow scope for fiscal policy as they severely limit both the objectives and means of fiscal policy. Moreover, none of these effectively address how to make successful institutions for the purpose of revenue collection and government expenditure that could strengthen the process of state-building. In other words, from their vantage point, state fiscal policy does not function as an instrument of change but simply serves to moderate the more dysfunctional consequences of a basically sound economic system. This framework demonstrates that fiscal policy is shaped by the political process, grounded on three pillars—a) political settlement (distribution of power), b) citizenship (legitimacy and public order) and c) value system (human sociality as opposed to self-interest)—and the objectives are to accelerate the rate of capital formation and investment by expanding investment and distribution of income, with the objective of employment-led capital formation and growth.

Orthodox views of fiscal policy

Mainstream views of fiscal policy do not deal with questions like what the appropriate level of taxation should be. Conversely, the orthodox policy promotes tax cuts, severely limits fiscal policy's part in economic stabilisation and forgoes the government's role in ensuring full employment, development and state-building. The orthodox economic models of public finance own the concept of optimal taxation. According to the orthodox models, the problem of taxation is essentially an optimisation problem that arises because of the discrepancy between some specific choices provided by the state and its realisation subject to certain constraints. The assumption is that the state can implement any policies it wants, like a king, without any limitation. Therefore, if the state is aware of the results of different tax plans, it can select the one best suited for its purpose. The idea of optimal taxation can be traced back to the doctrine of sacrifice, which was first proposed by J. S. Mill in his book *Principles of Political Economy* in 1848. Mill's concept (1848) generally holds that a tax system is just if it involves equal sacrifice or suffering on the part of each taxpayer. Modern welfare economics construes sacrifices as loss of utility and thereby utilises the concept of marginal utility for the calculation caused by taxation (Hettich & Winer, 1999).

The normative question that orthodox economic models usually ask takes the following form: what is the best policy to attain a certain goal? The constraints or ways to evaluate different policy options are decided based on equity and efficiency. A familiar problem on the basis of efficiency criteria is how a tax system could achieve an independently determined amount of revenue at the lowest cost (Brennan & Eusepi, 2004). On the welfare side, taxes reduce the disposable income of taxpayers. Thus, they have to endure a sacrifice. The magnitude of the sacrifice, however, depends on the utility that the taxpayers receive from the forgone income, similar to the Pareto efficiency point, which projects maximum efficiency without making someone worse off. If an assumption were made that the marginal utility of income declines as the level of income rises, the least sacrifice of utility from the imposition of taxes would come first from the highest income group in any society. That means the top income group has to pay a higher amount of tax (Backhaus & Wagner, 2004). This school is important as it can effectively say how best a certain sum can be raised, but it normally does not say what an appropriate level of taxation is. The tendency of this approach is to argue for a small government compatible with the concept of liberal democracy and limit fiscal policy within a secondary and narrower scope, such as stabilisation. As described by Seccareccia (2011):

> This fiscal policy consensus of the past decade was, in part, ideologically driven and the outcome of a policy movement in favour of a minimalist state that found its theoretical justification in the classic writings of economists such as Milton Friedman and Friedrich von Hayek. This policy consensus was further strengthened by the *realpolitik* of globalisation. In the context of globalisation, all that was politically feasible was a more restricted role for the state, which necessitated a passive disengagement from important pillars of the Keynesian welfare state.

Another problem with orthodox preference is its adherence to tax cuts. Such adherence is especially problematic for countries that find it difficult to increase tax revenue. In developing countries, the collection of the bulk of the revenues depends on indirect taxes. The tax base and tax compliance are narrow while tax avoidance and tax evasion are high. When international organisations like the International Monetary Fund (IMF) emphasise the following austerity in fiscal matters in line with such orthodox policies and do not consider the different economic circumstances of these countries, the resulting policy usually constrains economic growth and investments in health and education, causing most harm to the poor (Neto & Vernengo, 2004). Additionally, whereas raising income has become difficult, bringing down government consumption expenditure has also become demanding. Orthodoxy calls for lowering the tax rate without really expanding the tax base (Nayyar, 2011).

Similarly, the "new consensus" or its equivalent models permit little role for fiscal policy, and a limited role for monetary policy based on the assumption that "there is a feasible 'equilibrium rate' of interest which will secure a level of aggregate demand equal to the capacity level of output, which itself is compatible with constant inflation" (Arestis & Sawyer, 2004a). Moreover, orthodox macroeconomic policy functions by targeting intermediate variables such as government deficits. The measures are, however, criticised because of their failure to provide a solution (Nayyar, 2011).

The orthodox economy believes that during periods of economic crisis, attaining full employment should not be a concern of the government. Instead, accepting the pain of adjustment, the governments have to focus on a higher output tomorrow than that of a lower output today. The social cost of adopting such fiscal policies is high for developing countries experiencing "a pro-cyclical pattern" to macroeconomic policy, especially in the case of fiscal policy. Such measures result in inefficient government expenditure as, during recessions, lower public investment in the social sector may dampen long-term growth. On the other hand, during the boom, increased finances may see the government investing in sectors that accrue lower returns (Nayyar, 2011).

Mainstream economics also promotes the view that there exists a trade-off between efficiency and equality. Fiscal policy therefore should not be used to promote greater equality as it generally leads to "misallocations of resources" (Browning & Johnson, 1984). Moreover, it is supposed that efforts to bring about equality decrease people's incentive to work (Wade, 2011). Many economists have rejected the canon that allocative and distributional issues are separable due to a theoretical concern. The Fundamental Theorem of Welfare Economics states that markets with complete information and perfect competition would end up in Pareto efficiency, meaning no one would be better off without making other ones worse off, and Pareto efficiency can be achieved through wealth redistribution. However, the theorem is based on stringent assumptions. The Coase theorem, which also theorised Pareto efficiency from the viewpoint of transaction cost and externalities, had initially established this separable result and eventually had to recognise the stringency of the assumptions (Bardhan, Bowles & Gintis, 1999).

The possibility of longer-term effects of debts and deficits is ignored by the mainstream schools. What can be called the "older perspective" in economics, which can be traced back to the monetarist revolution of the 1970s and early 1980s, conceptualised expansionary fiscal policy to inevitably lead to either the crowding out of the private investment, lower consumption expenditure or lower net exports. "A still more exotic version" believed in Barro's Ricardian equivalence" (Seccareccia, 2011).

In contrast, the fiscal policy view of the New Consensus economics can be considered "a significant advance when compared to the older neoclassical perspectives that reject fiscal deficits altogether", i.e., any effect altogether (Seccareccia, 2011). Nonetheless, this new consensus macroeconomics and fiscal policy, which was the result of a major shift within macroeconomic policy over the last two decades of the twentieth century or so, opposes "the use of discretionary fiscal policy and of long-term budget deficits" (Arestis & Sawyer, 2004b). As the reason behind such a move, the cases of crowding out and of the Ricardian Equivalence Theorem (RET) are widely put forward (Arestis & Sawyer, 2004b).

Other than crowding out, other reasons are also available that can make fiscal policy ineffective, which originate from the institutional side of fiscal policy (Arestis and Sawyer, 2004b). They discussed the following five such aspects and their strengths. First, a forecast of the future course of the economy is required in order to operate fiscal policy. When there is uncertainty over these forecasts, the difficulties in making decisions about fiscal policy increase. Second, fiscal decision-making and implementation involve various lags, meaning that the intended objective may already be achieved before the proposed fiscal policy actually comes into effect. In this context, the difference between inside and outside lags is very important. The time taken by the policymakers to appreciate the necessity of fiscal policy action and to make the required decisions is referred to as the *inside lag*. Third, fiscal policy is accused of showing a "deficit bias", e.g., changing the tax rate "during upswings may be politically unrealistic". Again, the effectiveness of the fiscal policy does not decrease due to the presence of a deficit bias. Despite constraining governments to engage in further deficit spending in the face of a recession, the fiscal policy does not become ineffective. Fourth, changes in tax rate impact labour and capital (i.e., savings and investments) and therefore growth. However, the implementation of an active monetary policy also involves interest rate volatility, which could result in similar supply-side inefficiencies. Finally, the effectiveness of fiscal policies has been centred on the developed economies. Unfortunately, there are differences in the reality of developing countries. For example, a classic argument shows that in order to generate savings, the governments in developing countries run surpluses (Arestis & Sawyer, 2004b).

Critics have argued against the expansionary fiscal policy from two other standpoints as well (Stiglitz, 2012). First, a government is unlikely to finance areas with high-return investments, and the effects of fiscal multipliers are either small or even negative. It is therefore very likely that the ultimate gains may prove to be elusive, while short-run gains from such fiscal policies may prove to be minimal at best. About the first objection, Stiglitz (2012) has rightly argued that

> studies of the average returns on government spending on investments in technology show extraordinarily high returns, with returns on investments in infrastructure and education returns well above the cost of borrowing. Thus, from a national point of view, investments in these areas make sense, even if the government fails to make the investments with the absolute highest returns.

About the second objection, similarly he has pointed out the many variants of the argument that the fiscal multiplier is small. One of these variations typically rests on the notion that with an increase in government spending, some categories of private expenditure will decline to offset this increase. The GDP cannot increase, certainly, given the economy is at full employment and capital is fully utilised. Hence, the multiplier must be zero under these circumstances (Stiglitz, 2012).

State–citizen relationship and mainstream fiscal policy

Mainstream theories of taxation failed to consider differences in state capacity, the process of state-building and different forms of state–citizen relations. When policies are formulated without considering the nature of the dominating class and how fiscal policies can weaken or reinforce the interest of the class, the state-building capacity of the fiscal policy is compromised.

An assumption of the Edgeworthian type choice theoretic approach to taxation, for example, is that the state is a benevolent entity. The problem with this benevolent assumption remains that the actors that operate in the market economy in their own self-interest as a maximising entity are supposed to assume not only a different but also an opposite ideology in their state positions, which is benevolence. Another problem with the models remains that this school does not often take account of the political process.

Economic and technical factors alone are responsible for inducing tax policy change, and it is all too often taken for granted that the economic pressures emanating from an inadequate tax system (insufficient revenue, economic inefficiency) will be enough to foster its reform. Moreover, politics is often considered as an obstacle in tax policy change. However, through negotiation and the accommodation of various interests, the reformer may be able to enhance the long-term viability of the policy innovation (Sanchez, 2011).

As a result, these models often come up with plans that do not receive support from the mass population. Reform programmes are hardly implemented, and where they are carried out, the changes are often partial.

In contrast, based on the assumption of rational choice, fiscal contract models put a greater focus on taxation as a whole by shifting the power of the state to people by emphasising a contract. The rational choice theory emerged in the 1950s in an attempt to understand how elections are organised and carried out and how competition between opposing political parties produces different results (Downs, 1957). Since that period, the approach has been widely used by political scientists to study the decision-making process of the government arising from a combination of individual interests and constraints to the fulfilment of those interests (Watson, 2001). By incorporating the concept of the self-interest of the participants, rational choice theory repeats what is expressed by the liberalist ideology that individuals are utility maximisers (Watson, 2001).

Fiscal contract models see the problem of taxation mainly arising from the gap between what the state wants and what citizens would pay. In other words, fiscal contract models view taxation as a collective action problem where the state wishes to maximise revenue while taxpayers wish to minimise payment. This makes the state offer taxpayers something such as representation or services in exchange for their payment. As a result, what is promoted is a form of government which is more accountable to the public, such as representative democracies. Thus, the anti-democratic aspect of orthodox economic models is checked to some extent.

The composition of the taxation process, however, still centres around two classes—taxpayers and the state. Moreover, taxes can be considered as a public good—that they are non-rival and non-excludable. Therefore, the problem of free-riding arises. People attempt to consume public goods by paying as little as possible, if anything, and the transferring of costs of public goods to others is a natural feature of rational individuals (Sanchez, 2011). The main shortcoming regarding the questions asked remains that although these models can say why taxes are low, they are however unable to decide on the appropriate level of taxation and what transformation is required.

It is also interesting to note that the relationship between citizens and the state is not the same as the one between, say, retail buyers and sellers. The buyer can decide to purchase or not to purchase a commodity from the seller and is generally allowed to return any defective products. This, however, is not possible for taxation. Here, choosing not to pay your taxes is punishable by law, and one cannot ask for the return of the payment made as taxes because one argues that the goods and services provided by the state as inferior to the payment. Thus, contractual and exploitative attributes can be provided to political relationships (Backhaus & Wagner, 2004).

Alternatively, there is the process-centric Wicksellian School, which attempts to understand the issue of taxation by studying people's behaviour and interaction to achieve their respective goals. In this model, the investigative importance is mainly placed on the institutions that govern both the market and politics, as opposed to the attention placed upon prices and resource allocations in the Edgeworthian or contract-based models (Backhaus & Wagner, 2004).

In the Wicksellian model, the course of fiscal affairs actually results from complicated dealings among participants from both the fiscal and political arenas, the nature of which is determined by the prevailing institutional and constitutional framework. Thus, fiscal debates cannot be understood as the result of a process of the maximisation of choices by the ruler. The outcome of the interactions could be positive for almost everyone, or only for a small population. Moreover, the interactions may not be voluntarily decided by the participants. Whatever the result of the process or whatever the level of willingness of the participants, fiscal phenomena always arise from the interactions of people engaged with each other within the market economy (Backhaus & Wagner, 2004). In Wicksellian models, the median voter can achieve their goals, or at least some part of them, in a democratic system through the electoral process. Thus, the demand on the part of voters runs the system where competitions in elections are supposed to act to limit the outcome within a narrow range. The government does not have a characteristic, whether despotism or benevolence, in such models (Brennan & Buchanan, 2000).

It is noticeable that Wicksell was worried about the elite class's disproportionate appropriation of public expenditure, whereas the poor were paying the majority of the taxes. He, therefore, believed that the transformation of societies to democracy would turn the system in an opposite direction, in which the rich would be the only class to be paying taxes. As a result, Wicksell attempted to formulate a political procedure that would prevent any such extreme outcome, and therefore he emphasised the rule of anonymity and made taxation endogenous to the system. A major consequence of the system is that any taxation programme would require support from all parties, and thus the persons who would be most benefited by that programme would be required to pay the taxes (Brennan & Eusepi, 2004).

Finally, there is the constitutional model of economics famously associated with the work of James Buchanan and his followers. As opposed to the orthodox approach, in *The Power to Tax*, Brennan and Buchanan (2000) used what is called a "constitutional" approach, one different from the conventional constitutional perspective. They raise the question that even if the citizens prefer a government to prevent anarchy, would citizens like their government to exercise absolute power over them, or would they restrict the power of the government? They affirm that the traditional approach to public finance depends on the view that the government is a benevolent entity, yet it imposes restrictions on government activities through constitutions. At one end, the proponents of such beliefs view their government to be benevolent and are working to promote their interest; at the other end, constitutional constraints are put on government. They also point out that modern public choice theory puts forward the claim that the officials making decisions on behalf of the public behave in the same way as the people they represent; i.e., they have the same choice, motivations and preferences (Brennan & Buchanan, 2000).

A question was raised about the means that the citizens hope to use in such a setting to restrict the power of government to coerce and argued that the constitution is not enough to act as a protection (Brennan & Buchanan, 2000). The restrictions imposed on certain governments in providing services differ from one another. Moreover, they believe that:

> It is clear intuitively that the choice among alternative strategies that a player might make in the course of a game is categorically quite distinct from his prior choice among alternative sets of rules. A tennis player after hitting a particular shot may reasonably wish that the net was lower, yet prior to the game he may have agreed to a set of rules in which the height of the net was specified.
>
> (Brennan & Buchanan, 2000)

The possession of the power to tax does not mean that the government would use it in a certain manner. As a result, they argue that fiscal constraints can be used to restrict the government's power to tax, which can act as a more effective form of electoral constraint. The concentration of the current public choice theory, as well as the prevailing political ethos or public philosophy, was largely on voting rules and arrangements as the primary means of constraining governmental behaviour. Non-electoral means of achieving these ends have shifted the emphasis of the analysis (Brennan & Buchanan, 2000).

In the model, it is assumed that the government is not benevolent. Rather, it can be described as having a character of indifference, or even malevolence, which is a major modification of the benevolence principle of the orthodox school. The model also assumes that although the citizens could predict the level and distribution pattern of income and consumption in the post-constitutional period, they do not possess any knowledge about their own place and taste in that future society (Brennan & Buchanan, 2000). However, in a class society, even if a person does not have an idea about his ultimate position in the distribution of income, he could still form a fairly accurate prediction falling within a certain range.

The portrayal of government as revenue hungry for its own cause raises an old debate about fiscal policy—how much should a government raise? It is noticeable that they argued that "the taxpayers may be implicitly, but correctly, rejecting the equal yield postulate, in their predictions that *any* widening of the tax base must open up further taxing possibilities for a revenue-seeking government" (Brennan & Buchanan, 2000). Nevertheless, the question is not whether people really see government as revenue hungry. Rather, the main objection of the people seems to be against the inappropriate use of tax money, which does not provide them with any type of benefit.

In another book, Buchanan and Wagner (1978) were especially critical of Keynes. According to them, Keynes seemed to free the government from any leash. Before Keynes, the prevailing ideology was that of the classical economists, who had belief in a self-correcting market where government policy was nothing more than a source of disturbance. As a result, there was a strong inclination to limit the size of government, and a balanced budget was the preferred option. The Keynesian vision, however, made the expansive fiscal policy a requirement in the face of a plummeting economy as monetary policy was unsuccessful in promoting a self-correcting economy and thus nullified the principle of balanced budgets in the conduct of fiscal policy. What happened as a result was that the government no longer thought it necessary to remain dependent on taxes alone, and their plan to expend more on various programmes than the revenue could afford generally resulted in budget deficits (Buchanan & Wagner, 1978). Buchanan and Wagner (1978) therefore believed that Keynesian policy is suitable in a limited setting, not in a democracy.

Following the assumption of neoclassical thought, that human beings are self-interested agents and always try to maximise their own benefit, New Public Management (NPM) combines market-centric approaches. NPM calls for reducing the role of the government, cutting costs, introducing market mechanisms and putting private sector management in the public sector, which in turn will ensure efficient, effective and customer-oriented output (Ferlie, Fitzgerald & Pettigrew, 1996; Schedler & Proeller, 2000). NPM, therefore, downsizes the public sector and prescribes the market as the efficient solution to resource allocation.

Striking a balance between stabilisation and development is required for the proper use of fiscal policy in a developing country context. Deficits and debts have to be judged according to their impacts on the real economy (i.e. impacts on health, education, jobs, etc.). Besides, fiscal and monetary policies have an impact not only on effective demand. Rather they are likely to bring about significantly different consequences for virtually every element of society.

A government's character depends on the nature of the class that dominates it as opposed to negligence of it in Wicksell, assumption of benevolence in orthodox approach and malevolence in the choice approach. Fiscal policy can only achieve its primary goals when it is founded within a favourable political settlement—distribution of power. Besides, legitimacy and public order, as well as human sociality as opposed to self-interest, determine the nature of policy, which needs further critical scrutiny.

The growth in government size in the twentieth century can be interpreted from two opposing perspectives. The first sees size as a sign that the government has grown to an unnecessary extent as the constraints on revenue collection have withered. The second believes this growth in government size has promoted common goals in those respective economies (Besley, 2006). Unfortunately, the widespread agreement with the latter position in the literature has been ignored, reducing the role of fiscal policy in maximising public choice through the provision of public goods and generation of full employment, to promote a particular view of government.

As mentioned in an earlier chapter, Adam Smith was in favour of a minimal government. Such minimalism, however, seems to include a greater list of functions. According to Smith (1776), in addition to providing defence and justice, the state has certain other functions:

> The third and last duty of the sovereign or commonwealth is that of erecting and maintaining those public institutions and those public works, which, though they may be in the highest degree advantageous to a great society, are, how-ever, of such a nature, that the profit could never repay the expense to any individual or small number of individuals, and which it, therefore, cannot be expected that any individual or small number of individuals should erect or maintain.
>
> (Smith, 1776)

Liberalism itself recognised the principle of public good as a rationale for social intervention. As rightly put by Esping-Andersen (1996),

> merchant ships would run aground without light-houses, and the population similarly would die out without public sanitation. It was mainly in the force of circumstance that liberalism came to accept the must of social rights. As the British discovered in the Boer War, an empire is difficult to sustain without an army of healthy and educated soldiers.
>
> (Esping-Andersen, 1996)

Assessing the US experience as one in which "the shortfall between actual and potential unemployment is huge and that monetary policy has proven ineffective, at least in restoring the economy to anything near full employment," Stiglitz (2012) writes: "This happy state of affairs is especially likely given the ample supply of high-return investment opportunities in infrastructure, technology, and education resulting from underinvestment in these areas over the past quarter century."

Economists these days promote a fiscal policy of government spending under these circumstances. Government spending has gained traction because of its ability to increase output as well as employment in the long run. Higher economic growth will offset the cost of government spending through the lowering of national debt and interest rates in the medium term (Stiglitz, 2012).

As seen from the experience of other countries, the mission to reduce the function of government is a question of benefitting a certain class and a specific model of state-building which has not proved beneficial to developing countries, or the development efforts of the adopting nations. Rich countries in the twentieth century unexceptionally found themselves in a position of rising taxes. Tax expenditure to national income increased from less than a tenth to between a third and a half. The domain of state function has increased significantly, as governments have moved to set rules and regulations in more areas, such as the financial market. In the changing circumstances, taxes are used to build what can be called "social states" to meet the changing demands of societies. As a result, it is found that roughly half of taxes today go to health and education, and the other half to programmes related to income transfer and redistribution. Thus, only a tiny portion goes to those functions that have been traditionally considered basic functions of governments in a free-market economy (Piketty, 2014).

As endogenous growth theory predicts, although government expenditure could distort incentives, at the same time it could solve the problem of externalities. Such mixed results cannot be ruled out. Understandably, on the empirical side, the effect of government expenditure and taxes on the economic growth of a country has been found to be mixed (Angelopoulos & Philippopoulos, 2007). Moreover, some empirical evidence shows that although significant increases in government expenditure do produce strong growth effects in developing countries, such effects substantially vary across nations (Gregoriou & Ghosh, 2009). A particular reason could be how different classes interact and how available policy space contains them.

Similarly, the perceived trade-off between efficiency and inequality has faced challenges from a growing number of economists, both theoretically and empirically. In recent times, there has been a growing opinion that a high level of inequality may result in a low level of incentive and lower work effort (Zweimüller, 2000). It has been observed that the mandated redistribution of wealth from the rich to the poor in conjunction with other policies is sustainable in competitive equilibrium and allows the non-wealthy to engage in productive projects that would otherwise not be undertaken, or to operate such projects in a more nearly socially optimal manner; or it can support a more socially efficient use of common property resources (Bardhan, Bowles & Gintis, 1999). It is, therefore, acknowledged that asset inequality impedes economic performance since wealthy groups enjoy the distributional advantage and obstruct the evolution of productivity-enhancing institutions. The relationship between asset inequality and human capital is negative. As a result, human capital–enhancing policies will fail to produce the desired outcome when a high level of inequality persists in society (Deininger & Deininter, 2000). Higher inequality tends to retard growth in poor countries and encourage growth in rich countries (Barro, 1999).

Theoretical understanding of neoclassical thought and its derivatives, like new institutional economics, public choice, new public management and the traditional, Wicksellian and constitutional views of fiscal policy underpins its assumption that human beings are self-interested agents who would like to maximise benefit. Therefore, these approaches limit fiscal policy's part in economic stabilisation and forgo the government's role in ensuring full employment. These approaches thus ignore the process of state-building.

An alternative fiscal policy framework

Against the apolitical conceptualisation of fiscal policy, this framework demonstrates that the political process shapes policies. The political process is grounded on three pillars: a) political settlement, b) citizenship and c) value system. This framework uses political settlement to understand the distribution of power while the idea of citizenship raises the question of legitimacy and public order. On the other hand, the value system incorporates human sociality as opposed to the self-interest assumption of neoclassical economics.

These pillars are significant to understand the nature and scope of fiscal policies that aim to create stable, transformed and sustained growth. This framework includes various agents, means and institutions of fiscal policies that lead to the outcomes of employment-led capital formation and growth (Figure 3.1). State and household through different transmission mechanisms ensure employment-led growth. These mechanisms are influenced both by agents and institutions. For instance, public investment leads to employment-led growth when power distribution and checks and balances work. In the absence of institutions, the transmission mechanisms will not lead to desired growth and may lead to concentration and primitive accumulation. Again, if the existing power distribution and class composition favour a particular section, then such agents will result in the extraction of rents. Hence, the framework proposes that growth will only create employment when all the forces, including agents, means and institutions, work in coordination and in a positive way.

Agent

The nature of policies depends on the composition of class in a state. In postcolonial developing countries, intermediate classes—mainly comprised of

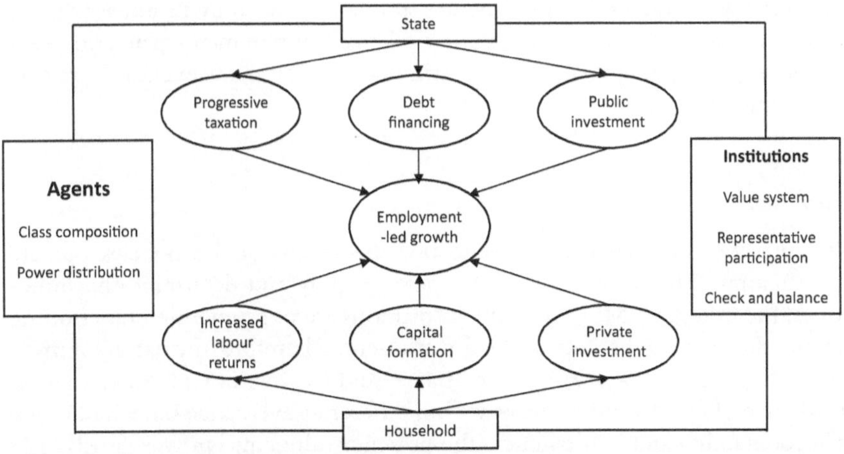

Figure 3.1 Conceptual framework of means, agents, institutions and outcomes. Source: Prepared by the author

bureaucrats, politicians and business elite—form clientelist networks that control the state apparatus. The appropriation of primitive accumulation is done through the monopoly power of the state. To continue this process, this class is always inclined to influence policies. Therefore, they use power to accumulate state resources on the one hand and, on the other hand, the state guarantees them that power. The absence of checks and balances in the post-colonial state provides absolute power to the executive, which is perpetuating a situation that is far from being a citizen-state. The unbalanced power distribution of different government branches—the executive, the judiciary and the legislative—has been leading these states to a situation where the state–citizen relationship is yet to be realised. As a result, the masses have remained detached from state affairs, which is reflected in various policies—particularly fiscal policy. The nature of the state-building process, which involves many of the attributes from colonial experience and the ongoing political culture in post-colonial states, seems to create obstacles on the road to a citizen-state. Therefore, various classes represent various forms of state–citizen relationships that act in shaping fiscal policy. Generally, power relations among various classes determine the nature and scope of fiscal policy. So the class has been considered as the agent of this framework.

Means

Increased aggregate demand is necessary for achieving employment-led capital formation and growth. Progressive taxation will lead to increased tax–GDP ratio, which is lower in developing countries. An increased tax–GDP ratio can only be granted with an increased return on labour. An increased return on labour will help to check inequality, which at the same time increases demand. Public investment needs to be expanded through debt financing if required. This framework agrees that fiscal deficit should be judged by its impact on the economy, not by the size of the deficit. Hence, employment-generating sectors boost aggregate demand, which stimulates investment, eventually raising the productive capacity of the economy.

Institutions

Neither different agents of the state nor the means of the policies operate in a vacuum. The institutions affect these severely and determine the direction of the outcome. Moreover, the institutions are not something functioning beyond the grasp of the state or the government. Therefore, the nature of institutions depends on the nature of the state—and its government. Since there is an absence of checks and balances within different governance branches, a lack of accountability and transparency, the presence of unequal power distribution among the state bodies and a lack of proper representation and participation of different classes, the institutions favour the powerful clientelist networks through various ways. These institutions, therefore, have remained exploitative and extractive, which has affected fiscal policies. This framework thus encourages inclusive institutions that secure stable, transformed and sustained growth and bring wellbeing to each citizen, irrespective of class, caste or creed.

Outcome

Progressive taxation and an increased tax–GDP ratio resulting from an increased return on labour boost public investment in infrastructure, education, health and social protection, which simultaneously would boost aggregate demand and productivity. Thus, the economy faces a virtuous cycle of employment-led growth and capital formation. The increased return on labour, on the other hand, depends on government expenditure and subsequent increased demand. This increased demand will not only raise the aggregate demand but will also raise aggregate investment in the economy. This investment will in return augment both employment and productive capacity in the economy, ensuring long-lasting economic growth.

On the other hand, government borrowing from the private sector constrains borrowing options for private firms. Private sector borrowing for financing deficits will reduce private investment and hence will result in lower economic growth. This restraint can be replaced by progressive taxation (Figure 3.2).

Securing these outcomes depends not only on necessary functional economic decisions but also on other sufficient conditions characterising agents and institutions, as this synthesis model argued. Based on the above discussion, this chapter underscores several propositions, which are to be tested in the empirical section which follows.

Investment and employment

The growth continuum is a function of employment, resulting from increased aggregate investment causing aggregate saving as the "income effects" produced by investment. Other means of growth will far outweigh the "substitution effects" resulting from price movements. The new framework aims to produce investment-led growth. This growth strategy affects employment in the economy as a by-product. Full employment is not targeted; rather it is market determined.

The hypothesis is that continuous growth requires expansion of employment opportunities, resulting from increased savings and investment in an economy. Growth without creating new employment cannot be sustained. Increased savings lead to increased investment. Investment needs to be such that it creates new employment opportunities, which leads to increased growth. When investment shifts upward at point *B* from point *A*, both employment and growth also shift upward (Figure 3.3). Growth reaches g^* from g when employment increases to E^* from *E*. New employment, in turn, raises the possibility of savings and thus postulates new investment and growth.

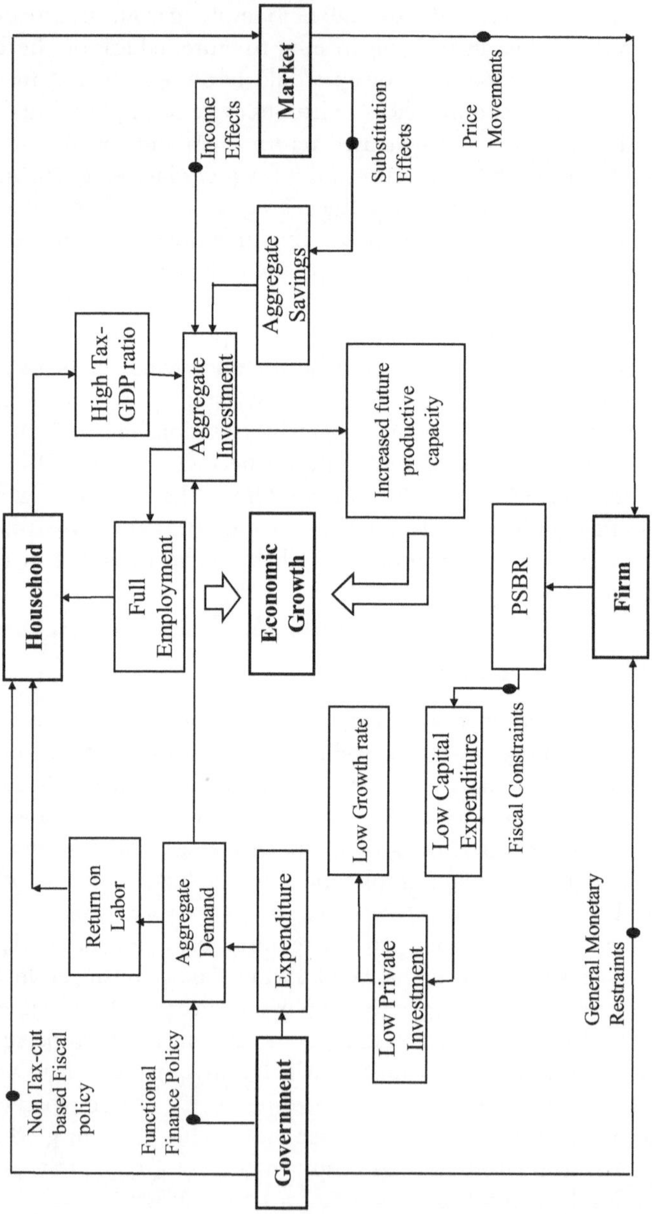

Figure 3.2 Conceptual framework. Source: Prepared by the author

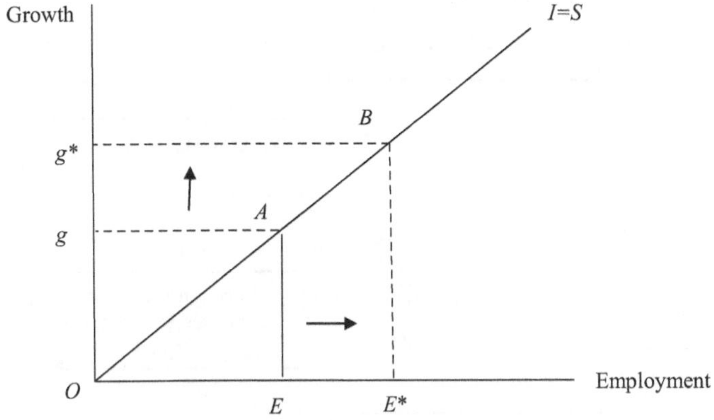

Figure 3.3 Growth generated from employment. Source: Prepared by the author

Generally, in developing countries, the gross capital formation has followed a vicious cycle in the economy where there is a low ratio of GDP to investment, which leads to the low investment in the manufacturing sector, the main source of economic growth. Low manufacturing investment then leads to a lower return on labour compared to the return on capital. Therefore, a low labour investment automatically generates lower returns, which then leads to lower gross investment. As a result, there is a very low capital formation in the economy as the cycle continues the process of lower generation of investment (Figure 3.4).

Looking at the gross capital formation of some selected countries, it can be seen that a percentage share of capital formation of most of the countries has declined in the last decade. Japan and Singapore have seen a lower capital formation than China and developing countries like India, Vietnam and Bangladesh (Figure 3.5). This is reflected in the rapid industrialisation of Asian countries, which in recent years have seen a transfer of technology and industries from developed countries.

The gross capital formation in Bangladesh was only 31.2 percent of the GDP in 2018. There is no doubt that it has increased in the last decade as it was 26 percent in 2009, but the rate of increase of the capital formation has not kept up with the rapid GDP growth. Another point is that the percentage of unemployed labour with advanced education has increased to 10.73 percent in 2018 from 3.89 percent in 2010.

Capital formation in Bangladesh is not reflected in the employment scenario of the country. The ratio of employment to population shows that for the last few years, it has remained stagnant in Bangladesh. When capital formation does not go in parallel with employment, one can assume that capital is being accumulated instead of investment. On the contrary, China and Vietnam have a much higher ratio of employment, which shows that capital formation results

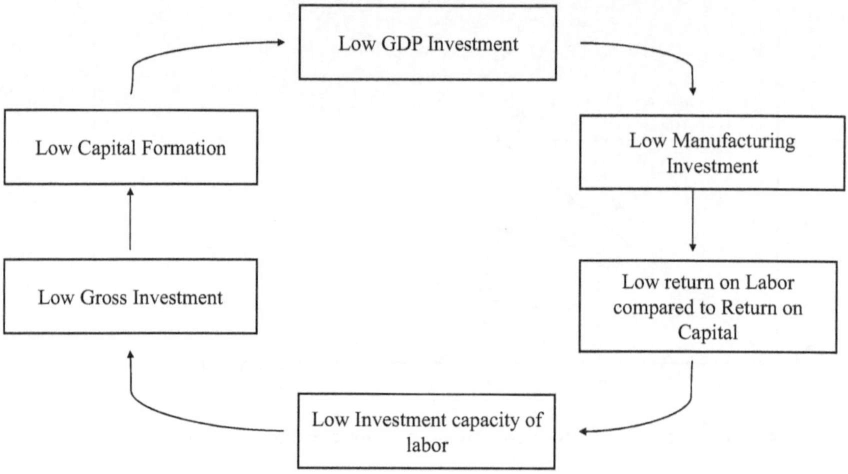

Figure 3.4 Vicious cycle of low capital formation. Source: Prepared by the author

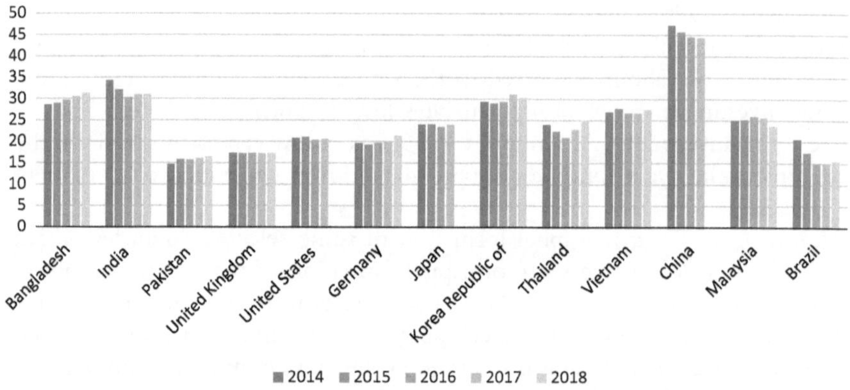

Figure 3.5 Gross capital formation of selected countries. Source: World Bank, 2020a

in employment generation (Table 3.1). The rapid GDP growth is lacking the incremental ratio of employment as it was supposed to be. As a result, the economy is showing a trend of jobless growth.

The GDP growth rate shows a positive trend in the macroeconomic situation in any country. The economy of Bangladesh has experienced acceleration since the 1990s and mostly in the last decade. Along with the GDP growth, the rate of Gross Domestic Savings (GDS) in the country has increased gradually. However, the gross savings has not materialised in investments that can generate employment. Except a few occasional spikes, employment growth in Bangladesh has largely been trending downward, contrasting with the increasing growth rate.

Table 3.1 Employment to population ratio (15+, total percent) in Bangladesh and some selected countries

Country	*2015*	*2016*	*2017*	*2018*
Bangladesh	53.98	53.97	56.13	56.19
India	50.75	50.71	50.71	50.60
Pakistan	51.26	51.33	51.48	51.69
United States	58.74	59.13	59.58	59.58
Germany	57.49	57.99	58.38	58.54
Japan	57.95	58.58	59.18	59.24
Korea (Rep.)	60.21	60.33	60.60	60.57
Thailand	68.65	67.63	67.36	67.05
Vietnam	76.39	75.95	76.03	75.96
China	66.67	66.42	66.16	65.68
Malaysia	62.34	62.13	62.20	62.42
Nigeria	52.20	51.75	51.90	51.87
South Africa	40.90	40.18	40.40	40.56
Egypt	42.03	42.15	42.35	42.57
Brazil	58.69	56.42	55.87	55.92

Source: World Bank, 2020a

The economy of Bangladesh grew at a rate of 7.86 percent in 2018, satisfactorily up from 5.44 percent growth in 1992 and 6.54 percent in 2005. The GDP growth rate has almost doubled in the last three decades (Figure 3.6). In comparison with 2009, both the domestic savings rate and national savings rate have decreased in 2018 (Table 3.2). In 2009–2010, national savings was 29.49 percent of total GDP (Table 3.2), which also declined to 28.41 percent. According to a primary estimation of 2018–2019, both domestic and national savings show an increasing trend. The statistics show that income has been reduced for most people, or consumption expenditure has reached such a high level that they cannot save. As a result, investment will not increase and will rather remain stagnant or decrease.

In addition, the ratio of private investment to GDP remained stagnant for the last few years. Bangladesh ranks on the lowest spectrum in the Ease of Doing Business indicator. In 2020, globally Bangladesh was ranked at 168th position whereas in South Asia ranked 7th, only ahead of Afghanistan (World Bank, 2020b). Institutional inefficiencies are the prime cause of low rank. Besides, political instability and low public investment in infrastructure leads to a lack of business confidence.

Public investment and tax mobilisation

Government spending is at least or more powerful with respect to aggregate demand than tax cut–based fiscal policy, as each unit of government spending

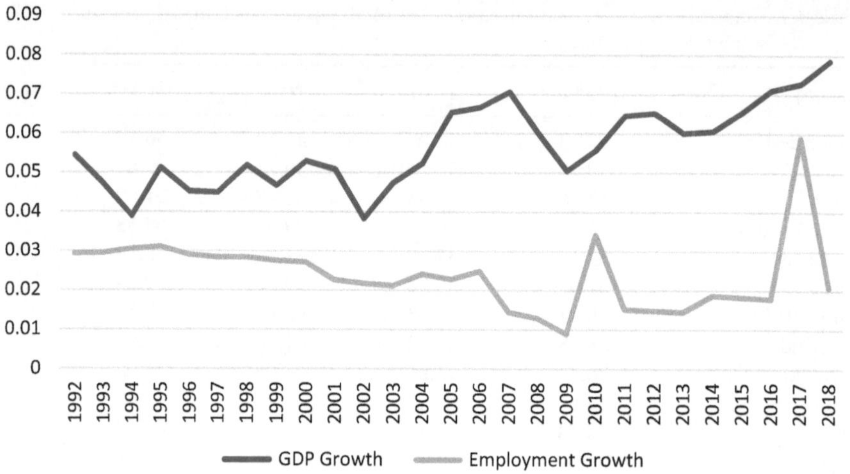

Figure 3.6 GDP and employment change over the years. Source: World Bank, 2020a; ILO 2020

Table 3.2 Consumption, investment and savings as a percentage of GDP in Bangladesh

Fiscal year	*Consumption (percent of GDP)*		*Investment (percent of GDP)*		*Savings (percent of GDP)*	
	Public	*Private*	*Public*	*Private*	*Domestic*	*National*
2009–2010	5.07	74.06	4.67	21.56	20.86	29.49
2010–2011	5.09	74.21	5.25	22.14	20.7	28.95
2011–2012	5.04	73.74	5.76	22.5	21.22	29.86
2012–2013	5.12	72.85	6.64	21.75	22.04	30.53
2013–2014	5.34	72.57	6.55	22.03	22.09	29.23
2014–2015	5.40	72.44	6.82	22.07	22.16	29.02
2015–2016	5.89	69.13	6.66	22.99	24.98	30.77
2016–2017	6.0	68.67	7.41	23.1	25.33	29.64
2017–2018	6.36	70.81	7.97	23.26	22.83	27.42
2018–2019	6.30	69.77	8.17	23.40	23.93	28.41

Source: Ministry of Finance, 2019.

adds a full unit to aggregate demand. This warrants, therefore, an increased tax–GDP ratio and such can only be granted with an increased return on labour. The hypothesis therefore demonstrates that increased government spending resulting from an increased tax–GDP ratio raises aggregate demand and employment. New employment opportunities and increases in real wages offset the instability in price level.

An increase in aggregate demand resulting from increased government spending shifts the *AD* schedule to the right from *AD* to *AD** (Figure 3.7,

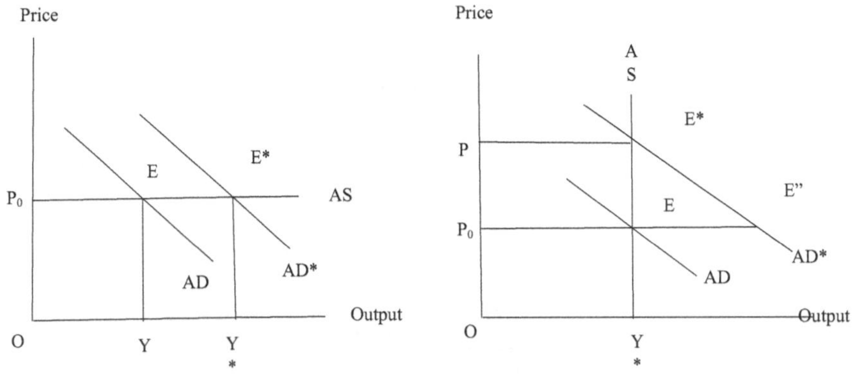

Panel a: Aggregate demand expansion when supply is perfectly elastic

Panel b: Aggregate demand expansion when supply is perfectly inelastic

Figure 3.7 Government spending boosting aggregate demand *Price*

Panel a). The perfectly elastic supply schedule *AS* postulates that firms are willing to supply any amount of output at the level of price P^0 There is, therefore, no effect on prices. The only effect is an increase in output and employment. Output increases to Y^* from *Y*. Firms, however, supply the full employment level of output (Y^*) at any level of prices since the supply schedule *AS* is perfectly inelastic (Figure 3.7, Panel b). In this case, the expansion shifts the aggregate demand schedule from *AD* to AD^* with an increase in the price level from P^0 to *P*.

The increase in the demand for goods therefore leads only to higher prices without increasing output, which reduces the real money stock and spending in the economy. As a result, the demand schedule keeps moving until the level of prices rises to the point where the real stock of money and spending falls to the level that is consistent with full employment output. Here, at *E"*, aggregate demand is once again equal to aggregate supply at price level *P*. The instability in the price level, however, is offset by new employment and increases in real wages (Figure 3.7).

Government spending on education, health, social security, infrastructure etc. boosts employment and the real wage of labour. The new employment opportunities and increases in real wages indemnify the increase in the price level as well as raising the tax–GDP ratio. When government spending on the horizontal axis moves to the right from G to G^*, employment and real wages on the vertical axis increase to E^* from *E*. Consequently, the tax–GDP ratio shifts upward from *T* to T^* (Figure 3.8). An increased tax–GDP ratio postulates a further rise in government spending. Government spending, however, must not serve the rent-seeking clientelist network.

Public investment in infrastructure, education, health and social security etc. would boost aggregate demand and productivity. The application of general

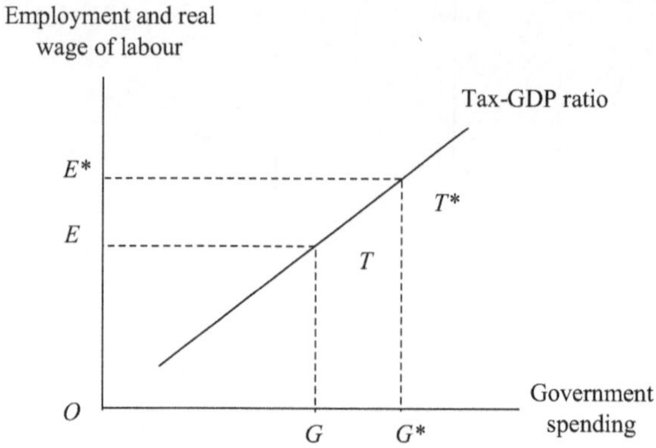

Figure 3.8 Increase in employment resulted from increased tax and government spending.
Source: Prepared by the author

monetary restraints, however, may unduly check demand even for necessary long-term industrial investment and thus hamper economic growth. Besides, fiscal restraint can hamper public investment in social sectors. When government exhausts its limit of public sector borrowing requirement (PSBR), there is a tendency of cutting allocation in social sectors like health, education and social security. This is why, during a recession, these sectors are the first ones to see a cut in expenditure.

Increased public investment raises aggregate demand in the economy (Figure 3.9). The line *AB* depicts that productivity also increases consistently with the expansion of public spending. The economy therefore realises productive expansion and the creation of new employment. Monetary restrains, however, repress this cycle. The proposition is a critique of Ricardian equivalence. The equivalence theory hypothesises that government expenditure affects the economy rather than the sources of funding. It postulates that private savings rise when the government goes for deficit financing to increase spending. The increased spending does not change consumption as consumers predict a rise in taxes in the future. Hence, consumers save for paying future taxes (Taylor, 2010). Hence, this theorem argues that tax cuts or increased spending do not result in higher aggregate demand.

The tax–GDP ratio is used as a global indicator for comparative revenue analysis. Countries with a higher tax–GDP ratio have higher tax revenues. For instance, Scandinavian countries have one of the highest tax–GDP ratios in the world followed by European countries. East Asian economies have recently seen higher tax revenues. South Asian countries in comparison have lower tax–GDP ratios, which implies that the tax structure in these countries fails to generate higher revenue and leaves room for tax evasion (Figure 3.10). Lower tax revenue in return results in lower government expenditure.

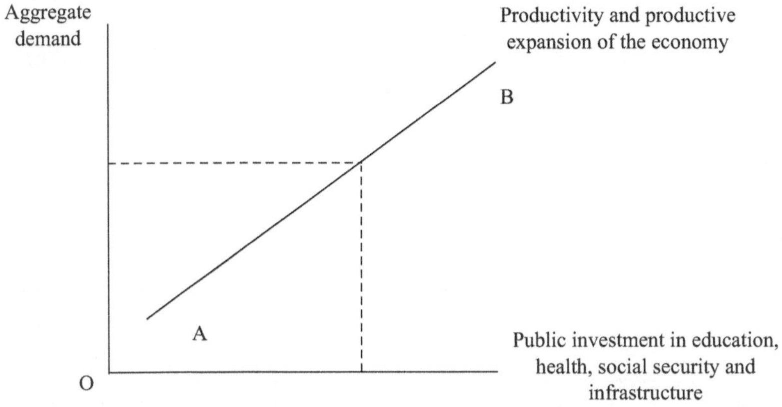

Figure 3.9 Public spending boosting aggregate demand and productivity. Source: Prepared by the author

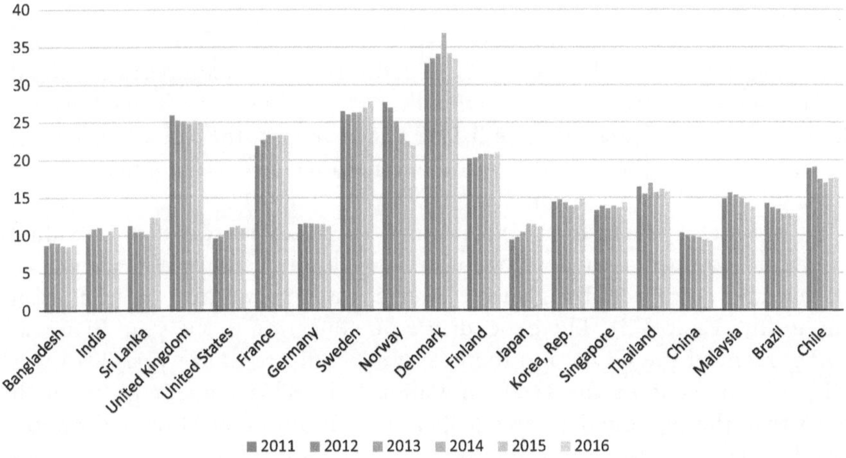

Figure 3.10 Tax revenue (percent of GDP) in Bangladesh and some selected economies. Source: World Bank, 2020a

Tax revenue in African countries shows a different picture. The ratio varies according to the geographical location of the countries. Resource-rich African countries in some cases show higher revenue compared to many Asian and developing states. The extraction of natural resources by state-owned enterprises results in higher tax revenue in these countries. For example, Tanzania and Mozambique had tax–GDP ratios of 11.6 and 21.3 respectively during 2015–2019. Recently LDC-graduated Botswana had a ratio of 20.8, much higher than Bangladesh or Cambodia where the ratios are 11.3 and 16.8 respectively (Chowdhury, 2020).

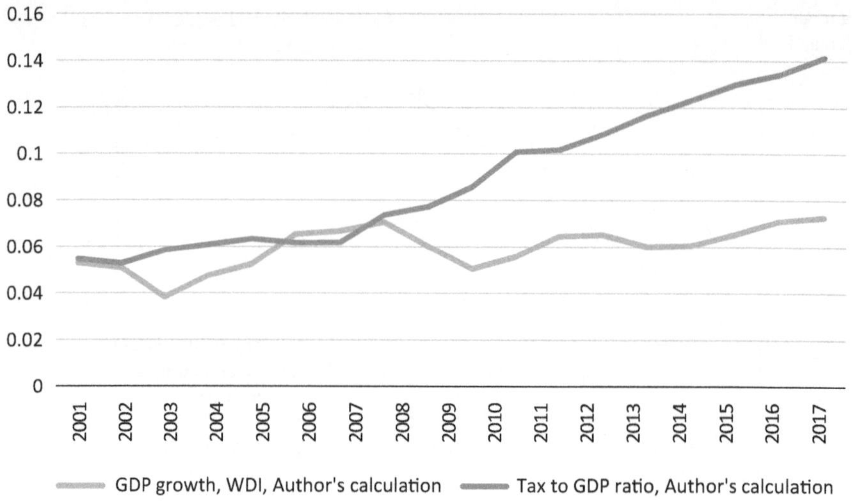

Figure 3.11 GDP growth and tax–GDP ratio. Source: World Bank, 2020a

During the last decade, the tax–GDP ratio has showed an increasing trend in Bangladesh. In 2017, the tax–GDP ratio was 14.14 percent, which means it almost tripled in 17 years (Figure 3.11). The change in the rate of growth of the tax–GDP ratio shows both positive and negative changes in different years and is still not as steep as economic growth.

As a result, government expenditure in social sectors has remained minuscule compared to developed and developing countries. Among all the selected countries, Bangladesh has the least expenditure on education and health (Table 3.3). The expenditure on education in the year 2016 was 1.92 percent of the GDP, and the health expenditure in the year 2014 was only 0.78 percent of the GDP in Bangladesh. This percentage is much lower than the suggested 5 percent spending on both education and health. Scandinavian countries with high revenue generation leave other countries far behind in the education and health sectors. This has affected both the quantitative and qualitative development of education and health in these countries.

Lower tax revenue also affects infrastructures in countries. Developed countries already have infrastructures in place. Infrastructure is required for progress in social and industrial sectors. The growth of East Asian developing economies has been reflected in their infrastructure as Japan and South Korea have been able to provide internet access to more than 92 percent of the population. Bangladesh, on the other hand, has the lowest electricity access in comparison to other countries. Only 62.4 percent of the population had access to electricity in 2014, whereas 79.16 percent, 97.53 percent and 92.19 percent of the total population had access to electricity in India, Pakistan and Sri Lanka

Table 3.3 State of education and health expenditure in Bangladesh and some selected economies

Country name	*Government expenditure on education, total (percent of GDP), 2013–2016*[a]	*Pupil-teacher ratio, primary, 2013–2015*[a]	*Health expenditure, public (percent of GDP), 2014*	*Hospital beds (per 1,000 people), 2009–2012*[a]
Bangladesh	1.92634	36.12701	0.786533	0.6
India	3.84236	31.49146	1.407238	0.7
Pakistan	2.64674	46.34065	0.918811	0.6
Sri Lanka	2.17912	23.15243	1.963953	3.6
United Kingdom	5.68427	17.3882	7.57885	2.9
United States	5.38078	14.53749	8.278518	2.9
Germany	4.95219	12.22305	8.697237	8.2
Norway	7.37329	8.86857	8.309618	3.3
Finland	7.1681	13.33204	7.289814	5.5
Japan	3.59184	16.44725	8.550082	13.7
Korea (Rep.)	4.62754	16.50455	3.985248	10.3
Thailand	4.12887	16.88246	3.208425	2.1
Vietnam	5.65873	19.23729	3.820019	2
China		16.29441	3.095174	3.8
South Africa	6.02955	33.59566	4.243269	
Argentina	5.32549		2.652674	4.7
Brazil	5.99395	20.91814	3.83176	2.3
Chile	4.92324	19.52587	3.851309	2.1

[a] Data refer to the most recent year available during the period specified.
Source: World Bank, 2020a; WHO, 2020

respectively (Table 3.4). In the other developed countries, 100 percent of the population has access to electricity.

It can be seen from the above statistical analysis that government spending is not as powerful with respect to aggregate demand as a tax cut–based fiscal policy, as each unit of government spending adds a full unit to aggregate demand in Bangladesh. As a result, it is evident that an increased tax–GDP ratio can only come about with an increased return on labour.

Debt, deficit and development

Macroeconomic policies in recent years have drifted away from their developmental role and have solely focused on their stabilisation role in the economy. As a result, budget deficit or public debt has been used more commonly as the indicator of the health of the economy.

Higher investment generally leads to higher national income. Increased national income will automatically generate higher revenue. Following this

Table 3.4 State of infrastructure in Bangladesh and some selected economies

Country name	*Access to electricity (percent of population), 2014*	*Individuals using the internet (percent of population), 2016*
Bangladesh	62.4	18.24694
India	79.16926	29.54716
Pakistan	97.53484	15.51456
Sri Lanka	92.19125	32.051
United Kingdom	100	94.7758
United States	100	76.17674
Germany	100	89.6471
Norway	100	97.2982
Finland	100	87.70365
Japan	100	92
Korea (Rep.)	100	92.71655
Thailand	100	47.50497
Vietnam	99.2	46.5
China	100	53.2
Chile	100	66.01

Source: World Bank, 2020a

notion, one cannot but reject the concept of "sound" finance that opposes government spending in times of higher debt. The concept of "functional finance" is more suitable in this scenario. However, the sustainability of the debt depends on the nature of government expenditure. Growth-enhancing investment will expand the economy, giving rise to government revenue through taxes later (Figure 3.12).

The concept of the deficit is more of an accounting construct than a neoclassical equation. Neoclassical schools do not include a deficit in equations (Kotlikoff, 1988). Hence, the neoclassical argument for low government deficit is problematic. The fiscal deficit is a useful indicator of stabilisation but not a well-defined indicator for measuring longer-term effects on economic growth. Japan has been facing the highest ratio of debt to GDP since the Japanese economic crisis. The ratio of debt to GDP has been high for the United States and the United Kingdom as well, mostly due to the financial crisis. These governments initiated bailouts to save the financial market in the aftermath of the crisis. Countries with lower ratios like Bangladesh often opt for a lower budget deficit and, as a result, social programmes are deprived of the necessary funding (Figure 3.13). Hence, debt is not the right indicator to measure the fiscal position of the country. Rather the debate must centre on sovereign debt. The economy of Greece faltered after the crisis because much of its debt was owed to external sources, whereas Japan and the United States kept much of their debt to themselves.

The source of deficit financing also has implications for debt sustainability. Borrowing from domestic sources is always preferable for the government as

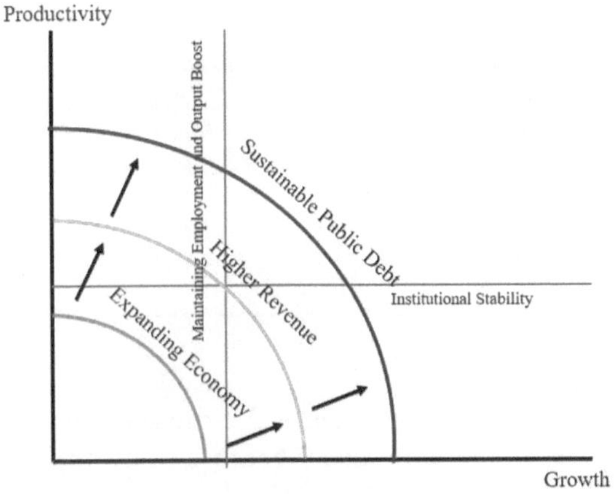

Figure 3.12 Sustainable public debt to GDP ratio in an economy. Source: Prepared by the author

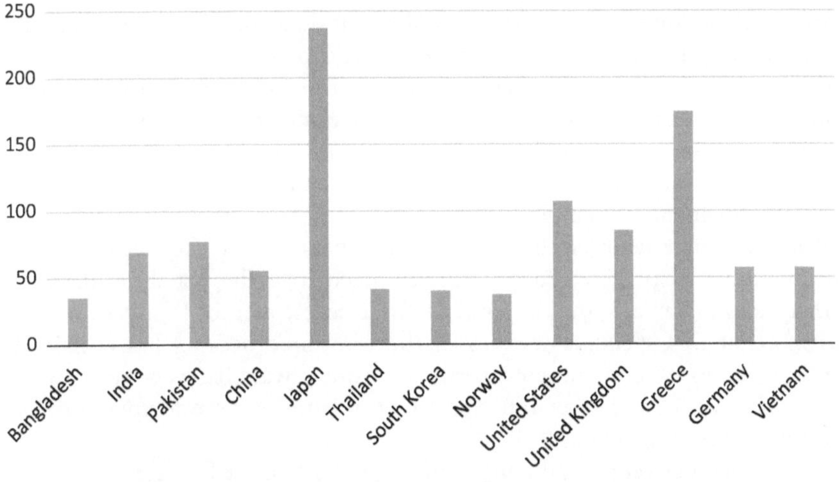

Figure 3.13 Debt to GDP ratio. Source: IMF, 2020a

doing so means there is little intervention from outsiders. However, there still exists some form of impediment. Firstly, borrowing from private banks may cause "crowding out" of private investments in the economy. Crowding out will result in an increased interest rate that may adversely affect businesses. However, the central bank can increase the liquidity in private banks through interest rates. This can encourage private investments. Secondly, the central bank can always help the government finance the spending. This is more prevalent in developing states due to the lack of a well-developed capital market (Chowdhury & Hart, 2016). The central bank has the authority

Table 3.5 Decadal average of fiscal deficit and private investment in Bangladesh as a percentage of GDP

Year	*Fiscal deficit (percent of GDP)*	*Private investment (percent of GDP)*	*Ratio of fiscal deficit to private investment (percent of GDP)*
1991–2000	2.74	14.74	5.38
2001–2010	3.47	18.91	5.45
2011–2018	4.11	22.64	5.51

Source: Ministry of Finance, 2019

to print money in addition to its role as the guardian of the banking sector. However, printing money has been opposed by many because of its impact on inflation.

Mere printing of money will not create inflation in a depressed economy. Rather, the objective is to keep total spending "neither greater nor less than that rate which at the current prices would buy all the goods that is possible to produce". Expansionary fiscal policy is expected to raise output as well as generate employment in the economy. When it does so, there is an expectation of increased demand. Higher demand needs to be met with an increased money supply. There is an expectation of price rises and some inflation in the economy from expansionary fiscal policy. Price increments for some goods will not result in runaway inflation. However, this should not discourage the government from undertaking fiscal measures to enhance productive capacity, which will maintain full employment.

With the increment of the average fiscal deficit over the decades, private investment has increased at a similar speed over the last three decades in Bangladesh (Table 3.5). The ratio of fiscal deficit to private investment is a measure of that speed. The ratio in the past three decades has remained identical. Increased government borrowing from private banks coupled with low public investment has retarded capital formulation and productive capacity (Titumir, Adiba & Haider, 2021).

The choice between fiscal and monetary policies must be based not only on economic but also on social and political considerations. While both sets of policies impinge on effective demand, they are likely to produce significantly different effects on virtually every element of the community. This would thus require rigorous empirical studies on the distributional consequences of fiscal and monetary policy instruments.

Checks and balances and human sociality

Macroeconomic policies are a function of checks, balances and human sociality, the absence of which may lead to widespread concentration of public resources, primitive accumulation and exploitation in society. The hypothesis is

Table 3.6 Function between human sociality and checks and balances

	Human sociality	*Absence of human sociality*
Check and balance	Policies guaranteeing equal access and benefit to citizen Forming a public society and citizen-state	Discrimination and exclusion Lack of struggle to form a citizen-state
Absence of checks and balances	Policies favouring clientelism and rent-seeking Coercive and exploitative state	Widespread concentration of public resources, primitive accumulation and exploitation Lack of public order and enforcement of contract between citizen and state

Source: Prepared by the author

that macroeconomic policies securing equal access and benefit sharing require a public society and citizen-state, which can be realised through a proper system of checks and balances and human sociality in the state. Human sociality helps foster the aspiration and struggle for a public society and citizen-state.

A society with checks and balances and human sociality secures equal access and benefit-sharing for citizens irrespective of class, caste, race or any kind of identity. Checks and balances establish an accountable and transparent governance system, which enforces the contract between the state and citizens.

The opposite case—an absence of both checks and balances and human sociality—leads to widespread concentration of public resources, primitive accumulation and exploitation. The lack of transparency and accountability due to the absence of checks and balances allows the group in power to grab rents, and a lack of human sociality makes the social contract between state and citizens void. In the absence of human sociality but the presence of checks and balances, public society fails to materialise, giving rise to discrimination. When human sociality exists but checks and balances are absent, the state becomes coercive and exploitative. Macroeconomic policies in the absence of any or both create discrimination and exploitation (Table 3.6).

Political settlement and class

Powerful groups tend to grab the policies for primitive accumulation and rent-seeking in absence of a public society, leaving the general populace to face widespread exclusion, discrimination and exploitation. The hypothesis is that macroeconomic policies tend to serve the interests of the ruling class in the absence of public society. Fiscal and monetary policies are based not only upon economic considerations but also upon social and political settlements.

Table 3.7 Clientelism vs. public society

	Clientelism	*Public society*
Powerful groups (ruling class)	Grabbing of wealth and power, rent-seeking, primitive accumulation	Equal access and benefit of citizens, a citizen-state
General people	Widespread exclusion, discrimination, exploitation	Decent standard of living with equal opportunity

Source: Prepared by the author

Political settlement in favour of clientelism provides benefits to the ruling class in forms of primitive accumulation, rent-seeking and illegal grabbing of wealth and power (Table 3.7). As a result, the general populace gets exploited. In contrast, a public society guarantees a decent standard of living and equal opportunities for every citizen. The absence of a public society leads to clientelism and primitive accumulation.

The political parties in Bangladesh are highly factional. The leaders can be described as charismatic and are from members of the intermediate classes, such as rich farmers, educated middle classes, urban petty-bourgeoisie and urban professionals. These intermediate classes organise much of the country's political activity, and their role is actually that of political entrepreneurs. As a result, the struggle never reaches the class-based nature of landlords or industrial capitalists observed elsewhere on the subcontinent. Different factions, for very pragmatic reasons, form alliances which involve changing loyalties and thus never form longstanding allegiances (Lewis, 2011).

The industrial policy adopted by the new government after the fall of the Awami League government led to the rapid growth of a new family-based industrial elite. Informed estimates estimate this new elite to have reached about 100–200 business groups by the late 1980s. Of them, 15–25 were quite large and the remaining were relatively small but growing (Kochanek, 1996).

Thus, the previous literature on class conflict and clientelism in the formation of the Bangladeshi state identified that the conflicts that exist in the country are between *factions* composed of various classes. However, only small groups of the winning factions have accrued benefits from conflicts. These groups, after getting hold of power, abandoned the interests of the class they belonged to. Later they went on to become the dominating force in politics (Khan, 2000). This class domination and transition in Bangladesh was fuelled by state-led primitive accumulation. Groups formed factions only to gain access to power and then to primitive accumulation. This has impaired the political process in the country, evident in the inefficiencies of parliamentarians. This has affected the budgetary process as well.

The Parliament of Bangladesh could not significantly influence the budget-making process. The inefficiency becomes visible when there exist inadequacies in terms of things like discussion and participation in budgeting as well as an absence of an opposition and Parliamentary standing committee (Khan, 2008). Various institutional impediments make the budgeting process more difficult for the parliamentarians. On average, 37 percent of MPs participate in budget discussions, and the discussions on the budget are too short and perfunctory with frequent opposition walkouts. Only 8 percent of cut motions were perfunctorily discussed and on average 92 percent of cut motions were guillotined. Moreover, most parliaments neither have adequate knowledge of budgetary matters nor adequate staff support for scrutinising the budget effectively (Khan, 2008).

If the members utilise 20 hours of discussion per week on an average (4 hours per day for 5 working days), they could have devoted on an average 60 hours to the budget discussion. However, the average time for discussion per budget was 35.1 hours, about 40 percent less than what could have been easily achieved on the given assumptions. The members of the parliament were given inadequate time for budget discussion and they also failed to utilise the insufficient time given to them (Table 3.8). On average, 129 members (about 37 percent of MPs) participated in the budget discussion in the eighth parliament (2002–2006). The average length of intervention made by an MP was 16.22 minutes (Table 3.8). The average is misleading since the senior leaders of the parties usurped most of the time allocated for discussion and the backbenchers were very often given 5–7 minutes (Khan, 2008).

There is a lack of enthusiasm among the members to discuss the budget (Table 3.9). This has resulted from the exclusion of MPs from the process of the allocation of resources. In many cases, the budget sessions became irrelevant as the major opposition party boycotted the budget sessions.

Table 3.8 Year-wise total discussion time on budget

Year	*Total budget discussion in hrs.*	*Total discussion in the Parliament in hrs.*	*Budget discussion as percent of total discussion time*
1996	40.25	252.81	15.9
1997	47.45	377.11	12.5
1998	21.28	391.76	5.4
1999	45.30	293.97	15.4
2000	33.66	176.76	19.0
2001	27.11	196.89	13.7
2002	29.88	244.56	12.2
2003	36.28	232.29	15.6
2004	39.75	267.75	14.8
2005	35.18	186.39	18.8
2006	30.08	248.46	12.1
Average	35.1	260.7	13.4

Source: Karya Nirbah reports of the Parliament (Adapted from Khan, 2008)

Table 3.9 No of MPs participating in budget discussion

Year	*No of participating MPs*	*Average length of intervention (in minutes)*
2002	118	15.2
2003	152	15.2
2004	152	15.7
2005	110	19.1
2006	113	15.9
Average	129	16.22

Source: Karya Nirbah reports of the Parliament (Adapted from Khan, 2008)

Crisis of the COVID-19 pandemic: Fiscal policy

Governments, central banks and supervisory authorities have responded promptly as a policy reaction to the ongoing COVID-19 pandemic. Given the nature of the shocks, fiscal policy has played a central role in ensuring a public health emergency with unprecedented real effects. Intensive fiscal policy actions were taken by governments, and stringent containment measures were adopted to reduce the infection rate of the spreading pandemic around the globe. As lockdowns relax and activity progressively resumes, a new round of fiscal stimulus is expected which will be more focused on supporting economic recovery (BIS, 2020).

The pandemic has caused an unprecedented economic crisis and has set back the progress of developing countries. Developed countries have been able to undertake recovery programmes because of their structured financial sector and ability to finance with debts. This has allowed developed nations to adopt policies like quantitative easing with "helicopter dropping". The United States passed fiscal stimulus designed to provide citizens with checks of 600 and 1,400 USD. Developing countries, on the other hand, faced challenges in initiating such projects. Developing countries have a higher percentage of informal and low-paid jobs compared to developed countries. Many countries depended greatly on tourism before the pandemic. Travel restrictions and closing off the borders have brought the tourism sector to a stop. Decline in demand in developed countries, on the other hand, has affected the manufacturing sectors, which provided much-needed government revenue to the countries. At the same time, much of the debt in developing countries is being financed by multilateral and international sources. A weak monetary structure, as well as fiscal ability, already puts the developing countries in the back seat when it comes to tackling the pandemic. The recovery and rebuilding process of countries depends on the developed nations. Multilateral organisations have already started the recovery phase in some of the poorest countries. The COVAX initiative by major multilateral organisations donated COVID-19 vaccines to these nations. Debt repayments have been halted, giving temporary relief to the countries. However, long-term rebuilding plans are needed in the face of the pandemic. This includes a structural shift in economic policies in the developing countries.

A common feature of developing countries has been cuts in expenditure on social sectors to maintain a deficit. This has affected the health sector during the pandemic as patients started flocking to hospitals with low capacity. There is no alternative to a public healthcare system to tackle the pandemic. Hence, government spending on healthcare has to be increased in the next fiscal years. The government in South Korea quickly responded to needs through a special fiscal budget allocation to social sectors. The health sector received an allocation of 10 percent of the budget for disease prevention and treatment. Mexico increased its spending in the health sector by 0.7 percent of the GDP.

Least developed countries (LDCs) in the Asia-Pacific fell short in creating required fiscal expansion due to lower capacities for government expenditure and higher debt burden. As the pandemic raged on, high income countries adopted strategies for expansion of fiscal policy in tackling the economic loss. The expansion helped the countries in providing necessary boost to healthcare sector as well as social protection that mitigated the income loss of citizens. Though the government expenditure rose slightly from the previous years, yet such level of measures could not be put in place in developing countries due to fiscal constraints. The government expenditure in Solomon Islands dropped to 36.9% in 2020 from 40.3% during 2016-19 while all other Asia Pacific LDCs increased government expenditure by 3-10%. Bangladesh recorded the smallest increase in government expenditure from 14.3% to 14.9% during the said period. At the same time, external debt grew significantly. External debt rose by 7.5% while government expenditure grew by less than one percent in Asia-Pacific LDCs.

The pandemic has put an additional burden on workers from informal sectors, as many lost their daily income due to lockdowns. To mitigate the income shocks, governments in developed countries have provided stimulus checks as well as increased unemployment benefits. South Korea, in their special budget, allocated 25 percent of the budget to support households through cash vouchers and an employment support package for youths (Ministry of Economy and Finance, 2020). However, developing countries do not usually provide such benefits. In Bangladesh, the government provides social security through social safety net programmes. Allocation in this sector due to COVID-19 increased by 8.1 percent, even though in real terms, the change was 2.5 percent. Around 30 percent of the allocation is composed of pensions for retired government officials. Hence, the allocation often fails to reach its targeted population (Titumir, Adiba & Haider, 2021). In Sri Lanka, the dedicated social security programme called "Samrudhi" could only reach 60 percent of the target population. The payments were concentrated in areas where the ruling party has higher votes (Brookings, 2020). The failure is not just linked to lower allocation but also to institutional incapacity. In such a scenario, Universal Basic Income has emerged as a new method of applying social security in developing countries. The majority of the population remains in poverty and has been impacted in some way due to the pandemic. In such scenarios, untargeted transfer will ensure maximum benefit to the population (Özler, 2020).

In the first year of the pandemic, governments across the globe increased their spending in the health sector. This included countries that already had high levels of expenditure on education as well as countries with low public spending. For instance, increased health expenditure accounts for 0.1 percent of the GDP in Argentina, Brazil and China, and up to 0.7 percent of the GDP in Mexico (IMF, 2020b). There will likely be a continuation of health expenditure as countries now look forward to vaccinating the population as vaccines are rolled out. However, the spending will vary according to the impact of the pandemic. Different variants of the virus have spread in different regions, and these regions have been affected differently. Hence, some countries have seen higher death tolls and infection rates. These include countries like Brazil, India and South Africa. Limited testing capacity in developing countries may have caused lower infection detection. Therefore, countries need to spend on preparedness as well as building infrastructure for better testing facilities.

Besides the spending in the health sector, social security should be prioritised in the face of income loss from the pandemic. Governments have rolled out stimulus packages to tackle economic damage. The stimulus packages should be aimed towards manufacturing enterprises who have suffered from the pandemic. Small and medium enterprises

Second, government expenditure should help remedy some of the economic losses created by containment and mitigation measures, reducing the direct pain inflicted on individuals and businesses and aligning incentives for social distancing. In fact, the support for shuttered businesses and furloughed workers without pay makes social distancing measures possible without causing catastrophic economic damage. Likewise, this support generates an incentive for people who should self-isolate to consider their symptoms and remain at home.

Fiscal inaction by the government will likely widen inequality in society. The International Labour Organization (ILO) estimates that due to the pandemic, worldwide income shrank by 10.7 percent or USD 3.5 trillion. At the same time, according to an Oxfam report, global billionaires increased their wealth by USD 3.9 trillion during the pandemic (Oxfam, 2021). Developing countries have more informal sector workers than formal ones and they have been the worst hit due to restrictions and lockdowns. The economic recovery path predicted by the economists are V, U, L and I curves. In most cases, economists predicted that developed countries would see a V-shaped recovery with a high growth after a short period of low growth during the pandemic. For instance, among the East Asian countries, China and Vietnam have seen a V-shaped recovery (World Bank, 2020c). The U-shaped recovery sees a prolonged recession before the economy takes off. However, in the face of the pandemic, economies are now facing a K-shaped recovery path, where the upper end of the English letter "K" shows the rate of concentration and the

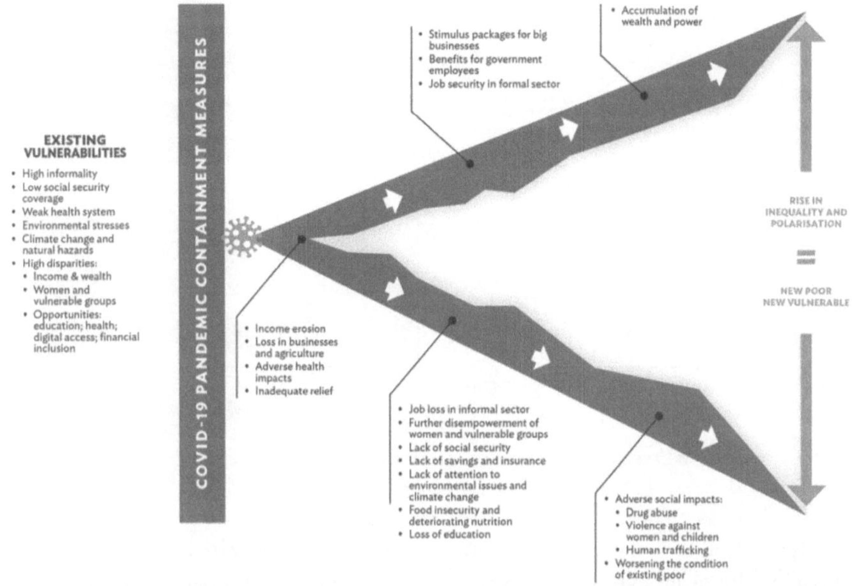

Figure 3.14 K-curve. Source: Adapted from Titumir (2020). Which recovery path may we pursue? New Age, 15 October. Available from www.newagebd.net/article/118990/which-recovery-path-may-we-pursue by United Nations, Asian Development Bank & United Nations Development Programme, 2021

lower end portrays the rate of pauperisation (Figure 3.14). The gap between both ends shows inequality (Titumir, 2021). This gap grows as containment measures can lead to inequality. Income erosion, job loss in the informal sector and a lack of social security worsen the conditions of the existing poor. On the other hand, government stimulus packages end up in big businesses. Loss of income and jobs are not high in formal sectors due to higher job security. Two contrasting pictures of two groups of the population give rise to polarisation.

Unless governments intervene, this gap is only expected to grow. Government intervention in the form of benefit packages and social security can reduce this gap. The government has to step in with active restraints. Active restraint measures include the presence of public goods provision, redistributive actions, macrofinancial interventions and structural policy reforms. These policies have the wealth redistribution effects necessary to improve the living standards of citizens. Such policies will reduce the wealth concentration gap (Figure 3.15a). On the contrary, active inaction or business-as-usual policies by the government can worsen the condition and widen the gap (Figure 3.15b).

The usual pro-cyclical spending cut in developing countries can be offset through multilateral finances (Hausmann, 2020). This will allow them to spend in sectors like health and social security. Countries have already requested help from multilateral financial institutions like the IMF. The World Bank will be

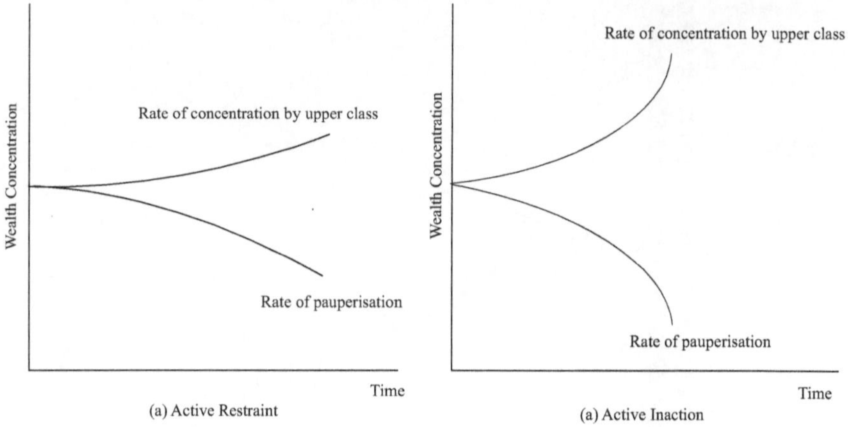

Figure 3.15 K-shaped recovery path. Source: Titumir, 2021

providing a USD 6 billion loan assistance programme to developing countries for improving the healthcare sector (World Bank, 2020d). Such financial institutions can provide dollar swaps to increase liquidity in the local market (Georgieva, 2020; Hausmann, 2020). These policies may increase the public debt in the economy. However, debt will increase for all countries during the pandemic and this will be regarded more as a "new normal" (Resende, Terra & Filho, 2021).

The effectiveness of both the monetary and fiscal stimulus in tackling COVID-19 remains in doubt as monetary transmission in developing countries is still weaker and fiscal space still limited. Stimulus measures may provide short-term relief; however, the fallout from the pandemic requires a long-term plan to support the citizens. This can only be done through continuous spending on social sectors.

Conclusion

Mainstream views of fiscal policy promote tax cuts, demonise fiscal deficit and debt and ditch the government's role in ensuring full employment, development and state-building. Liberal public expenditure theorists tend to advance an apolitical technocratic view of the state and state finances. From their vantage point, state fiscal policy does not function as an instrument of change but simply serves to moderate the more dysfunctional consequences of a sound economic system.

Neo-Keynesians view the state as a purely neutral technocratic and administrative apparatus standing above narrow class interests and class struggles. Rather, the state and political action itself are cast as the nexus or foci of structural continuity and change, in that the state (or portions thereof) must balance competing and often contradictory class interests while reproducing society at large. Hence come the ideas of political settlement (distribution of power), citizenship (legitimacy and public order) and value system (human sociality as opposed to self-interest and animal instincts). The state does not stand outside but rather becomes the arena in which the contradictions of civil society are displaced and manifest.

The alternative framework in this chapter demonstrates that the political process shapes policies against the backdrop of an apolitical conceptualisation of fiscal policy. Three pillars have been identified as the ground of the political process: political settlement, citizenship and value system. This framework uses political settlement to understand the distribution of power, while the idea of citizenship raises the question of legitimacy and public order. On the other hand, a value system incorporates human sociality as opposed to the assumption of self-interest made in neoclassical economics. These pillars are significant to understand the nature and scope of fiscal policies that aim at stable, transformed and sustained growth. This framework includes various agents, means and institutions of fiscal policies that result in employment-led capital formation and growth.

The path to recovery for developing countries becomes much harder than for developed countries because of their lower credit ratings. This makes it difficult for developing countries to borrow money for implementing emergency fiscal measures. Developed countries, on the other hand, had low interest rates before the pandemic arrived. On top of this, their higher credit rating allowed them to take extreme fiscal measures to tackle the pandemic. Fiscal policy tools also differ among countries. However, the fiscal policy tools available mostly align on one of two sides, government spending and revenue. Whatever the tool is, the target of fiscal measures is to stabilise income and consumption. Progressive taxation and unemployment benefits can provide relief and stabilise income. To ensure the smooth conduct of business, particularly for small and medium enterprises, governments can provide affordable loans. Again, developing countries require assistance in this regard. Temporary debt relief and suspensions can help these countries protect the livelihoods of the population in danger.

Finally, this chapter argues that if the state fails to create a tax system that can maximise public choice by providing for public goods and employment generation, ensuring optimal resource mobilisation, containing and transforming the nature of class relations and identity, state-building as well as development efforts could suffer. The discussion here thus involves the fiscal relationship between the state and the citizen—how fiscal policy can be developed to affect the relationship between the state and its citizens, which can strengthen the process of state-building. This chapter thus argues for a fiscal policy that caters for the revenue needs of the state and that incorporates class and accumulation into the system.

References

Angelopoulos, K., & Philippopoulos, A. (2007). The growth effects of fiscal policy in Greece 1960–2000. *Public Choice*, 131(1/2), 157–175.

Arestis, P., & Sawyer, M. (2004a). On the effectiveness of monetary policy and of fiscal policy. *Review of Social Economy*, 62(4), 441–463.

Arestis, P., & Sawyer, M. (2004b). *Re-examining Monetary and Fiscal Policy for the 21st Century*. Cheltenham, UK: Edward Elgar.

Backhaus, J. G., & Wagner, R. E. (2004). Society, state, and public finance: Setting the analytical stage. In J. G. Backhaus & R. E. Wagner (Eds.), *Handbook of Public Finance*. Boston: Kluwer Academic Publishers.

Bardhan, P., Bowles, S., & Gintis, H. (Eds.) (1999). *Wealth Inequality, Wealth Constraints and Economic Performance* (Vol. 1). Elsevier Science B.V., Amsterdam

Barro, R. J. (1999). Inequality, Growth, and Investment. NBER Working Paper No. 7038. National Bureau of Economic Research, Cambridge, MA.

Besley, T. (2006). *Principled Agents? The Political Economy of Good Government*. New York: Oxford University Press.

BIS. 2020. *The Fiscal Response to the Covid-19 Crisis in Advanced and Emerging Market Economies*. Bank for International Settlements. June 17.

Bräutigam, D. A. (2008). Introduction: Taxation and state-building in developing countries. In D. A. Bräutigam, O.-H. Fjeldstad, & M. Moore (Eds.), *Taxation and State-Building in Developing Countries*. New York: Cambridge University Press.

Brennan, G., & Buchanan, J. M. (2000). *The Power to Tax: Analytical Foundations of a Fiscal Constitution*. Cambridge University Press, New York.

Brennan, G., & Eusepi, G. (2004). Fiscal constitutionalism. In J. G. Backhaus & R. E. Wagner (Eds.), *Handbook of Public Finance*. Boston: Kluwer Academic Publishers.

Brookings. (2020). Fiscal policy for Covid 19 and beyond. World Bank Group. May 29.

Browning, E. K., & Johnson, W. R. (1984). The trade-off between equality and efficiency. *Journal of Political Economy*, 92(2), 175–203.

Buchanan, J. M., & Wagner, R. E. (1978). The political biases of Keynesian economics. In J. M. Buchanan & R. E. Wagner (Eds.), *Fiscal Responsibility in Constitutional Democracy*. Boston: Martinus Nijhoff.

Chowdhury, A. A. (2020). Growth and structural transformation in African LDCs (2000–2020).

Chowdhury, A., & Hart, N. (2016). Why worry about fiscal deficits? G24 Policy Briefs.

Deininger, K., & Deininter, P. (2000). Asset distribution, inequality, and growth. Policy Research Working Paper No. 2375. The World Bank, Washington, DC.

Downs, A. (1957). An economic theory of political action in a democracy. *Journal of Political Economy*, 65(2), 135–150.

Esping-Andersen, G. (1996). *The Three Worlds of Welfare Capitalism*. Cambridge, UK: Polity Press.

Ferlie, E., Fitzgerald, L., & Pettigrew, A. (1996). *The New Public Management in Action*. USA: Oxford University Press.

Georgieva, K. (2020). Policy action for a healthy global economy. IMF Blog, March 16. International Monetary Fund. Retrieved from https://blogs.imf.org/2020/03/16/policy-action-for-a-healthy-global- economy/

Gregoriou, A., & Ghosh, S. (2009). The impact of government expenditure on growth: Empirical evidence from a heterogenous panel. *Bulletin of Economic Research*, 61(1), 95–102.

Hausmann, R. (2020). Flattening the COVID-19 curve in developing countries. *Project Syndicate*. March 24. Retrieved from https://www.project-syndicate.org/commentary/flattening-covid19-curve-in- developing-countries-by-ricardo-hausmann-2020-03

Hettich, W., & Winer, S. L. (1999). *Democratic Choice and Taxation: A Theoretical and Empirical Analysis*. New York: Cambridge University Press.

IMF. (2020a). *IMF Data*. Washington, DC: International Monetary Fund.

IMF. (2020b). Policy responses to Covid-19. Retrieved from https://www.imf.org/en/Topics/imf-and- covid19/Policy-Responses-to-COVID-19#S

ILO. (2020). *ILOStats*. Geneva, Switzerland: International Labour Organization. Retrieved from https://ilostat.ilo.org/

Khan, M. H. (2000). Class, clientelism and communal politics in contemporary Bangladesh. In K. N. Panikkar, T. J. Byres, & U. Patnaik (Eds.), *The Making of History: Essays Presented to Irfan Habib*. New Delhi: Tulika.

Khan, A.A. (2008). *People's Participation in Budgetary Process in Bangladesh: In Search of Some Policy Reforms*. Shamunnay.

Kochanek, S. A. (1996). The rise of interest politics in Bangladesh. *Asian Survey*, 36(7), 704–722.

Kotlikoff, L. J. (1988). The deficit is not a well-defined measure of fiscal policy. *Science*, 241(4867), 791–795.

Lewis, D. (2011). *Bangladesh: Politics, Economy and Civil Society*. Cambridge University Press, Cambridge.

Mill, J. S. (1848). *Principles of Political Economy with Some of Their Applications to Social Philosophy*. Canada: University of Toronto.

Ministry of Economy and Finance. (2020). *Tackling COVID-19 Health, Quarantine and Economic Measures: Korean Experience*. Government of the Republic of Korea.

Ministry of Finance. (2019). *Bangladesh Economic Review 2019*. Ministry of Finance. Government of People's Republic of Bangladesh.

Nayyar, D. (2011). Rethinking macroeconomic policies for development. *Brazilian Journal of Political Economy*, 31(3 (123)), 339–351.

Neto, A. F. C., & Vernengo, M. (2004). Fiscal policy and the Washington consensus: A post Keynesian perspective. *Journal of Post Keynesian Economics*, 27(2), 333–343.

Oxfam. (2021). *World's Billionaires Have More Wealth Than 4.6 Billion People*. Press release. Retrieved from https://www.oxfam.org/en/press-releases/worlds-billionaires-have-more-wealth-46-billion-people

Özler, B. (2020). What can low-income countries do to provide relief for the poor and the vulnerable during the COVID-19 pandemic? *World Bank Development Impact Blog*. Retrieved from https://blogs.worldbank.org/impactevaluations/what-can-low-income-countries-do-provide- relief-poor-and-vulnerable-during-covid

Piketty, T. (2014). *Capital in the Twenty-first Century*. Cambridge, Massachusetts: Harvard University Press.

Prichard, W. (2010). *Taxation and State Building: Towards a Governance Focused Tax Reform Agenda*. IDS Working Paper No. 341. University of Sussex, Brighton, UK: Institute of Development Studies.

Resende, M. F. D. C., Terra, F. H. B., & Filho, F. F. (2021). Conventions, money creation and public debt to face the covid-19 crisis and its aftermath: A post-Keynesian view. *Brazilian Journal of Political Economy*, 41(2), 254–270.

Sanchez, O. (2011). *Mobilizing Resources in Latin America : The Political Economy of Tax Reform in Chile and Argentina*. New York: Palgrave Macmillan.

Schedler, K., & Proeller, I. (2000). *New Public Management*. Stuttgart/Wien.

Seccareccia, M. (2011). The role of public investment as principal macroeconomic tool to promote long-term growth: Keynes's legacy. *International Journal of Political Economy*, 40(4), 62–82.

Smith, A. (1776). *An Inquiry into the Nature and Causes of the Wealth of Nations* (Vol. 2). Indianapolis, Indiana: Liberty Classics.

Stiglitz, J. E. (2012). Stimulating the economy in an era of debt and deficit. *The Economists' Voice*.

Stuckler, D., & Basu, S. (2013). *The Body Economic: Why Austerity Kills*. Basic Books, New York

Taylor, L. (2010). *Maynard's Revenge*. Harvard University Press, Cambridge MA

Titumir, R. A. M. (2020). Which recovery path may we pursue? *New Age*, 15 October. Retrieved from www.newagebd.net/article/118990/which-recovery-path-may-we-pursue.

Titumir, R. A. M., Adiba, A. I. J., & Haider, W. (2021). *Structural and Redistributive Trends of Budgeting in Bangladesh: Planning Ahead with Lessons from the Fifty Years* [unpublished manuscript].

Titumir, R. A. M. (2021). Class, power and inequality in Bangladesh. In R. A. Mahmud Titumir, N. Georgeou, & A. Chowdhury (Eds.), *COVID-19 and Bangladesh: Response, Rights & Resilience, 2020*. Dhaka: University Press Ltd.

United Nations, Asian Development Bank & United Nations Development Programme. (2021). *Responding to the COVID-19 Pandemic: Leaving No Country Behind*. Bangkok, Thailand: United Nations.

Wade, R. (2011). Global trends in income inequality: What is happening, and should we worry? *Challenge*, 54(5), 54–75.

Watson, A. M. S. (Ed.) (2001). *Routledge Encyclopedia of International Political Economy* (Vols. 3). New York: Routledge.

WHO. (2020). *WHO The Global Health Observatory*. World Health Organization

World Bank. (2020a). *World Bank Development Indicator*. Washington, DC: World Bank.

World Bank. (2020b). *Doing Business 2021*. Washington, DC: The World Bank.

World Bank. (2020c). COVID-19 and the East Asia and Pacific Region, East Asia and Pacific Economic Update, April, Washington, DC: The World Bank. Retrieved from http://www.worldbank.org/eapupdate

World Bank. (2020d). World Bank Group increases COVID-19 response to $14 Billion to Help Sustain Economies, Protect Jobs. March 17. Retrieved from https://www.worldbank.org/en/news/press-release/ 2020/03/17/world-bank-group-increases-covid-19-response-to-14-billion-to-help-sustain-economies-protect-jobs

Zweimüller, J. (2000). Inequality, redistribution, and economic growth. *Empirica*, 27, 1–20.

4 Fiscal policy and productive capacity

Introduction

The diverging trajectory of former East and West Germany, despite starting from the same standpoint, is a striking example of the edge in productivity. In 1987, productivity in East Germany, measured as comparative levels of census value added per hour worked in manufacturing, stood at 28.2 percent as a proportion of that of West Germany. In 1990, the productivity level of East Germany fell further to about 25 percent of the productivity level of West Germany, while the wage rate in East Germany stood at about 35 percent of the wage rate of its western counterpart (Klodt, 2000). After the German reunification, the labour productivity measured as the East–West ratio of GDP per employee observed a significant increase, reaching 0.78 in 2010 (Fuchs-Schündeln & Izem, 2012).

From 1973 to 1979, the government of South Korea initiated the heavy chemical and industry (HCI) drive that earmarked trade policies constituting subsidies on imported inputs and heavily discounted credit to allow for investment capital–intensive production processes. The targeted industries in this drive recorded a rise in labour productivity and a decline in their output prices, compared to non-targeted industries. Similarly, in the post-Soviet space, Uzbekistan experienced a doubling in its GDP from 1989 to 2012, following similar strategies as South Korea. The country invested in creating an automobile industry, now known for its high-speed railways, which resulted in a significant increase in the share of industry in GDP, and greater acquisition of machinery and equipment in industrial output and export.

This chapter demonstrates how productivity can be influenced by existing power relations, the role political settlement plays in this regard and how the endogeneity of politics affects the advancement of the whole process. Much of the literature predominantly falls within the realm of either the neoclassical growth theory or the new growth theory, and thus there is negligence of how the state, underwritten by appropriate political settlement, plays an active role in ensuring and maintaining high rates of investment and the shift to higher productivity-inducing technology acquisition, catching-up and deepening.

DOI: 10.4324/9781003201847-4

This chapter shows that productivity in factors of production—labour, capital and technology—are brought about through the endogeneity of political settlement or social property relationships, and informal institutions, as understood in terms of nature and distribution of power in a given society. It utilises instruments such as technology acquisition and organisational capabilities to determine the level of productivity contributed by the role of fiscal policy. In the time of COVID-19, developing countries may choose to use these instruments to boost productive economic sectors and induce effective policy responses to improve productivity, where many fell short. For instance, in India, the central government had left state governments to their own devices in combating the blows of the global pandemic without compensating them by the dues it owed to the state governments, damaging fiscal federalism in the country (Chandrasekhar & Ghosh, 2021).

This chapter contributes to the debates on the necessary and sufficient conditions for sustained and rapid improvements in living standards. The factors of production—labour and capital (technology induced)—are discussed through the endogeneity of political settlement. Following a critical analysis of different schools of thought, the chapter identifies the rent-seeking behaviour of powerful clientelist networks and the rentier motives of the state and attempts to find their relationship with the expansion of productive capital in the economy, which is the main driving force for productivity in the long run.

To begin with, the neoclassical growth theory put forward by Robert Solow (1956) had been intended to explain the continuing rise in per capita income. In Solow's model, capital accumulation was the driver of output growth, where a greater capital stock generates greater per capita production, although with diminishing returns when technology is held constant. The long-term growth model builds upon the Keynesian Harrod-Domar model, while forgoing the assumption of fixed proportions, to allow for capital-labour substitution. In contrast, the literature on endogenous growth theory shifted attention to human capital accumulation and assumed that diminishing returns to investment in education, training and research may not be inevitable (Dowrick, 2004). Thus, endogenous growth theory developed numerous models where the rate of growth is determined by the savings decision of households and that technological advances are the result of the deliberate or undeliberate maximising tendency of economic agents (D'Agata & Freni, 2003).

Nonetheless, not all capitalist economies, especially those that have adopted free-market policies lately, have shown success in this regard. Productive expansion is often credited to "technological progress" due to the reorganisation of production, more efficient capital goods or better use of capital. Changes in productivity, however, take place within the overall institutions and macroeconomic indicators. In reality, it may arise from greater labour exploitation or sharper competitive practices between firms and households in the circular flow, leading to inevitable market failure in the form of dependence, lack of diversification or institutional capabilities. For example, despite strong growth in both total value added and exports in Bangladesh since the 1990s, the country has failed to achieve the level of productivity observed in China and India (Dollar, Hallward-Driemeier & TayeMengistae, 2005; Fernandes, 2008). Although it has been believed that the process of achieving higher productivity may not be difficult, as it may involve a desire to adopt policies and institutions as per the experiences of successful economies, the number of countries failing to do so indicates otherwise (Pagés, 2010).

Studies so far have failed to pay any attention to how productivity can be influenced by existing power relations, what kind of role political settlement plays in this regard and how the endogeneity of politics affects the advancement of the whole process. One way or the other, the existing literature predominantly falls within the realm of either the neoclassical growth theory or the new growth theory, and thus there is also negligence of how the state, underwritten by appropriate political settlement, plays an active role in ensuring and maintaining high rates of investment and the shift to higher productivity technologies. Thus, questions about the necessary and sufficient conditions for sustained and rapid improvements in living standards remain unanswered. This chapter makes an attempt to demonstrate that productivity in factors of production—labour and capital (technology induced)—are brought about through endogeneity of political settlement or social property relationships as understood in terms of nature and distribution of power in a given society.

Fiscal policies for transformation: A review

Often, low productivity is portrayed as an unintentional product of market failures and poorly formulated economic policies that disrupt the incentives provided for innovation inhibit efficient businesses from expanding in scale and often encourage the persistence and growth of inefficient firms (Pagés, 2010). In terms of the productivity gap between East Germany and West Germany, for example, the gap between the two Germanies cannot be accredited to a mediocre capital endowment or qualification insufficiencies of the East German labour force. Instead, it turns out to be the outcome of an unsuitable design of industrial policy, which focused on the subsidisation of physical capital and mostly discounted the advancement of human capital- and service-intensive industrial structures (Klodt, 2000).

The factors that have frequently come up as important targets for state policies in the literature, including in the empirical literature, represent elements as diverse as export market participation, investments in research and development (R&D), worker training, foreign acquisition of firms, market competition, technological differences, process innovations, foreign direct investment, networks, state–business relations, investment climate reform, business environment trade, innovation and wage dispersion (Augier, Dovis & Gasiorek, 2012; Aw, Roberts & Winston, 2007; Inui, Kawakami & Miyagawa, 2012; Lee, 2011; Mahy, Rycx & Volral, 2011; Qureshi & Velde, 2013; Ricci & Trionfetti, 2012; Rochina-Barrachina, Mañez & Sanchis-Llopis, 2010; Salis, 2008; Xu & Sheng, 2012).

Not all factors, however, work for every economy. In the case of Japan, it has been a combination of policy failures such as import restrictions along with structural changes in the economy in the form of poor skill embodiment of the entering labour force and shifting of manufacturing plants in foreign countries that have aggravated the productivity problem (Mosk, 2008). Shifting of resources like labour from low-productivity areas such as agriculture to a higher productivity activity like manufacturing had a moderate influence on Japanese productivity and growth (Mosk, 2008). Since resource allocation in Singapore was not suffering from any significant misallocation from microeconomic policy distortions, the country only achieved limited productivity growth from structural policy reforms (Ghesquiere, 2007). Total factor productivity growth in Singapore, estimated as the residual item, mirrors numerous influences. Interpretations have emphasised the implementation of more innovative production techniques in manufacturing and advances in the quality of imported capital equipment, which included advanced foreign technologies. Cost reductions that were brought about by increasing returns to scale as Multi-national corporations (MNCs) expanded their activity were also significant (Ghesquiere, 2007).

Essentially, most of these studies follow either the neoclassical growth theory or the endogenous or new growth theory, and their coverage is economy-wide. The neoclassical growth theory emphasises the accumulation of capital as the source of productivity and assumes diminishing returns in production. The implication is that investment does not drive long-term growth in the neoclassical model (Dowrick, 2004). Neoclassical growth theory, however, has been criticised both on theoretical and empirical grounds. A major criticism has been that the rate of growth of economies should be dependent upon the frugality of the economy and that technical change should be the consequence of deliberate planned decisions of economic agents (D'Agata & Freni, 2003). Moreover, as the marginal product has a tendency to decrease, poorer countries are expected to grow faster than rich ones, thus leading to convergence (Miles & Scott, 2005).

An important difference between the new growth theories and the neoclassical growth theories involves the role of public policies in the long-term growth process of the economy. That is, whereas new growth theories acknowledge the ability of policies and institutions to determine the level of physical and/or human capital and therefore the long-term performance of the economy, the neoclassical alternative assumes a negative outlook (Dowrick, 2004). There ought to be no negative correlation between the initial income endowment and resultant growth, as per endogenous growth theories (Miles & Scott, 2005).

In this context, the positioning of rent in the orthodox economics remains problematic. Rents, often simplistically referred to as excess incomes, should exist in efficient markets (Khan, 2000). This is because despite being an excess income for recipients, rents are not necessarily the payments made to pay for the production of a certain good, provision of a service or execution of any relevant activity. Rents are differentiable, and it becomes imperative to distinguish between some rents that are inefficient and dampen growth and other rents that can be relatively more productive for growth and development. These productive rents can therefore challenge the predicament that institutions safeguard rents and should thus be removed in order to reduce inefficiency. Although the conclusion is simple, it may not be effective. It is of greater importance to rather differentiate between productive and unproductive rents in order to determine the complex institutional and market reforms required for efficiency and growth. The process of managing development, hence, is about the persistent process of discriminating between productive and unproductive rents to allow for continued productive capacity expansion. Moreover, a stringent governance capability will smoothen the implementation of industrial policy and the equitable disbursement of productive rents.

It is clear that real economies, especially developing ones, often do not have these conditions met. The truth is exactly the opposite, and therefore rents can occasionally be efficient, and in other instances they may be necessary for stimulating growth and development (Khan, 2000). Moreover, the lower the intricacy of the technology used in production, the lower the significance of learning. Along with that, the wage advantage of the developing country is expected to rise for low-productivity technologies where the developing countries have a lower unit cost of production compared to potentially high productivity technologies. Thus, a "comparative advantage" is had by developing countries in producing low-technology products (Khan & Blankenburg, 2009). Smoother functioning of the market is a requirement for technological catching up in late-developing countries.

Market failures are a common occurrence in all economies, especially in developing ones. Liberal economists, particularly public choice theorists and new public administration approaches, make the assumption that market failures mainly happen because of "bad states." They therefore want the state to stay out of the economic sphere, which they believe would solve the problem. Many important types of market failures do not originate from state interventions. They therefore would continue to remain. In fact, a realistically effective market is challenging to construct for structural reasons that include the cost of providing the essential governance-related public goods, and because of this, the opposite is likely to happen. In such circumstances, identifying market failures determines successful development, which can be unique to each country, and solutions to them are to be discovered in order to minimise the risk of government failure. The engagement of the state is needed for exercising this option, not its refusal (Khan, 2000).

Understanding productivity expansion

This section argues that productivity expansion requires the engagement of the state in addressing market failures, restructuring of political settlement or social property relationship to redistribute rents and the right to generate productivity, and provision of performance-based fiscal policies (e.g., *ex post* subsidies), which is designed to maintain compulsion of the market considering the endogeneity of politics.

Capitalist economy, technology and market failures

Capitalist economies came into existence in the now-advanced economies long before the market was established both as a self-correcting and an optimising mechanism (Haynes & Husan, 2002). This self-correcting and optimising behaviour of the market is held as such an absolute truth that the existence of endemic market failures is often overlooked. Since new technology involves market failure, it requires the intervention of the state to address those market failures. Moreover, for economic development to take place, the importance of the allocative function of markets over their creative functions is evident; this, however, is largely underrepresented in the literature relating to market failure as a cause and symptom of underdevelopment or the unceasing free-market debate in developing countries (Arndt, 1988).

Moreover, historical data advocates that the key mechanism for convergence at the international as well as the national level is the dissemination of knowledge (Piketty, 2014), and this depends on the efficacy of a country in organising funds and institutions which promote large-scale investment in education and training, along with a stable legal framework (Piketty, 2014). Thus, market failures in financing and organisational capabilities hinder new start-ups in developing countries.

To illustrate how market failure affects financing, suppose that the price of a product is set through the functioning of a competitive international market. The price of the product therefore would be decided on the basis of the movement of two forces: the cost of factors of production and the productivity of the labour. In such a situation, since technology acquisition requires time, the level of productivity in the beginning generally stays at a lower level than is observed for the competitors. Under this circumstance, one way to make the product competitive at the international level is to reduce the price by reducing the cost of inputs in the interim period. Since the market cannot capture the externalities fully, a competitive market does not solve this problem of financing (Khan, 2015). Moreover, even though technology and capital can be borrowed or emulated from developed countries, not many countries have succeeded in achieving the desirable results. The fundamental problem is the lack of organisational capabilities that continues to affect firms from the beginning. The matching of imported machinery and domestic worker capabilities to maximise team productivity again suffers from market failures (Khan, 2014).

Rent-seeking and rentier state

The framework of rent-seeking necessitates a shift from the traditional viewpoint of the creation and retention of monopoly rents. Monopoly rents arise from the benefits accrued from the ownership of an asset possessing unique or all-encompassing qualities, such as patents or copyrights, or by denying access to a market, such as monopoly (Birch, 2020). Rent-seeking primarily originates in the processes of institutional change, which leads to a change in the economic rights of individuals. The rentier state is one that emerges when the state sources its income from external sources, instead of from tax revenue levied on the citizenry. In such a case, the government is the key recipient of rents and does not need to depend on the citizenry for tax revenue, which in turn ensures that citizens make no political demands and have no ability to pressurise the state. This is because the citizenry is not required to bear tax burdens in return for the services provided by the state.

As a result, the rentier state alters the social contract between state and citizens into one in which citizens do not possess the motivation to question the legitimacy of the government or uphold a countervailing power against the political settlements enacted by clientelist networks. The state, on the other hand, is not expected to demonstrate fiscal accountability towards citizens as the financing for state-provided services is not sourced from taxpayers, but from independent, external sources. In addition, clientelist networks end up receiving state-directed funds on their basis of loyalty to the regime, and it serves as the only source of economic gain, thus fuelling the political settlement between these networks and the state.

Restructuring of rents for productive capital

Restructuring of rents is required to avoid the pitfalls of market failure and for the maintenance of compulsion into the fiscal policy. Moreover, enhancing productivity and growth involve not just the strengthening of some rents but also the weakening of others.

When a lately developing country can borrow technology from already developed ones and actually put it into worthy applications in the industrial sector, the industry has the potential to achieve even greater profitability than in the more developed country where the technology was created. There are mainly two reasons for this. First, the borrower does not have to incur the full cost of developing the technology. Second, the borrower country has the advantage of cheaper labour (Chang, 1996). As already stated, this argument is not valid for all borrowers since technology is not a plan in itself and it contains elements that cannot be categorised, and thus involves a relatively long period of learning (Chang, 1996). There also involves "the notion of adaptability", which puts forward that there is an association between social capability and technological opportunity (Abramovitz, 1986). Firms in developing countries will require extra incentives to embrace new technology, and these incentives are what many late-developing countries have been offering through tariff protection and other state-created rents (Chang, 1996). Careful distribution of rents by the state is therefore a requirement for technology acquisition and productivity growth.

Moreover, even if it is agreed that redistributing the rights and rent is required, the question still remains about the actual arrangement. In this regard, an industrial policy which fails to consider the nature of market failures and provides rents *ex ante* to infant industries through different financial instruments like subsidised interest rates, tariff protection and export and budgetary subsidies are bound to produce bad results (Khan, 2014). Intended results were attained only when these compulsions encouraged firms to invest high levels of effort in problem-solving, including learning organisational capabilities (Khan, 2014).

Compulsion and performance-based fiscal policy

A major step towards productivity expansion within an economy involves the introduction of performance-based fiscal policy for compulsion. Capitalism is generally defined as "a market system" that fulfils "two main conditions". The first condition is the private ownership of the "vast majority of the physical means of production". The owners of these, who are either private individuals or corporations, can use and profit from the productive means as they wish. The second condition is that the majority of the production is done by labourers, who come to terms with the employers on a daily basis and in return for their work receive a wage (Schutz, 2011). Private ownership was present in many societies before the advent of capitalism.

The central characteristic of the capitalist system is actually one of compulsion. This compulsion makes the labour and capital work harder, which makes the capitalist economy more productive. Examples of compulsion observed for labour are described the following way:

> Illustrative of this is the essential role played by physical force and the state in the creation of the proletariat, including the police, the army, the tax and justice systems, and so on, rather than the smooth operation of market forces. This contrasts with most present-day labour relations, where the dull compulsion of economic needs and their development through tradition, education and habit induces the working class to look upon the conditions of the capitalist mode of production as self-evident and morally justified. Force rarely needs to be at the forefront now (although it is available if required) because labour is deeply tied to capital and appears as if it always has been and always will be.
>
> (Fine & Saad-Filho, 2004)

As further explained by Heinrich (2012):

> In a society based upon commodity exchange, everyone must follow the logic of exchange if he or she wants to survive. It is not merely the result of my "utility maximising" behaviour if I want to sell my own commodities dearly and buy other commodities cheaply. Rather, I have no other

> choice (unless I am so rich that I can choose to ignore exchange relationships). And since I am not capable of seeing an alternative, maybe I even perceive my own behaviour as "natural." When the majority behaves in the manner indicated, they also reproduce the social relations that commodity exchange is based upon, and therefore the compulsion for every individual to continue to behave accordingly.

An application of market compulsion is required for increasing productivity. This guaranteed that the performance of both capitalists and workers constantly had to undergo development in order to survive, and an adjustment made in the market logic to that of market compulsion compared to an extension of the prevailing role of the market as a provider of profit opportunities. If these modifications do not correspond to market-enhancing reforms, then ascertaining what they are, and the class and political constraints inhibiting their emergence will be of utmost importance (Khan, 2005).

Class and endogeneity, not only climate

The institutional side of economic transactions has to be taken care of to account for the costs or benefits associated with them. Achieving aggregate efficiency gains is a multifaceted issue that surpasses the bounds of technological growth. It needs incentives to be aligned, unbiased competition for resources and the opportunity for firms with good ideas to flourish and expand. Overall, what is required is a dynamic institutional setting that is capable of containing the negative influences of changing economic elites over time (Pagés, 2010).

In this regard, it is important to differentiate "the non-targeted, investment climate type of industrial policy" from the targeted "type of industrial policy that aims to accelerate technology acquisition and productivity growth in particular areas". Whereas the former is weak in its effectiveness, the latter is strong, as it is more likely to produce better outcomes. Rapid catching up hence entails robust industrial policy, containing strategies for targeted technology acquisition that allows a country to catch up swiftly with leader countries. Moreover, while technical progress is feasible along the route put forth by a market-driven strategy, the progression up the technology ladder tends to be relatively slower than with a dynamic technology acquisition and learning strategy (Khan & Blankenburg, 2009).

Finally, if some rents are indispensable for efficiency and growth while others are detrimental, sophisticated institutional and market reforms may be necessary. Managing development may involve the continuous discrimination of efficient from inefficient rents by policymakers and analysts. Subsequently, constructing the right institutional framework might prove to be more complex than shifting to the benchmark of a no-rent competitive market economy. On the contrary, the lack of diligence by policymakers, changes in political and technological circumstances or even undeliberated institutional growth may make an efficient system of rents inefficient over time (Khan, 2000).

The restraints levied by social capability on the successful implementation of more innovative technology steadily weaken and permit its better exploitation (Abramovitz, 1986). Nobel laureate Ronald Coase has rightly argued that it seems illogical for economists to assess the process of exchange without identifying the specific institutional setting within which the transaction occurs, as it impacts the incentives to produce and the costs of transacting (Vane & Mulhearn, 2005).

Technology, market failures and the state

Despite the United States being often portrayed as an example of "private sector–led wealth creation", it has been actually the state that has played "on a massive scale in entrepreneurial risk taking to spur innovation." The importance of the state in playing an entrepreneurial role has gained new importance in the face of newer technologies. For instance, the United States actively gets involved in investments and strategic choices when it comes to technology acquisition (Mazzucato, 2013).

Nanotechnology and Apple are two examples in this regard. Nanotechnology has become the future of technology. Most modern and advanced technological products require nanotechnologies. While the emergence of nanotechnologies is a recent phenomenon, the development process, however, began much earlier, in the 1990s. The United States government then had an active role in deciding the strategies of the technology (Mazzucato, 2013; Motoyama, Appelbaum & Parker, 2011). This government funding and involvement have been proven to be helpful to private companies as well. Apple is the most valuable company on earth. Much of its profit comes from computers and phones made by the company. However, in terms of the R&D/sales ratio, Apple falls in the bottom three when compared to its rivals (Schmidt, 2012). So how could Apple become so popular with their cutting-edge technological products? The answer is Apple has ridden on the back of government-funded technological innovations. Their innovativeness lies in utilising these innovations in their own products (Mazzucato, 2013).

Capitalist transition and productivity

Neoclassical economists define capitalism as the private ownership of assets and market coordination of all activities not organised within firms (Williamson, 1986). The Marxist definition of capitalism, however, differs from the neoclassical one on the grounds of the relationship between two classes: owners and non-owners of means of production. Owners of the means of production are capitalists, whereas the non-owners work for the capitalists. An important issue with the neoclassical definition is that economic systems existing prior to capitalism had private ownership of assets as well as extensive markets. In this context, the Marxist definition defines the new economic system that had emerged in sixteenth-century England in a more distinct manner.

One other merit that lies in the Marxist approach is that while the new institutional economics can explain why a system that allows private property ownership can be efficient through the reduction of transaction costs, the Marxist definition aims to explain the reasons behind the unexpected productivity growth in successful capitalist economies. The neoclassical understanding of capitalism is a derivation from the argument that well-defined private property rights reduce transaction costs, and this in turn creates an environment where the markets reach their full potential in terms of efficiency.

In the Marxist approach, capitalism is not only defined by the existence of market opportunities, which had been present in many economies before; it is also defined by the introduction of market compulsions that make both the capitalists and workers strive for survival through the improvement of performance (Wood, 2002). The Marxist approach had brought around a change in the understanding of the market. Previously, the market was thought to be a provider of profit opportunities. The Marxist definition of property rights and class relationships, however, was understood from the point of view of market compulsion.

Fiscal policy and productivity: A new framework

Sustaining growth in poor countries is a challenge, and there is a broad consensus about that. This is not only because of the necessity of identification of the right economic policies but also because the demand for support to be fulfilled by appropriate governance capabilities. The new framework (Figure 4.1) proposed, therefore, is based on the necessary and sufficient conditions for creating productive capacity expansion, which highlights the key conditions of fiscal policy to circulate between the state, firms and other intervening variables in increasing capital formation and expanding productivity. For the firm, the necessary conditions for fiscal policy to lead to productive expansion are drawn from active technology acquisition, the diversification of key industries, investment in creating human capital and capital accumulation to increase competitiveness (Figure 4.1).

Simultaneously, the necessary conditions of the state lie in a strong industrial policy that targets specific productive sectors, productive rents for allowing aggressive technology acquisition and organisational capability in harnessing the inclusivity and equitability of fiscal policy for all citizens. At the same time, these necessary conditions have to be supported by their sufficient conditions, which are rooted in institutions, including institutional capability, the ability to enforce contracts and the ability to recognise market and government failures in the economy.

Necessary conditions

The necessary conditions for expansion in productive capacity are an orchestration of the concerted efforts of the firm and the state. The firm will be responsible for an aggressive technology acquisition that leads to capital formation in

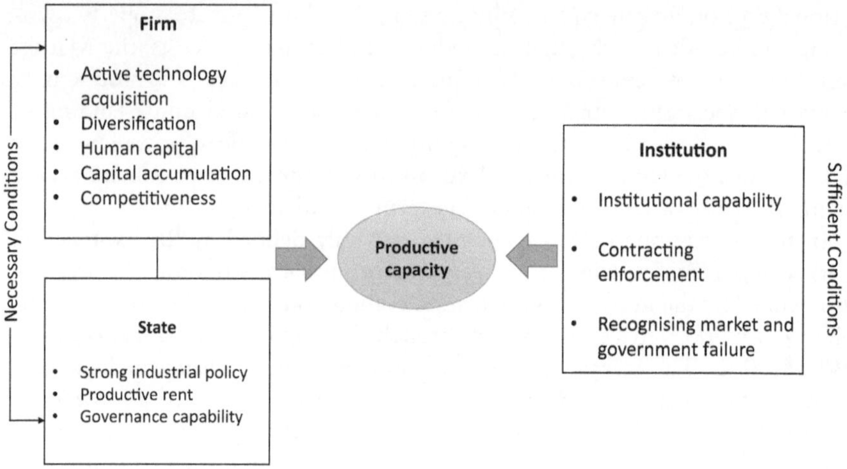

Figure 4.1 Fiscal policy and productive capacity. Source: Prepared by the author

such a manner that it contributes to the enhancement of the skill formation of the workforce, and is not accumulated by resource-dependent networks. Moreover, diversification in production is likely to lead to investments in new industries or sectors. Investment in these sectors will require an initial large-scale technology acquisition which will significantly increase capital formation in the economy. New capital formation or accumulation, along with the expansion of new sectors, will subsequently demand the formation of new skills, thus increasing the productive capacity in the economy. This triggers the other necessary conditions, as skill formation will enhance human capital, and the adoption of new technologies is likely to improve competitiveness. As a result, a concerted effort of these necessary conditions altogether will lead towards productive capacity expansion (Figure 4.1).

The state, on the other hand, has an equally important role in fulfilling the necessary conditions for productive capacity expansion (Figure 4.1). Firstly, the state should devise a strong industrial policy; industrial policies that are non-targeted and dependent on the investment climate are referred to as "weak" or "horizontal" policies, while industrial policies that are geared towards specific sectors and are designed to catalyse the process of active technology acquisition are known as "strong" industrial policies. A trade policy may not be substituted for an industrial policy either; growth in exports will not necessarily lead to industrialisation, economic growth or efficiency (Nanda, 2021). The absence of a targeted industrial policy may lead to growth that is contributed primarily by commodity-driven growth in services and traditional agriculture, with no rise in value added in high-productive sectors such as manufacturing, which was the case for 20 African countries that accounted for over 80 percent of the African GDP (Chowdhury, 2021). Therefore, the state requires the formulation of a strong, targeted industrial policy that will accelerate the processes of diversification, technology acquisition and capital accumulation of firms. In addition, with the help of the industrial policy, the state will be responsible for the provision of productive rents or incentives for firms to adopt technology acquisition.

Sufficient conditions

Sufficient conditions are inputs required to expand productive capacity over and above the provision of necessary conditions, and they include conditions such as institutional capability, recognising market and government failures and contracting enforcement (Figure 4.1). Failure to fulfil the sufficient conditions is likely to thwart the efficacy of necessary conditions and transformation trajectory. As mentioned earlier, institutions safeguard productive rents for firms to undertake the expansion of productive capacity, and accordingly, the institutional capability or strength will determine the efficacy of these rents. This is due to the fact that often an unprecedented change in political and technological conditions, shift in institutional aims or a lack thereof may render productive rents inefficient over time. Both formal and informal institutions protect these rents, and therefore the institutional capability ensures that continuous discrimination of productive from unproductive rent is carried out in order to prevent inefficient rents seeping into the economy.

Market failures occur in all economies and more often in developing ones. Liberal economics often assumes that the bad state is responsible for most market failures. In this approach, the dominant solution is thus to get the state out of the economy and enhance the governance arena to allow the market to function better. But this would still create significant market failures, especially in developing countries where it is difficult to construct an effective market for structural reasons related to the cost of provision of vital governance-related public goods. Thus, market failures need to be recognised for development, but it must be kept in mind that different types of market failures may occur in different country contexts because of differing political and social conditions.

In terms of the adoption of existing technologies, developing countries often encounter challenges in contracting. These complications arise due to the externalities accompanying technology and principal-agent transactions. The externalities affect the skill of the workforce and the providers of technology in developing countries in the presence of technology rents, new industries, failures of coordination and principal-agent problems for investment in the learning-by-doing processes. When private contracting is unable to formulate suitable solutions to these and other problems, policy interventions are needed. The effectiveness of a policy, however, lies in identifying a problem correctly and addressing it sufficiently.

The process of productive capacity expansion demonstrates the pathway for capability development and the emergence of new competitive sectors through the channel of learning in order to maintain discipline and regulation in the

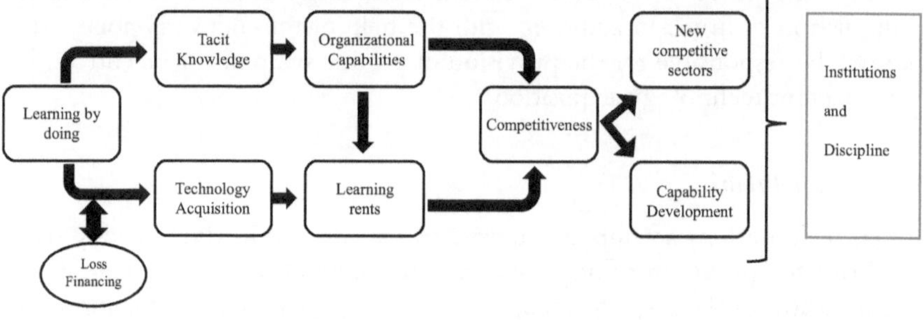

Figure 4.2 Productive capacity flowchart. Source: Prepared by the author

institutions (Figure 4.2). The chain starts with learning by doing, which incubates a financial loss but enhances tacit knowledge and acquisition of technology to achieve organisational capabilities and learning rents. These, however, lead to increasing competitiveness in the market, which ultimately produces new competitive sectors and increases the capability of both individuals and firms. Thus, the foundation of the institutions and discipline becomes strong.

Organisational capabilities and learning rents

The economic growth history has consisted of a series of "revolutions". The first of these occurred from the late 1700s through the middle 1800s and was characterised by a transition from hand to mechanised manufacturing using water and steam power. The second revolution began in the late 1800s and extended into the first part of the twentieth century. It was dominated by mass production, powered by electricity. The specification and control of the multiple steps in production led to reduced costs (economies of scale). The third revolution began in the late 1900s and has been characterised by automation, based on the widespread use of computers, which has led to more diversified and higher quality products and services (economies of scope).

The proposition is that organising competitive production processes requires a knowledge of organising production in highly demanding global chains of production, and such "tacit knowledge" is embedded in organisational procedures that can be learnt only through "learning by doing". There are three reasons why today's transformations represent not merely a prolongation of the Third Industrial Revolution but rather the arrival of a fourth and distinct one: velocity, scope and systems impact. This is characterised by a fusion of technologies that is blurring the lines between the physical, digital and biological spheres, collectively referred to as cyber-physical systems.

A case where *ex ante* incentives such as rent-seeking arise, leading to a misalignment problem, is represented by the profit-maximising point on the demand curve at A (Figure 4.3). The marginal revenue MR is equal to marginal

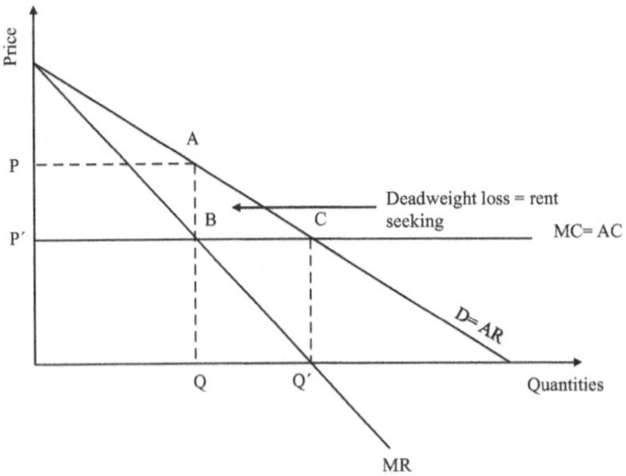

Figure 4.3 Rent-seeking and misalignment problem. Source: Prepared by the author

cost *MC* at point *B*, denoting that market price is at *P*, bringing in supernormal profits. However, the socially desirable equilibrium is *Q*' where the demand is equal to the supply, given by the *MC* curve, at point *C*. The shift from point *C* to point *A* denotes a fall in the total economic surplus of *ABC* which is referred to as the rent-seeking amount. Thus, point *A* denotes a misalignment problem of *ex ante* incentives.

Given that the aforementioned misalignment problem does not arise, competitiveness will be affected by the degree of loss financing undertaken during the period of learning by doing and the acquisition of technology afterwards. Periods of learning by doing and technology acquisition can be illustrated as an upward sloping curve (Figure 4.4). It increases slowly during the learning-by-doing phase as firm undertakes financing of the loss-making period, followed by a higher spurt in the growth of competitiveness brought on by technology acquisition. Firms therefore will require productive rents as part of a targeted industrial policy in order to finance the learning-by-doing phase of capital formation so as to progress into the second phase that allows firms to take advantage of the merits of technology acquisition in terms of higher competitiveness.

Technology acquisition

A key shortcoming of the concept of market failure in understanding the role of the government in advances in technology is its innate negligence of the history of innovation. Government has always been at the central standpoint of creating the most radical types of innovation, such that it has not only fixed markets but also dynamically created markets. (Mazzucato, 2013). Three areas of intervention can be identified. They are setting off direction, arrangement of funding and setting up of organisational structure.

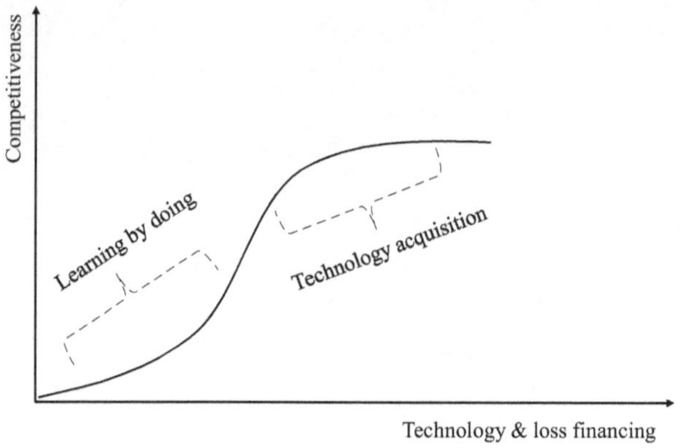

Figure 4.4 Competitiveness and technology acquisition. Source: Prepared by the author

The proposition is that acquiring competitiveness will require the acquisition of technology and financing of a loss-making period of production while learning by doing is taking place, while stringently avoiding *ex ante* incentive misalignment problems, including rent diversion, rent dissipation and rent-seeking, which are in preponderance in the developing world.

The production capacity depending on the level of tacit knowledge acquired by organisations may be expressed using two production functions: when tacit knowledge is low and when it is high. An organisation or firm that has low tacit knowledge, an increase in the availability of capital and/or labour will produce at a level insufficient for broad-based growth, *Y* (Figure 4.5). A higher level of tacit knowledge represents a higher production function *Y'*, also known as broad-based growth, while a lower level of tacit knowledge will yield a lower production function, *Y*. This implies that with the same quantity of capital and labour inputs, the output will differ between firms acquiring different levels of tacit knowledge. As a result, with the same quantity of inputs, the firm with high tacit knowledge will be able to produce a higher quantity of output. Simultaneously, for a small change in capital and labour, a firm with high levels of tacit knowledge will produce a proportionally higher amount of output, *B*, than the other firm, *A*.

Tacit knowledge determines the level of organisational capabilities acquired by the firm. A higher level of tacit knowledge therefore determines higher organisational capabilities, which enable firms to produce a proportionally higher output with a small increase in the use of input factors.

The phenomenon whereby a firm lacks the required organisational capabilities in order to produce at an efficient, equilibrium level can be illustrated using a factor demand and supply equilibrium (Figure 4.6). Such a firm is likely to face a constraint on acquiring factors, as represented by the horizontal line passing through the factor supply and demand curve at *B* and *C* respectively below

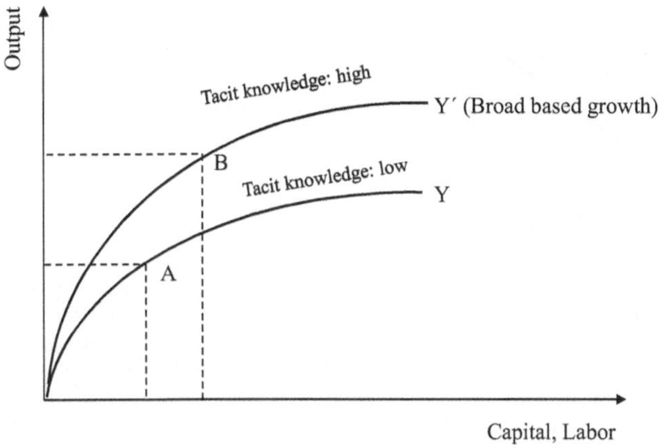

Figure 4.5 Organisational capabilities and tacit knowledge. Source: Prepared by author

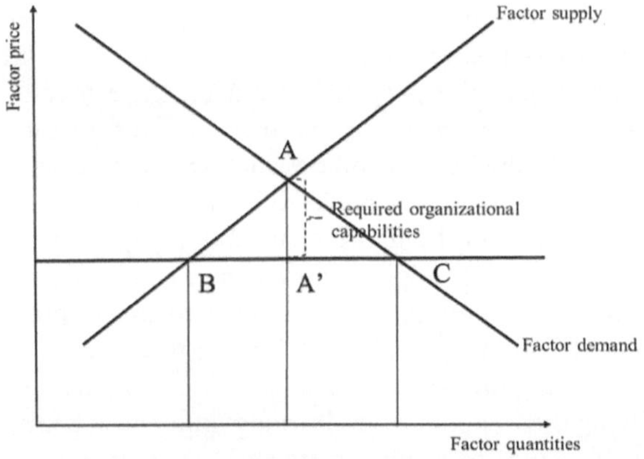

Figure 4.6 Disequilibrium in factor utilisation. Source: Prepared by the author

the equilibrium level. This shows that an attempt to correct the disequilibrium *AA′* or market failure will be constrained by the lack of organisational capabilities. Once these capabilities are achieved, factor demand and supply will likely reach the equilibrium level *A* and lead to a correction of market failures.

New sectors emerged when fortunate accidents created *ex post* rents for private investors in capability development, who invested in capability development first using bank credit and their own resources. A model using two supply curves demonstrates the emergence of *ex post* incentives and its impact on the market of a new sector (Figure 4.7). Supply curves shift from *S* to *S′* as *ex post* rents are acquired, leading to a rise in production from Q to Q′, and a fall in price from *P* to *P′*. As a result of the expansion in supply, often caused

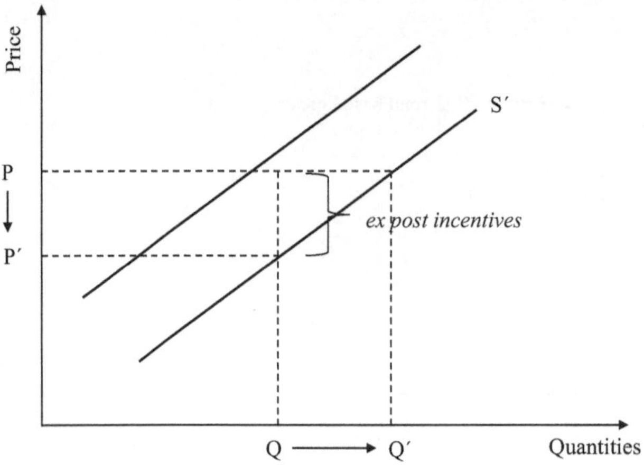

Figure 4.7 *Ex post* rent. Source: Prepared by the author

by a larger scale of production or new firms entering the market, production expands, leading to the emergence of the new sector.

Banks were willing to lend because the potential return on these investments with the rent justified the investments in learning, and the private investors who acted as catalysts had sufficient capabilities and incentives to self-monitor high levels of effort. The willingness of banks to lend to the investors in the presence of rent is demonstrated in the figure given above (Figure 4.8). At the initial equilibrium *E*, demand and supply were on the *D* and *S* curve respectively, with the interest rate at *r*. As investors decided to make more investments in learning, demand shifted from *D* to *D′* leading to a rent *r′r* as denoted in the graph at the prevailing interest rate. The interest rate *r′*, including the rent needed for justifying the investments in learning, influenced banks to expand its supply of loanable funds to these investors. As a result, supply shifts from *S* to *S′*, while prevailing at the interest rate *r*, along with the rent, and achieves the new equilibrium *E′*.

A cross-country comparison of the advances of the fourth technological revolution is investigated, the indicators of which are the new and redefined infrastructures i.e., road connectivity and quality of road infrastructure (Perez, 2009).

On the two axes, a scatterplot is used to demonstrate the quality of infrastructure on a scale of *1* to *7*, and road connectivity on a scale of *0* to *100*, thus depicting the relative position of several countries deemed successful and unsuccessful in technology acquisition (Figure 4.9). At the farthest end of the spectrum lies the United States, along with other developed countries such as Germany and Canada. The best quality of road infrastructure among these countries is Japan, although it ranks much lower in road connectivity. Nevertheless, at the innermost end lies Bangladesh, with a relatively worse

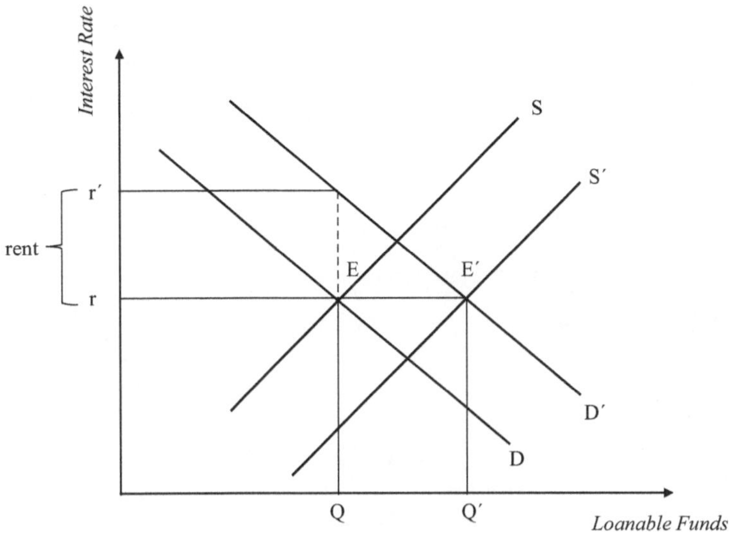

Figure 4.8 The market for investment. Source: Prepared by the author

position than all other countries. Countries such as Sri Lanka, Kenya, India and Thailand rank much higher in terms of both the indicators. While Bangladesh remains better off in terms of quality of road infrastructure than Nepal, Brazil and Nigeria, it still lags behind significantly in terms of road connectivity.

The trend of total factor productivity for countries successful in technology acquisition is shown in (Figure 4.10).

The analysis includes the most innovative countries, such as the United States, Germany and Canada; and the most rapidly innovating countries such as the Korean Republic and Japan. The trend shows the advances in productivity made by each country from 1999 to 2014. Japan exhibited remarkable growth patterns in productivity, despite having significantly lower productivity growth than the other countries from 2004 to 2008. Some countries including Japan recorded a fall in their total factor productivity after 2011. The only countries recording a rising trend were the United States and South Korea.

Akin to the experiences of industrial policy in South Korea and Uzbekistan mentioned earlier, this section investigates the trends of public investment and capital formation in Bangladesh over the years. Capital formation has been used in its logarithmic form for ease of analysis and is expressed in US dollars constant for 2010 (Figure 4.11). Government expenditure is expressed as a percentage of GDP in order to be comparable between countries with different national production levels. The bars represent gross capital formation, and the trend lines represent how government expenditure as a percentage of GDP changed over time for each country. Government expenditure has been highest in Germany, while capital formation has maintained a somewhat

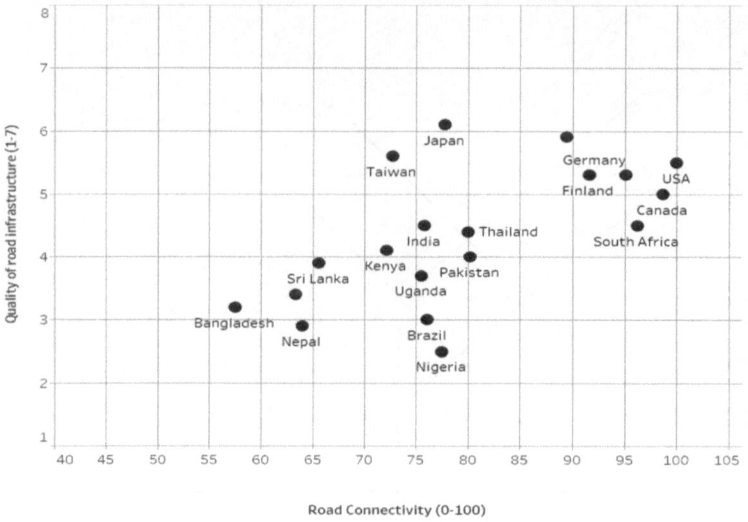

Figure 4.9 Cross country scatterplot of transport infrastructure. Source: WEF, 2020

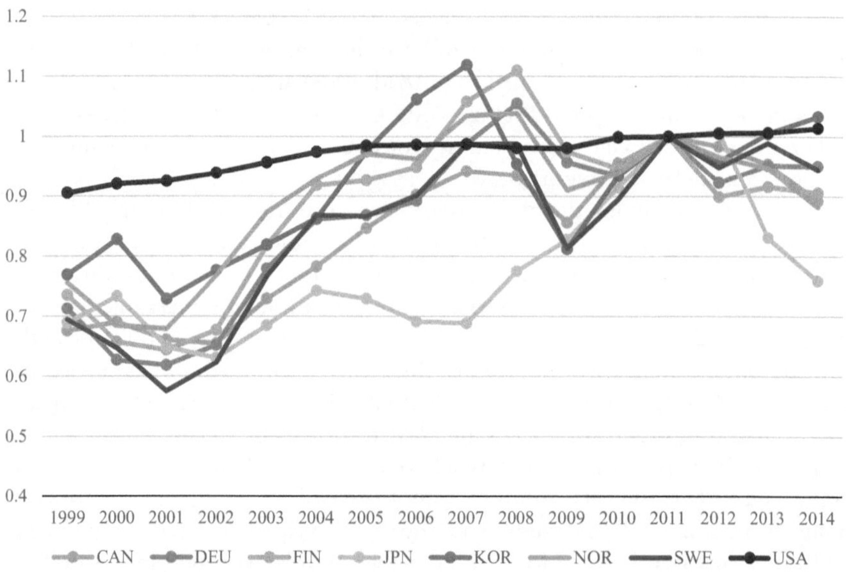

Figure 4.10 Cross-country trends for total factor productivity, 1999–2014. Source: Sanz-Córdoba, 2019

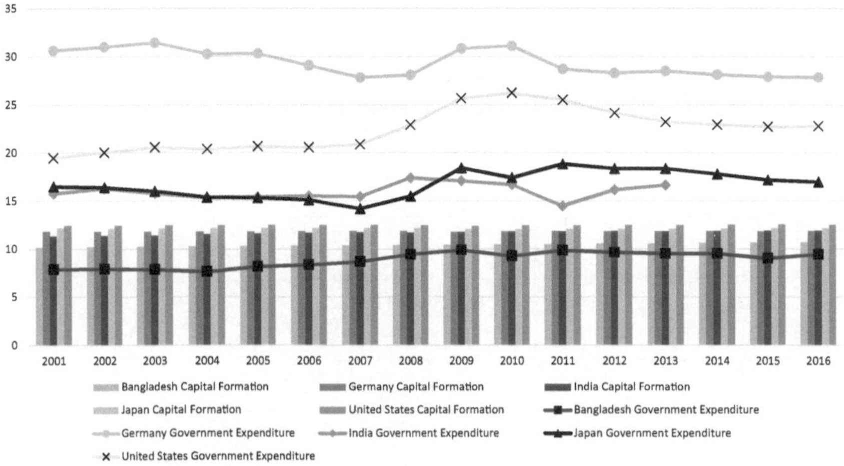

Figure 4.11 Correlating government expenditure and capital formation over time. Source: Titumir, Adiba & Haider, 2021

constantly high level over the entire period. Government expenditure in India took off soon after 1974. Japan started off from the lows as well but very soon took off, showing the sharpest rise till 1980, and then peaking in 1995–1996, akin to Germany. At the other end, Bangladesh recorded significantly lower rates of government expenditure as a percentage of an even lower GDP than the other countries included in this model, implying a lower absolute amount in monetary terms as well. Capital formation maintained a somewhat constant, slow-growing stance, despite the trend in government expenditure, proving the lack of financial incentives, i.e., fiscal supports, to bolster the growth of capital formation.

Institutions and discipline

In the new framework proposed earlier in this chapter, institutions served as sufficient conditions for fiscal policy to create productive capacity expansion. The trade-off for the initiatives for catching up through the provision of non-market incentives can be illustrated through a payoff matrix.

The proposition is that if non-market incentives are required for catching up, the effective implementation of such strategies typically also requires institutional systems of compulsion to impose discipline on the market. In a market with weak institutions of compulsion and little to no non-market incentives, businesses will go on as usual. The existence of a weak set of institutions is likely to lead to a more clientelist and unregulated market, not fit for catching up. On the other hand, if strong institutions of compulsion exist but no efforts are made in providing non-market incentives,

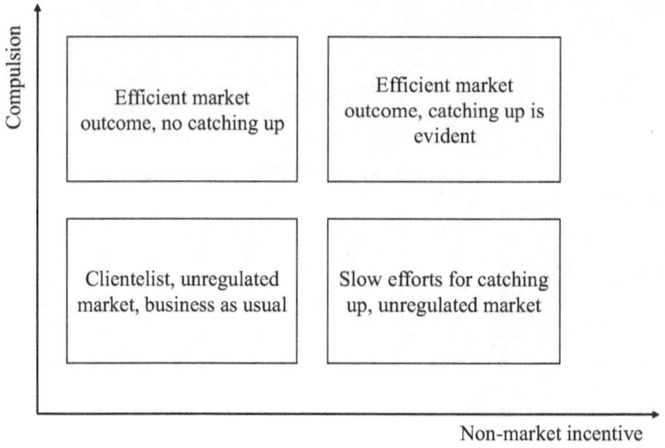

Figure 4.12 Institutions and discipline. Source: Prepared by the author

catching up will be slow to achieve. Thus, when non-market incentives are in place, coupled with institutions of compulsion acting to create discipline in the market, catching up can be achieved in an effective manner. The different outcomes can be expressed in a matrix representing the combination of outcomes of different levels of non-market incentives and compulsion from institutions (Figure 4.12). A higher amount of non-market incentives will incentivise firms to undertake more effective strategies of catching up, while higher compulsion from institutions on the market will introduce discipline and regulation, thereby leading to efficient market outcomes. Therefore, the top-right quadrant represents the desirable outcome where markets are regulated, market outcomes are efficient and catching up is evident (Figure 4.12). On the contrary, the point that is least preferred for goals of productive capacity expansion lies in the bottom-left quadrant, where both compulsion and non-market incentives are low, thereby leading to a clientelist, unregulated market, with no efforts to catch up by firms, as most of the economic decisions are taken with clientelist motives.

Crisis of the pandemic: Recovering productivity

The ability to effectively formulate and execute policies to tackle the pandemic is lower in developing countries, while their vulnerability to the pandemic is higher. In addition to the direct health crisis, developing countries that export to foreign markets are facing a sharp demand shock from its external consumers due to COVID-19. For example, in the countries of East Asia, tourism and trade constitute a large part of the economy (World Bank, 2020a). Countries that heavily rely on exports and remittances for revenue will also face increased issues (The Economist, 2020a; Hausmann, 2020).

Developing countries have been more susceptible to the crisis due to poor structural conditions. Low capacity in healthcare systems, lack of access to existing healthcare services and lack of effective health insurance are some reasons why people in developing countries are at a risk of high and sudden health expenditures. There is a large gap between the ideal and current health status of people in developing countries (Wagstaff & Neelsen, 2019). While developing countries have a younger demography and warmer climates (conditions that might be related to low COVID-19 risks), they also have higher proportions of malnourished population, higher incidences of HIV/AIDS, and other medical conditions that make them more vulnerable (The Economist, 2020b; The Washington Post, 2020). Developing countries also have large amounts of employment in the informal sector (Loayza, 2018). Of the total employment, 50–90 percent is in the informal sector in low and middle-income countries. This poses a serious issue since informal workers do not have access to services like unemployment insurance, paid leave and health insurance. This means that they are not only exposed to the virus COVID-19 itself but also to the mitigation and containment policies adopted to reduce the spread of the disease.

The productive capacity framework outlines the two-fold response to COVID-19 and related shocks (Figure 4.13). Based on the proposed framework for productive capacity expansion, as explained earlier in this chapter, the key responsibilities of the government include financing learning-by-doing processes for technology acquisition and capability development through learning or productive rents, buttressed by the organisational capabilities of institutions. These inputs move into firms and, later, households through human capital and skill formation. State and the market are conjoined in the shared interests

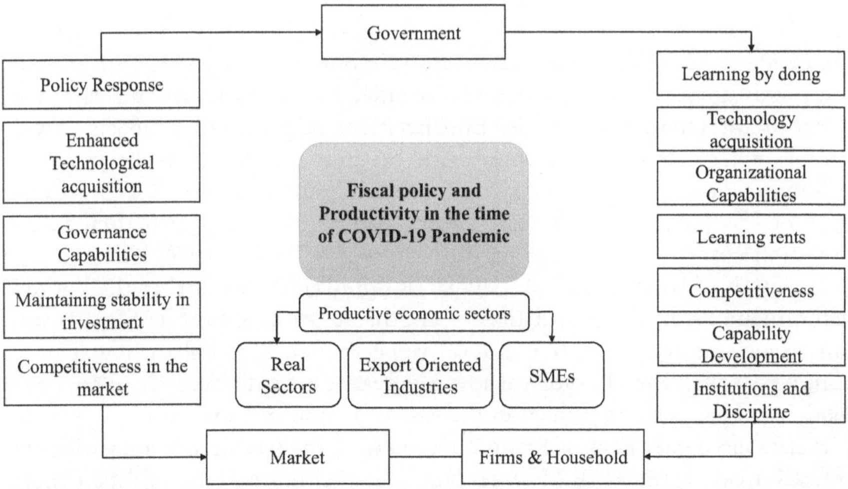

Figure 4.13 Productive capacity framework amid COVID-19. Source: Prepared by the author

of policy response to COVID-19 shocks, aggressive technology acquisition to meet the needs of new physically disjointed markets, improved governance and other determinants of competitiveness and stability.

Structural transformation and diversification

In the wake of COVID-19, developing countries such as Bangladesh should revisit their state of structural transformation for several reasons. Firstly, the country saw rising poverty and inequality and a decreasing GDP growth rate, which could have a serious impact on its graduation from the list of the Least Developed Countries (LDC) as it earlier full-filled the eligibility criteria in terms of per capita income, human assets, and economic and environmental vulnerability, set by the United Nations. Secondly, the agriculture and service sector of the country employs a large portion of its labour force, but the stimulus package was mostly distributed among the large industries. Both sectors have little capital generation capacity. The recovery and reconstruction policy of the government has to take into account the existing leakages that caused the downfall in the first place.

The LDCs are also marred with a relatively slower and stagnating structural transformation which hampers expansion of productive capacities. Coupled with fragile infrastructure, low private investment, concentrated export markets and high external dependence, the LDCs have recorded slower economic growth in the pandemic period. LDCs such as Bangladesh and Cambodia record similar productive capacity index in 2018, that ranks countries in terms of human capital and structural transformation levels.

The impediments have emphasised the crucial role of expansion of productive capacity in building resilience to shocks. Expansion of productive capacity will allow these countries to shift labour from the lowest productive sector to its highest productive sector, and fasten the pace of structural transformation. Concerted policies and collaborative efforts in building capacity to expand into new goods and services, markets, and diversified industries, will in turn enhance prospects for international trade. Enhancement of productive capacities will entail capital accumulation, technological progress and structural change.

Low total factor productivity (TFP) growth is also a concern for the country. Total factor productivity is a more reliable indicator of structural transformation compared to labour productivity (UNCTAD, 2016). The average TFP growth of Bangladesh is 0.2, which is significantly lower than the United States, members of the Association of Southeast Asian Nations (ASEAN) and East Asian countries (0.8, 0.3 and 1.3 respectively). Skill enhancement programmes, as well as technological advancement, can significantly raise the productivity of the country as seen in the case of China and Vietnam.

Relatively higher rates of economic growth in the past decade are attributed to ready-made garment (RMG) exports, which comprise 80% of total export earnings and represent the largest manufacturing sector of the country. As a result of overreliance on a single sector, export contraction caused by global lockdown had a major impact on export earnings and the economy as a whole.

Consequently, the largest share of the decline in exports was in the RMG sector. Germany, the United Kingdom and the United States are three major export destinations of Bangladesh, and lockdown in these countries caused a sharp drop in exports from Bangladesh. Of the total decrease in exports to Germany, 98 percent was in RMG goods, while other goods (e.g., leather, jute and handicraft) faced a 2 percent reduction. For the United Kingdom and the United States, the share of RMG export decline was 96 percent and 95 percent respectively (Figure 4.14). This draws a fair picture of the dependence of Bangladesh on other countries and on its RMG sector, which indicates the lack of structural transformation of economy and the risk it poses to employment and growth.

Diversification requires a strong policy from the government like the case of Thailand and Vietnam, where aggressive technology acquisition by the government resulted in technology-heavy industries shifting there from developed countries. Institutional barriers in the country pose the biggest threat to private and foreign investment as indicated by the Ease of Doing Business index. Bangladesh ranks 168th in this indicator, with poor conditions in enforcing contracts and corruption (World Bank, 2020b).

The pandemic and subsequent economic shutdown halted economic activity for all, leading to income erosion and loss of wellbeing for many. The lion's share of informal workers, especially the self-employed, depends on daily earnings to pay for basic household amenities. Not working for long periods during the pandemic put the subsistence of their households at risk. This means that radical policies such as complete and extended lockdowns are not pragmatic when it comes to developing countries, since people would be ready to work illegally rather than die of hunger. Workers in the informal sector are also unable to access the aid and relief provided to the formal labour force, such as reduced income taxes and paid sick leave. Low and middle-income countries

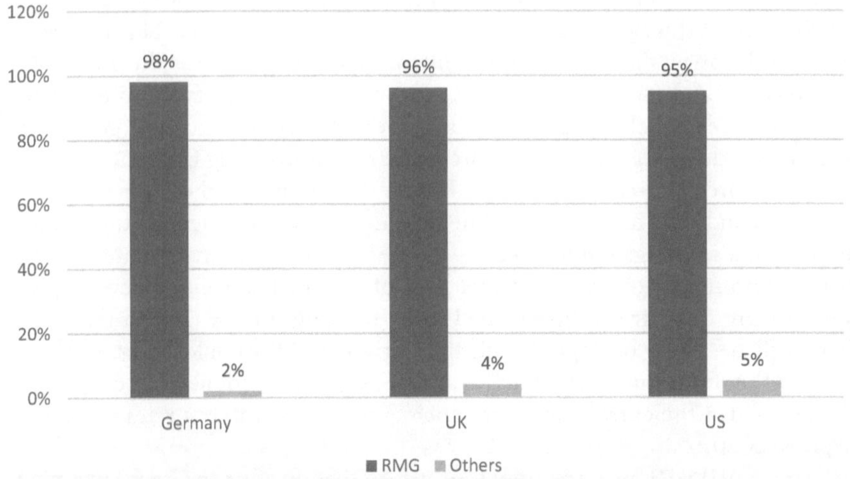

Figure 4.14 Percentage share of RMG in a total decrease of export. Source: Unnayan Onneshan, 2021

also do not have ample "fiscal space" that will allow them to make large sums of public expenditures available to counter economic shock (Kose, Ohnsorge & Sugawara, 2018).

Compared to developed countries, developing countries do not have large public debt-to-GDP ratios. However, unlike developed countries, their debt is subject to higher maturity and exchange rate risks. In addition, they have more shallow financial markets and lower credit ratings. A lax tax administration and small tax base also mean that it will be more difficult to implement a counter-cyclical fiscal policy in developing countries. In these uncertain times, the "flight to quality" in financial markets may mean that it will be more difficult to borrow to cover the fiscal deficit for some countries (Hausmann, 2020).

The circumstances of developing countries disproportionately affected by the adverse impacts of COVID-19 may be further illustrated by studying the case of Bangladesh. The COVID-19 crisis is already impeding the economic growth of Bangladesh. Moreover, on one hand, it will cause a reduction in government revenue and, on the other, it will cause increased spending. This altered economic scenario will result in what may be described as "parameter changes". All the estimates are likely to be guesswork since the government really cannot get a firm handle on the size of the decline in economic activity and how quickly it might recover. COVID-19 has resulted in a bigger budget for the fiscal year. The next budget is likely to be even bigger with rises in unemployment and declining outputs. It is unlikely that the recovery would be "V" shaped (characterised by a sharp decline and then a sharp increase). Hence, the fiscal response will continue to grow (Financial Express, 2020).

The estimated revenue collection for the coming fiscal year is 3,780 billion BDT, but the total expenditure is Tk. 5,680 billion, leaving a budget deficit of 1,900 billion BDT. The public debt is now equivalent to 34 per cent of GDP (of this, 38 percent is external debt), and this fiscal deficit will add to it. By 2022–2023 this percentage is likely to rise to 38.3 per cent. This increased ratio is still lower than that of the United States (84 percent), the Eurozone (69 percent), and Japan (154 percent). However, if output falls more sharply than expected and the deficit increases, the debt–GDP ratio will go up. In Bangladesh, the budget deficit is sourced through borrowing from internal and external sources, foreign grants and bonds. The bond markets are not deep and liquid and thus not effective. The government would increase the money supply and also mitigate inflationary pressure on the economy, as stated by the finance minister. However, the meaning of an "increase in money supply" is not totally clear. It can be assumed to be printing money. But in that case, there will be a risk of depreciating the currency. This could boost inflation considerably for Bangladesh which is a trade-dependent country. Fiscal deficits can also widen the current account deficit and increase interest rates (Financial Express, 2020).

The COVID-19 fiscal response is similar to that during the Great Recession in many ways. Three important implications can be yielded from the evidence of past fiscal stimulus. First, when unemployment is high and liquidity constraints are bound, the marginal propensity to consume out of individual transfers is particularly high. This implies fiscal multipliers near or above one. Second, during times of fiscal strain, the marginal propensities to spend out of federal transfers by state and local governments are particularly high. This suggests a dollar-for-dollar pass-through to spending a dollar. Third, the fiscal multiplier on government spending is around 1.5 when monetary policy is by the zero-lower bound (Wilson, 2020). Overall, the evidence suggests that the output boost is likely to be large from this fiscal response.

Conclusion

While there exists a consensus that sustaining growth in poor countries is a challenge, it is not only because the right economic policies have to be identified, but also because those policies have to be buttressed by suitable governance capabilities for aggressive technological acquisition and productive expansion to take place. Studies so far have failed to pay attention to how productivity can be manoeuvred by pre-existing power relations, the role political settlement plays in this regard and how endogeneity of politics affects the progression of the whole process.

Therefore, organising competitive production processes requires a knowledge of organising production in highly demanding global chains of production, and such "tacit knowledge" is embedded in organisational procedures that can be learnt only through "learning by doing". Despite some problems not arising, competitiveness will be affected by the degree of loss in financing undertaken during the period of learning by doing and the acquisition of technology afterwards. The periods of learning by doing and technology acquisition and their effect on the level of competitiveness increases slowly during the learning-by-doing phase as firms undertake financing of the loss-making period, followed by a higher spurt in growth of competitiveness brought on by technology acquisition.

Another major argument of this chapter is that acquiring competitiveness will require the acquisition of technology and financing of a loss-making period of production while learning by doing is taking place. It is necessary to stringently avoid *ex ante* incentive misalignment problems, including rent diversion, rent dissipation and rent-seeking, which are in preponderance in the developing world. Tacit knowledge, however, determines the level of organisational capabilities acquired by the firm. A higher level of tacit knowledge therefore determines higher organisational capabilities, which enable firms to produce a proportionally higher output with a small increase in the use of input factors. New sectors emerged when fortunate accidents created *ex post* rents for private investors in capability development, who invested in capability development first using bank credit and their own resources.

If non-market incentives are required for catching up, the effective implementation of such strategies typically also requires institutional systems of compulsion to impose discipline on the market. In a market with weak institutions of compulsion and little to no non-market incentives, businesses will go on as usual. The existence of a weak set of institutions is likely to lead to a more clientelist and unregulated market, not fit for catching up. On the other hand, if strong institutions of compulsion exist but no efforts are made to provide non-market incentives, catching up will be slow to achieve. Thus, when non-market incentives are in place, coupled with institutions of compulsion acting to create discipline in the market, catching up can be achieved in an effective manner. The COVID-19 pandemic has increased doubt, devastated economies in a heartbeat and above all increased uncertainty in an already malfunctioning state of affairs.

Nevertheless, the previous studies predominantly fall within the realm of either the neoclassical growth theory or the new growth theory, and thus there is also negligence of how the state, underwritten by appropriate political settlement, plays an active role in ensuring and maintaining high rates of investment and the shift to higher productivity technologies. Thus, debates on the necessary and sufficient conditions for sustained and rapid improvements in living standards remained unresolved. This chapter thus contributed to this debate and demonstrated that productivity in factors of production—labour and capital (technology induced)—are brought about through the endogeneity of political settlement or social property relationships as understood in terms of nature and distribution of power in a given society.

References

Abramovitz, M. (1986). Catching up, forging ahead, and falling behind. *The Journal of Economic History*, 46(2), 385–406.

Arndt, H. W. (1988). "Market failure" and underdevelopment. *World Development*, 16(2), 219–229.

Augier, P., Dovis, M., & Gasiorek, M. (2012). The business environment and Moroccan firm productivity. *Economics of Transition*, 20(2), 369–399.

Aw, Y., Roberts, M. J., & Winston, T. (2007). Export market participation, investments in R&D and worker training, and the evolution of firm productivity. *The World Economy*, 30(1), 83–104.

Birch, K. (2020). Technoscience rent: Toward a theory of rentiership for technoscientific capitalism. *Science, Technology, & Human Values*, 45(1), 3–33.

Chang, T. L. (1996). Cultivating global experience curve advantage on technology and marketing capabilities. *International Marketing Review*, 13(6), 22–42. https://doi.org/10.1108/02651339610151908

Chandrasekhar, C. P., & Ghosh, J. (2021). Wrecking fiscal federalism. International Development Economics Associates. Retrieved March 4, 2021 from https://www.networkideas.org/featured-articles/2021/01/wrecking-fiscal-federalism/

Chowdhury, A. (2021). Growth and structural transformation in African LDCs (2000–2020), mimeo, personal communication. .

D'Agata, A., & Freni, G. (2003). The structure of growth models: A comparative survey. In N. Salvadori (Ed.), *The Theory of Economic Growth: A 'Classical' Perspective*. Cheltenham, UK: Edward Elgar.

Dollar, D., Hallward-Driemeier, M., & TayeMengistae. (2005). Investment climate and firm performance in developing economies. *Economic Development and Cultural Change*, 54(1), 1–31.

Dowrick, S. (2004). Ideas and education: Level or growth effects and their implications for Australia. In T. I. & A. K. Rose (Eds.), *Growth and Productivity in East Asia*. Chicago: The University of Chicago Press.

The Economist. (2020a). Commodity economies face their own reckoning due to Covid-19. March 5. Retrieved from https://www.economist.com/finance-and-economics/2020/03/05/commodity-economies- face-their-own-reckoning-due-to-covid-19

The Economist. (2020b). Fatality rates for Covid-19 could vary enormously. March 12. Retrieved from https://www. economist.com/international/2020/03/12/fatality-rates-for-covid-19-could-vary-enormously

Fernandes, A. M. (2008). Firm productivity in Bangladesh manufacturing industries. *World Development*, 36(10), 1725–1744.

Financial Express. (2020). Covid-19, Bangladesh Budget 20–21 and public debt. June 20. Retrieved from https://thefinancialexpress.com.bd/print/covid-19-bangladesh-budget-20-21-and-public-debt-1592670051

Fine, B., & Saad-Filho, A. (2004). *Marx's Capital* (4th ed.). London: Pluto Press.

Fuchs-Schündeln, N., & Izem, R. (2012). Explaining the low labor productivity in East Germany—A spatial analysis. *Journal of Comparative Economics*, 40, 1–21.

Ghesquiere, H. (2007). *Singapore's Success: Engineering Economic Growth*. Singapore: Cengage Learning.

Hausmann, R. (2020). Flattening the COVID-19 curve in developing countries. Project Syndicate. March 24. Retrieved from https://www.project-syndicate.org/commentary/flattening-covid19-curve-in- developing-countries-by-ricardo-hausmann-2020-03

Haynes, M., & Husan, R. (2002). Market failure, state failure, institutions, and historical constraints in the East European transition. *Journal of European Area Studies*, 10(1), 105–129.

Heinrich, M. (2012). *An Introduction to the Three Volumes of Karl Marx's Capital*. New York: English translation by Alexander Locascio. Monthly Review Press. Originally published as *Kritik der politischen Vkonomie: Eine Einfhrung* by Schmetterling Verlag GmbH, Stuttgart, Germany, c2004.

Inui, T., Kawakami, A., & Miyagawa, T. (2012). Market competition, differences in technology, and productivity improvement: An empirical analysis based on Japanese manufacturing firm data. *Japan and the World Economy*, 24(3), 197–206.

Kose, A., Ohnsorge, F. L., & Sugawara, N. (2018). *Fiscal Space: Concept, Measurement, and Policy Implications*. Research & Policy Brief No. 19, World Bank, Washington, DC.

Khan, M. H. (2000). Rents, efficiency and growth. In M. H. Khan & K. S. Jomo (Eds.), *Rents, Rent-Seeking and Economic Development: Theory and Evidence in Asia* (pp. 21–69). Cambridge: Cambridge University Press.

Khan, M. H. (2005). The capitalist transformation. In K. S. Jomo & E. S. Reinert (Eds.), *The Origins of Development Economics: How Schools of Economic Thought Have Addressed Development* (pp. 69–80). New Delhi: Tulika Books and London: Zed Press.

Khan, M. H. (2014). *The Design of Financing for Developing New Competitive Sectors: Theory and Evidence*. Paper presented at seminar organised by Bangladesh Institute of Bank Management (BIBM), October 26, Dhaka, Bangladesh.

Khan, M. H. (2015). Industrial policy design and implementation challenges. In J. Felipe (Ed.), *Development and Modern Industrial Policy in Practice: Issues and Country Experiences* (pp. 94–126). Cheltenham: Edward Elgar.

Khan, M. H., & Blankenburg, S. (2009). The political economy of industrial policy in Asia and Latin America. In G. Dosi & M. Cimoli (Eds.), *Industrial Policy and Development*. Oxford: Oxford University Press.

Klodt, H. (2000). Industrial policy and the East German productivity puzzle. *German Economic Review*, 1(3), 315–333.

Lee, C. (2011). Trade, productivity, and innovation: Firm-level evidence from Malaysian manufacturing. *Journal of Asian Economics*, 22(4), 284–294.

Loayza, N. V. (2018). *Informality: Why Is It So Widespread and How Can It Be Reduced?* Research & Policy Brief No. 20, World Bank, Washington, DC.

Mahy, B., Rycx, F., & Volral, M. (2011). Wage dispersion and firm productivity in different working environments. *British Journal of Industrial Relations*, 49(3), 460–485.

Mazzucato, M. (2013). *The Entrepreneurial State: Debunking Public vs. Private Sector Myths*. London: Anthem Press.

Miles, D., & Scott, A. (2005). *Macroeconomics: Understanding the Wealth of Nations*. Chichester, West Sussex, England: John Wiley & Sons.

Mosk, C. (2008). *Japanese Economic Development: Markets, Norms, Structures*. New York: Routledge.

Motoyama, Y., Appelbaum, R., & Parker, R. (2011). The National Nanotechnology Initiative: Federal support for science and technology, or hidden industrial policy? *Technology in Society*, 33, 109–118.

Nanda, N. (2021). *India's Industrial Policy and Performance: Growth, Competition and Competitiveness*. England: Routledge.

Pagés, C. (2010). The age of productivity. In C. Pagés (Ed.), *The Age of Productivity: Transforming Economies from the Bottom Up* (pp. 1–21). New York: Palgrave Macmillan.

Perez, C. (2009). Technological Revolutions and Techno-economic Paradigms. The Other Canon Foundation and Tallinn University of Technology Working Papers in Technology Governance and Economic Dynamics 20, TUT Ragnar Nurkse Department of Innovation and Governance.

Piketty, T. (2014). *Capital in the Twenty-first Century*. Cambridge, Massachusetts: Harvard University Press.

Qureshi, M. S., & Velde, D. W. t. (2013). State–business relations, investment climate reform and firm productivity in Sub-Saharan Africa. *Journal of International Development*, 25(7), 912–935.

Ricci, L. A., & Trionfetti, F. (2012). Productivity, networks, and export performance: Evidence from a cross-country firm dataset. *Review of International Economics*, 20(3), 552–562.

Rochina-Barrachina, M. E., Mañez, J. A., & Sanchis-Llopis, J. A. (2010). Process innovations and firm productivity growth. *Small Business Economics*, 34(2), 147–166.

Salis, S. (2008). Foreign acquisition and firm productivity: Evidence from Slovenia. *The World Economy*, 31(8), 1030–1048.

Sanz-Córdoba, P. (2019). Data for: The Role of Infrastructure Investment and Factor Productivity in International Tax Competition. *Mendeley Data*, V1, doi:10.17632/w5vfp2yv66.1

Schmidt, H. D. D. (2012). You cannot buy innovation. Retrieved October 13, 2018 from http://www.asymco.com/2012/01/30/you-cannot-buy-innovation/?utm_source=feedburner&utm_medium=feed&utm_campaign=Feed%3A+Asymco+%about28asymco%29

Schutz, E. A. (2011). *Inequality and Power: The Economics of Class*. New York: Routledge.

Solow, R. M. (1956). A contribution to the theory of economic growth. *The Quarterly Journal of Economics*, 70(1), 65–94.

Titumir, R. A. M., Adiba, A. I. J., & Haider, W. (2021). *Structural and Redistributive Trends of Budgeting in Bangladesh: Planning Ahead with Lessons from the Fifty Years* [unpublished manuscript].

UNCTAD. (2016). Virtual Institute Teaching Material on Structural Transformation and Industrial Policy.

Unnayan Onneshan. (2021). *From Squeeze to Expansion: Policy and Institutional Reforms for Averting K-Shaped Recovery*. Pre-Budget Policy Paper.

Vane, H. R., & Mulhearn, C. (2005). *The Nobel Memorial Laureates in Economics: An Introduction to Their Careers and Main Published Works*. Cheltenham, UK: Edward Elgar.

Wagstaff, A., & Neelsen, S. (2019). *A Comprehensive Assessment of Universal Health Coverage in One Hundred and Fifteen Countries and Territories: A Retrospective Observational Study*. World Bank, Washington, DC.

The Washington Post. (2020). Warm, humid weather could slow coronavirus, new research finds. March 24. Retrieved from https://www.washingtonpost.com/weather/2020/03/24/warm- humid-weather-coronavirus/

Williamson, O. (1986). *The Economic Institutions of Capitalism: firms, markets, relational contracting*. Free Press, London.

Wilson, D. J. (2020). The COVID-19 Fiscal multiplier: Lessons from the great recession. *FRBSF Economic Letter*, 2020(13), 1–5.

Wood, E. M. (2002). *The Origin of Capitalism: A Longer View*. Verso, London.

World Bank. (2020a). COVID-19 and the East Asia and Pacific Region, East Asia and Pacific Economic Update, April, The World Bank, Washington, DC. Retrieved from http://www.worldbank.org/eapupdate

World Bank. (2020b). *Doing Business 2020*. World Bank Group, Washington DC, United States.

WEF. (2020). *Global Competitiveness Report 2020*. World Economic Forum, Davos, Switzerland.

Xu, X., & Sheng, Y. (2012). Productivity spillovers from foreign direct investment: Firm-level evidence from China. *The World Development*, 40(1), 62–74.

5 Equality, welfare and state

Introduction

In 2011, South Sudan, after going through a period of civil war, finally went for a referendum and later, based on the votes, acceded to become an independent state. The reason for the separation and the civil war was largely the widespread disparity between the two regions of Sudan. While the Northern part had seen higher economic activities and growth, the Southern part was experiencing abject poverty. The inequality between North and South Sudan is an ideal example of both vertical and horizontal inequality. The inequality between two larger groups in Sudan shows a vertical inequality, while the overall inequality regardless of the location depicts horizontal inequality (Roden, 1974). The inequality was not just an inequality of income; it was an inequality of power as well. North Sudan had seen higher growth due to their control over the political and state institutions, whereas the Southern part had little representation in the political establishment. The state policies were thus unequal towards the other group, which eventually led to civil war (Thomas, 2015).

Recently, the issue of inequality once again has come into the forefront, especially in developed countries. Not only is inequality believed to be "morally wrong", it is also linked to lower growth performance and higher economic instability—a conviction that has become more mainstream nowadays and has received the support and endorsement of the International Monetary Fund (IMF) (Stiglitz, 2015). At the same time, traditional welfare states have come under severe criticism. For example, welfare states in Europe have been accused of expanding in size and cost from the early 1980s while also becoming more bureaucratic and too market-centric. Their services have also been accused of failing to address market failures and impeding economic efficiency, growth and the collective efforts of the people (Clasen, 2005). As a result, measures were taken, such as the reduction of taxes on profits and income from capital and the establishment of low wage sectors at the demand of employers, which led to the weakening of the welfare state in Europe. The impacts of the system are harmful for economies, their citizens and the democratic systems of those countries (Eißel, 2014).

DOI: 10.4324/9781003201847-5

Inequality can be both reduced and widened by a state's economic policy. Fiscal policy can also be the answer to the problem of inequality in developing countries. Government expenditure programmes in the social sector like health, education and employment may ensure access to these, which can increase the capability of the population. Skills-enhancing education programmes sponsored by the government create a skilled population. Universal healthcare ensures the basic healthcare required for strong human capital. Government policies that increase productive capacity can employ a large population. A progressive tax structure for wealth redistribution can reduce the tax burden on poorer populations as well as funding government expenditure on social programmes. All these measures can reduce societal inequality. This solution though is often shelved as a faraway dream for developing countries. Instead, these countries have seen the responsible institutions being used by clientelist groups which have shifted the policies in a way that benefits them. Global bodies like the IMF or the World Bank have also worsened the situation in the developing world through ferrying unfettered market-centric policies and squeezing the role of the state through structural adjustment reforms. Unplanned and extractive policies have also put developing countries under a burden of debt, which has forced them to initiate austerity measures. Such measures include reduced government expenditure and regressive tax structures, adding a burden to the poorest population of a country. This has also widened the income gap and inequality.

The role of informal institutions plays a major role in determining fiscal policy. Developed countries to a larger extent have enforced strict regulations on taxes. Citizens also seem to abide by the laws and regulations. As a result, developed countries have seen higher tax–GDP ratio, which has allowed them to increase government funding in direct cash programmes like unemployment benefits. Developing countries, on the other hand, see a lower revenue turnout, as citizens often remain outside the tax nets while the powerful evade taxes. Like their rich fraternity in the Western world, the *nouveau riche* relocate money to offshore banking facilities to avoid taxes. Hence, developing countries have in recent years witnessed higher capital flight as well as a faster rate of wealth creation.

This chapter provides a new framework for understanding inequality while being mindful of systemic escalating inequality arising out of low returns on labour vis-à-vis capital in capitalism (permanent systemic inequality). Here, an elaborate theoretical distinction has been made between demand, want and need in support of each according to his ability, to each according to his need as opposed to the neoclassical theory of demand—the relationship between consumer demand for goods and services and their prices, which is intrinsically inequalising. This chapter also demonstrates the factors needed for a welfare state and the nature of being, which puts a predominant focus on the relationship between fiscal policy and political settlement.

To illustrate, this chapter uses the case of Bangladesh. The success of Bangladesh, especially regarding the reduction of income poverty since the

1990s, has been considered to be noticeable among other comparable developing countries by development agencies such as the World Bank. The progress of the country regarding the achievement of the Millennium Development Goals (MDGs) has also received a positive response. However, inequality has remained a concern as it has kept worsening (Lewis, 2011). The Gini coefficient of income increased from 0.388 in 1991–1992 to 0.432, 0.451 and 0.467 in 1995–1996, 2000 and 2005, respectively, and then slightly decreased to 0.458 in 2010 (GoB, 2014). On the other hand, in case of the provision of social welfare, only the 1990s observed a change in the government approach to welfare when it came up with a different kind of schemes directed towards addressing risks across the lifecycle. Thus, whatever praise the Bangladesh government received worldwide, there could be little denying that the growth and development have not benefitted every class equally and thus remain a threat to social order and solidarity.

Fiscal policies, inequality and welfare state: An assessment

Despite growing concerns about inequality, there is little consensus about how to fight it. Moreover, although a good many countries have embraced the concept of the welfare state in the post-war period, the objectives they have adopted remain non-uniform. This section argues that the neoclassical theory of income distribution, along with its political project, neoliberalism, has promoted an atomistic conception of the individual, though individuals are socially embedded, limiting both objectives and means of fiscal policy and the scope of the state to fight inequality and achieve a welfare state. This has contributed to the worsening of income distribution.

Neoclassical distribution theory

Despite the neoclassical theory of income distribution forming an integral and more traditional part of the marginal revolution developed in contrast to classical economic thought, it nonetheless finds itself a more divisive component of neoclassical theory (Pasinetti, 2000). Distribution and growth theory came into existence in the 1870s through the writings of William Stanley Jevons, Carl Menger and Leon Walras in an endeavour to supplant the classical theory of price, distribution and growth (Hein, 2014). The neoclassical theory of distribution can also be found "in one form or another" in the works of "Haavelmo, Hicks, Meade, Samuelson, Solow and Swan, among others" (Sen, 1963). Moreover, the studies conducted in microeconomics following the re-emergence of inequality as a social and political economic problem in the 1980s formulated arguments "almost exclusively in pre-Sraffian and anti-Keynesian terms; that is, in terms of the pricing of underlying factors of production and their marginal productivities" (Galbraith, 2001).

The neoclassical explanation of income distribution attempts to portray the distribution of income between wage and profits as determined through technological conditions of production prevailing in the market, i.e., it is the marginal productivity labour and capital that determines the distribution pattern of wage and profits in a market economy. Not only do they attempt to explain the income distribution law through the factors of production, but they also claim that the basis for the distribution between factors is decided according to the contribution of those factors, thus forming a theory of income distribution on a "functional" basis (Zhou, 2016).

The negligence of mainstream economists to curb income and wealth inequality through government intervention is furthered by the perceived trade-off between efficiency and equality. Since mainstream economists approach the issue of income distribution from a technical point of view and believe that fair distribution of income among factors equalling its marginal productivity in the production automatically originates from well-functioning markets, they consider any type of government intervention undesirable. They associate inefficiency with any such move and believe the resulting costs to be normally large. Inequality is also supposed to have a positive impact on the incentive to work (Wade, 2011).

Neoclassical economics interpreted factor income as a set of returns and marginal productivities under constant returns to scale. Such a notion was met with objections from the likes of Joan Robinson and Piero Sraffa (Galbraith, 2001). Their question mainly focused on the measurement of aggregate capital. They argued that capital could not be determined independently from the distribution of income between wages and profits (Brown, 2005). Robinson questioned the aggregation of capital when it is heterogeneous (Pressman, 2005).

The neoclassical income distribution theory has two main parts. First, in a perfectly operating market, employment of a factor of production occurs up to the particular point where the marginal product of that factor of production equals its marginal cost. Second, competition among entrepreneurs ensures that factor compensation of the last unit does not fall below its value addition to that unit, and hence the possibility of exploitation can be ruled out under a perfectly competitive capitalist system (Gerdes & Gerdes, 1977). Thus, from its sloppy basis in two-factor production functions, neoclassical marginal productivity or distribution theory asserts that "profits are the just reward of capital and wages are proportional to personal productivities, duly adjusted by stocks of human capital" (Galbraith, 2001). For Kalecki, however, "Unlike neoclassical theory, but like classical economic theory", it is the monopoly and its level of control over the market that dictates "how high firms can set prices, and thus the distribution of income between wages and profits" (Galbraith, 2001). Additionally, the neoclassical concept of factor productivity does not mean that competition and exploitation are mutually exclusive of each other since:

> It is one thing to argue that under competition a factor will be used to the point at which its cost to the user will equal the revenue its addition to the factor mix produces. It is quite another thing to make the ideological

> statement that "a factor gets what it creates", that is, that its contribution to output is exactly matched by an equivalent reward in money, physical goods, or other forms of compensation. It takes two entirely different sets of assumptions to sustain both interpretations of the marginal productivity principle. The former can be found proven as convincingly as one needs in any standard microeconomic text. The "proof" of the latter aspect of this doctrine, which relies directly on the fundamental and companion assumptions, will rarely be found in any but the most superficial form in any standard exposition, and nowhere will it be found in a complete form.
> (Gerdes & Gerdes, 1977)

The major shortcoming of neoclassical theory is that the mathematical explanation is far from the reality. The perfect symmetry of labour and capital as explained by neoclassical theory is not logical (Pasinetti, 2000). There also exists inequality within labour and within capital. It is also important to make distinction between those who are employed and who are unemployed against their will or unemployed because they are unable to work. There is also a problem of lack of diffusion of technological knowledge among societies competing with or contrasting each other (Pasinetti, 2000).

Moreover, the efficiency–equality trade-off has been challenged on both theoretical and empirical grounds. High levels of inequality have a detrimental effect on growth, since they result in lower levels of effort. The general consensus from cross-country studies is that inequality retards growth in poor countries (Zweimüller, 2000; Deininger & Deininter, 2000; Barro, 1999). Another reason why inequality is bad for the economy is that it leads to weakening of demand, since it reduces the purchasing power of people at the bottom who spend a greater proportion of their income. This problem has greater implications when monetary authorities respond to weak demand. In most cases, they do this by lowering interest rates, which can give rise to a bubble and risks the economy (Stiglitz, 2015).

Re-reading Piketty and others

In his masterpiece *Capital in the Twenty-First Century*, Piketty (2014) argues in favour of a broader notion of capital and proposes progressive taxation on it. According to him, whereas income represents "the quantity of goods produced and distributed in a given period", capital stands for "the total wealth owned at a given point in time", originating from "the wealth appropriated or accumulated in all prior years combined". Thus, what he actually did was to use "the words *capital* and *wealth* interchangeably, as if they were perfectly synonymous" (Piketty, 2014).

The rate of return on capital estimated by Piketty is the yield on capital over the course of a year. Capital includes both the financial and non-financial assets, excluding liabilities and debt. Hence, "National capital" is the aggregate value of everything owned by a state at a given point (Piketty, 2014).

Based on these definitions, Piketty discovers the way fundamental inequality is created in a society and expresses it in algebraic form: $r > g$, where r equals the average annual rate of return on capital, whereas g stands for the rate of growth of the economy. In other words:

> when the rate of return on capital exceeds the rate of growth of output and income, as it did in the nineteenth century and seems quite likely to do again in the twenty-first, capitalism automatically generates arbitrary and unsustainable inequalities that radically undermine the meritocratic values on which democratic societies are based.
>
> (Piketty, 2014)

Piketty proposes the introduction of progressive taxation on this wealth. Progressive taxation would bring two benefits. Firstly, progressive taxation on wealth is necessary to retain globalisation. Without such taxation, the least benefitted group from global trade would resort to protectionist policies to protect their interests. Secondly, such progressive taxation would keep financial institutions in check through democratic scrutiny. This is necessary to protect competition, as such policies will deter private interests (Piketty, 2014).

However, a particular objection against Piketty's analysis involves the expression $r > g$ in *Capital in the 21st Century*. Piketty did not take into account the effect of population growth in estimating the rate of output growth (Nardi, Fella & Yang, 2016). After testing the empirical validity of Piketty's argument, Nardi, Fella and Yang (2016) argue that

> changes in the rates of return on capital and TFP have only small effects on wealth inequality, while changes in output growth due to population growth have very large effects. The key intuition is that the rate of return and the TFP growth rate affect all households in a similar way. In contrast, a change in the population growth rate affects different categories of individuals through two main channels.
>
> (Nardi, Fella & Yang, 2016)

Soskice (2014), however, criticises Piketty's analysis mainly for two reasons. The first criticism emerges as the role of business was ignored in favour of the neoclassical conception of "investment as driven by the decisions of savers". The second criticism arises from the fact that Piketty's "mathematical model" ignored politics and technological change, which brought a great change in economics after the Second World War and gained importance in the study of inequality. However, it is not clear how Soskice's (2014) criticism of ignoring businesses' role in saving changes Piketty's main point. About the accusation of ignoring the other factors and use of a parsimonious equation, the following reply by Piketty applies:

> That said, the way in which I perceive the relationship between $r > g$ and inequality is often not well captured in the discussion that has surrounded

> my book. For example, I do not view $r > g$ as the only or even the primary tool for considering changes in income and wealth in the 20th century, or for forecasting the path of inequality in the 21st century. Institutional changes and political shocks—which to a large extent can be viewed as endogenous to the inequality and development process itself—played a major role in the past, and it will probably be the same in the future. In addition, I certainly do not believe that $r > g$ is a useful tool for the discussion of rising inequality of labour income; other mechanisms and policies are much more relevant here, e.g., the supply and demand of skills and education.
>
> (Piketty, 2015)

Piketty accepts the fact that there are demographic and other factors. The shocks include demographic shocks such as loss of family members, shocks to rates of return, shocks to labour market outcomes and shocks to personal preferences and tastes (Piketty, 2015). According to Piketty,

> I now clarify the role played by $r > g$ in my analysis of the long-run level of wealth inequality. Specifically, a larger positive $r - g$ gap will tend to greatly amplify the steady-state inequality of a wealth distribution that arises out of a given mixture of shocks (including labour income shocks).
>
> (Piketty, 2015)

Piketty's fundamental $r > g$ inequality is not associated directly with market imperfection. Contrarily, he posits that a more perfect capital market will lead to a greater divergence between r and g (Piketty, 2014). The notion of the exclusion of residential real estate had been ruled out by Piketty, often labelled as unproductive, when compared to the more productive capital in use by firms and the government. In reality, all forms of wealth have to be treated as productive and represent the two major economic functions of capital, as residential real estate can also be viewed as an asset that generates housing services equal to its rental equivalent (Piketty, 2014).

Piketty's theory has a number of limitations as well. First, it is also important to consider that whether the focus is the capitalist sector proper, consisting only of the workers and the capitalists, or the capitalist sector together with the setting in which it exists, which includes its pre-capitalist surroundings (Patnaik, 2015). The work does not mention the spatial or geographical whereabouts of capital. Capital accumulation in one place effects capital in other places. The work lacks a description of a capital-less society, which cannot be left out of discussions (Jones, 2014). According to Holmwood (2014):

> Piketty's book sets out a research agenda for social science, but it also implies a political and normative agenda. The latter needs to address global issues and interconnections in the past as well as the present. But we need to grasp them in their local contexts and recognise that the "same"

> processes will have different consequences deriving from local social structures and interests. Indeed, the arguments necessary to build a "coalition" to address the inequalities of patrimonial capitalism will differ depending on past path dependencies and new paths taken. One problem, however, is that the emphasis on the "global", and formulaic hostility to methodological nationalism, will potentially lead us toward a bland "internationalism", rather than *a globally-aware localism*. The new market regime of higher education stresses the role of universities in an international knowledge economy and audit measures stress international rankings. Whereas, in the past, "professional standards" and the aspiration for "objective knowledge" could occur alongside a "value-relevant" project of modernisation and democratisation, the "internationalisation" of professional standards occurs alongside their regulation by market forces that are themselves at issue.
>
> (Holmwood, 2014)

Second, Piketty's proposal is mainly global and is supportive of progressive taxation and global capital levy schemes. While tax on global capital may seem unrealistic, the realistic measure according to Piketty is coordination regarding taxation to stop capital flights and tax evasions, which is very prevalent in developing countries (Piachaud, 2014). In Piketty's own words: "It is possible to imagine public institutions and policies that would counter the effects of this implacable logic: for instance, a progressive global tax on capital". Piketty himself seems aware of the challenge as he subsequently writes: "But establishing such institutions and policies would require a considerable degree of international coordination. It is unfortunately likely that actual responses to the problem—including various nationalist responses—will in practice be far more modest and less effective" (Piketty, 2014). Third, the primitive accumulation of capital or the dispossession of petty producers leads to wealth inequality. Inequality is also exacerbated by declining real wages, even when productivity is higher, where a large section of the labour force remains stuck in low-paying jobs (Patnaik, 2015).

The role of social policy and welfare state assumes little prominence in Piketty's analysis. The analysis missed two important roles of the state. Firstly, the analysis ignored the role of social policies in the redistribution of income along the lines of gender and race. Secondly, health inequality or social security affects the income of a person. Policies like social security and healthcare are simplified or ignored in his analysis (Piachaud, 2014).

Social welfare regimes

It is also important to understand that there are other dimensions of inequality apart from income, e.g., health, exposure to environmental hazards and access to basic necessities (Stiglitz, 2015). Tax structure and redistribution depend on the type of welfare regime the country decides to follow. It therefore is of immense importance to work out what kind of welfare state a country requires.

There are three main variations of welfare states: the Nordic-style welfare regime, the American-style welfare regime and the continental European–style welfare regime. The principle of economic redistribution is more markedly applied in the Nordic-style welfare regime, which makes it more redistributive compared to continental European welfare regimes. First, social assistance is much better developed in social democratic welfare states for people with even a tenuous attachment to the labour market. These people enjoy rights to higher basic transfers. Second, the former provides more free or subsidised social services than the latter do. The American-style welfare regimes rely more heavily on targeting than the general provision of benefits compared to the other two types of welfare regime (Huber, Pribble & Stephens, 2009). However, the redistribution of wealth does not mean a direct cash transfer from the rich to the poor. Rather, the redistribution works indirectly in the form of healthcare, education and social security (Piketty, 2014).

The result of these three different welfare regimes in reducing inequality and poverty varies markedly from each other. The Nordic-style social democratic welfare states observe the most reduction in inequality and poverty. In contrast, American-style welfare regimes end up with the highest level of poverty and inequality of the three while continental European welfare regimes fall somewhere in the middle (Huber, Pribble & Stephens, 2009).

The liberal welfare regime has three characteristics: (1) liberal politics, (2) capitalist economics and (3) residualist social policies. The liberal welfare regime aims to promote high economic growth, which is also supposed to play the main role in poverty reduction and thus promoting the welfare of society. The residualist system of social welfare in forms such as transfer payments plays a secondary role. This type of welfare regime originated from the great transformation associated with the industrial revolution and observed its peak in England with the New Poor Law of 1832 (Goodin et al., 1999).

In a liberal welfare regime, policy support is used only as a last resort, and emphasis is placed on the proper use of public policy, the underlying belief behind which is that the wrong policy choice could discourage people from looking for employment (Smith, 2004). Thus, what a liberal welfare regime does is to limit access to services that are free or subsidised so as to regulate the behaviour of the citizens (McLaughlin, 2006).

The result has not been that satisfactory in the case of inequalities in liberal welfare regimes, despite such policies. The United States, for example, has seen the production of many more luxury homes than basic affordable housing. The healthcare system there has left a large share of the population without health insurance. Private transportation has grown over time at the expense of public transportation, and lower-income groups are finding it difficult to find transportation to get to work (Ulbrich, 2011). Generally, it is seen that this type of economy has lower taxes, weak labour laws and higher inequality, but greater availability of jobs (Smith, 2004).

Like the liberal welfare regime, the social democratic welfare regime has three characteristics: (1) class politics, (2) socialist economics and (3) redistributive social policies. It is the model that is followed in Scandinavia (Goodin et al., 1999). The welfare regime of the region is universalistic, with much emphasis put on the ideal of solidarity. These economies have high-income taxes, universal social services, low unemployment and income inequality and almost no poverty. The prevention of poverty and the employment of everyone who wishes to work are two major purposes of the state (Smith, 2004).

The fundamental value that drives the social democratic welfare regime is social equality (Goodin et al., 1999). Two distinctive characteristics of the welfare regime of this type, as has been found in Sweden, are universalism and non-discrimination. The rights of individuals in this type of welfare state take the form of social rights—rights which are decided by needs and not by performance in the market. It is also believed that as the rights offered are universal, this type of regime enjoys a high level of support from the public (Kurian, 2005). The introduction of social security programmes and progressive taxation was actually a compromise between labour and capital to achieve distributive equality in the Scandinavian welfare states and provided the experience on which the concept of de-commodification relies (Kato, 2003). The policy response of the state thus works across three dimensions. First, the power of private capital is weakened through strategies such as introducing regulations and restrictions. Second, the bargaining power of labour is improved through full employment policies. Finally, active intervention is carried out in the labour market, such as "legislatively regulating working hours, conditions and wages; providing education, training and labour exchanges to assist those not in work; and public employment for those for whom no work is to be found in the private sector" to protect individual workers (Goodin et al., 1999).

The corporatist welfare regime also has three characteristics: (1) group politics, (2) communitarian economics and (3) mutualist social policies. This model of welfare regime is believed to be residual of pre-industrial feudal forms and is supposed to be following the social teachings of the Roman Catholic Church. It remains as the welfare regime found in Germany and Austria and across the Catholic world (Goodin et al., 1999). This group is also called "continental conservative welfare states". Spain, Greece, Portugal and Belgium share many of the traits of this model as well (Smith, 2004).

In the corporatist/continental model, most social services are "intermediary bodies (corps) and are in some way linked to one's occupational status, or to a particular insurance fund with which one is affiliated", not by a single provider such as the national or provincial governments, which provide social services on equal terms to all citizens in Canada or the United Kingdom. The benefits are widespread but not universal in nature, as has been observed in the French model. Different occupations such as the self-employed, civil servants, teachers, highly paid professionals or cadres, farmers, miners, merchant sailors and train conductors negotiate to reach more favourable deals within the welfare state. Such a style of bargaining makes the corporatist system more prone to being hijacked by the most powerful interest groups, often the skilled and organised male workforce (Smith, 2004). The corporatist model in some ways is said to have been directed towards the prevention of the social disruption caused by rapid economic change. This ideology, however, has been criticised because of its protection of existing workers at the expense of aspiring ones. Taxes and social expenditure are found to be almost as high in this type of system as in social democratic welfare regimes. Nonetheless, unemployment in this system is much higher, "income inequality is substantially higher, and female labour participation is lower (especially in Germany and Italy)" (Smith, 2004).

A welfare state does not necessarily imply economic redistribution. A particular example is the French state whose social policy is not overwhelmingly redistributive, and as opposed to the progressive income tax system of Denmark and Sweden, and the mix of progressive income taxes and payroll taxes used in Germany, Canada and Britain. The French government finances their social sector from a mix of regressive payroll taxes, regressive sales taxes and sometimes a smaller general social contribution tax (Smith, 2004). It is also seen that myth and ceremony allow politicians and the public to paper over the massive contradictions of welfare policy. Welfare policy purports to address poverty and inequality but refuses to deal with the structural causes of poverty and inequality or the reality of welfare recipients (Handler & Hasenfeld, 2007). In addition, it should not be expected that more unequal societies would redistribute more. Unequal societies are characterised by a greater capacity of their richer members to affect the state's policies in their favour. Increases in inequality translate into a greater share of resources in the hands of individuals with the capacity to extract fiscal favours from policymakers, resulting in a decrease in the resources a society is able to devote to redistribution (Rodríguez, 2004).

In a free-market economy, states are traditionally expected to provide for law and order and public goods. Issues like poverty and inequality are usually considered to fall within the basic functions of state. Even welfare states could not cross the line when it comes the question of income inequality and redistribution. Promoting equality and meeting the needs of the hard pressed are two choices that every society faces. Whereas activities in the second area are identified as a sufficient requirement of a welfare state, activity in the first area is thought to be neither necessary nor sufficient (Goodin, 1988).

There is also a debate over how to fight inequality. The emphasis on tax progressivity and economic fairness arises from similar concerns of who would bear the burdens of a tax code. Tax progressivity decides tax burdens and thus in turn economic efficiency and economic fairness. However, the term *progressivity* has mainly been used to mean economic fairness (Inman, 1996). Thus, the implication is that the state needs to generate revenue, and it is asked how fairly it can do so. It is even argued that sometimes the tax structure cannot counter income inequality, with an example being that of the pre-tax income inequality that has occurred since the 1970s in the United States. Sometimes factors such as family composition change, and the changing wage structure has such a dominant effect on income inequality that it cannot be altered by progressive tax (Karoly, 1996).

At the theoretical level, different classes (such as the intermediate class and the elite class) are identified as being responsible for making poverty and inequality play a pivotal role in the political process, whether national or local. For example, as an alternative to Piketty (2014), Soskice (2014) develops a politico-economic framework describing the role of politics in "institutionalising" technological change. Essentially, what Soskice's framework does is to portray how political decisions made in the face of certain technological improvements or innovations like Fordism and the Information and communication technology (ICT) revolution have led to undesirable consequences like poverty. For example, Fordism "produced low unemployment and wage compression" in advanced economies because of the functioning of three elements: a massive rise in aggregate demand, the easy integration of labour with poor education and social skills into a semi-skilled workforce and a fall in the wage difference between skilled and semi-skilled labour because of existence of complementarities between them in production process and resulting collective bargaining (Soskice, 2014).

It is easy to see how Soskice's (2014) analysis is sometimes value driven and selective. For example, the argument that "majoritarian systems" are averse to being "generous in redistribution" and then claiming that only in Scandinavian countries with paradoxically strong right parties are the interests of the low-skilled included in coalitions between centrist and left parties. Again, to summarise, the idea that the general limits to redistribution via the political system are the result of democratic decision-making, not the effect of capital itself, seems "paradoxical". Moreover, the claim that "It is therefore not obvious that the political power of advanced capitalist companies has increased in recent decades" also does not seem to be true and especially does not reflect the reality of developing countries.

The notion of inequality has been ignored by international organisations as well. Rather, their agenda has focused more on reducing poverty. The first United Nations resolutions mentioned poverty but failed to recognise inequalities (Mestrum, 2009). This has been followed by international campaigns in poorer regions (e.g., "Make Poverty History", "ONE campaign", "Stand Against Poverty"), which have focused explicitly on global poverty. The World Bank in its flagship human World Development Report showed similar trends. The reason was clear. Inequality, a more political agenda, was less favourable than a relatively apolitical agenda such as poverty (Wade, 2011).

Nevertheless, the importance of politics and institutions cannot be denied. According to Stiglitz (2015), inequality is largely a result of policies. The law of economics is universal. Hence, differing inequalities among countries can only be answered through politics, not through economics. Some countries have done exceedingly well in keeping inequality in check, whereas in some countries, inequality has increased over time. There is no denying that education and healthcare positively effects income. The level of education and healthcare, however, is not same across countries. Some countries opt for policies to ensure healthcare for all, whereas some prefer private healthcare. This is an issue of policymaking rather than economics (Stiglitz, 2015). The institutional and political backing behind the definition and distribution of property rights has to be taken into consideration. The economic forces explained by Piketty are fundamentally related to political phenomena. The process of capital accumulation is also a political phenomenon rather than an economic one (Hopkin, 2014).

It is clear from the above discussion that the welfare state is not an anti-market entity. Societies in which some groups have systemically inferior access to the reciprocal benefits of market participation are faced with the problem of reconciling democracy with a distribution of social surplus that is unequal and may be inequitable (Williams, 2001). In distinguishing the welfare state from other sorts of state, we must first stipulate that the welfare state is set in the context of a market economy. Of course, planned economies do ordinarily contain a social security or social service sector. That is not the same a "welfare state", though. The point of welfare state interventions is to remedy unplanned and unwelcome outcomes (Goodin, 1988).

As opposed to the first line of position mentioned above regarding the birth of the welfare state, it is the employer's interests that are argued to have led to the formation of the welfare state in the second line of argument. Moreover, the interests of employers may vary from country to country. For example, in the case of Sweden, employers' decision to support collective bargaining and a legal framework to protect their own interests in labour markets have been mentioned to lead to welfare policies, which, because of different interests, led to a different kind of state in the United States. From the employers' point of view, wages determine the supply and quality of labour they can employ in the production process. Employers are also interested in controlling the wage rate of their own products as well as that of their competitors. They also understand the importance of a high wage rate as a source of high demand in the product markets. There are different means present both at the individual and the collective level available to employers through which they can try to achieve these related but varied and often contradictory objectives. It is also assumed that because of pragmatic and profit-seeking reasons, and sometimes probably from humanitarian ones, employers may suffer from regret that market competition compels them to shift the burden onto their workers (Swenson, 2002).

In this respect, the prominent manufacturers in the United States and Sweden adopted completely opposite strategies to address issues related to labour markets and labour unions. As the United States has experienced technological change and a shortage of skilled labour, they could not use abusive methods to deal with labour unions and thus failed to establish collective control of the labour. Therefore, leading manufacturing employers' inability to join a cartel in steel, machine and foundry production led them to set off on a distinctive individualistic and decentralised course of action. Many employers came up with the strategy of offering higher wages than was required (efficiency wages) along with relatively generous social benefits (welfare capitalism) for the purpose of fighting the harmful effects of labour unions, reducing turnover costs and ensuring the supply of efficient labour (Swenson, 2002).

In contrast, some other industries, mainly the coal, clothing and construction industries, formed cartels as technology and competition provided suitable conditions. As opposed to the United States, Swedish employers started organising themselves from early in the century and followed a thoroughly different strategy. They collectively became involved in repressing wages, as opposed to the US strategy of individually raising them, and took steps that stopped differentiating pay across firms and industries.

Income distribution mechanisms

This section identifies a number of mechanisms that together affect the income distribution in a country. The fulfilment of people's aspirations for equality requires the identification of the forces responsible for worsening inequality and the employment of tools to counter these. Moreover, there is no single strategy that governments can apply to achieve the objective of economic redistribution.

The reduction of inequality requires two major changes in the tax structure. First, the tax system has to be progressive. Second, rather than aggregating different sources of income and different wealth and assets into a single type, each has to be taxed differently considering the entirety of its impact on the economy.

Despite the counter-arguments, the importance of a progressive tax system still cannot be denied. As has frequently been found, the tax structure in the currently developed countries has been mostly progressive. Tax policy, measured by the progressivity at the top of the individual income tax system, seems to play a big role in shaping income concentration. High top tax rates reduce the pre-tax income gap without, so far, having a clear negative effect on economic growth (Saez, 2017).

At this time, all the countries concerned operated highly progressive personal income taxes. There were progressive taxes on wealth, or on the transfer of wealth via inheritance. It was the time of the expansion of the welfare state, which meant that the safety net became more effective and that those at the bottom of the income distribution pile were able to share in rising prosperity (Atkinson, 2013). Until the 1970s, the United States had rates of income tax that were much more progressive than those in many European countries. It still continues to have corporate taxation that is higher than that found in most European countries (Holmwood, 2014).

There is also little use denying that the poor and the rich are subjected to different rates of return on the assets they hold. It is therefore important to keep into account different types of assets the poor and the wealthy could possess. A particularly important asset in this regard is real estate housing.

Taxes on rent require additional attention:

> My sense is really that the public will favour more progressive taxation only if it is convinced that top income gains are detrimental to economic

> growth of the 99 percent, and that taxation can ameliorate this. In America, people do not have a strong view against inequality per se, as long as inequality is fair. And what does fair mean? As an economist, you would say fair means that individual income and wealth reflect the value of what people produce or otherwise contribute to the economic system. This is why distinguishing between the standard supply side scenario versus the rent-seeking scenario is so important.
>
> (Saez, 2017)

Increasing labour share in income requires a number of actions, in which government can play an important role. In this regard, government should improve the employment opportunities and bargaining power available to the labour and pay attention to what the labour is paid. First, to increase the bargaining power, a living wage and public employment can be a useful tool: "The government should offer guaranteed employment at the living wage to everyone who seeks it" (Atkinson, 2014). Public employment programmes have the ability to generate an active labour market.

Additionally, the government should work to ensure a fairer distribution of surplus within the firm. Government has to ensure that workers get their share when a surplus is divided between employers and workers. Regulating the firms would ensure that they maintain ethics. This should also mean maintaining equal opportunities for women. This can significantly reduce the pay gap as well as unequal opportunities for women (Atkinson, 2014). Another proposal in this regard is the changing relative bargaining power of capital and labour. Besides giving bargaining power to the workers, one other way of doing this is to reduce the mark-ups to consumers (Kristal, 2010).

Citizens have become more aware in the aftermath of the financial crisis that their pay is not determined by the market but rather by the existing institutions. It is ultimately the bargaining power of the worker that determines their pay from public employment models. Relatively lower bargaining power and a lack of trade unions for workers in the lower spectrum of pay allows employers to get away with a higher proportion of surplus. The surplus, however, shifts more in favour of those working as executives because of their ability and capacity to bargain (Atkinson, 2013).

The provision of public goods has income redistribution characteristics besides taxation. Government through its fiscal policy measures can influence the directions in market. Public investment in technological change for example can influence future markets. This leads to the government getting monopoly power, which was previously ruled out by the assumption of perfect competition (Atkinson, 2014)

Hence, austerity programmes initiated by governments during economic recessions reverse the economic redistribution from the rich to the poor. Cuts in the public budget thus lead to the transfer of income from labour to capital (Atkinson, 2014). This widens inequality. Thus, economic recession and subsequent austerity measures cause more damage to the poor.

As argued by Piketty (2014), there is in principle real equality for everyone in the case of access to education and health and redistribution in modern welfare states, where a logic of rights and a principle of equal access to a certain number of goods is deemed to be fundamental.

> Perhaps the most invidious aspect of inequality is that affecting opportunity. Equality of opportunity—the "American dream"—has always been a cherished American ideal. But data now show that this is a myth: America has become the advanced country not only with the highest level of inequality, but one of those with the least equality of opportunity. The life prospects of a young American are more dependent on the income and education of his parents than in other developed countries. We have betrayed a fundamental value. And the result is that we are wasting a most valuable resource, our human resources: millions of those at the bottom are not able to live up to their potential.
>
> (Stiglitz, 2015)

Here a distinction has to be made between the poor and the wealthy in terms of the opportunities they enjoy in entrepreneurial and productive activities. An important tool to ensure equality of opportunity is better utilisation of credit. Access to credit provides citizens in lower-income groups a higher purchasing power for consumption. Credit thus can be a tool for smoothing out class differences. However, this also bolsters the belief of those who do not support economic redistribution (Kus & Fan, 2015). The window of opportunity shrinks even more for lower-income groups as education and healthcare becomes more expensive.

Rising inequality from capital accumulation can be offset through taxation, equal opportunities for citizens and an increased state net worth that allows higher spending (Atkinson, 2014). Of these three, taxation policy has the ability to significantly reduce the wealth gap. However, government intervention in the form of transfer payments and public goods provision can reduce the inequality faster. A combination of taxes and public spending can do even better (Aaron, 2015). Hence, the welfare regime, in order to reduce inequality in society, opts for a balanced fiscal policy consisting of the provision of public goods and progressive taxation.

Social democrats view the commodities in the realm of capitalist economy but only take certain goods and services, leaving out the rest. For instance, privately provided healthcare, education and housing in a market economy is provided by the state in a social democratic approach. This now allows more equitable distribution of welfare goods in society, hence reducing inequality (Goodin et al., 1999).

The above discussions lay out the role of governments and, more precisely, discusses the tools at hand to reduce societal inequality. However, such measures or tools depend on the society where they will be implemented. Without solidarity among the members of the society and a functioning state, such policies will not work. It is ultimately the role of the state to maintain social order in society and subsequently its solidarity and stratification (Eißel, Leaman & Rokicka, 2014; Esping-Andersen, 1996). The popularity of redistributive measures have gained renewed interest in an increasingly unequal world. Studies have shown that increasing inequality leads to higher support for economic redistribution (Olivera, 2015).

The increasing support, however, is yet to make any significant difference in the redistribution paradigm. Inequality can also be capitalised on by policymakers, which is evident by the lack of action to tackle inequality. Inequality generates political distortions, which cause disincentives to capital accumulation. Economic redistribution barely reaches the hands of the poor. Rather, the resources are shifted to the pockets of the politicians in an unequal society (Rodríguez, 2004). The arguments against redistribution are mostly related to the inefficiencies of redistribution measures. However, redistribution can only work when institutions function to ensure the transfer of payment. The policies fail because the institutions in unequal societies favour those in power, subsequently shifting resources towards the capitalists and the non-poor (Mello & Tiongson, 2006).

In light of the study above, a framework has been developed. The framework depicts the interaction between household and government in a market system (Figure 5.1). Institutions, both formal and informal, influence this interaction. States, with the help of formal institutions, internalise the externality created by the market system. The distribution of power within the government determines the level of public goods provision. A citizen-state is directed

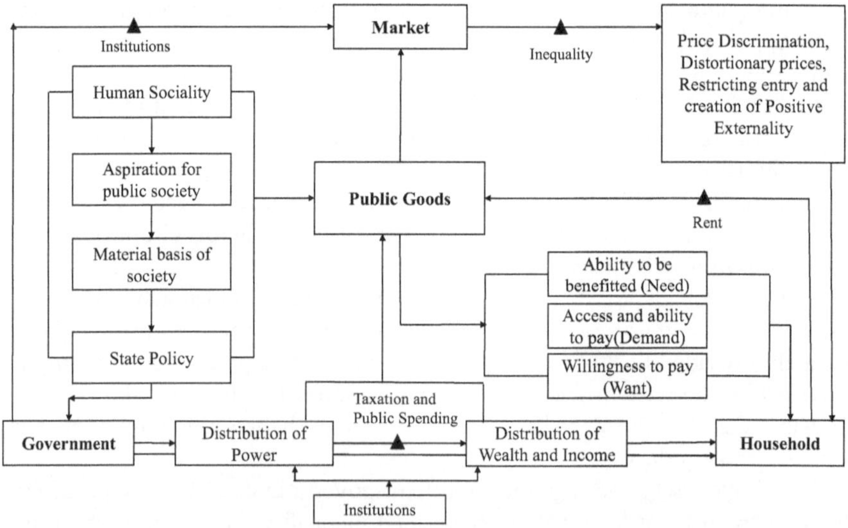

Figure 5.1 Conceptual framework for the analysis of the chapter. Source: Prepared by the author

by the idea of providing public goods to its citizens. Based on the framework, four propositions are outlined here which will be proven in the next section of the chapter.

Inequality, rent and taxation

The distribution of wealth and income through taxation and public spending is determined by, and contingent upon, the distribution of power. The proposition is that the distribution of power works as a precursor in determining the capacity of the state to collect taxes and spend in public affairs.

The relation between taxation and the political power of rent-seeking groups is negative. This is due to the political power the clientelist groups hold and their ability to shape tax policies according to their needs. Hence, when political power is confined to clientelist groups, the occurrence of tax exemption and tax evasion rises. As a result, the amount of tax collection falls, which negatively affects the amount of public spending. The more the rent-seeking group enjoy political power, the lower the taxes they pay (Figure 5.2). The grabbing of wealth through primitive accumulation increases, with more political power confined to rent-seeking clientelist groups.

In 2018, 26 of the richest people on earth possessed the same amount of wealth as the poorer half of the population. The wealth of 2,200 billionaires increased by 12 percent, while that of the poorest half reduced by 11 percent. Wealth is more difficult to measure than income. In the developed nations, many are subject to student loans, credit card debts, etc., so wealth can also be negative (Oxfam, 2018). The richest 147 people control about 1 percent of global wealth but represent only 0.000002 percent of the population (Oxfam,

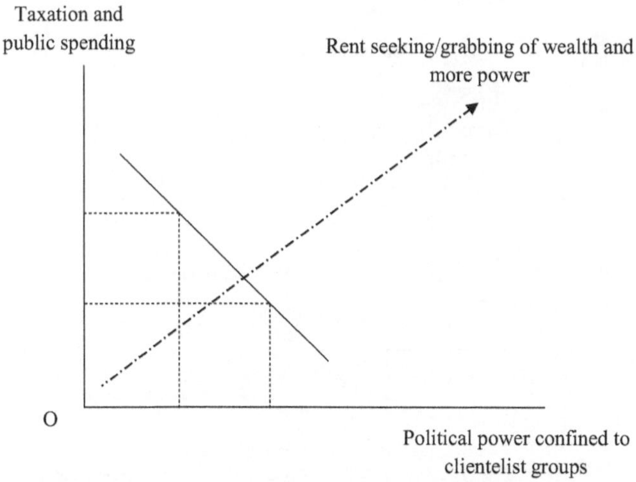

Figure 5.2 Political power affecting taxation and public spending. Source: Prepared by the author

2018). Around 0.8 percent of the global population—42 million people—have a net worth greater than a million. This 0.8 percent controls 44.8 percent of the world's wealth (Oxfam, 2018). The lowest group in the wealth pyramid consists of 64 percent of the world's population, but their share in world health is barely 2 percent (Figure 5.3).

There is rising inequality throughout most of the world, but it varies in magnitude (Figure 5.4). In 1980, the top share was only 30–35 percent in Europe, North America, China and India. It was only about 20–25 percent in Russia. However, by 2015, the national income held by the top share rose drastically in India and China. The change in Europe was much slower than the rest. The economic boom in China and India is a much more recent phenomenon than rest of the groups. This change in the income share of the top 10 percent goes to show that the economic progress of these countries has greatly benefitted top income groups.

While the income share of the top 10 percent has been increasing sharply, the bottom 50 percent of the population have seen the opposite. The share in India and China has shrunk rapidly over the years, while the decline is slower for Europe. Developing countries including Brazil and Sub-Saharan Africa have seen a steady increase in their share (Figure 5.5). The differing rates of inequality within different income groups across the globe also show that policy institutions matter, and inequality is not merely a by-product of globalisation.

The magnitude of the top 10 percent income shares varies from 20–25 percent to 60–65 percent of total income. The same aggregate income of countries can result in a widely varying distribution of income (Alvaredo et al., 2018). The top income shares vary from about 5 percent to 30 percent, just

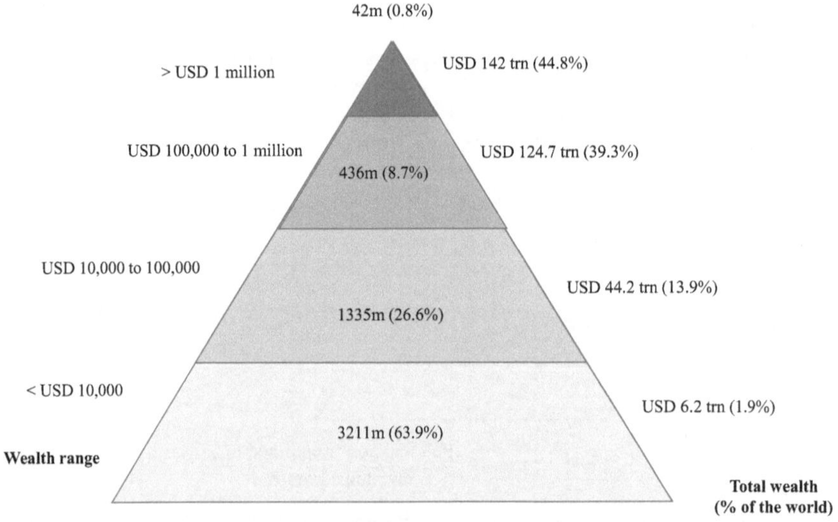

Figure 5.3 Global wealth pyramid 2018. Source: OXFAM, 2018

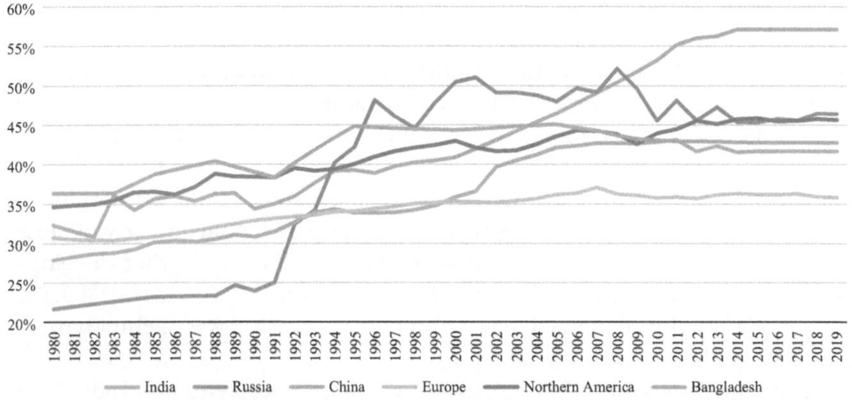

Figure 5.4 Top 10 percent income shares across the world, 1980–2017. Source: Alvaredo et al. (2018) (World Inequality Report, 2018)

Figure 5.5 Bottom 50 percent income shares across the world, 1980–2016. Source: Alvaredo et al. (2018) (World Inequality Report 2018)

like the share of income that goes to the bottom 50 percent of the population. In other words, the same aggregate income level can give rise to widely different income levels or the bottom and top groups, depending on the distribution of income prevailing in the specific country and the time period under consideration (Alvaredo et al., 2018).

The LDCs in Asia and the Pacific have witnessed a reversal in reduction in poverty, with upward trends in 2020. Poverty persists as a significant determinant in the region as around 33% of the population in the Asia-Pacific LDCs still live below the poverty line of USD 3.20 for middle-income countries (Sachs et al. 2021). The poverty headcount ratio shows a wide gap between LDCs and developing countries such as China and Viet Nam. Poverty in Asia Pacific LDCs increased by one percentage point, whereas poverty still fell for countries like China and Viet Nam during the pandemic. The working poverty rate, which illustrates the percentage of population in poverty despite being employed, shows a vivid gap between the LDCs and other developing countries in the region. The rate of working poor is 8.3% in Asia-Pacific LDCs while developed countries have none, meaning all those in employment receive wages higher than the poverty line.

Income growth has been impressive in China (831 percent) and India (223 percent) in terms of real per-adult national income growth. This has been relatively low in Europe (40 percent), Russia (34 percent) and North America (63 percent). It is apparent that in all the groups, the growth rate of the upper income groups is higher than that of the lower-income groups. For example, the income of top 0.001 percent grew by more than 3,750 percent, while the income of bottom 50 percent grew less than 420 percent. The same income growth levels in India are more than 3,000 percent versus less than 110 percent. In Russia too, the higher income group saw greater increases (Table 5.1). This is due to a change in policy from a communist system to a market economy. Europe appears to be the region with the lowest income gap.

All the populations and their incomes have been pooled together and adjusted using purchasing power parity (PPP). This means that a given income can buy the same bundle of goods in different countries. The global average income growth is lower (60 percent) than that of individual emerging economies. A high growth for top 1 percent (>100 percent), low growth in the middle 40 percent (43 percent) and high growth in the bottom 50 percent (94

Table 5.1 Global income growth and inequality, 1980–2016

	Total cumulative real growth per adult (%)					
Income group	*China*	*Europe*	*India*	*Russia*	*US and Canada*	*World*
Full population	831	40	223	34	63	60
Bottom 50%	417	26	107	−26	5	94
Middle 40%	785	34	112	5	44	43
Top 10%	1,316	58	469	190	123	70
Top 1%	1,920	72	857	686	206	101
Top 0.1%	2,421	76	1,295	2,562	320	133
Top 0.01%	3,112	87	2,078	8,239	452	185
Top 0.001%	3,752	120	3,083	25,269	629	235

Source: Alvaredo et al. 2017

percent) can be observed at the global level. Global income growth is even higher in the case of the top 0.001 percent (about 235 percent).

In the United States and Canada, 35 percent was captured by the top 1 percent income group. This same rate in Russia was 69 percent. Globally, the top 1 percent of the population captured twice as much (27 percent) as the share of the bottom 50 percent of the population (Table 5.2).

The inequality widens more in terms of the share of wealth. Globally, the top 10 percent of the population held around 81 percent from 2015 to 2019. The top 1 percent has accumulated 44 percent of the wealth. The total wealth held by the top 10 percent of the population has gone down significantly. The top 1 percent has kept accumulating wealth at a similar rate (Table 5.3).

Bangladesh has been facing similar trends in inequality. The Commitment to Reducing Inequality (CRI) index measures the performance of a country in reducing inequality based on three indicators: public service or government spending in social sectors, progressive taxation policies and labour rights. Bangladesh was ranked 113th among 158 countries in the CRI Index 2020 (Oxfam, 2020). That is, the country is doing very little to reduce the wealth gap. Bangladesh ranks poorly in public service and labour rights compared to

Table 5.2 Share of global growth captured by income groups, 1980–2016

	Share of global growth captured by income groups (%)					
Income group	*China*	*Europe*	*India*	*Russia*	*US and Canada*	*World*
Full population	100	100	100	100	100	100
Bottom 50%	13	14	11	−24	2	12
Middle 40%	43	38	23	7	32	31
Top 10%	43	48	66	117	67	57
Top 1%	15	18	28	69	35	27
Top 0.1%	7	7	12	41	18	13
Top 0.01%	4	3	5	20	9	7
Top 0.001%	2	1	3	10	4	4

Source: Credit Suisse, 2019 (Global Wealth Databook 2019)

Table 5.3 World wealth inequality, 2000–2019

		Share of wealth held by		
Year	*Gini*	*Top 10%*	*Top 5%*	*Top 1%*
2000–2004	91.66	88.2	74.78	45.66
2005–2009	90.36	85.98	72.38	43.52
2010–2014	88.94	82.9	70.24	42.52
2015–2019	88.46	81.7	70.12	44.8

Source: Credit Suisse, 2019 (Global Wealth Databook 2019)

taxation policies. This shows that government initiatives in reducing inequality fall far short of what needs to be done. Spending on health and education has been much lower than in other countries, which is evident from the rank of 142 in public services. The poorest 10 percent of the population in Bangladesh has seen a reduction of their share in national income from 2 percent in 2010 to 1.01 percent in 2016. On the other hand, the share of the richest 10 percent increased from 35.84 percent in 2010 to 38.16 percent in 2016 (BBS, 2019). The rich are thus getting richer and poor are getting poorer. The Gini coefficient is used globally for measuring inequality. The coefficient ranges from 0 to 1, with 1 being the highest level of inequality and 0 being the lowest level of inequality. In Bangladesh, the coefficient value has increased to 0.48 in 2016 from 0.46 in 2010.

The official growth statistics shows that Bangladesh has experienced unprecedented GDP growth rate since 2013, with the recent GDP growth being the greatest in the country's history. Overall, the GDP growth has remained high while job growth is slow and there has been a slight increase in real wage growth. This lack of proportional job creation and growth in wage rate contributes to increasing inequality in Bangladesh. The country is thus going through a period of jobless growth. The poor are thus not getting enough opportunities to engage in productive employment activities.

Small-scale firms and low-income households face impediments in accessing financial services because of a lack of financial know-how, difficult paperwork, complicated processes and other market failures. Also, the current social protection programmes in Bangladesh are inadequate in terms of reducing poverty and inequality. There needs to be increased and leakage-free distribution of social protection funds.

Regressive tax policies benefit the rich more than the poor. This contributes to the growing inequality. Programmes targeted specifically at the poor are susceptible to leakages to the wealthier class due to corruption. The poor do not have access to the privileges that result from the patron–client relationship between interest groups and the government. These include debt bailouts, tax exemptions, subsidies, etc.

The gap between the bottom 5 percent (0.23 percent of the total income) and top 5 percent (27.82 percent of the total income) is extremely high (BBS, 2019). In 2010, the percentages were 0.78 percent and 24.61 percent respectively. Thus, the gap has increased over this period (Table 5.4).

It is also evident that income accruing to households belonging to groups from decile-1 to decile-5 remained almost the same in 2016, apart from for decile-1 and decile-10. In 2016, the income share of the households belonging to groups from decile-6 to decile-9 slightly decreased, except that of decile-10, which increased corresponding to those of 2010. In 2010, the income share of decile-10 was 35.85 percent, which increased to 38.09 percent in 2016.

The Gini coefficient of income increased to 0.482 in 2016 from 0.458 in 2010. The increase in the Gini coefficient is evidence that the concentration of income increased from 2010 to 2016. Both rural and urban areas show a

Table 5.4 Percentage share of income households by decile groups and Gini coefficient

	HIES 2016			*HIES 2010*		
Household income group	*Total*	*Rural*	*Urban*	*Total*	*Rural*	*Urban*
National	100	100	100	100	100	100
Bottom 5%	0.23	0.25	0.27	0.78	0.88	0.76
Decile-1	1.02	1.06	1.17	2.00	2.23	1.98
Decile-2	2.83	2.99	3.04	6.22	3.53	3.09
Decile-3	4.05	4.36	4.1	4.1	4.49	3.95
Decile-4	5.13	5.52	5.00	5.00	5.43	5.01
Decile-5	6.24	6.58	6.15	6.01	6.43	6.31
Decile-6	7.48	7.89	6.88	7.32	7.65	7.64
Decile-7	9.06	9.52	8.44	9.06	9.31	9.30
Decile-8	11.25	11.8	10.4	11.50	11.50	11.87
Decile-9	14.86	15.51	13.47	15.94	15.54	16.08
Decile-10	38.09	34.78	41.37	35.85	33.89	34.77
Top 5%	27.82	24.19	32.09	24.61	22.93	23.39
Income Gini coefficient	0.482	0.454	0.498	0.458	0.431	0.452

Source: BBS, 2019

similar changing pattern of decile distribution of income at the national level. Inequality is not consequential to economic growth but rather to policies.

Tax structure and progressivity

A tax system is defined as progressive if the post-tax income is more equitable than the pre-tax income. However, it is difficult to assume progressiveness simply looking at the tax rates due to the existence of deductions and exemptions. The tax rates do not reflect the actual tax burdens. Traditionally, income in the form of capital has faced lower tax rates. The high-income tax payers tend to benefit more from this. Corporate income tax faces mixed reactions partly because of the distributed tax burden (Piketty & Saez, 2007).

By looking at numbers and tax rates, one might assume that Bangladesh has progressive taxation. The income tax rates in Bangladesh certainly show progressivity. However, the tax composition and burdening paints a different picture. The Household Income and Expenditure Survey of 2005 showed that the burden of tax on goods and products, called Value Added Tax (VAT), in the lowest income range in Bangladesh is 6.92. This is very high and shows a low progressivity in terms of VAT since the VAT burden of the highest income group is 4.56. Even the fourth highest income group has a VAT burden lower than the effective VAT rate of 6.01 percent. This shows that VAT in Bangladesh is rather regressive. The same conclusion is obtained from Suit's Index of Progressivity. For rural people, VAT is less regressive compared to urban people, both with and without exemptions. The relative burden for VAT is higher for members of the lower-income monthly household per capita income groups. For example, for households that have less than BDT 200 per capita income, the relative tax burden is 404 percent. On the contrary, for households that have BDT 3,500 and above, the relative tax burden is 63 percent. The tax burden for VAT without exemptions is similar as the burden is 648 percent for the first and 54 percent for the second group (Faridy & Sarker, 2011).

There is hidden regressive pattern in the tax system. The French (and Italian) tax collection agencies are less efficient and less vigilant than their German, British and North American counterparts. Occasionally a high-flying French businessman/politician like Bernard Tapie might end up in jail for a year for evading taxes. However, someone not so well-known has a higher chance of evading taxes and punishment. The incarceration rate for egregious cases of tax evasion is lower in France than in most other OECD nations. "Low levels of social trust hinder efforts to reform" (Smith, 2004).

The tax pattern in Bangladesh becomes regressive as it unduly gives benefits to those with illegal earnings; one of these is allowing citizens to make any illegally earned money legal through tax proceedings. The process is more commonly referred as "whitening of the black money". The black economy may be defined as that sector of an economy which does not show up in official figures. The figure of about Tk. 16.609 billion for 1985-1986 is more than one-third of the country's GDP (Reza, 1989). There is no evidence to identify the size of black income, be it in terms of local or foreign currency that flows via this channel. It is estimated that black money amounts to about 10 percent of profits in the context of business and industry. It is obvious that the magnitude of illegal income from all these sources will significantly vary from one year to another depending on supply–demand conditions and administrative loopholes. Therefore, any estimate in this respect is bound to remain highly conjectural (Reza, 1989).

The definition of black money by the NBR also downplays the process of acquiring of such money. According to NBR, any money that is not shown to government agencies and hence not being taxed upon is black money. This definition puts more emphasis on the payment of taxes, downplaying the issue of money that is earned or obtained through illegal or unjust means. Thus, black money may also be the money illegally obtained by political, and/or bureaucratic corruption in government, semi-government, business or non-government organisations. Thus, black money can also be formal if it is declared but still illegally obtained.

Emerging groups of millionaire businessmen are contributing only a low proportion of their personal income tax collection every year to the government. This is evident from the contradictory remarks from two of the most influential financial institutions in Bangladesh. While the central bank declared that there are 23,212 multi-millionaires in Bangladesh, the National Board of Revenue published that the number of persons paying > BDT 100,000 as personal income tax in the 2011–2012 taxation year was lower than 1,000. This clearly shows that only a fraction of the multi-millionaires are paying taxes. By definition, in Bangladesh, black money can be turned into white money simply by paying taxes. And if someone pays taxes on just a fraction of their black money, they now have the necessary papers that will be useful to protect them against investigations. The lowest tax rate in Bangladesh is 10 percent and the highest is 25 percent. Owners of black money tend to only pay taxes on income that is in the 10 percent range. The Finance Act proposed to accept any amount of undeclared legally or illegally obtained money without conditions in 2005. In the 2009–2010 fiscal year, it was declared that it was the first budget where the black money whitening law was properly enacted (Waris & Latif, 2014).

Since 1976, governments have had such opportunities to whiten illegal money. Right after the aforementioned announcement in 2009, the prices of apartments increased by three to four times and the general expectation was that it was the black money holders who were buying or who were able to buy these flats (Byron, 2009). Through tax evasion, bureaucratic hassle can be avoided and money can be saved. For example, a person earning BDT 500,000 a year should pay a tax of 25 percent, which is BDT 125,000. However, if the person decides to hide part of the black income and instead pays tax at a 10 percent rate only, he will be able to pay less tax as well as to have papers showing he has paid the tax. If he later pays whitening tax, the actual rate of tax (given that he has already earned interest with the black money) will be less than what he was to pay at first. So any reasonable person with pecuniary logic may want to follow this path. (Solaiman, 2014).

Black money can be whitened through purchasing apartments and lands. This prompted a gigantic rise in the prices of apartments and lands in Dhaka, the capital of Bangladesh (Tables 5.5 and 5.6). Prior to such laws, the increase in prices from 1990 to 2000 was only 12 percent. However, after the introduction of the law, the price of apartments shot up, and from 2000 to 2010, it increased by 483 percent. (REHAB, 2012; Solaiman, 2016). This astounding rise in apartment prices comes from the increased demand in a short period of time, mainly because of the whitening of black money.

The increase in the price of apartments has also caused the price of land to rise. The price of land also increased exponentially from 2000 to 2010. In Dhaka city, the price of land increased many times in the first 10 years of this century compared to the increase in prices in the decade before. The rate of increase has almost doubled on average and has increased by up to 3–10 times in many areas (REHAB, 2012).

Land has been the cause of inequality in urban cities in Bangladesh, especially in Dhaka. The government leased lands in Dhaka at a miniscule price after the liberation war. The valuation of these lands has increased magnanimously in just 50 years. Thus, the price of land has created a generational inequality as those who want to buy land now face a much higher cost than those who leased from the government.

The increase in the number of millionaires can also be linked to the increase in the sale of assets, cars and other luxury goods. The number of millionaires was only 22 in pre-independence Bangladesh. It increased to

Table 5.5 Price arrangement of apartments based on regions of Dhaka city

	Average price of apartments (Taka/Sq. feet)					*% Increase in price over the past two decades*	
	Year						
Area	*1990*	*1995*	*2000*	*2005*	*2010*	*Between 1990–2000*	*Between 2000–2010*
Dhanmondi	2150	2200	2400	3300	14000	12%	483%
Gulshan	2115	2080	2450	4500	14000	16%	471%
Banani	1,750	1,950	2,200	3,100	12,500	26%	468%
Baridhara	1,850	1,950	2,150	4,000	20,000	16%	830%
Lalmatia	1,800	1,950	2,400	3,400	8,500	33%	254%
Mirpur	1,250	1,300	1,500	2,500	5,500	20%	267%
Uttara	1,650	1,750	2,000	2,700	5,300	21%	165%
Shantinagar	1,850	1,900	2,200	2,700	5,000	19%	127%
Siddeswari	1,450	1,800	2,250	2,750	5,500	55%	144%
Malibag	1,600	1,850	2,250	2,500	7,000	41%	211%
Mohammadpur	1,450	1,600	1,800	3,500	4,500	24%	150%
Shamoli	1,350	1,500	1,600	2,100	7,000	19%	338%
Kolabagan	1,800	2,000	2,250	2,100	5,500	25%	144%
Monipuripara	1,850	2,000	2,250	3,300	5,500	22%	144%
Green Road	1,600	1,700	2,000	2,500	5,500	25%	175%
Elephant Road	1,600	1,800	2,200	2,500	5,500	38%	150%
Segun Bagicha	1,450	1,550	1,900	2,500	6,000	31%	216%

Source: REHAB, 2012

Table 5.6 Distribution of price of land in regions of Dhaka city

	Price of land (Taka/Katha)			*% Increase in price over the past two decades*	
	Year			*Between*	*Between*
Area	*1975*	*2000*	*2010*	*1990–2000*	*2000–2010*
Baridhara	25,000	5,000,000	40,000,000	733%	700%
Gulshan	25,000	2,200,000	25,000,000	267%	1036%
Banani	25,000	2,000,000	15,000,000	233%	650%
Dhanmondi	25,000	2,200,000	20,000,000	267%	809%
Lalmatia	20,000	1,800,000	15,000,000	200%	733%
Uttara	20,000	1,000,000	7,500,000	233%	650%
Cantonment	20,000	1,000,000	7,500,000	150%	650%
Mirpur	10,000	700,000	4,000,000	250%	471%
Demra	4,000	600,000	18,000,000	200%	2900%
Motijheel	50,000	3,500,000	20,000,000	192%	471%

Source: REHAB, 2012

47 in 1975 and then to a striking 5,799 in 2001 based on bank deposits (Sarkar, 2011). The number kept rising in the following years to 23,130 in 2009 and 27,400 in 2010 (Sarkar, 2011). But as previously stated, the rise in tax payers did not rise in accordance with this number. It implied a failure of the government to have motivated or made the people accountable to pay taxes (Solaiman, 2014).

Public goods and market provisioning

If a public good is provisioned through the market, there is a possibility of excludability in forms of access, leading to unequal distribution due to imperfect market and entry barriers. The hypothesis states that market provisioning considers public good as a demand from citizens rather than a need. Such a notion leads to price discrimination and exclusion.

A perfectly elastic curve illustrates that the price remains unchanged in a market where demand for the good is infinite. Similarly, when a public good is being provided through public provisioning, individual benefit remains unchanged as the number of users increases (Figure 5.6: Panel a). Universal public provision keeps the benefit constant and the number of beneficiaries does not change, which means that no excludability occurs in public provision. The benefit, however, does not remain constant when a public good is provisioned through market. People, irrespective of their ability to pay, socio-economic status, gender or any other identity, cannot afford the prices set by the market. Those who have ability to demand from market can have access to public goods, while others remain excluded. Market provisioning thus allows N people to get access to public goods—those who are able to buy services

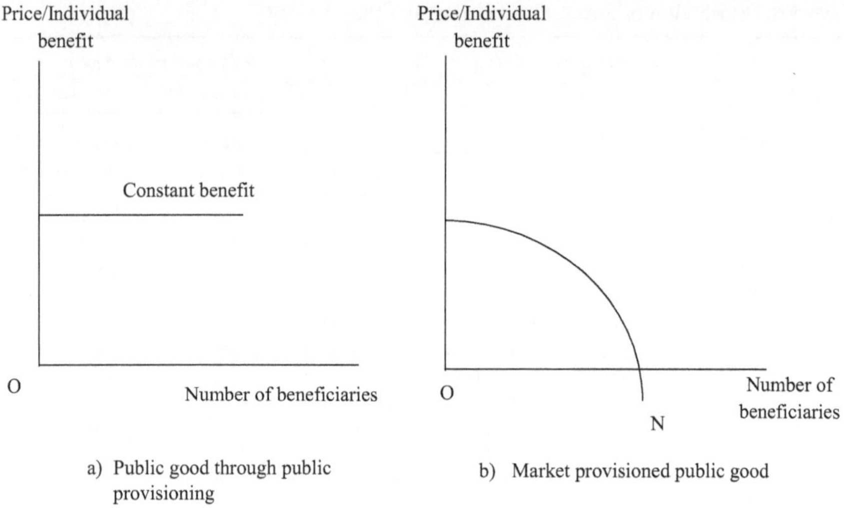

Figure 5.6 a) Public goods through public provisioning b) Market provisioned public goods. Source: Prepared by author

from market. Hence, many people become excluded (Figure 5.6: Panel b). At the same time, the transition to a market economy may lead to an increase in the use of resources by the government that are allocated on non-market criteria while, at the same time, its direct involvement in terms of owning and/or managing various factors of production decline.

The economic system of Bangladesh has moved towards a market economy dominated by the private sector by the mid-1990s from a planned economy dominated by the public sector in the early 1970s. But a market economy cannot operate in a vacuum. The existence of an effective government that ensures property rights is a pre-condition for the proper functioning of a free-market economy. Otherwise, "chaos" will prevail (Buchanan, 1976). Indeed, "state is essential to the functioning of a modem economy—to prevent such "chaos" developing by legitimising property rights, by controlling monetary and financial operations, by regulating economic activities etc." (Atkinson & Stiglitz, 2015). In the United States, Franklin D. Roosevelt enacted the Social Security Act of 1935, the first government-mandated social security programme to protect citizens from economic loss, right after the "Great Depression". It was the first female secretary of United States, Secretary of Labor Frances Perkins, as well as physician Francis Townsend, who were behind the enactment law. The act included unemployment benefits and old-age allowance for Americans (Achenbaum, 1988; Norton et al., 2011).

Even though the GDP growth has been high, large-scale job creation has been scarce. The economy has not been able to produce employment in sync with the growth of GDP. Hence, the economy of Bangladesh is facing "jobless growth". As aforementioned, the people from poor households are not getting enough productive opportunities to generate income. Thus, poverty reduction rates have reduced and the Gini coefficient has increased. Government expenditure on human capital aspects such as health and education as a share of GDP has reduced in recent years. This low investment in human capital aspects results in low increases in labour productivity and hence low increases in returns to labour. Thus, it does not aid in reducing poverty and inequality. Inequality does not only exist in terms of income but also exists in terms of access to healthcare, education, financial services, social safety nets etc. Overcoming this bias towards the high-income groups requires policies that will help to enhance the human capital of the poor and allow them to engage in productive economic activities. An analysis of the Scandinavian countries reveals how taxation and social spending (fiscal policies) can help to reduce income inequality. They have a progressive tax system and use the tax incurred to finance human capital and social services for the poor and disadvantaged population.

Total health expenditure per capita in Bangladesh increased from USD 27 in 2012 to USD 37 in 2015 (Figure 5.7). Only 3.0 percent of the GDP is spent in the health sector in Bangladesh, making Bangladesh one of the countries that spend the least on health in South-East Asia. Moreover, estimations suggest that 67 percent of the total health expenditure is made using households' out-of-pocket expenditures. It is the highest in South-East Asia, closely followed by India (62 percent) and far more than the Maldives (18 percent).

Government spending on education for Bangladesh was 2.4 percent of the GDP (Figure 5.8). The same percentage for Argentina is 6.0, and it is 4.6 and 5.8 for Indonesia and Malaysia respectively. Scandinavian nations such as

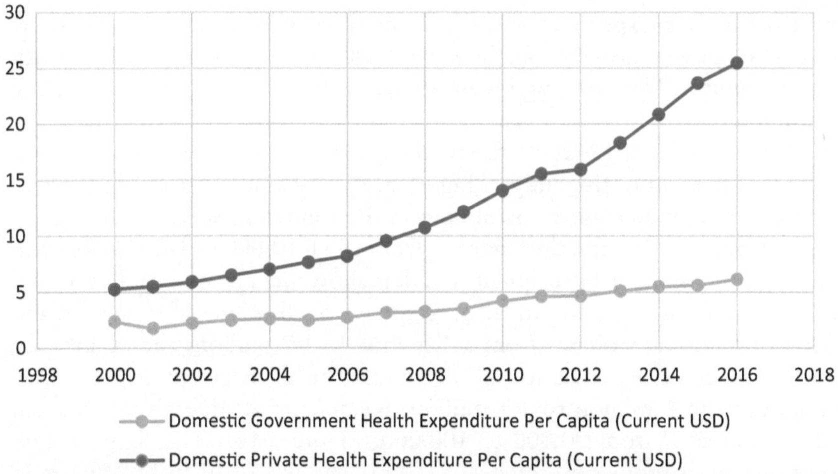

Figure 5.7 Health expenditure of Bangladesh. Source: World Bank, 2020

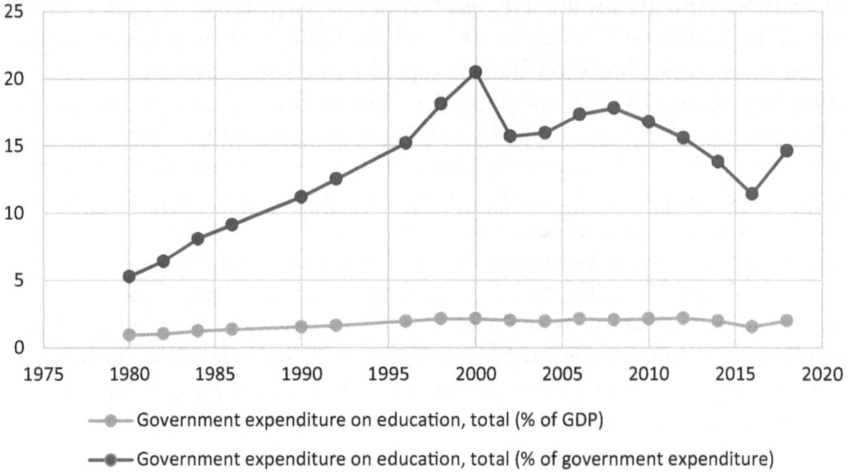

Figure 5.8 Public expenditure on education of Bangladesh. Source: World Bank, 2020

Norway and Sweden spend about 6.8 percent and 6.5 per cent of GDP on education respectively.

One more factor that has contributed to the low-income inequality in Europe is social protection. On average, European countries spend 12–19 percent of the GDP in this sector. This is done mostly in the form of income transfers to poor and vulnerable families. In Bangladesh, social protection spending is only 2.2 percent of the GDP; excluding civil service pensions, this amounts to a meagre 1.6 percent.

The progression of growth can be seen from the economic trends. Bangladesh is now the 31st-largest economy in the world in terms of purchase power parity. It is expected to be the 23rd-largest economy in the world by 2050. This growth progression, however, will be fruitless if it is a "growth without equity". The growing inequality has to be addressed in the first place for development.

In the fiscal year 2019–2020, the total expenditure on social safety nets was set at 14.21 percent of the budget (Figure 5.9). The amount was 2.58 percent of the GDP. The increase is distributed in the following way: an increase in the state honourees for freedom fighters from BDT 10,000 to BDT 12,000; an increase in the number of recipients of adult allowances from 4 million to 4.4 million; an increase in the number of recipients of allowances for widows and victims of domestic violence from 1.4 million to 1.7 million; and an increase in the number of beneficiaries of allowances for all insolvent persons with disabilities from 1 million to 1.5 million. Recipients of stipends for disabled students increased from 90,000 to 100,000 (Figure 5.10). The figure below shows the social protection budget, fiscal budget and GDP in fiscal years in Bangladesh.

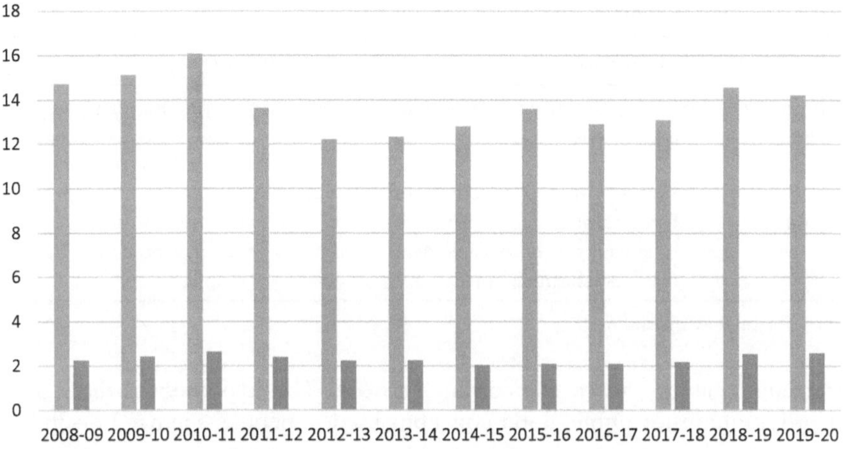

Figure 5.9 Percentage of social protection to fiscal budget and GDP in fiscal year. Source: Planning Commission, 2021 (Social Security Policy Support Programme)

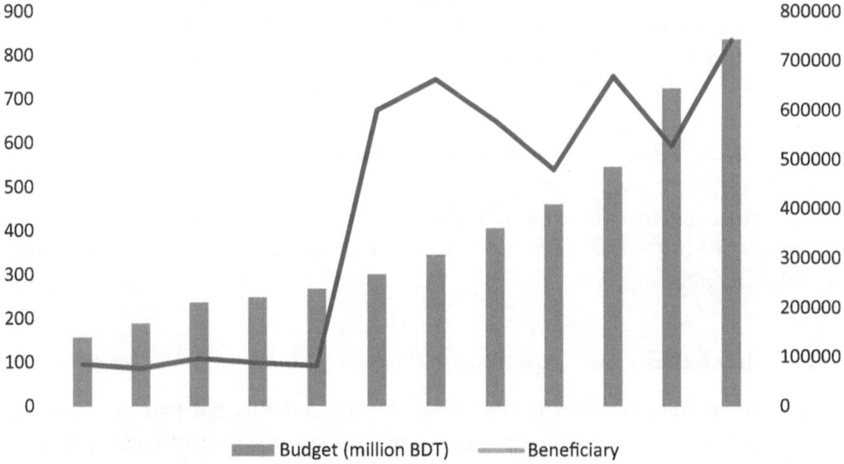

Figure 5.10 Social protection budget and beneficiaries in Bangladesh by fiscal year. Source: Ministry of Finance, 2020a

Need and demand

Need, demand and want are to be differentiated, as need relates to the ability to benefit from public goods, whereas demand is a function of preferences and the ability to pay, implying an acceptance of the need for an equitable distribution of, and access to, public goods, adhering to the principle of each

Table 5.7 Provision of public good: need vs. demand

	Universal benefit	*Ability to pay*
According to need	Public good: universal and equitable access and benefit	Market provisioning: excludes those who have no ability to pay
According to demand	Market provisioning: function of preferences based on ability to pay, excludes those who have no ability to demand based on market-determined price	Market provisioning through price mechanism: excludes those who have no ability to pay

Source: Prepared by the author

according to ability, to each according to need. The hypothesis is that market provisioning for public good conceptualised as people's demand excludes many and hinders universal and equitable access and benefit sharing. Public good should be conceptualised as people's need, which requires universal and equitable provisioning.

Market provisioning of public goods works through using a price mechanism. If people have the ability to pay at a market-determined price, they can demand public goods or services. The function of demand and supply implies individual preferences based on the ability to pay. As a result, people who have no ability to pay cannot demand, which leaves many people excluded from equitable access and benefit sharing of public goods. The misleading conceptualisation of public good as people's demand rather than people's need obstructs the universal and equitable provisioning of public good (Table 5.7).

When public good is provided in accordance with need, universal benefits ensure access to everyone including those who cannot pay for the good. However, without universal benefit, access remains limited to those who have the ability to pay.

Active citizenship and equalising tendencies

The nature of state policies is embedded in, and an integral part of, society, which is contingent upon the aspiration for a public society and human sociality. The hypothesis demonstrates that macroeconomic policies are supposed to ensure distributive justice and equal access to benefit when there is presence of both human sociality and a struggle for a public society.

The continuous struggle of people for a public society is an important yardstick of enforcing a contract between state and citizen. At the same time, prosocial behaviour and reciprocity among human beings suggests that humans maintain strong sociality, which posits the possibility of establishing an equitable society and citizen-state. Prosocial behaviour involves citizens helping other members of society even at their own expense. This behaviour arises when citizens believe that they are a part of the community (Twenge et al.,

Table 5.8 Human sociality and struggle for public society determining the nature of policies

	Human sociality	*Absence of human sociality*
Aspiration and struggle for a public society	Policies ensuring equitable distribution of wealth and benefit	Discrimination
Absence of struggle for a public society	Clientelism, discrimination	Coercion, clientelism, rent-seeking, primitive accumulation, exploitation, exclusion

Source: Prepared by the author

2007). The presence of both the aspiration for a public society and human sociality ascertains the equitable distribution of wealth and benefit in a society. The aspiration for a public society can lead to discrimination towards certain groups in the absence of human sociality. If citizens do not aspire to a public society then political groups get bolstered, giving rise to clientelism. An absence of both leads to policies purporting exploitation and exclusion (Table 5.8).

Politics is linked with state policies like spending in social sectors, particularly in developing countries. It is both the formal and informal institutions that shape policies like social protection in developing countries. For instance, in Africa, social protection measures see a positive change at election time. However, this is true for countries with democratic representation. A lack of active citizenship enables political elites to grab much of the benefits from social policy measures in developing countries (Hickey, 2008). The patron–client relationship in less democratic countries results in the elite groups designing policies that lead to the exclusion of vulnerable groups (Brock, McGee & Ssewakiryanga, 2002). In Uganda, the absence of a contract between the ruling regime and citizens in Northern Uganda arguably informs the tendency to deal with the high levels of chronic poverty in that region through piecemeal social funds that are further diluted by the politics of patronage (Hickey, 2008).

In Bangladesh, a much wider range of actors and organisations, including non-state NGOs and informal community-level institutions, supranational organisations, International Financial Institutions (IFIs) and international donors, has been seen to be contributing to social policy inputs than has been seen in conventional welfare regimes. Similarly, the welfare strategies used represent a wider range of formal and informal welfare strategies (Davis, 2001).

Customs and social institutions also provide social protection in Bangladesh. Memberships of social groups such as kinship groups and community come with a range of entitlements that tend to provide social protection during crises. There exists the culture of Zakat, fitra, gifts, loans and help with medical expenses from a range of both formal and informal actors in the economy and society (Davis, 2001).

Although the proportion of foreign aid in overall government expenditure has reduced, the importance of foreign aid in meeting social protection measures should not be underestimated. Many observers conclude through evidence that aid has rather reduced domestic resource mobilisation and has reinforced political associations that exasperate external dependence (Sobhan, 1998). The issue here is a lack of political connection between welfare funding and those towards whom the fund is targeted. The state becomes the sole controller of these funds and thus this enhances the scope of clientelism and other corrupt practices in a state that is susceptible to corruption. Thus, no amount of discussions about participation can supplant the need for in-practice democracy and the devolution of aid management power away from the state and to the local beneficiaries or their representatives.

Moreover, the Community leaders may use the obtained power for personal gain and enhance own resources through corrupt practices. The informal hierarchies inhibit action against such malpractices. Thus, this makes the bottom-up approach to aid distribution problematic, since the leaders or representatives such as Union Parishad chairpersons can use the social hierarchies for their personal gain and to benefit other clientelist interest groups (Davis, 2001).

Reducing inequality during the pandemic

COVID-19 has caused a distinct type of shock in the sense that it consists of both demand-side and supply-side shocks. This has led to humanitarian and economic crises, creating a situation where conventional macroeconomic policies are turning out to be inadequate. Macroeconomic policy should work in harmony with the policies and measures of social protection, urban management, public communication etc. (World Bank, 2013). Developing countries also face the issue of a limited fiscal capacity and thus must identify priority areas for best utilisation of the finances. A government may resort to a higher fiscal deficit depending on its national income and fiscal space. If the deficit is too expensive under the current conditions, a budget-neutral reallocation of funds should be done based on pragmatism (Figure 5.11).

Inequality is expected to rise due to the pandemic as mentioned in the third chapter of this book. Fiscal policies do have the capability to widen the gap between the richest and poorest class. Economic redistribution has drawn renewed interest amid the pandemic. Developing countries in particular face income erosion, job losses, unemployment, decreased social spending and fragile health sectors.

The fiscal measures taken by governments during the pandemic fall broadly into two categories. Firstly, governments have initiated fiscal stimulus packages. These are short-term measures to tackle immediate shocks from the economic loss. The stimulus includes a wide range of measures varying from individual paycheques to relief packages for businesses. Compared to the financial crisis of 2008–2009, developed countries announced stimulus packages worth 9.73 percent of GDP, as opposed to 2.63 percent in 2008–2009; on the other hand, developing countries that disbursed a stimulus package of 4.62 percent of GDP in 2008–2009 announced packages worth only 5.46 percent of GDP in the

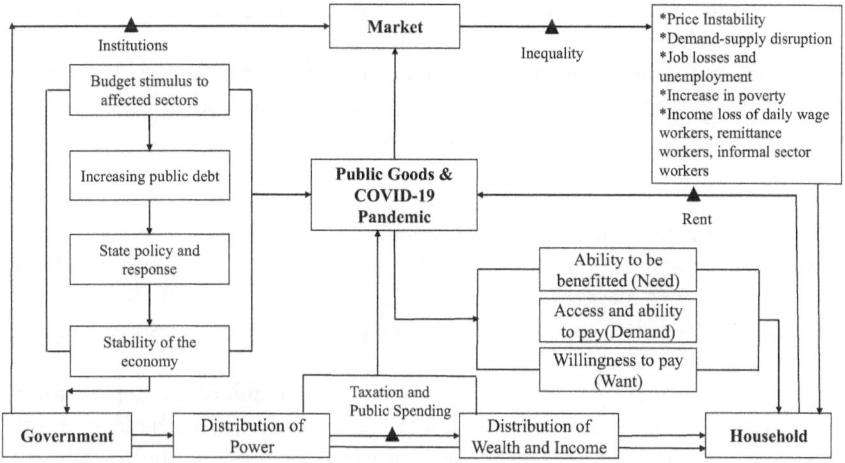

Figure 5.11 COVID-19 and equality. Source: Prepared by the author

post-pandemic period (Carpentier et al., 2021). Developing countries, with their limited fiscal space, have provided citizens with individual benefits similar to those of developed countries. The Bangladesh government announced a stimulus package worth 11.90 billion USD in the first phase (Ministry of Finance, 2020b). These stimuli have gone to different sectors of the economy which suffered from the pandemic, including the agricultural sector, the ready-made garments sector and small and micro industries.

Secondly, governments have taken recovery measures to cope with long-term shocks from the pandemic. These measures are reflected in government budgeting. For instance, social sectors will require increased spending in the next few years as the pandemic has dealt a heavy blow to the health and employment sectors. Hence, there will be increased spending on the health sector in the coming years. Government revenue will also fall due to the shrinking economy. As a result, taxation policies will also see a change in economic redistribution.

Finally, a government may also rely on grants and low-interest (concessional) lending from agencies (particularly for low-income countries). The practices of macroeconomic stability must still be maintained even during the ongoing crisis. For this reason, inflation causing finance for public deficit is not advised. Also, reallocation should not ignore basic public services and/or government accountability. Macroeconomic policies to deal with the crisis can be divided into relief measures, recovery policies, and international coordination (Loayza & Pennings, 2020).

Many economists are planning a slow opening of the economy post-pandemic. The question that arises here is how the economy can be catapulted and aggregate demand stimulated towards growth (Furman, 2020). Given the limitation of the monetary and fiscal policies due to the debt burden, unconventional policies are being pushed. The German government has announced an unfathomable stimulus package of 130 billion Euro. A very unexpected fiscal policy measure is the form of changes in VAT rates to stimulate future sales tax and spending at impact. Germany planned a reduction in VAT rates from July 2020 until December of the same year. This will increase households' expected inflation in 2021 and thus stimulate the demand by households in 2020 until prices rise again. A similar effect may be obtained by suddenly announcing increases in future VAT rates without reducing tax rates. Both stimulate households in a similar way, although they have varying implications for the government budget (D'Acunto, Hoang & Weber, 2020). This unconventional approach has been designed to help the European crisis during the Great Recession.

It is clear that the impact of Keynesian policy will be different in an economy facing lockdown and in an economy not facing a lockdown. In the former, the demand for all goods by the entire spectrum of people belonging to different income groups needs to be maintained. The small size of fiscal stimulus may thus sound less impactful, but one must remember that there is also a supply-side issue that has arisen from the lockdown. If enough relief is provided to the poor and middle income sectors from the sectors producing non-essential items, this will likely generate demand from them for the essential items. Given that there is close to full employment in the essential items–producing sector, this sector may not be provided with stimulus if demand is maintained along with supply (Singh, 2020).

Income-support policies alone cannot solve the economic crisis during a pandemic. A direct fiscal stimulus may result in a negative shock in the economy as a health crisis will also affect the supply of goods. This can also result in prolonging the financial crisis (Baldwin & Mauro, 2020). Some policies that intend to stimulate demand can be formulated now in order to stimulate demand later.

Monetary policies may not work in developing countries during the crisis. The interest rates in developing countries are not determined by the market, hence any intervention to control the rates will not work. The capital market is either not fully formed or functioning to the extent that it will stimulate the market (Mishra, Montiel & Spilimbergo, 2012). The flexibility of prices in developing countries weakens transmission policies. This is more serious in countries with high inflation (Klenow & Malin, 2010). Monetary policy has less effect in such scenarios. Hence, fiscal policy is more preferred in developing countries. However, the smaller fiscal multiplier may reduce the overall effect of fiscal policies (Ilzetzki, Mendoza & Végh, 2013; Kraay, 2012).

Fiscal policies can only influence the economy when the investments made are utilised in time. It is extremely important that policies are implemented during the crisis, rather than after the crisis. Developing countries have a tendency to delays and long planning, which reduces the efficiency of the projects

(Leeper, Walker & Yang 2010; Ilzetzki, Mendoza & Végh, 2013; Huidrom et al., 2019).

Tax exemptions can be relatively less effective in the context of developing countries. This is due to the existence of a large informal sector. For example, a tax exemption on income will not benefit a low-income informal sector worker. This makes such tax exemptions less equitable. Countries with low tax collection capacity may not be equipped for a fiscal stimulus. This is because the stimulus will create a greater rise in debt than in revenue, and thus there may be a risk of crowding out other important investments necessary for development.

While the costs of debt-financed stimulus have been reduced by all-time low interest rates in developed countries, borrowing costs are rising in developing countries since investors are moving towards safer assets. Since the start of the pandemic, investors have withdrawn more than USD 83 billion from emerging markets, the largest outflow ever recorded (IMF, 2020). A temporary fiscal stimulus can become permanent due to a country's weak fiscal institutions. This happened to some Latin American countries after the global financial crisis (Celasun et al., 2015).

A very vital question is how the additional expenditure due to the crisis will be financed. A textbook answer is that the government should borrow rather than increase taxes (Blanchard & Johnson, 2013). This is because taxes reduce purchasing power in the private sector. But is it the same in the case of a lockdown? Since the upper income class cannot spend on non-essential items anyway given the lockdown, a tax increase will not reduce purchasing power more than lockdown already has. Thus, imposing a tax is unlikely to reduce the aggregate demand of the economy (Singh, 2020).

Conclusion

This chapter identified an alternative framework consisting of mechanisms that together affect the income distribution in a country. Fulfilment of people's aspirations for equality requires the identification of forces responsible for worsening conditions of inequality and the employment of tools to counter them. Moreover, there is no single strategy that governments can apply to achieve the objective of economic redistribution. For that purpose, the state needs to decide on the stats of tax progressivity and redistribution and adopt the policy tools referred to here within the concept of the welfare state.

Fiscal policy is considered to have significant effects both on micro-decisions of economic agents and on aggregate economic activity. As fiscal policy is to a large extent a consequence of political and not only economically based decisions, it is difficult to model this field of economic policy, which by definition is very complex and has important distributional dimensions. It is generally accepted that the effects of fiscal policy depend to a large extent on the instrument used. In general, multipliers associated with changes in spending and, within that, in targeted transfers are higher than those related to tax cuts.

On the other hand, the multipliers associated with tax cuts are much higher than spending multipliers.

The major strategies available to policymakers are strengthening of the position of labour, through, among other things, a commitment to ensuring full employment, ensuring equal opportunity or participation in productive activities and a progressive tax system, along with some form of redistributive social safety net. Finally, for acceptance, feasibility and sustainability, class and the welfare regime need to be taken into consideration.

The current COVID-19 pandemic is posing a different type of shock. The effects are massive and highly contagious, affecting both demand and supply and leading to human and economic crises. In this context, macroeconomic policy cannot be restricted to conventional measures. It should work in order to achieve the equal distribution of responses in terms of emergency support from governments. Along with complementary policies in social protection, urban management, public communication and financial and goods markets, a whole-of-government approach to deal with the health emergency posed by COVID-19 is the need of the hour. Bringing the shocks of the pandemic to a minimum level and recovering the economy from the catastrophic effects of shutdown should be the main target of the government when implementing fiscal policy. Providing fiscal stimulus to the most affected sectors, marginalised groups and vulnerable entrepreneurs is the main focus of the governments of the developing states in order to bring stability to the economy.

Increasing public expenditure as well as targeting healthcare as the most vital sector to fight the pandemic should be the major concern of policymakers. Public goods are essential for the economic growth of developing countries. Therefore, investing in public goods, tax reliefs and consolidated fiscal policy can be strong tools for the government to build up resilience in the economy amid the COVID-19 pandemic.

Furthermore, this chapter has argued that public goods, while provisioned through the market, do not work effectively and cannot reach the public. The current situation of the pandemic has proved this statement already. The low efficiency of social protection systems in developing countries and low public expenditure on essential public goods like education and health make developing countries more vulnerable to the crises like this. The alternative framework shown in this chapter is concerned with changing the traditional approaches in the developing states as, without this, economic growth and state-building cannot be possible in developing states given that the capability of adjusting to shocks is very low. Thus, state policies are to be made and implemented that favour the public in these countries, focusing on the equal distribution of income and wealth along with a major focus on public goods.

References

Aaron, H. J. (2015). *Can Taxing The Rich Reduce Inequality? You Bet It Can! Economic Studies at Brookings*. Washington, DC: The Brookings Institution.

Achenbaum, W. A. (1988). *Social Security: Visions and Revisions: A Twentieth Century Fund Study*. Cambridge University Pres, New York.

Alvaredo, F., Chancel, L., Piketty, T., Saez, E., & Zucman, G. (2017). *The Elephant Curve of Global Inequality and Growth*. Working Paper.

Alvaredo, F., Chancel, L., Piketty, T., Saez, E., & Zucman, G. (Eds.) (2018). *World Inequality Report 2018*. Belknap Press.

Atkinson, A. B. (2013). Reducing income inequality in Europe. *IZA Journal of European Labor Studies*, 2(12), 1–11. doi:10.1186/2193-9012-2-12

Atkinson, A. B. (2014). After Piketty? *The British Journal of Sociology*, 65(4), 619–638.

Atkinson, A. B., & Stiglitz, J. E. (2015). *Lectures on Public Economics: Updated Edition*. Princeton University Press.

Baldwin, R., & Weder di Mauro, B. (2020). Introduction. In R. Baldwin & B. Weder di Mauro (Eds.), *Mitigating the COVID Economic Crisis: Act Fast and Do Whatever It Takes* (pp. 1–24). Center for Economic Policy and Research. Washington, DC: CEPR Press.

Barro, R. J. (1999). *Inequality, Growth, and Investment*. NBER Working Paper No. 7038. National Bureau of Economic Research, Cambridge, MA.

BBS. (2019). *Final Report on Household Income and Expenditure Survey 2016*. Dhaka, Bangladesh: Bangladesh Bureau of Statistics.

Blanchard, O., & Johnson, D. R. (2013). *Macroeconomics*. Essex: Pearson.

Brock, K., McGee, R., & Ssewakiryanga, R. (2002) *Poverty Knowledge and Policy Processes: A Case Study of Ugandan National Poverty Reduction Policy*. IDS Research Paper. Brighton, UK: Institute of Development Studies.

Buchanan, J. M. (1976). Taxation in fiscal exchange. *Journal of Public Economics*, 6(1–2), 17–29.

Byron, R. K. (2009). Boon for tax-dodgers, bane for taxpayers. *The Daily Star*, 18 June.

Brown, C. (2005). Is there an institutional theory of distribution? *Journal of Economic Issues*, 39(4), 1–17.

Carpentier, L. C., D'Alelio, D., Zuccolo, B. C., Combe, O., & Landveld, R. (2020). Unprecedented COVID-19 stimulus packages are not being leveraged to accelerate SDG investment. Geneva. Switzerland: UNCTAD. https://unctad.org/news/unprecedented-covid-19-stimulus-packages-are-not-being-leveraged-accelerate-sdg-investment accessed on July 12, 2021

Celasun, O., Grigoli, F., Honjo, K., Kapsoli, J., Klemm, A., Lissovolik, B., Luksic, J., Moreno-Badia, M., Pereira, J., Poplawski-Ribeiro, M., Shang, B., & Ustyugova, Y. (2015). Fiscal Policy in Latin America: Lessons and Legacies of the Global Financial Crisis. IMF Staff Discussion Note No. 15/06, International Monetary Fund, Washington, DC.

Clasen, J. (2005). *Reforming European Welfare States Germany and the United Kingdom Compared*. New York: Oxford University Press.

Credit Suisse. (2019). *Global Wealth Databook 2019*. Zürich: CS, 120.

D'Acunto, F. Hoang, D., & Weber, M. (2020). Unconventional fiscal policy to exit the COVID-19 crisis. *Vox. CEPR Policy Portal*. June 8.

Davis, P. R. (2001). Rethinking the welfare regime approach: The case of Bangladesh. *Global Social Policy*, 1(1), 79–107.

Deininger, K., & Deininter, P. (2000). *Asset Distribution, Inequality, and Growth*. Policy Research Working Paper No. 2375. The World Bank, Washington, DC.

Eißel, D. (2014). Inequality and the role of redistributive policy. In D. Eißel, E. Rokicka, & J. Leaman (Eds.), *Welfare State at Risk: Rising Inequality in Europe*. Cham: Springer.

Eißel, D., Leaman, J., & Rokicka, E. (2014). Introduction. In D. Eißel, E. Rokicka, & J. Leaman (Eds.), *Welfare State at Risk: Rising Inequality in Europe*. Cham: Springer.

Esping-Andersen, G. (1996). *The Three Worlds of Welfare Capitalism*. Cambridge, UK: Polity Press.

Faridy, N., & Sarker, T. (2011). Incidence of Value Added Tax (Vat) in the developing countries: A case in Bangladesh. *International Journal of Trade, Economics and Finance*, 2(5), 437.

Furman, J (2020). Protecting people now, helping the economy rebound later. *VoxEU.org* , 31 May.

Galbraith, J. K. (2001). The distribution of income. In R. P. F. Holt & S. Pressman (Eds.), *A New Guide to Post Keynesian Economics*. New York: Routledge.

Gerdes, C., & Gerdes, C. (1977). The fundamental contradiction in the neoclassical theory of income distribution. *Review of Radical Political Economics*, 9(2), 39–64.

GoB. (2014). *The Millennium Development Goals: Bangladesh Progress Report 2013*. Dhaka, Bangladesh: General Economics Division (GED), Planning Commission, Government of the People's Republic of Bangladesh.

Goodin, R. E. (1988). *Reasons for Welfare The Political Theory of the Welfare State*. Princeton, NJ: Princeton University Press.

Goodin, R. E., Headey, B., Muffels, R., & Dirven, H.-J. (1999). *The Real Worlds of Welfare Capitalism*. Cambridge, UK: Cambridge University Press.

Handler, J., & Hasenfeld, Y. (2007). *Blame Welfare, Ignore Poverty and Inequality*. Cambridge.

Hein, E. (2014). *Distribution and Growth after Keynes: A Post-Keynesian Guide*. Cheltenham, UK: Edward Elgar Publishing.

Hickey, S. (2008). Conceptualising the politics of social protection in Africa. In *Social Protection for the Poor and Poorest* (pp. 247–263). London: Palgrave Macmillan.

Holmwood, J. (2014). Beyond capital? The challenge for sociology in Britain. *The British Journal of Sociology*, 65(4), 607–618.

Hopkin, J. (2014). The politics of Piketty: What political science can learn from, and contribute to, the debate on capital in the twenty-first century. *The British Journal of Sociology*, 65(4), 678–695.

Huber, E., Pribble, J., & Stephens, J. D. (2009). The politics of effective and sustainable redistribution. In A. Estache & D. Leipziger (Eds.), *Stuck in the Middle: Is Fiscal Policy Failing the Middle Class*. Washington, DC: Brookings Institution Press.

Huidrom, R., Lim, J., Kose, A., & Ohnsorge, F. (2019). Why do fiscal multipliers depend on fiscal positions? *Journal of Monetary Economics*, 114(C), 109–125. doi:10.1016/j.jmoneco.2019.03.004

Ilzetzki, E., Mendoza, E. G., & Végh, C. A. (2013). How big (small?) are fiscal multipliers? *Journal of Monetary Economics*, 60(2), 239–54.

IMF. (2020). *The Great Lockdown: Worst Economic Downturn Since the Great Depression*. Washington, DC: International Monetary Fund.

Inman, R. P. (1996). *Do Balanced Budget Rules Work? US Experience and Possible Lessons for the EMU* (No. w5838). National Bureau of Economic Research.

Jones, G. A. (2014). Where's the capital? A geographical essay. *The British Journal of Sociology*, 65(4), 721–735.

Karoly, L. A. (1996). Trends in income inequality: The impact of, and implications for, tax policy. In J. Slemrod (Ed.), *Tax Progressivity and Income Inequality*. New York: Cambridge University Press.

Kato, J. (2003). *Regressive Taxation and the Welfare State*. New York: Cambridge University Press.

Kurian, N. (2005). The Swedish welfare state and new challenges. In B. Vivekanandan & N. Kurian (Eds.), *Welfare States and the Future*. New York: Palgrave Macmillan.

Kus, B., & Fan, W. (2015). Income inequality, credit and public support for redistribution. *Intereconomics*, 50(4), 198–205.

Klenow, P., & Malin, B. (2010). Microeconomic evidence on price-setting. In B. Friedman and M. Woodford (Eds.), *Handbook of Monetary Economics 3A* (pp. 231–284). Elsevier, Amsterdam.

Kraay, A. (2012). How large is the government spending multiplier? Evidence from world bank lending. *The Quarterly Journal of Economics* 127(2), 829–887.

Kristal, T. (2010). Good times, bad times: Postwar labor's share of national income in capitalist democracies. *American Sociological Review*, 75(5), 729–763.

Leeper, E. M., Walker, T. B., & Yang, S. C. S.. (2010). Government investment and fiscal stimulus. *Journal of Monetary Economics*, 57, 1000–1012.

Loayza, N., & Pennings, S. M. (2020). Macroeconomic policy in the time of COVID-19: A primer for developing countries. *World Bank Research and Policy Briefs*, (147291). World Bank Group, Washington D.C.

Lewis, D. (2011). *Bangladesh: Politics, Economy and Civil Society*. New York: Cambridge University Press.

McLaughlin, E. (2006). 'Pseudo-democracy and spurious precision': Knowledge dilemmas in the new welfare state. In C. Glendinning & P. A. Kemp (Eds.), *Cash and Care Policy Challenges in the Welfare State*. University of Bristol: The Policy Press, Bristol.

Mello, L. d., & Tiongson, E. R. (2006). Income inequality and redistributive government spending. *Public Finance Review*, 34(3), 282–305.

Mestrum, F. (2009). Why we have to fight global income inequality. In M. Kohonen & F. Mestrum (Eds.), *Tax Justice Putting Global Inequality on the Agenda*. London: Pluto Press.

Ministry of Finance. (2020a). *Bangladesh Economic Review 2020*. Government of People's Republic of Bangladesh.

Ministry of Finance. (2020b). *Socio-Economic Development in Bangladesh & Stimulus Packages to Combat COVID-19*. Government of People's Republic of Bangladesh.

Mishra, P., Montiel, P., & Spilimbergo, A. (2012). Monetary transmission in low-income countries: Effectiveness and policy implications. *IMF Economic Review* 60, 270–302.

Nardi, M. D., Fella, G., & Yang, F. (2016). Piketty's Book and Macro Models of Wealth Inequality. Chicago Fed Letter, No. 352: Federal Reserve Bank of Chicago.

Norton, M. B., Sheriff, C., Blight, D. W., & Chudacoff, H. (2011). *A People and a Nation: A History of the United States, Volume II: Since 1865*. Cengage Learning.

Olivera, J. (2015). Preferences for redistribution in Europe. *IZA Journal of European Labor Studies*, 4(14), 1–18. doi:10.1186/s40174-015-0037-y.

Oxfam. (2018). *Reward Work, Not Wealth*. Oxfam Briefing Paper. Oxfam, United Kingdom.

Oxfam. (2020). *Fighting Inequality in the Time of Covid-19: The Commitment to Reducing Inequality Index 2020*. Oxfam, United Kingdom.

Pasinetti, L. L. (2000). Critique of the neoclassical theory of growth and distribution. *BNL Quarterly Review*, 53(215), 383–431.

Patnaik, P. (2015). Capitalism and inequality. *Agrarian South: Journal of Political Economy*, 4(2), 153–168.

Piachaud, D. (2014). Piketty's capital and social policy. *The British Journal of Sociology*, 65(4), 696–707.

Piketty, T. (2014). *Capital in the Twenty-first Century*. Cambridge, MA: Harvard University Press.

Piketty, T. (2015). Capital and wealth in the 21st century. *National Tax Journal*, 68(2), 449–458.

Piketty, T., & Saez, E. (2007). How progressive is the U.S. Federal Tax System? A historical and international perspective. *Journal of Economic Perspectives*, 21(1), 3–24.

Planning Commission. (2021). *Social Security Policy Support Programme*. Planning Commission, Government of People's Republic of Bangladesh.

Pressman, S. (2005). What is wrong with the aggregate production function? *Eastern Economic Journal*, 31(3), 422–425.

REHAB. (2012). *A Comprehensive Study on the Real Estate Sector of Bangladesh.* Dhaka, Bangladesh: Real Estate and Housing Association of Bangladesh (REHAB).

Reza, S. (1989). The black economy in Bangladesh: Some preliminary observations. *Savings and Development*, 13(1), 23–43.

Roden, D. (1974). Regional inequality and rebellion in the Sudan. *Geographical Review*, 64(4), 498–516.

Rodríguez, F. (2004). Inequality, redistribution, and rent-seeking. *Economics & Politics*, 16(3), 287–320.

Saez, E. (2017). Income and wealth inequality: Evidence and policy implications. *Contemporary Economic Policy*, 35(1), 7–25.

Sarkar, J. U. (2011). 27 Millionaires in 10 Years. *The Daily Samakal*, 16 February (translated from Bengali).

Sen, A. K. (1963). Neo-classical and Neo-Keynesian theories of distribution. *Economic Record*, 39(85), 53–64.

Singh, G. (2020). Covid-19: Getting the fiscal policy right. *Ideas for India*. June 26.

Smith, T. B. (2004). *France in Crisis: Welfare, Inequality, and Globalisation since 1980.* New York: Cambridge University Press.

Sobhan, R. (1998). "How Bad Governance Impedes Poverty Alleviation in Bangladesh", OECD Development Centre Working Papers, No. 143, OECD Publishing, Paris, https://doi.org/10.1787/466441620275.

Solaiman, S. M. (2014). Laws whitening black money for boosting national economy: Prevention or legalisation of corruption in Bangladesh? *Journal of Money Laundering Control*, 17(2), 141–165.

Solaiman, S. M. (2016). Black money, "white" owners, and "blue" tenants in the Bangladesh housing market. *Journal of Financial Crime*, 23(2), 501–526.

Soskice, D. (2014). Capital in the twenty-first century: A critique. *The British Journal of Sociology*, 65(4), 650–666.

Stiglitz, J. E. (2015). *The Price of Inequality: How Today's Divided Society Endangers our Future.* Paper presented at the Sustainable Humanity, Sustainable Nature: Our Responsibility, Proceedings of the Joint Workshop 2–6 May 2014, Extra Series 41, Vatican City.

Swenson, P. A. (2002). *Capitalists Against Markets: The Making of Labor Markets and Welfare States in the United States and Sweden.* New York: Oxford University Press.

Thomas, E. (2015). *South Sudan: A Slow Liberation.* Zed Books Ltd, London.

Twenge, J. M., Baumeister, R. F., DeWall, C. N., Ciarocco, N. J., & Bartels, J. M. (2007). Social exclusion decreases prosocial behavior. *Journal of Personality and Social Psychology*, 92(1), 56.

Ulbrich, H. H. (2011). *Public Finance in Theory and Practice.* New York: Routledge.

Wade, R. (2011). Global trends in income inequality: What is happening, and should we worry? *Challenge*, 54(5), 54–75.

Waris, A., & Latif, L. A. (2014). The effect of tax amnesty on anti-money laundering in Bangladesh. *Journal of Money Laundering Control*, 17(2), 243–255.

Williams, M. (2001). Welfare state. In R. J. B. Jones (Ed.), *Routledge Encyclopedia of International Political Economy.* New York: Routledge.

World Bank. (2013). *World Development Report 2014: Managing Risk for Development.* Washington, DC: World Bank.

World Bank. (2020). *World Development Indicator.* Washington, DC: World Bank.

Zhou, M. (2016). *Labor's Share of Income: Another Key to Understand China's Income Inequality* (1 ed.). Singapore: Springer.

Zweimüller, J. (2000). Inequality, Redistribution, and Economic Growth. *Empirica*, 27(1), 1–20.

6 Monetary policy, growth and employment

Introduction

Most central banks around the world follow two major channels of operation: a stability-focused approach targeted at financial stability and inflation, and a broader target-focused approach, often directed at growth and employment in the economy. While a price stability-focused, inflation-targeting monetary policy has rapidly gained traction in many economies, the real effects of monetary policy on growth and employment remain unexplored for many developing countries. An inflation-targeting monetary policy is generally contractionary, which puts controls on money supply and interest rates. However, countries in Sub-Saharan Africa have experienced a constraint on domestic investment as a result of limiting domestic credit in order to contain inflation (Ndikumana, 2016). Restraining credit by increasing interest rates and decreasing money supply therefore restricts the expansion of productive capacity through technology acquisition in developing countries, thereby dampening the creation of employment and growth. As a more employment-targeting policy, the Reserve Bank of India mandated commercial banks to allocate a percentage of their lending portfolios to specific industries targeted by policymakers as key strategic industries which could benefit from directed credit and investment to generate more employment.

The chapter challenges the mainstream consensus of the money–inflation trade-off and the neutrality of money to present ways through which monetary policy exerts real effects on growth and employment in the long run. It recognises that growth requires a continuous flow of credit, and establishes additional channels through which monetary policy can augur credit to sectors that are crucial for long-term growth, employment creation and productivity augmentation. It does so in mainly three ways. It first re-examines different schools of thought regarding the use of Phillips curve. The argument that is put forward here is that a particular version of the Phillips curve has been promoted by the dominant narrative to establish the trade-off between inflation and employment, which, although not always appropriately, has further restricted the role of monetary policy in promoting national output. Additionally, there exists a considerable consensus in the literature that depicts how monetary variables

DOI: 10.4324/9781003201847-6

can be linked to long-term economic growth. It then establishes additional channels through which monetary policy matters. The first condition here to meet is channelling credit through discretionary policy to important sectors that are crucial for long-term growth, employment creation and productivity augmentation. The second condition is to fulfil capital market liberalisation in a way that supports rather than hinders the process.

Finally, the chapter analyses monetary policy in the context of developing countries during the economic shutdown, which put the financial sector under major strain. Finally, it discusses the particular fiscal–monetary policy combinations (known as the fiscal–monetary policy mix) that can reinforce long-term stability. In order to recover from the economic slowdown due to the COVID-19 crisis, the chapter determines monetary policy to seek to ensure that financial conditions are sufficiently accommodative to incentivise high capital investments and deficit-financed spending. The transmissions in such a context are driven by variations in wage and employment outcomes in the real economy.

In the literature, there seems a general acceptance that nominal variables (such as price level and inflation) can be influenced by monetary policy, but there is little agreement regarding monetary policy's ability to affect real variables (such as unemployment and real GDP). Additionally, the 1960s observed the rise of economists like Edmund Phelps and Milton Friedman, who came to argue that any trade-off that was earlier believed to be possible can only be short-lived, since as soon as people start to expect higher inflation, monetary policy ceases to produce unemployment below the long-term equilibrium (or natural) level (Lansing & Thalhammer, 2002). As explained by Espinosa-Vega (2002),

> the basis for this view is the assumption that the only way monetary policy can affect real economic activity is via "money illusion"–that is, by creating changes in the price level that are misunderstood by households and firms and cause them to make bad economic decisions. If monetary policy can affect real economic activity by means other than money illusion, then it may be possible for money to be non-super-neutral in the long run.

Following these changes, many countries have increasingly followed inflation control as the objective of monetary policy in the belief that monetary policy only has a limited impact on economic growth, especially in the long term. For example, although the number of inflation-targeting countries where monetary policy targets price stability as the sole or primary objective, and where a publicly announced numerical target for inflation has been announced, increased from 23 to 44, this remains an understatement of the new trend as price stability has become the main focus of many other central banks (Bhattacharyya, 2012). Moreover, the notion behind such a step is the idea that the growth impact of monetary policy will not be achievable without a low inflation economy (Stiglitz, 2010).

The use of monetary policy for the sake of long-term economic growth and employment creation is further complicated because of the interactions between the different target variables. For example, the objectives of economic growth and structural change in a developing country are supposed to be linked with price stability and external-sector balance (Hossain, 2009). It is also challenging to determine how any monetary policy would interact with fiscal policy to cancel out or reinforce their potential targets of growth and employment.

These theoretical positions of the mainstream economies impose serious limitations on the possibility of using monetary policy, especially in developing countries like Bangladesh, for growth and employment creation purposes. As these countries seriously lag behind their developed counterparts in terms of the effective management of the economy, leaving any policy options would be limiting their ability to promote growth, employment and state-building.

Monetary policies, growth and employment: A review

The dominant strand in the literature follows the conception of the neutrality of money in terms of the role of monetary policy in influencing long-term growth, employment and investment in the economy. The debate mainly involves whether an expansionary monetary policy does have an effect on growth. The groups here are strong supporters of no state intervention in the monetary arena in this manner. However, there exists some consensus in the economic literature supporting the concept of the non-neutrality of money in the long term; that the classical school believed in the non-neutrality of money is actually a partial or wrong representation of their position. In order to undertake a comprehensive review of the different schools of thought, this section categorises dominant and heterodox monetary theories as the sceptics, the relative optimists, the credit path and the capital control path.

The sceptics

A useful starting point regarding the role of monetary policy in economic growth could be the concepts of the neutrality and super-neutrality of money. The long-term neutrality postulate of money is linked to classical orthodoxy which, based on the classical quantity theory, states that changes in money supply affect only the price level and do not have any effect on real variables such as real output and employment. The classical economists believe that as relative prices are flexible enough to adjust, the markets for goods and labour are continuously in equilibrium. As a result, all resources are totally employed in the production process, and the economy stays at full employment level except with some brief deviations. Money in such an economy acts as a measure for value in which commodity prices are expressed. Thus, money only facilitates transactions and does not play any role in the determination of relative prices, real interest rates, the equilibrium level and, consequently, aggregate real income. Thus, money is neutral in terms of what is happening in the real economy (Papademos & Modigliani, 1990).

Later, monetarists attempted to add to the neutrality proposition of money by providing an explanation as to why any change in monetary policy would only have a short-lived impact on real economic activity (Espinosa-Vega, 2002). The tool used here to establish the monetary policy's non-effectiveness in the long-term determination of growth and employment is the Phillips curve. However, the Phillips curve used for this purpose is not the original Phillips curve developed by Phillips, but the one developed by P. Samuelson and R. Solow in 1960. Instead of representing the relationship between the rate of change in money wages and the rate of unemployment, the new curve represented a relationship between the rate of inflation and the rate of unemployment. In this way, the Phillips curve has become an instrument for policymakers that shows how much employment can be bought by a particular level of inflation (Frisch, 1983).

To elucidate monetarists' argument, an economy may start with an equilibrium whereby both prices and wages are stable. An expansionary monetary policy is applied that starts to grow nominal aggregate demand, which in turn produces a rise in prices and wages. Initially, workers would predict this as an increase, and firms would assume the same as an increase in their products sold. This would reduce the unemployment rate up to a certain period. After that period, however, a realisation would occur to both parties that the economy is actually experiencing higher inflation. As a result, they would revise their anticipated rate of inflation and expected wage rate upward and the level of production downward. Thus, the trade-off between inflation and unemployment would be short term (Friedman, 1975).

The inflation rate thus has two components: one anticipated and the other unanticipated. If output or employment has to be influenced by the growing money supply, the latter has to be increased constantly at an increasing rate. It is therefore only the unanticipated component that has a positive influence on unemployment as described by the Phillips curve. Therefore, at the rate in which inflation rate is fully anticipated, the economy is said to be in a steady state, and the corresponding unemployment rate is labelled by Friedman and Phelps as the "natural" rate of unemployment. In other words, it is the rate at which inflation arising from greater money supply is fully anticipated and thus produces no real effects (Frisch, 1983).

It is, however, difficult to set up an empirically reliable Phillips curve and a reliable estimate of the non-accelerating inflationary rate of unemployment, or NAIRU. NAIRU is defined as the theoretical rate of unemployment below which inflation would rise. For example, at times in the past, the US unemployment rate has been found to be lower than any NAIRU estimates. Nonetheless, the inflation rate showed no indication of acceleration. It is also reported that economists sometimes revise their NAIRU estimates downward to account for the sustenance of low unemployment rates along with low inflation, which raises an important question of reliability (Espinosa-Vega &

Russell, 1997). On the other hand, there is some empirical evidence, such as that of German inflation of the 1920s, where there were significant real effects of inflation on the real economy (Hall, 1982).

The idea of the neutrality of money was later extended by the neoclassical school. In this respect, the article of Lucas of 1972 is praised for setting the standards for neoclassical macroeconomics (Espinosa-Vega, 2002). In his paper, Lucas stated that:

> Information on the current state of these real and monetary disturbances is transmitted to agents only through prices in the market where each agent happens to be. … prices convey this information only imperfectly, forcing agents to hedge on whether a particular price movement results from a relative demand shift or a nominal (monetary) one. This hedging behaviour results in a non-neutrality of money, or broadly speaking a Phillips curve, similar in nature to that which can be observed in reality. At the same time, classical results on the long-run neutrality of money, or independence of real and nominal magnitudes, continue to hold.
>
> (Lucas, 1972)

Friedman and Phelps assumed that price and wage changes make economic agents take "bad" economic decisions (Frisch, 1983). On the other hand, Lucas (1973) argued that such a way of making decisions is still a process of efficient economic decision making, as people use the information available to them to make the best forecasts about the future. In other words, it was implicit in the argument of Friedman and Phelps that people have full information. Nonetheless, they fail to make efficient use of it. Alternatively, Lucas explicitly assumed that economic agents use all the information available to them as efficiently as possible when making economic decisions. But they do not always have access to all the information (Espinosa-Vega, 2002). Thus, in Lucas, the blame for any poor decision is placed on the shortage of information, which is more in line with the rationality hypothesis.

Neoclassical economists, however, point out in particular the fact that utilisation of inflation–unemployment trade-off to produce any real effects in the short term still involves great difficulty as "people might respond to government demand-management policy in ways that would frustrate the goals of the policy" (Espinosa-Vega & Russell, 1997). On the basis of an empirical study of real output–inflation trade-offs from 18 countries over the period 1951–1967, Lucas found that policies that are aimed at increasing nominal income will be likely to have a significant initial effect on real output and a smaller positive initial effect on inflation rate. For a rather volatile country such as Argentina, the nominal income difference is usually coupled with "equal, contemporaneous price movements with no discernible effect on real output" which are inconsistent with the Phillips curve. Contrarily, they believe that inflation will trigger real output, if only it "succeeds in 'fooling' suppliers of labour and goods into thinking relative prices are moving in their favour" (Lucas, 1973).

Unlike Friedman, authors pertaining to the "new consensus" or "new neoclassical synthesis" embrace the concept of a "vertical long-run Phillips curve", meaning that

> Although monetary variables play a role in the determination of the level of economic activity in the short run, they have no real effects in the long run. The basic role of monetary variables is to push the economy to its long run equilibrium, although they play no role in the determination of that equilibrium.
>
> (Kriesler & Lavoie, 2007)

Later, the pioneer thinkers of financial liberalisation, McKinnon (1973) and Shaw (1973), suggested that inflationary monetary policy and financial repression impede growth by depressing savings and diminishing the efficiency of investment. This was in contrast to the belief of inflationary finance that saving and investment are limiting factors of growth (Hossain & Chowdhury, 2000).

The relative optimists

The position of classical economists regarding money's role in the economy as presented in mainstream economics has been discussed in the previous section. However, among the classical economists, Humphrey (1991) studied those who are predominantly British and wrote during the period 1750–1870. Regarding the contention that those economists denied the idea that any change in money-stock has an impact on output and employment even in the short term, such understanding is incorrect. In his own words, ".the classical theory held that money affects output and employment certainly in the short run and perhaps to some extent in the long run too ... they identified at least nine reasons for the occurrence of such effects" (Humphrey, 1991). In other words, of the 11 prominent classical monetary theorists— Thomas Attwood, Jeremy Bentham, David Hume, Thomas Robert Malthus, John Ramsay McCulloch, James Mill, John Stuart Mill, David Ricardo, Henry Thornton, Robert Torrens and John Wheatley—at least 8 were found to reject the proposition that "money is always neutral and that continuous market-clearing and perfect wage-price flexibility prevail" (Humphrey, 1991). Similarly, Frisch opines that the views of classical economists such as Smith, Ricardo and Mill did not did not correspond to the idea of the neutrality of money (Frisch, 1983).

Keynes also held the same position. It is a common belief that Keynes proposed fiscal policy as the best method for maintaining full employment in an economy. Similarly, he relied on incomes policy to curb inflation. Keynes is well justified in his argument, as in his *General Theory*, he described a situation famously known as the liquidity trap, in which monetary policy becomes unable to further reduce the rate of interest, and therefore fails to stimulate demand. In this case, fiscal policy becomes the tool of choice for the authorities to produce any effect (Congdon, 2007). The empirical evidence is also in favour of Keynes's argument, as explained in Asimakopulos (1995): substantial increases in the money supply lead to higher interest rates because of their impact on expectations or anticipations. The monetary authorities were not authorised to manipulate the rate of interest by an expansion in the supply of money along an unaffected liquidity-preference function. The experience of very low and even negative real rates of interest in the period 1973–1980, as the rate of inflation surpassed the rate of interest, distorted bond markets. This wasted the capacity of the monetary authorities to regulate the rate of interest by increasing the supply of money. Therefore,

> it was not only the increase in uncertainty about the future mentioned by Keynes that shifted the liquidity function, but also the belief that substantial increases in the money supply would have inflationary consequences for the future that would lead to higher interest rates.
>
> (Asimakopulos, 1995)

Keynes, however, was not totally sceptical about the use of monetary policy. As is discussed in both the second chapter and the fifth chapter of his *General Theory*, Keynes linked money supply with both employment and inflation: if there is unemployment in the economy, an increasing money supply would generally reduce the unemployment level. This nevertheless does not represent the entire scenario. Certain cases, according to him, invalidated the application of monetary policy:

> For whilst an increase in the quantity of money may be expected, *cet. par.*, to reduce the rate of interest, this will not happen if the liquidity-preferences of the public are increasing more than the quantity of money; and whilst a decline in the rate of interest may be expected, *cet. par.*, to increase the volume of investment, this will not happen if the schedule of the marginal efficiency of capital is falling more rapidly than the rate of interest; and whilst an increase in the volume of investment may be expected, *cet. par.*, to increase employment, this may not happen if the propensity to consume is falling off. Finally, if employment increases, prices will rise in a degree partly governed by the shapes of the physical supply functions, and partly by the liability of the wage-unit to rise in terms of money. And when output has increased and prices have risen, the effect of this on liquidity-preference will be to increase the quantity of money necessary to maintain a given rate of interest.
>
> (Keynes, 1937)

The first formalisation of the Keynesian view of the ability of monetary policy to affect real economy in the long term was presented by James Tobin. Unlike his classical predecessors, but like Metzler, Tobin argued that monetary policy along with economic fundamentals defines real economic activity generally and real interest rates, particularly even in the long run (Espinosa-Vega, 2002).

Furthermore, demand management has important long-term supply-side effects with respect to both human and physical capital (Tobin, 1980).

Modern literature regarding the effects of money growth on any real variables in the economy starts with Tobin's paper of 1965 (Orphanides & Solow, 1990). The attempt was to explain the Keynesian difficulty of deviation between warranted and natural rates of growth arising from the "unwillingness of investors" to save because of unattractive rates of return on capital (Tobin, 1965). He argued that a community's willingness to save could be enhanced if there were other stores of value other than capital. The rate of return of these alternatives competes with that of capital. The minimal rate of return on capital (alternatively, a required rate of profit) therefore depends on these other destinations for saving. Monetary assets are considered important alternative stores of value in an economy, and it is their yields of these assets which are a key determinant of "acceptable rates of return on real capital and on the acceptable degree of capital intensity". If government can cause such a change, capital deepening can continue (Tobin, 1965). A higher inflation rate introduces a portfolio change from money to capital when asset demand for capital is determined not only by its own real rate of return, but also on the real return on the alternative available assets, known as the "Tobin effect" or the "Mundell effect" (Haliassos & Tobin, 1990).

Monetary policy and long-term growth: The credit path

This section argues that monetary policy can be effectively used to promote long-term growth and employment creation because of the presence of a credit route. To argue this position, it begins by putting money within the production function approach to growth accounting developed by Solow. Solow in his influential paper in 1957 deconstructed US growth over the period 1909–1949 to find that production function shifted upward at an average rate of about 1 and 2 percent per year for the first half and the second half of the period, respectively. This shift had brought about two times the increase in gross output per man hour over the period, of which 87.5 percent of which can be attributed to technical change while the remaining 12.5 percent to a greater use of capital. Finally, the technical change was on average "neutral" in nature, by which he meant shifts in the production function that left "marginal rates of substitution untouched but simply increase or decrease the output attainable from given inputs" (Solow, 1957).

Productivity is thus supposed to be "the key factor behind long-run economic" growth, and the primary driver of productivity is technological improvement. Moreover, it is also assumed that "technological change holds an endogenous component which makes it at least partly dependent on growth itself". Finally, technology is supposed to have a strong interaction "with investment in physical and human capital as well as with changes in historical, political and institutional settings" (Ark, Kuipers & Kuper, 2000). Solow's attempt was criticised by Stern first for using aggregate production functions for the above purpose, and second for leaving the key source of growth to be dependent on "exogenous" technical change (Stern, 1991). One major explanation for whether monetary and financial policies can promote growth comes from "whether they can induce technical progress and/or raise capital deepening" (Hossain & Chowdhury, 2000).

It therefore becomes important to look to a different class of models that attempt to explain the long-term growth rate of the economy endogenously, whereby technical progress occurs from sectors generating new ideas. In these models, the endogenous factor for growth is explained by how many resources are allocated to the productivity enhancing sector. The ideas from this sector may then have a spill-over effect on other sectors at zero cost. The optimal allocation of resources to this sector then would be allocated based on what is collectively beneficial for the society, which would surely be higher than what would be allocated by a free market economy at the equilibrium. Individuals would only invest in research as much as would be possible to make profit, therefore raising the necessity of government action such as government funding of research (Stern, 1991). Thus, these models open a place for monetary policy to play a long-term growth enhancing role.

Markets cannot automatically bring about the solution to technology problems. Economists since the time of Adam Smith have been questioning the respective ability of the free market and government regarding this issue, and for the neoclassical growth model, because of its reliance on the "assumptions of exogenous technology and full appropriation of investment", in terms of the government, the answer is a clear "no". Such a negative view of government however comes with a condition—it is the condition that the individuals are "far-sighted in their savings behaviour and take into account the well-being of" of the present as well as the future generations. "The equilibrium growth path will be socially efficient" (Grossman & Helpman, 1994) only under this condition. With Romer began the incorporation of research and development (R&D) theories and the idea of imperfect competition into the growth framework from the 1980s. In the new models, government research funding and granting of *ex post* monopoly power for the purpose of promoting technological advance results in a higher growth rate. If there is no predisposition for the economy to run out of ideas, the growth rate may remain positive in the long run (Barro & Sala-i-Martin, 2004). The rate of growth and the scope of innovative activity, nevertheless, may not be Pareto optimal because of "distortions related to the creation of the new goods and methods of production". Instead, the long-term growth rate relies on governmental interventions and initiatives, such as taxation, law and order, provision of infrastructure services, protection of intellectual property rights and regulations of international trade, financial markets and other aspects of the economy. The government thus encumbers the possibility for good or evil through its ability to influence the long-term rate of growth.

The problem with this new or endogenous growth theory, however, remains that it assumes that the capital/output ratio, or the amount of capital needed to produce one unit of output, remains constant. Furthermore, it makes the extremely limiting assumption that international production functions in all sectors are symmetrical in nature. Therefore, it does not take into account the growth-generating reallocation of labour and capital and thus fails to consider the process of structural transformation (Naqvi, 1996). Moreover, two other challenges exist for the above type of growth theory; that is, two factors may hinder market efficiency when growth is led by endogenous innovation. Firstly, efficiency will determine the marginal cost pricing, while innovation necessitates monopoly profits to be gained. Secondly, efficiency requires returns on investment to be fully appropriable, but spill-overs of knowledge will be inevitable (Grossman & Helpman, 1994).

Selective and other qualitative credit control measures enter as an important tool at this point as they can be used for capital accumulation, both human and physical, in the areas that generate subsequent increasing returns to scale. This comes in strict opposition to the present mainstream position:

> The focus on inflation means that the central bank should not be concerned with other goals such as promoting full employment, supporting industrial policy or allocating credit to sectors of special social need, such as housing … Using indirect tools of monetary policy means that central banks should not use credit allocation techniques such as subsidised interest rates, credit ceilings, and capital controls to affect the quantity or the allocation of credit. These tenets are promoted not only in developed countries, but also with great vigour in the developing world.
>
> (Epstein, 2007a)

In case of directed credit, the purpose is to "channel credit to priority sectors, groups or regions to support activities that are either considered to be socially beneficial, or inherently riskier, and borrower groups that are likely to be marginalised in the credit markets". The decision to exploit investment opportunities in such a manner has both efficiency and equity criteria as the theoretical justification—to equate social return of investment with that private return and to create a more equal distribution of resources (Kohli, 1997). Selective credit policies work to achieve two immediate objectives for authorities (Odedokun, 1987). By changing the direction of credit flow, they attempt to address credit market imperfections in the financial sector and commodity market imperfections in the real sector. Since markets in developing countries typically suffer from a "greater degree of credit and commodity market imperfections" than their developed-country counterparts, such policies are of greater significance in the former countries.

The complementary requirement of capital control path

To be successful, the policy of selective credit control has to be complemented by capital management techniques and the scrutiny of capital movement across countries. Since the 1980s, the opening of capital accounts went hand in hand with domestic financial market liberalisation in many countries (Ocampo, Spiegel & Stiglitz, 2008). It was mostly performed according to the recommendations of the wealthy nations whose ultimate goal was the total liberalisation of capital flows and the removal of all types of sharing of information about asset ownership among nations. This wave of liberalisation came with a broader reform of market controls from international organisations like the International Monetary Fund (IMF), the World Bank and the OECD—sometimes in connection with measures promoted by the latest economics knowledge (Piketty, 2014).

Attention to capital control is of special importance for the least developed countries, both "in absolute as well as relative terms" since capital flight "poses a threat to national solvency and economic growth perspectives" (Hermes & Lensink, 2001). Moreover, according to Pastor (1990), the objection to capital control by the IMF deserves special scrutiny since it is in contrast both to historical examples and to empirical evidence (Pastor, 1990).

As can be seen from various discussions, among the number of ways that capital account management benefits the economy, the focus is usually on growth, poverty reduction, technological benefits, employment generation and the removal of investment bottle-necks. The negative effect is usually supposed to occur through the instability in the output and employment and the fall in revenue from capital outflow. The state-building effect has always been overlooked. Along with directed credit programmes, capital control can affect state-building variables such as the creation of a new class and the building of new class consciousness. Moreover, providing credit at below the market rate faces challenges in terms of providing long-term benefits to the economy if its outflow is not checked. According to Epstein (2007b), consumer monetary theory (CMT), a framework for understanding the role of money in giving consumers access to the economy's output, can decrease the intensity of currency risk and thus permit authorities to safeguard a currency peg; they can make space for the government and/or the central bank to chase growth-promoting and/or reflationary macroeconomic policies by counterbalancing the danger of capital flight; by decreasing the risk of financial crisis in the first place, CMTs can diminish the possibility that governments may be bound to use contractionary macro- and microeconomic and social policy to be conducive to foreign investment; and finally, CMTs can also ease the threat of foreign control or ownership of domestic resources. It therefore "follows that capital management can enhance democracy by reducing the potential for speculators and external actors to exercise undue influence over domestic decision making directly or indirectly". CMTs can hence lessen "the veto power of the financial community and the IMF, and create space for the interests of other groups (such as advocates for the poor) to play a role in the design of policy". They can consequently be said to enrich democracy as they generate the "opportunity for pluralism in policy design" (Epstein, 2007b).

Trade and financial sector liberalisation increases capital flight by making the capital easier to move from one place to another. Rather, it is regulation that can put a limit on capital flight (Brada, Kutan & Vukšić, 2011). The approach taken by the IMF has helped little in this case. The IMF opted to solve the economic crisis in order to combat capital flight from debtor countries. In the process, the IMF ignored factors such as political instability, tax evasion and money laundering. Deflationary measures taken by countries also encouraged more illicit capital flows as capital accrued lower returns in the home country. The orthodox approach was also criticised for the failure to question whether the domestic elites should have had the right to move money abroad (Helleiner, 1995).

In this regard, it is reasonable to assume that capital flight, which occurs as individuals reallocate their wealth from domestic to foreign assets, comes in three basic forms. These include holdings made up of currency, savings in domestic banks or financial institutions and investments in real productive sectors or activity (Pastor, 1990). Thus, the signal that capital flight shows sometimes has to be understood. However, the unattractiveness of domestic alternatives is not the only reason behind capital flight. Often rapidly accumulated rent is also secured from state scrutiny through capital flight.

To solve debt crisis resulting from capital flight, economists like David Felix suggested that governments in debt capture citizens' foreign assets in order to service their existing debts or as collateral for further borrowing (Helleiner, 1995). However, this is not an easy task in the face of international disagreement, and prevention will always remain a better option than such cures. It is therefore suggested that in order to achieve economic growth, it is necessary to improve the information infrastructures, i.e., in terms of the legal, accounting and monitoring systems of banks. This is because if some countries possess better infrastructures than others, they will attract investments from the latter to the former, inciting a higher outflow of capital. In such cases, the latter countries—naturally developing countries—may fall into a poverty trap if a capital market integration is introduced (Sakuragawa & Hamada, 2001).

Moreover, in developing countries, money markets are mostly fragmented, and thus the impacts of monetary policy are narrowly incident. As a result, monetary policy is lower in effectiveness, aggravated by the deregulation of domestic financial sectors and capital account liberalisation. In order to correct these lapses, it becomes imperative for monetary policy to assume a broader set of objectives rather than just managing inflation and using interest rates as the only instrument. Allowing a broader space for monetary policy will develop financial markets, strengthen institutions and diversify the use of monetary tools and instruments, leading to a greater effectiveness of monetary policy in the real economy (Nayyar, 2011). At the same time, time and country-specific factors will have to be taken into consideration, as opening the capital account in the primary stages of development may harm developing countries and push them into greater impoverishment (Sakuragawa & Hamada, 2001).

Evidence linking credit and capital control with growth

Technological change in a country requires several additional conditions to be met, and selective credit policy has historically played an important role in all the areas. First, the provision of selective credit for technological catching-up requires prior identification of national interests and priority sectors. Second, coordination between firms and sectors remains of utmost importance so as to make such investment profitable. Third, technological up-gradation often requires large-scale investment. Fourth, risk reduction strategies have been undertaken in the face of the uncertainty associated with new technology.

While the first two of the above conditions involve the direction of funds, the third and the last one address how to determine the amount of funds to be directed and how uncertainty and risk is to be reduced. Country case studies and historical data comparison mostly show how monetary policy through selective credit policies has been effectively used to shape the type and path of economic activity in the long term.

The selection of technology to be transferred, especially for late-coming countries that lack sources to produce their own technology, has to occur according to each country's economic and social structure, technological capability and human capital (Tiryakioğlu, 2012). This step, however, is also crucial for countries that want to develop and upgrade their own technologies. Whether a country wants to produce its own technology and whether it wants to enable technology transfer, government banks can perform an important role, as was performed by Japanese government banks. First, government banks can provide loans at subsidised rates. Second, such loans can signal to the private banks which industries are in accordance with national priority, have potential and are relatively safe. Finally, government banks can investment in infrastructure related to loan-supported activities that have high productivity; these can enhance potential at the national level, but at the same time involve long gestation periods, and thus are not usually financed by private banks (Cargill & Yoshino, 2000).

In terms of providing signals about which industries are of national priority and at the same time increasing the attractiveness of those industries, selective credit can be of vital importance. An example in this regard is the Japan Development Bank (JDB), which provided long-term loans at less than the market rate to firms for pursuing the goals specified by the industrial policy. Instead of a direct government intervention into industrial activities, the industrial policy of Japan is based on indirectly leading private firms and influencing behaviour to achieve an outcome that is considered socially desirable. The role assigned to the Japan Development Bank in this regard was appropriate for the implementation of such indicative planning (Horiuchi & Sui, 1993).

Later, the difference of performance in Japanese machine-tools firms was attributed directly to differences in government credit: the key targets of the industrial policy plans in the 1960s and 1970s were machinery manufacturers. The Japanese government's intervention through the Ministry of International

Trade and Industry (MITI) has been crucial for this purpose. In 1956, MITI introduced the Extraordinary Measures Law for the Promotion of the Machine Industry to stimulate the machine tool industry to make its production processes more efficient, thereby strengthening its international competitiveness (Calomiris & Himmelberg, 1994). This was done according to the industrial policy of the late 1950s, which aimed at strengthening industries and/or stimulating the development of new production technology. Accordingly, the government passed a new law allowing policymakers the opportunity to intervene and provided financial facilities to those industries through the JDB's loans (Horiuchi & Sui, 1993).

Cooperation between firms and sectors is of the utmost importance. Cooperation often means working with government agencies as well as private-sector businesses. In continental Europe, for example, central banks historically played a very important role in the nineteenth century as lenders not only to the state, but also to industry. Virtually all European countries had then been facing different circumstances than those in England and in both North and South America. Compared to England, other European countries started their industrialisation process later and generally held the view that they needed state assistance in the catching-up process. Financial institutions, especially banks, were considered to be of crucial importance in the financing of industries. Therefore, the large universal banks with close connections with large-scale industry emerged there, which was essentially the Austro-German model. Moreover, the charters of several European central banks made it possible for them to conduct business with both the commercial banks and other customers. For example, both the Bank of France and the Reichsbank of Germany belonged to this category. Besides, the Bank of France, the Bank of the Netherlands and the Bank of Italy enjoyed an extensive branch network and close relationships with industrial customers. Even the loans of the Bank of the Netherlands still accounted for half of all bank loans to the industrial sector in 1900 (Capie, Goodhart & Schnadt, 2008).

Like its European counterparts, Japan pooled funds from postal savings, insurance and other such programmes to mainly fund what can be called diverse "strategically conceived programs" through the Fiscal Investment and Loan Program (FILP) (Calder, 1990). The Japanese government thus used policy-based financial institutions in the early 1950s as part of an official policy to provide long-term funds for industrial investment, infrastructure, housing and other purposes (Vittas & Kawaura, 1995). These included welfare objectives implicit in public savings with government efforts at industrial transformation, summarised in the notion of the developmental state (Calder, 1990).

The new application of technology, whether domestic or foreign imported, involves "substantial problems of adaptation and absorption" and requires both tangible and intangible investments. The neoclassical view takes technology and productive inputs and outputs as perfectly known. However, in the real world, this is not the case. It is actually the opposite—the "knowledge is not instantaneously and costlessly available to all firms" and entails investments in a wide range of skills, technological know-how and supportive organisational structures to initiate and run the whole process successfully (Archibugi & Pietrobelli, 2003). Because of the existence of asymmetric information between firms and their lenders (such as commercial banks), the cost of investment from external sources exceeds that of internal financing. This implies that financing constraints would be greater for an innovative and new firm compared to a mature and well-established one (Fazzari, Hubbard & Petersen, 1988; Leoni, 1997). Moreover, the payback period in technological investment involves a greater level of uncertainty, and even all investment could be lost despite the best efforts on the part of the entrepreneur. Such higher risk necessitates the presence of institutions that can enable risk-sharing, without which the entire responsibility of raising collateral for the investment as well as engrossing the entire loss falls on the entrepreneur. For investments of this kind, the projects are more likely to go forward if more investors decide to participate (Khan, 2010).

The positive impact of selective credit policies cannot be denied for the above cases. According to Werner (2002):

> There is a rich literature on the institutional details and role of credit directed by the Ministry of Finance's Fiscal Investment and Loan Program (FILP), which, among others, provides funds for subsidised credit by government financial institutions. However, government lending institutions account for less than 20 percent of all bank loans. A far more wide-ranging tool of official intervention in the credit market to direct funds exists in the form of credit allocation policies imposed by the central bank on the entire commercial banking sector … Despite its neglect in the recent literature, the direction of bank credit by the central bank has played an important role in Japan, as well as in Korea, Taiwan, India, Indonesia, Malaysia, and Thailand.

Abundant subsidised loans were provided to targeted industries by the National Investment Fund (NIF) in South Korea. Therefore, real bank interest rates were negative during most of the 1970s. The directed credit instrument of the government reached 41 percent and 51 percent of domestic credit in 1975 and 1978, respectively. In comparison, light industries like textiles were fiercely discriminated against in terms of credit provision and had to resort to more expensive sources (Kai-Sun et al., 2001). In comparing the experience of Korea with that of Mexico, a key factor was observed, showing that the different economic performance between the two countries is the result of the use of selective dynamic intervention (Aboites & Cimoli, 2005). For example, South Korea influenced the level and composition of non-competitive intermediate and capital goods by interventionist policies. South Korea used quotas, directed credits and targeting to select industries that had high foreign exchange earning potential through exports (Aboites & Cimoli, 2005). Selective credit policy thus can be used to carry out supporting activities conducive to the development and use of technology.

Similarly, after its establishment in 1951, the Japan Development Bank started lending to the development of the power sector, which it believes forms the basis of the economy and industry, and to the rationalisation, modernisation and cultivation of coal, steel, marine transportation and other major industries. During 1956–1965, the bank promoted energy and transportation activities so as to underpin the industrial infrastructure. The bank's focus shifted to industrial system improvements and independent technological development in the period 1966–1971 (Development Bank of Japan, 2016).

The importance of directed credit policies cannot be understood simply from the size of the directed credit programmes or the level of interest rates and subsidies, which often supersedes these aspects. as the Japanese example shows. During the early reconstruction and high growth era of Japan, industrial investments were mostly funded through policy-based finance. The percentage of this investment shrank as Japan drove towards industrialisation. From 31 percent in 1961, it fell to 7 percent in 1991. The programme though kept funding declining industries (Vittas & Cho, 1996).

The Japan Development Bank played a crucial role as it offered long-term credit at a lower interest rate than the market long-term prime rate to firms that were regarded to contribute to the objectives of the industrial policy. Between 1951 and 1960, four key industries, constituting electric power, marine shipping, iron and steel and coal, received almost 77 percent of the total loans from JDB (Horiuchi & Sui, 1993).

Furthermore, small firms often face more difficulty in terms of financing than their larger counterparts. In India, large and small firms faced different environments regarding financial constraint. While large firms were able to finance their new investments from external sources at the margin, this cost was higher for small firms (Eastwood & Kohli, 1999). Research by Gertler and Gilchrist (1991) reveals that such an outcome is also possible in the context of an advanced country, the United States, where a restrictive monetary policy was followed by a fall in bank lending to small firms while that to large firms increased. Moreover, small firms observed a decline in their sales at a faster pace than their large counterparts. In such cases, directed credit policies can help in the growth of these firms.

Additionally, support for industries did not only mean that specific sectors were provided with a special fund. It also meant hindering speculative and unimportant sectors from receiving loans. In Japan, for example:

> In particular, the Bank of Japan had considerable leverage in discouraging city banks from lending for speculative purposes, such as real estate development, or for lending to the household sector for housing finance or consumer credit. It is perhaps not surprising that Japanese banks engaged in substantial direct and indirect lending for housing and real estate purposes in the 1980s when they were no longer dependent on Bank of Japan funds for financing their loans and the moral suasion of the authorities carried less weight.
>
> (Vittas & Kawaura, 1995)

Bank loans have been also used to achieve multiple economic and social objectives in different countries. In terms of the use of indicative planning and administered credit as industrial policy instruments, post-war France was the first country to take this approach, and it was soon followed by a second wave of industrialising continental countries in Europe such as Spain and Greece. Apart from the above objective, some European countries used selective credit instruments in the post-war decades for meeting the objectives of combining development with social redistribution: interregional redistribution and the development of the periphery in Italy, Spain, France and Greece; the subsidisation of low-cost housing construction, especially in Scandinavia; and financial support for agriculture and the small business sector in most of Europe (Pagoulatos, 2003). In Greece, selective credit policies have been used along with industrial and tax policies to direct the creation of an entrepreneurial class, plan and direct business life and watch over the course of economic development (Pagoulatos, 2003).

In the history of the United States, there was a huge expansion of banks after 1812 and there had been numerous bank failures by 1830 (Chown, 2005). Many of the banks, which were from the southern and western states, were encouraged by the governments to finance large quantities of farm credit by issuing convertible notes. The move towards freeing banking laws reflected the desire to reform the chartering process in the direction of free entry under the Jackson and Van Buren Administrations (Martin Van Buren, who was elected president in 1836, had been Jackson's vice president). The term "free banking" however is incorrect, as the free banking of that period was not in any sense laissez-faire or unregulated banking. The standardised charters that were accepted by the states imposed numerous and relatively strict restrictions on the banking sector: on their capitalisation and reserves, the conditions of note issue and the types of assets banks could hold (Russell, 1991).

As opposed to the fight in the United States between the private banks and the central banks as well as between the federal government and states regarding their respective rights, "the role of the central bank in helping, through monetary means, to reinforce national unity and identity was generally seen as one of its positive and important functions" in most of Continental Europe and Russia. Moreover, the establishment of a united and standard currency system and the creation of nationwide payment systems and clearing-houses were not only important and valuable on their own, but also key to the nation-building process, especially in Germany and Italy (Capie, Goodhart & Schnadt, 2008).

It has to be understood that the reality of rapidly growing countries in their early days are different from the late growers. Moreover, countries that have used selective credit policies in the past to ensure a long-term steady growth path sometimes resort to greater markets as their financial markets became more capable. However, they still use selective credit policies from time to time. According to Vittas and Cho (1996), markets that exist in the early stages of development are often imperfect or missing, and private institutions may be poorly structured; any intervention from the government may assist in promoting healthy economic growth. On the other hand, during later stages, as markets become more sophisticated, such benefits from government intervention reduce considerably (Vittas & Cho, 1996).

As can be seen from the history of the central bank of England, the bank introduced a system of quantitative ceilings and requests to control the volume of bank lending to the private sector, especially in the 1960s, to supplement its control over short-term interest rates. Although these policies were initially applied to the clearing banks, starting from 1965 they were broadened to include alternate institutional channels, including other banks, discount houses and finance houses, in an effort to regulate the flow of credit to the private sector. Among the objectives of this policy were to permit the financing of central and local government borrowing and nationalised industry at lower interest rates than would have been possible in a free financial system, and to escape any negative implications that high interest-rate levels could have on domestic income distribution.

Selective credit policy, likewise, has different potential under differing institutional systems. In France, selective credit policy is a primary instrument of the state in industrial territory. In Germany, selective credit measures are implemented by the banks in the long-term interests of German industry, but the state plays only a very insignificant role. In Sweden, selective credit measures play a crucial role in covering finance, but they mostly have been avoided for industrial purposes (Reuss, 1981). Selective credit discounting was abandoned in Spain in 1971 and replaced with compulsory credit coefficients that required banks to allot a certain percentage of their deposits as lending to targeted sectors at pre-determined lending rates, often with some leeway (Perez & Westrup, 2010).

Hodgman's review of attitudes towards and experience with credit controls in six west European countries since the Second World War identified that experience of credit controls has been motivated by a variety of purposes. These objectives have been to finance government debt at lower interest rates; keep a check on private-sector credit so that domestic interest rates do not rise and the country attracts foreign funds, allocating resources to priority uses; "block channels of financial intermediation" "by impeding a rise in velocity" "to assist a restrictive general monetary policy"; and strengthen public support for price and wage controls "holding down interest income to credit granting institutions and private investors" (Hodgman, 1973).

Central banks in the post-war United States, Europe and Japan have used a variety of means to help direct credit to preferred sectors to support a number of social and economic goals. Among those means include asset-based reserve requirements, loan guarantees, support for pooling and underwriting small loans and utilisation of the discount window in support of labour-intensive industries. In asset-based reserve requirements, the central bank or government assigns lower requirements to preferred assets, thereby creating an incentive for banks to hold those types of assets relative to less desirable assets. Another important instrument is to create a loan guarantee programme for banks that lend to certain types of activities, such as cooperatives and small businesses that create employment. Another way of using the directed credit programme is to provide the opportunity for liquidity and risk-sharing to institutions (Epstein, 2007b).

Experience with capital account movement

Although capital market liberalisations are supposed to bring foreign investment into the reforming countries and brought about significant economic gains, such attempts to remove monetary policy rules from the capital market has important negative implications for growth and state-building in developing countries. As far as capital account liberalisation is concerned, it has been argued by Cobham (2001), based on the results of a number of papers, that for developing countries, the net benefits of capital account liberalisation have not been recognised, and thus that it can be concluded that these rarely exist for relatively poorer countries. As a result, this conclusion stands in contrast to the pre-conceived notion that any country that follows the right policies and establishes the right institutional and supervisory standards will enjoy the benefits (Cobham, 2001). Similarly, the time-series study of Durham found in a study based on four countries, Nigeria, Zimbabwe, India and Pakistan, that either the Foreign Direct Investment (FDI) or Foreign Private Investment (FPI) will adversely affect growth or savings, while two other countries, Uganda and Sri Lanka, suggest a positive relationship. On the other hand, the findings for Kenya, Zambia and Bangladesh demonstrate a more ambiguous association. The predominance of adverse impacts is mostly consistent with the conception that lower income countries have insufficient "absorptive capacity" to utilise foreign investment (Durham, 2000). Thus, even after disregarding the instability arising from capital flight, the real effects of capital account liberalisation on the key economic variables are not robust. Pastor (1990) previously associated capital flight with growth costs, tax-base erosion and the worsening of income distribution in Latin American countries in the 1970s and 1980s.

Without some sort of capital control, the creation of new class and class consciousness suffers. The experience of Pakistan in this regard is a clear example. In the 1960s, Pakistan established financial intermediaries as a major channel of industrial finance. The major role was played by the government-owned Industrial Development Bank of Pakistan (IDBP) and the privately owned Pakistan Industrial Credit and Investment Corporation (PICIC) as a source of long-term lending.

Other institutions, such as the Investment Corporation of Pakistan (ICP), the National Investment Trust (NIT) and their mutual funds, as well as insurance companies, also acted as important sources of finance (World Bank, 1970). The government created new enterprises and thus absorbed the risk of failure. Subsequently, when the project became profitable, they sold the enterprises to the capitalist class (Khan, 1999). Later, however, it was observed that Pakistan's capitalist class increased their personal wealth at the expense of the common people, and 22 of them became industrial barons within a period of less than two decades. Their ownership accounted for about 66 percent of industry, 97 percent of insurance and 80 percent of banking. There had also been some reports that they possessed more than Rs 300 crores worth of foreign exchange in foreign banks, concealed from the government (Farooqi, 1972).

Capital control along with selective credit use has a long history in the real world. Its successful use can be traced back to the period after the Second World War, when the central banks under government direction utilised a variety of credit allocation techniques, accompanied mostly by measures of capital and exchange controls on international capital movements to accomplish the rebuilding and restructuring of national economies and providing for social needs (Epstein, 2007a). According to Pastor (1990):

> Historically, however, developing countries with capital controls have tended to exhibit lower levels of capital flight (for example, South Korea). Four of the five low-flight countries in our sample—Brazil, Chile, Colombia, and Peru—are reported to have had at least creaky exchange controls through most of the period. Meanwhile, Argentina, Mexico, and Venezuela, free of the "impediments to social welfare" imposed by capital controls, literally haemorrhaged resources throughout the same period.
>
> (Pastor, 1990)

Similarly, in the case of China, despite significant capital flight, experts pointed out that the case may have been much more severe in the absence of the capital management techniques that were involved. Moreover, these capital management policies had enabled China to implement an expansionary monetary policy against the significant deflationary pressures in the economy (Epstein, Grabel & Jomo, 2008). It has never been a choice between no movements of capital versus complete opening of capital control without any kind of supervision. For instance, China levies control on capital, such that foreign nationals are not allowed to invest freely in the country. These controls, however, have not limited the rise of capital accumulation owing to domestic savings, such as in the case of Japan, South Korea and Taiwan (Piketty, 2014).

Monetary policy and growth: A new framework

The key elements of money growth, capital and employment as discussed in the previous sections and the relationship defined between them forms the groundwork for the alternative framework proposed in this chapter. The alternative framework is based on the virtuous cycle leading from lowering interest rates to productive expansion and capacity utilisation, which eventually results in a rise in effective demand, creating new employment opportunities. The link between the variables is strengthened by case studies of the failure of four economies that undertook inflation-targeting monetary policies with no subsequent improvements in employment levels. The transmission mechanism of the monetary policy to the creation of employment and growth begins with lowering interest rates, which incentivises investment in technology to increase due to the relatively lower costs of borrowing from banks (Figure 6.1). Aggressive technology acquisition resulting from increased investment will lead to capital formation, which will result in the expansion of productive capacity, as explained in Chapter 4. A higher productive capacity will ensure firms can achieve capacity utilisation and redistribute rents between profits and wages. An increase in wages is likely to augment liquidity for buyers, encouraging more spending in the form of effective demand. Finally, the rise in effective demand will lead to the creation of employment in the economy. In addition, parts of the process, such as productive capacity expansion, rise in effective demand, employment creation and its multiplier effects will lead to a significant upsurge in growth.

Monetary policy consists of pathways or transmission mechanisms in which the employment-targeting monetary policy is likely to be beneficial by utilising the institutions in the financial sector and money market. Apart from the inflation-targeting frameworks, the new framework addresses the links between institutions in the money market and central bank that govern the transmission mechanism of money, leading to a virtuous or vicious cycle (Figure 6.2). Money is transferred from the central bank to the money market, which then flows to the credit market. Firms avail of long-term loans and working capital from the credit market in order to finance costs and investment in technology acquisition. The returns to labour and capital flow to households, which in turn put money back into the credit market through savings deposits and investment in the capital market. The Securities and Exchange Commission oversees the transmission channels through regulation and controls that introduce compulsion and discipline into the circular flow.

Monetary policy and productivity

Monetary policy induces growth through capital formation and the productive expansion of the economy by technology financing. Monetary policy is supposed to generate capital formation. The more the capital forms, the more the growth occurs (Figure 6.3). The hypothesis is that the nature of monetary policy needs to be such that it helps capital formation and technological financing, which contributes to greater growth in the economy. When capital formation in an economy is accelerated, it results in an increase in growth, demonstrated by an upward sloping curve that reaches a plateau as the economy nears its maximum productive capacity with the existing labour and capital. Capital formation is generated by the monetary policy through the credit channel (Figure 6.2). Therefore, greater domestic credit is likely to shift the point P on the curve to Q (Figure 6.3).

At the same time, through financing technological acquisition and advancement, monetary policy prompts productivity. The increased amount of capital formation results in more investment in technological acquisition and productivity growth, which leads to higher growth performance of the economy. This relationship can be further solidified by regressing both capital formation

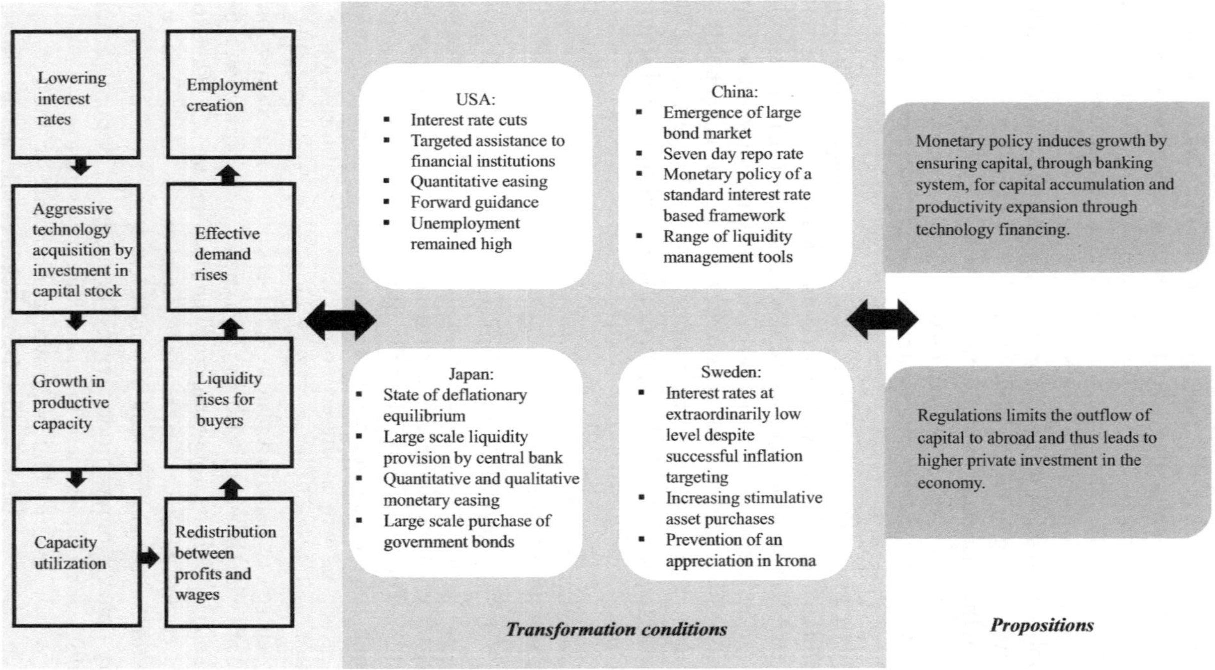

Figure 6.1 Preparation of the Alternative Framework. Source: Prepared by the author

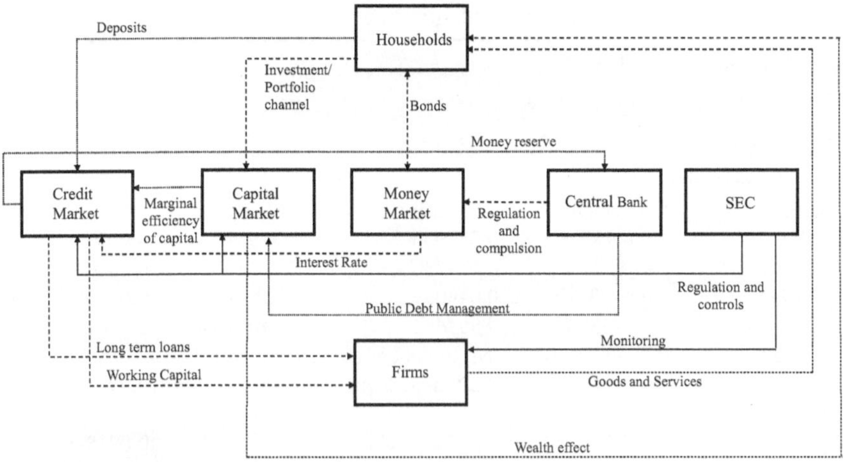

Figure 6.2 Alternative Framework. Source: Prepared by the author

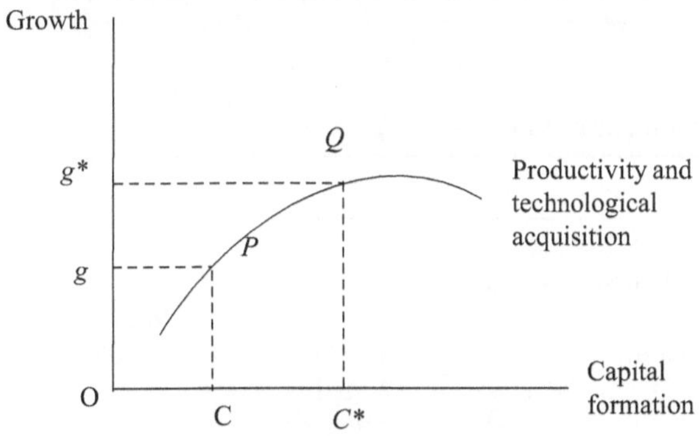

Figure 6.3 Capital formation, growth and productivity. Source: Prepared by the author

and inflation on interest payments in order to find whether a long-term relationship exists between the variables (Table 6.1).

A regression was undertaken on interest payments for gross capital formation and inflation in the United States during the period 1972–2018. Interest payments and gross capital formation are taken in their log form and the inflation rate given by the Consumer Price Index, including a deterministic time trend in the time-series equation. Unit roots have been tested using Augmented Dickey-Fuller statistics, and all variables are integrated of order 1, or in other words, in first difference form. An ordinary linear regression was run, showing capital formation to have had a more than proportional positive change in interest payments over time (Table 6.1).

Table 6.1 Time-series regression of capital formation and CPI on interest payments

Dependent Variable: LINTPAY
Method: Least Squares
Date: 04/01/20 Time: 17:14
Sample: 1972–2018
Included observations: 47

Variable	Coefficient	Std. error	t-Statistic	Prob.
LCAPFOR	1.040909	0.357636	2.910526	0.0057
CPI	0.181997	0.021730	8.375411	0.0000
@TREND	−0.350831	0.048061	−7.299695	0.0000
C	−8.036594	9.884654	−0.813037	0.4207
R-squared	0.944097	Mean dependent var		25.85326
Adjusted R-squared	0.940197	S.D. dependent var		0.994717
S.E. of regression	0.243254	Akaike info criterion		0.091846
Sum squared resid.	2.544422	Schwarz criterion		0.249305
Log likelihood	1.841622	Hannan-Quinn criter.		0.151099
F-statistic	242.0650	Durbin-Watson stat		0.449513
Prob(F-statistic)	0.000000			

Source: Author's calculation

Table 6.2 Engle Granger Test for residual term

Null Hypothesis: RESID02 has a unit root

Exogenous: None
Lag Length: 0 (Automatic—based on SIC, maxlag = 9)

		t-Statistic	Prob.*
Augmented Dickey-Fuller test statistic		−3.627331	0.0005
Test critical values:	1% level	−2.616203	
	5% level	−1.948140	
	10% level	−1.612320	

Source: Author's calculation
*MacKinnon (1996) one-sided p-values.

An Engle Granger Test carried out on the residual term of the regression shows that the residual does not have a unit root in its level form with no intercept or trend (Table 6.2). As a result, the variables of the regression are thus cointegrated, that is, there exists a long-term relationship between them. A Johansen Cointegration test further reinforced this conclusion.

Regulations and investment

Regulations limit loan defaults and outflow of capital abroad and thus lead to higher private investment in the economy. Strict enforcement of rules and

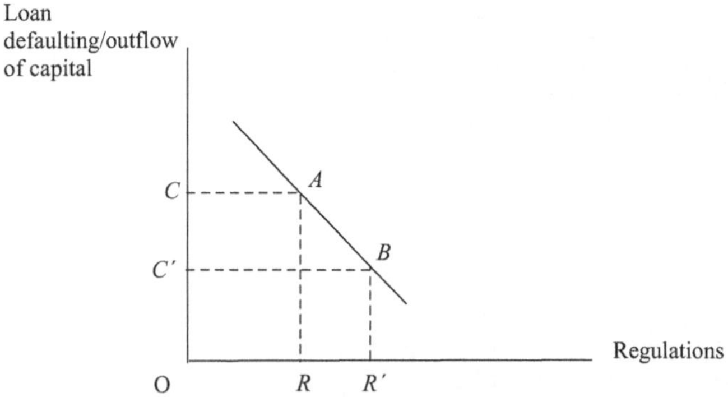

Figure 6.4 Regulations limiting irregularities in the economy. Source: Prepared by the author

regulations reduces the risks in the financial sector. There is an inverse relation between regulations and irregularities in the economy (Figure 6.4). The hypothesis proposes that the enforcement of regulations through monetary policy can effectively check irregularities, i.e., loan defaulting and capital flight in the economy, which results in the productive expansion of the economy and new employment generation. In the absence of adequate, stringent regulations *R*, loan defaulting and illicit capital outflows remain high at *C*, thereby resulting in a less desirable outcome, *A*. When regulations are made more stringent and compulsive, *R'*, loan defaults and capital outflows will decrease from *C* to *C'*, leading to a more desirable outcome at *B*.

The stronger the enforcement of regulations, the lower the occurrence of loan defaults in the banking sector or the case of capital flight. Checking capital flight and loan defaults leads to more investment in the economy, which results in productive expansion and new employment creation. This may be proved through a cross-country analysis of the stringency of regulations regarding illicit capital outflows. This is undertaken by analysing the capital flight scores for each country in relation to their polity index and competitiveness scores for a measure of regulation and discipline (Table 6.3).

The analysis of regulation and discipline may be computed using competitiveness scores, percentages of illicit capital outflows and polity scores across Asian countries. According to the figures (Table 6.3), China has a relatively higher competitiveness score, albeit with a high capital flight percentage as well, whereas India has a relatively lower competitiveness score but also a lower capital flight score. The key difference between the two countries is their respective polity score. China has a much worse polity score (−7) than that of India (9). This therefore implies that countries with better regulation reflected in higher polity scores will be less likely to have high capital flight percentages.

Table 6.3 Cross-country analysis of capital flight

Countries	*Competitiveness index*	*Capital illicit outflows*	*Polity index*
Malaysia	5.23	13.3	5
China	4.89	8.6	−7
Thailand	4.64	9.9	−3
Indonesia	4.52	7.9	9
India	4.31	7.8	9
Vietnam	4.3	7.5	−7
Sri Lanka	4.21	9	6
Cambodia	3.94	7.6	2
Nepal	3.85	10.2	6
Bangladesh	3.76	7.2	1

Source: WEF 2015, Global Financial Integrity, 2019

COVID-19 crisis and monetary policy

COVID-19 has had broad-based adverse effects on domestic consumption, with a plunge in confidence indicators as financial frictions and uncertainty pertaining to the scope and the extent of fiscal transfers and targeted funding schemes have exacerbated recessionary fears. Economically, the synchronicity of interest-rate cuts, asset purchases, money market operations and fiscal policy should re-engineer a faster recovery. While a recovery is inevitable amidst global clouds dispersed by monetary accommodation and crisis-centric fiscal policy, it hinges on the extent of a recovery in terms of domestic consumption and fixed business investment. It can be argued that fiscal transfers and unemployment insurance will sustain demand for household goods and consumer products.

Meanwhile, it is widely expected that deferred spending will serve as an anchor for a consumption-driven economy; this is argued against a V-shaped recovery given the circumstances for two reasons. Firstly, small and medium-sized enterprises who furloughed workers are unlikely to rehire them once the lockdown ends; additionally, the gradualist approach through which countries remove social distancing suggests that some business in the service sectors, such as those servicing events, might take slightly longer to recover as virus fears prevent large gatherings in the very short term. Admittedly, one cannot discount the socioeconomic implications of consumption-driven social activity, which suggests that risks of a recovery, faster than suggested, are evenly balanced. Secondly, some businesses will rely on part-time workers in the near term or freelancers due to the uncertainty over the elimination of social distancing methods. The salience of these arguments hinges on differing outcomes from COVID-19 and investments in the healthcare sectors (Kouam, 2020).

A mechanism for providing cash support to firms and households facing losses and income erosion in the face of the pandemic was to channel eased credit through the banking sector. The discrepancies in rates of allocation and disbursement of stimulus to the various groups was discussed earlier. Now, an analysis of the monetary sector will help gain insight into the extent of the credit support availed of by firms and households. Despite the provision of the stimulus package, monetary expansion in the economy was stifled. Cash entered the banking system to provide eased credit to firms in distress, but a significant share of the available credit support was not availed of. As a result, money did not reach firms and households, but rather was left in the banks, leading to an excess liquidity situation in the domestic credit sector.

Monetary expansion has been subdued. The growth of domestic credit has been sluggish, particularly as both public and private investment opportunities looked bleak in the rising uncertainty of the pandemic. The growth rate stood at 8 percent, significantly below the targeted 14.8 percent declared by Bangladesh Bank. Investors and borrowers remain relatively disenchanted in increasing private-sector investment, despite lending rates being at a record low of 5–7 percent. Simultaneously, public sector borrowing stalled due to slower project implementation. In addition, complexities in investment conditions for small depositors and investors and low and middle-income groups have largely hindered the flow of credit. As a result of these three conditions, the channelling of domestic credit into the eventual monetary expansion of the economy was deterred (Unnayan Onneshan, 2021).

Several business-as-usual measures were adopted in using the monetary policy to correct the fallouts from the pandemic that targeted industries and real sectors. These included lending policy relaxation and injecting fresh money into the banking system to increase the flow of domestic credit. However, the policies may have misjudged the inflow of remittances into the country. High rates of remittance deposits, coupled with the insertion of extra money, amidst curtailed options for spending and investment during the pandemic period left banks with excess liquidity. At the same time, remittances have increased foreign exchange reserves, flaring up the excess liquidity as Bangladesh Bank purchases dollars from the banking sector.

Apart from the year-end spike in December 2019, the excess liquidity in the banking sector maintained a steady, manageable level from the month of July 2018. Liquidity levels began to see a persistent increase, venturing much higher than the minimum liquidity required, from the month of June 2020 as the stimulus packages and national budget were announced, further fuelled by high inflow of remittances (Figure 6.5). The excess liquidity lying idle in the banks, with no mechanism of flowing out as credit and later retracted as savings deposits, pressurises interest rates to remain persistently low and impedes the profitability of banks.

In LDCs, incomes in informal employment eroded significantly. Around 68% of the informal employment has been affected significantly compared to only 15% in high income countries (Figure 2). The income of the informal workers is expected to decline by 60% globally, and 82% in low-income countries (ILO, 2021a). Informal employment is highest in the low-income

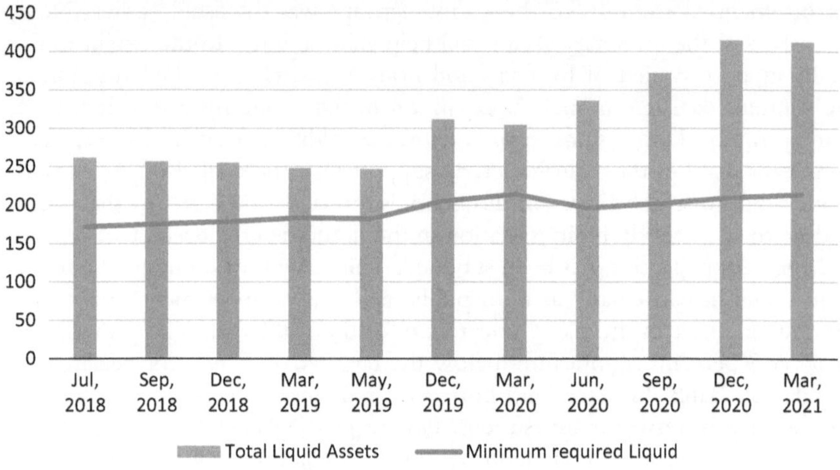

Figure 6.5 Excess liquidity assets in banks. Source: Bangladesh Bank, 2021

countries, 88% to be precise, compared to 25% in high income countries. Asia Pacific LDCs employ an average of 78.7% of their labour force in the informal sector, among which Bangladesh and Cambodia employ over 90% in the informal sector.

In order to promote inclusive growth policies to avert the K-shaped recovery path, priorities should be phased out gradually, targeting low-income populations, informal sector, and small and medium enterprises first, and then later on, delving into the pursuit of achieving inclusive and green recovery.

For economic recovery and mitigation of the divergence between countries, it is imperative to instituting a full-fledged universal life-cycle-based National Social Security System, particularly in view of the fact that the existing social safety net programmes are inadequate, ineffective and not universal, sometimes entirely seasonal or are devised on an ad hoc basis after disaster with a low coverage.

Economic recovery from COVID-19 calls for a concerted framework that harmonises the tools of both fiscal and monetary policies. The proposed policy framework highlights important instruments such as refinancing schemes for productive sectors, low interest rates and digital financing, which will aid the effectiveness of fiscal measures and targeted stimulus packages (Figure 6.6). In Bangladesh, for instance, the sectors that require dedicated assistance are agriculture, as farmers counted losses due to the shutdown of transportation to markets; small and medium-sized enterprises that employ a significant portion of the labour force; women entrepreneurs, due to the disproportionate impacts of COVID-19; and export-oriented industries such as readymade garments. The related institutions that should provide oversight and accountability in the policy processes are the central bank, other commercial and state-owned banks and Foreign Private Investment (NBFIs) (Figure 6.6).

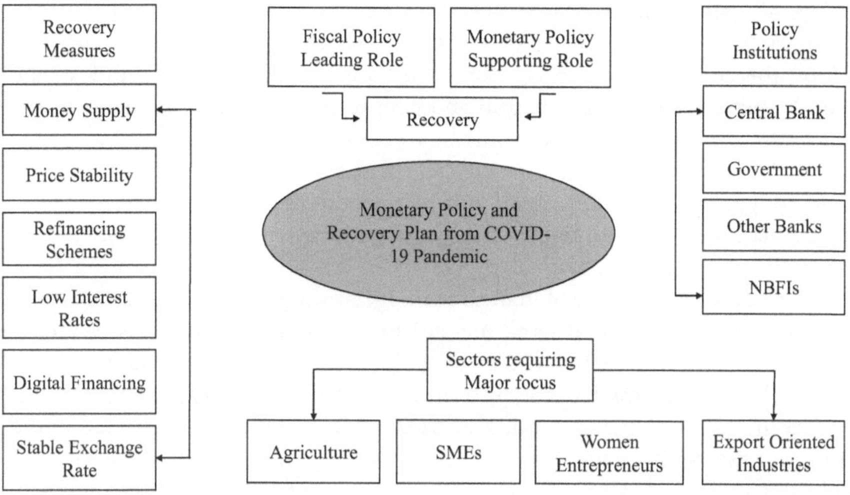

Figure 6.6 Policy framework for recovering from COVID-19 Pandemic. Source: Prepared by the author

Covid-19 pandemic resulted in significant reduction in the GDP of the global economy. The IMF projects that the global economy will shrink by 3 percent and that of Bangladesh by at least 4 percent (IMF, 2020). The government in the fiscal year 2019–2020 projected a growth rate of 8.15. In the budget for the fiscal year 2020–2021, the government significantly revised the number to 5.2 percent, an almost 3 percent decrease in GDP growth rate. The growth rate dampens the employment scenario of a country. As businesses shut down to prevent the spread of the virus, jobs were lost and as a result there was an income erosion in the economy. The role of the monetary policy was to put the economy back on track from the crisis.

In addition to the global economy, the pandemic has dismantled stability in developing economies as well. In Bangladesh, for instance, the COVID-19 crisis has dealt a massive blow to revenue collection by the government. Revenue collection may face a negative growth of 6 percent in 2020—2021 due to the economic shutdown. Revenue collected by the NBR in the first 10 months of 2019–2020 was BDT 62,000 crores less than the revised target due to economic halts and losses in real sectors as an impact of coronavirus. Tax collection was BDT 1, 73,797 crores in July–April of 2020 against a target of BDT 2, 35,796 set for the period (Unnayan Onneshan, 2020). Losses faced by businesses as well as income reduction due to the shutdown will result in lowered tax collection in 2020–2021 as well. VAT collection may also shrink due to low consumption spending. Revenue collection has been poor even for the last few years. Government expenditure has grown many times faster than revenue collection, resulting in a higher fiscal deficit (Unnayan Onneshan,

2020). The central bank must provide a larger financial package to vulnerable groups like micro-finance borrowers. Given that some banks' overexposure in the advance–deposit ratio and deposits to banks may not increase in the near future, the central bank can opt for a working capital taka loan window and need-based statutory liquidity ratio and cash reserve ratio requirements in the short term. Another objective would be to ensure stability in the exchange rate to avoid disruption in trade flows. A selective capital control measure to discourage speculative trading could also be introduced. For the maintenance of an adequate supply of foreign exchange, negotiations should be initiated with the IMF and other multilateral organisations for relief and suspension from debt servicing and additional grants for budgetary support.

Monetary policy should work in a certain way during a crisis. As seen during the financial crisis, when the financial institutions faced a liquidity crunch, that is when the central bank stepped in to ease the crunch. "Quantitative easing", a money supply augmenting instrument, was initiated to provide liquid money to the banks in order to overcome bankruptcy. Both the financial crisis and the pandemic have similarities as businesses suffer and job losses result in lower consumption expenditure and aggregate demand. The COVID-19 crisis or a pandemic is also very different from a financial crisis. During a pandemic, the shutdown of the economy for an indefinite period results in lower production and supply-chain disruption. The goal of monetary policy has to be different than that in a financial crisis, as during a pandemic, the central bank also needs to ensure the flow of credit from banks. Money supply increased through various instruments will benefit the economy only when the credit flow is directed by the central bank. Any deviation from the flow results in primitive accumulation and capital flight.

Monetary policy seeks, first, to ensure financial conditions are sufficiently accommodative to incentivise high capital investments and deficit-financed spending; the transmissions under such a context are driven by variations in wage and employment outcomes in the real economy. The latter determines the pass-through of monetary policy, via the real economy, to inflation.

Monetary policy achieves its mandate of an explicit inflation target or one with a variation band. The transmission from monetary policy and reserve management approaches to inflation operates via monetary and non-monetary targets. Monetary targets are driven by changes in the level of policy rates, which increase or reduce money supply. While lower interest rates cause banks to pay less for their deposits held at the central bank, they can transmit the perceived benefits of lower interest rates via the credit channel. Lending from businesses and corporations triggers investments in fixed assets and machinery, with additional employment created to utilise the infrastructure and transform inputs into outputs. For example, an apparel shop can borrow money from the bank to open a factory rather than import inputs from China or the United States in an attempt to reduce operating costs. The entrepreneur takes a loan from the commercial bank at favourable rates of interest and expands their manufacturing activity. This practice, in turn, creates further employment and higher incomes, which in turn support domestic consumption. The latter comprises of an increase in domestic demand, an anchor for a gradual increase in prices. Furthermore, inputs needed for the factory and the manufacturing process will place upward pressure on prices (Kouam, 2020).

In order to revive the economy, there is a need to reopen closed-down businesses. Such businesses will require capital, and the central bank has to ensure access to it. However, restoring the economy to the path of growth will depend on the ability to create new jobs. Hence, credit should flow towards new investments. Ensuring jobs and productivity will result in higher aggregate demand in the economy. The Bangladesh government has initiated various stimulus and recovery packages to ensure access to capital to the businesses that have suffered. The stimulus packages vary from the industrial sector to the agricultural sector.

The flow of credit to newer investment can open the door for diversification in the economy as new businesses may get the capital required, thus leading to a structural change.

Conclusion

Existing theories about monetary policy mostly posit that monetary policy only has a limited impact on economic growth, especially in the long run. Moreover, this impact is supposed to be delivered only through achieving a low inflation economy. This chapter, based on case studies and historical data comparison, argues that as opposed to monetarist beliefs, monetary policy can be effectively used to shape the type and path of economic activity in the long run. It can initiate diversification and structural change in the economy, especially through the credit channel. Additionally, the policy of capital management increases the state-building ability of the government.

The critique of the mainstream consensus concerning the money–inflation trade-off and the neutrality of money presents ways through which monetary policy exerts real effects on growth and employment in the long run. The long-term neutrality postulate of money is linked to classical orthodoxy which, based on the classical quantity theory, states that changes in money supply affect only the price level and do not have any effect on real variables such as real output and employment. Later, monetarists attempted to add to the neutrality proposition of money by providing the explanation as to why any change in monetary policy would only have a short-lived impact on real economic activity using the Phillips curve. This chapters finds from the works of writers who were predominantly British and wrote during the period 1750–1870, regarding the contention that those economists denied the idea that any change in money-stock has impact on output and employment even in the short run, that such an understanding is incorrect.

As a result, alterations in monetary policy can have real impact on employment and growth in the economy. The proposed framework, apart from the inflation-targeting frameworks, addresses the links between institutions in the money market and central bank that govern the transmission mechanism of money, leading to a virtuous or vicious cycle. The enforcement of regulations through monetary policy can effectively check irregularities i.e., loan defaulting and capital flight in the economy, which results in the productive expansion of the economy and new employment generation.

It then establishes additional channels through which monetary policy augurs credit to sectors that are crucial for long-term growth, employment creation and productivity augmentation. The chapter also analyses monetary policy in the context of developing countries during the economic shutdown, which put the financial sector under major strains. Finally, it discusses the particular fiscal–monetary policy combinations (known as the fiscal–monetary policy mix) that can reinforce long-term stability. In order to recover from the economic slowdown due to the COVID-19 crisis, the chapter determines that monetary policy seek to ensure financial conditions are sufficiently accommodative to incentivise high capital investments and deficit-financed spending. The transmissions under such a context are driven by variations in wage and employment outcomes in the real economy.

Finally, monetary policy induces growth through capital formation and the productive expansion of the economy by technology financing. Monetary policy is supposed to generate capital formation. The more capital forms, the more growth occurs. At the same time, through financing technological acquisition and advancement, monetary policy prompts productivity. The increased amount of capital formation results in more investment in technological acquisition and productivity growth, which leads to the higher growth performance of the economy. The nature of monetary policy needs to be such that it helps capital formation and technological financing, which contributes to increased growth in the economy.

Regulations limit loan defaulting and the outflow of capital abroad, and thus lead to higher private investment in the economy. Strict enforcement of rules and regulations reduces the possibilities of risk in the financial sector. There is an inverse relationship between regulations and irregularities in the economy. The stricter the enforcement of regulations, the lower the occurrence of loan defaults in the banking sector or cases of capital flight. Checking capital flight and loan defaults leads to more investment in the economy, which results in productive expansion and new employment creation. Therefore, it can be concluded that the enforcement of regulations through monetary policy can effectively check irregularities i.e., loan defaulting and capital flight in the economy, which results in the productive expansion of the economy and new employment generation.

References

Aboites, J., & Cimoli, M. (2005). Intellectual property rights and national innovation systems: Lessons from Mexico and Korea. In C. Lapavitsas & M. Noguchi (Eds.), *Beyond Market-Driven Development: Drawing on the Experience of Asia and Latin America*. New York: Routledge.

Archibugi, D., & Pietrobelli, C. (2003). The globalisation of technology and its implications for developing countries windows of opportunity or further burden? *Technological Forecasting & Social Change*, 70, 861–883.

Ark, B. v., Kuipers, S. K., & Kuper, G. H. (2000). Introduction. In B. v. Ark, S. K. Kuipers & G. H. Kuper (Eds.), *Productivity, Technology and Economic Growth* (pp. 1–17). New York: Springer Science+Business Media.

Asimakopulos, A. (1995). *Keynes's General Theory and Accumulation*. New York: Cambridge University Press.

Barro, R. J., & Sala-i-Martin, X. (2004). *Economic Growth*. Cambridge, MA: The MIT Press.

Bangladesh Bank. (2021). *Major Economic Indicators*. Dhaka, Bangladesh: Bangladesh Bank.

Bhattacharyya, N. (2012). *Monetary Policy and Employment in Developing Asia*. ILO Regional Office for Asia and the Pacific, Bangkok: International Labour Organization.

Brada, J. C., Kutan, A. M., & Vukšić, G. (2011). The costs of moving money across borders and the volume of capital flight: The case of Russia and other CIS countries. *Review of World Economics*, 147(4), 717–744.

Calder, K. E. (1990). Linking welfare and the developmental state: Postal savings in Japan. *Journal of Japanese Studies*, 16(1), 31–59.

Calomiris, C. W., & Himmelberg, C. P. (1994). *Directed Credit Programs for Agriculture and Industry: Arguments from Theory and Fact*. Paper presented at the Proceedings of the World Bank Annual Conference on Development Economics 1993.

Capie, F., Goodhart, C., & Schnadt, N. (2008). The development of central banking. In F. Capie, C. Goodhart, S. Fischer, & N. Schnadt (Eds.), *The Future of Central Banking: The Tercentenary Symposium of the Bank of England*. New York: Cambridge University Press.

Cargill, T. F., & Yoshino, N. (2000). The postal savings system, fiscal investment and loan program, and modernization of Japan's financial system. In T. Hoshi & H. Patrick (Eds.), *Crisis and Change in the Japanese Financial System* (pp. 201–230). New York: Springer Science+Business Media.

Chown, J. (2005). *A History of Money from AD 800*. New York: Routledge.

Cobham, A. (2001). *Capital Account Liberalisation and Poverty*. QEH Working Paper Series—QEHWPS70.

Congdon, T. (2007). *Keynes, the Keynesians and Monetarism*. Edward Elgar Publishing.

Development Bank of Japan. (2016). *Applying Financial Expertise to Design the Future*. Annual Report & CSR Report. Development Bank of Japan.

Durham, J. B. (2000). *Time-Series Econometrics of the Real and Financial Effects of Capital Flows: Selected Cases in Africa and Southern Asia*. QEH Working Paper: Queen Elizabeth House.

Eastwood, R., & Kohli, R. (1999). Directed credit and investment in small-scale industry in India: Evidence from firm-level data 1965–78. *The Journal of Development Studies*, 35(4), 42–63.

Epstein, G. (2007a). Central banks as agents of economic development. In H.-J. Chang (Ed.), *Institutional Change and Economic Development*. New York: United Nations University Press.

Epstein, G. (2007b). *Central Banks, Inflation Targeting and Employment Creation* Economic and Labour Market Papers. International Labour Office, Geneva, Switzerland: International Labour Organization.

Epstein, G., Grabel, I., & Jomo, K. S. (2008). Capital management techniques in developing countries: Managing capital flows in Malaysia, India, and China. In J. A. Ocampo & J. E. Stiglitz (Eds.), *Capital Market Liberalisation and Development*. New York: Oxford University Press.

Espinosa-Vega, M. A. (2002). How powerful is monetary policy in the long run? In J. Rabin & G. L. Stevens (Eds.), *Handbook of Monetary Policy*. New York: Marcel Dekker.

Espinosa-Vega, M., & Russell, S. (1997). History and theory of the NAIRU: A critical review. *Economic Review (Vol. Second Quarter): Federal Reserve Bank of Atlanta.*

Farooqi, M. (1972). *Pakistan: Policies that Led to Break-up*. New Delhi: New Age Printing Press.

Fazzari, S. M., Hubbard, R.G., and Petersen, B.C. (1988). Financing constraints and corporate investment. *Brookings Papers on Economic Activity*, 1, 141–195.

Friedman, M. (1975). *Unemployment versus Inflation? An Evaluation of the Phillips Curve*. IEA Occasional Paper 44. Institute of Economic Affairs, London.

Frisch, H. (1983). *Theories of Inflation*. New York: Cambridge University Press.

Gertler, M., & Gilchrist, S. (1991). *Monetary Policy, Business Cycles and the Behaviour of Small Manufacturing Firms* Working Paper (No. 3892). National Bureau of Economic Research, Cambridge, MA.

Grossman, G. M., & Helpman, E. (1994). Endogenous innovation in the theory of growth. *The Journal of Economic Perspectives*, 8(1), 23–44.

Haliassos, M., & Tobin, J. (1990). The macroeconomics of government finance. In B. M. Friedman & F. H. Hahn (Eds.), *Handbook of Monetary Economics* (Vol. 2, Chapter 17, pp. 889–959). Elsevier, Amsterdam.

Hall, R. E. (1982). *Inflation: Causes and Effects*. Chicago, IL: The University of Chicago Press.

Helleiner, E. (1995). Handling "hot money": US policy toward Latin American capital flight in historical perspective. *Alternatives: Global, Local, Political*, 20(1), 81–110.

Hermes, N., & Lensink, R. (2001). Capital flight and the uncertainty of government policies. *Economics Letters*, 71, 377–381.

Hodgman, D. R. (1973). Credit controls in western Europe: An evaluative review. *Credit Allocation Techniques and Monetary Policy*. Boston, MA: Federal Reserve Bank of Boston.

Horiuchi, A., & Sui, Q.-Y. (1993). Influence of the Japan development bank loans on corporate investment behaviour. *Journal of the Japanese and International Economies*, 7, 441–465.

Hossain, A., & Chowdhury, A. (2000). *Monetary and Financial Policies in Developing Countries Growth and Stabilisation*. New York: Routledge.

Hossain, A. A. (2009). *Central Banking and Monetary Policy in the Asia-Pacific*. Cheltenham, UK: Edward Elgar.

Humphrey, T. M. (1991). Nonneutrality of money in classical monetary thought. *Economic Review* (Vol. March/April): Federal Reserve Bank of Richmond.

IMF. (2020). *World Economic Outlook Databases*. Washington, DC: International Monetary Fund.

Integrity, G. F. (2019). Illicit Financial Flows to and from Developing Countries: 2005–2016. Global Financial Integrity (GFI), Washington, DC.

Kai-Sun, K., Leung-Chuen, C., Lui, F. T., & Qiu, L. D. (2001). *Industrial Development in Singapore, Taiwan, and South Korea*. Singapore: World Scientific Publishing.

Keynes, J. M. (1937). The general theory of employment. *The Quarterly Journal of Economics*, 51(2), 209–223.

Khan, M. (1999). *The Political Economy of Industrial Policy in Pakistan 1947–1971*.

Khan, M. (2010). *Political Settlements and the Governance of Growth-enhancing Institutions*.

Kohli, R. (1997). Directed credit and financial reform. *Economic and Political Weekly*, 32(42), 2667–2676.

Kouam, H. (2020). COVID-19: Crisis-averse versus growth-centric monetary policy. Retrieved from SSRN 3655315.

Kriesler, P., & Lavoie, M. (2007). The new consensus on monetary policy and its post-Keynesian critique. *Review of Political Economy*, 19(3), 387–404.

Lansing, K., & Thalhammer, J. (2002). Output and inflation: A 100-year perspective. In J. Rabin & G. L. Stevens (Eds.), *Handbook of Monetary Policy*. New York: Marcel Dekker.

Leoni, R. (1997). Human resources constraints in technological innovation processes: Theoretical considerations and empirical evidence. In G. Antonelli & N. D. Liso (Eds.), *Economics of Structural and Technological Change* (pp. 213–228). New York: Routledge.

Lucas, R. E. (1972). Expectations and the neutrality of money. *Journal of Economic Theory* (Vol.4, pp. 103–124).

Lucas, R. E. (1973). Some international evidence on output–inflation tradeoffs. *The American Economic Review*, 63(3), 326–334.

MacKinnon, J. G. (1996). Numerical distribution functions for unit root and cointegration tests. *Journal of Applied Econometrics*, 11(6), 601–618.

McKinnon, R. I. (1973). *Money and Capital in Economic Development*. Brookings Institution, Washington, DC.

Naqvi, S. N. H. (1996). The significance of development economics. *World Development*, 24(6), 975–987.

Nayyar, D. (2011). Rethinking macroeconomic policies for development. *Brazilian Journal of Political Economy*, 31(3 (123)), 339–351.

Ndikumana, L. (2016). Implications of monetary policy for credit and investment in sub-Saharan African countries. *Journal of African Development*, 18(2), 1–18.

Ocampo, J. A., Spiegel, S., & Stiglitz, J. E. (2008). Capital market liberalisation and development. In J. A. Ocampo & J. E. Stiglitz (Eds.), *Capital Market Liberalisation and Development*. New York: Oxford University Press.

Odedokun, M. O. (1987). Fungibility and effectiveness of selective credit policies: Evidence from Nigerian data. *The Developing Economies*, 25(3), 234–248.

Orphanides, A., & Solow, R. (1990). Money, inflation and growth. In B. M. Friedman & F. H. Hahn (Eds.), *Handbook of Monetary Economics* (Vol. 1, pp. 223–261). Elsevier, Amsterdam.

Pagoulatos, G. (2003). *Greece's New Political Economy State, Finance, and Growth from Postwar to EMU*. New York: Palgrave Macmillan.

Papademos, L., & Modigliani, F. (1990). The supply of money and the control of nominal income. In B. M. Friedman & F. H. Hahn (Eds.), *Handbook of Monetary Economics* (Vol. 1, pp. 399–494). North-Holland, Amsterdam.

Pastor, M. (1990). Capital flight from Latin America. *World Development*, 18(1), 1–18.

Perez, S. A., & Westrup, J. (2010). Finance and the macroeconomy: The politics of regulatory reform in Europe. *Journal of European Public Policy*, 17(8), 1171–1192.

Piketty, T. (2014). *Capital in the Twenty-first Century*. Cambridge, MA: Harvard University Press.

Reuss, H. S. (1981). Introduction. In J. K. Galbraith (Ed.), *Monetary Policy, Selective Credit Policy, and Industrial Policy in France, Britain, West Germany, and Sweden*. Washington, DC: Joint Economic Committee, Congress of the United States, U.S. Government Printing Office.

Russell, S. (1991). The U.S. currency system: A historical perspective. *Federal Reserve Bank of St Louis* (September/October), 34–61.

Sakuragawa, M., & Hamada, K. (2001). Capital flight, North–South lending, and stages of economic development. *International Economic Review*, 42(1), 1–24.

Shaw, E. S. (1973). *Financial Deepening in Economic Development*. New York: Oxford University Press.

Solow, R. M. (1957). Technical change and the aggregate production function. *The Review of Economics and Statistics*, 39(3), 312–320.

Stern, N. (1991). The determinants of growth. *The Economic Journal*, 101(404), 122–133.

Stiglitz, J. E. (2010). *The Stiglitz Report: Reforming the International Monetary and Financial Systems in the Wake of the Global Crisis*. New York: The New Press.

Tiryakioğlu, M. (2012). Learning-based technology transfer policies and late development: The South Korea experience. In M. A. Yülek & T. K. Taylor (Eds.), *Designing Public Procurement Policy in Developing Countries* (pp. 141–156). New York: Springer Science+Business Media.

Tobin, J. (1965). Money and economic growth. *Econometrica*, 33(4), 671–684.

Tobin, J. (1980). *Stabilization Policy Ten Years After*. Brookings Papers on Economic Activity: Brookings Institution.

Unnayan Onneshan. (2020). *Whither Bending the Curves for Life and Livelihood: A Rapid Assessment of National Budget 2020–21*. Dhaka. Bangladesh.

Unnayan Onneshan. (2021). *From Squeeze to Expansion: Policy and Institutional Reforms For Averting K-Shaped Recovery*. Pre-Budget Policy Paper.

Vittas, D., & Cho, Y. J. (1996). Credit policies: Lessons from Japan and Korea. *The World Bank Research Observer*, 11(2), 277–298.

Vittas, D., & Kawaura, A. (1995). *Policy-Based Finance, Financial Regulation, and Financial Sector Development in Japan*. Policy Research Working Paper (No. 1443). Washington, DC: Financial Sector Development Department, The World Bank.

WEF. (2015). *Global Competitiveness Report 2015*. Davos, Switzerland: World Economic Forum.

Werner, R. A. (2002). A reconsideration of the rationale for bank-centered economic systems and the effectiveness of directed credit policies in the light of Japanese evidence. *The Japanese Economy*, 30(3), 3–45.

World Bank. (1970). *Industrialization in Pakistan: The Records, the Problems and the Prospect* (Vol. 1). The World Bank, Washington, DC.

7 Price, Inflation and Monetary Policy

Introduction

The policy of central banks changed significantly from the late 1970s in favour of a policy that solely focused on price stability, in contrast to a previous policy perspective that kept an employment objective along with a price stability objective. This period marks the beginning of neoliberal ideas, of which an integral part was a shift in monetary policy stance on the global stage (Stanford, 2008). Despite putting a greater emphasis on inflation, however, many Western countries observed the persistence of high inflation starting from the mid-1960s. What made inflation in this period special compared to that in earlier periods was its continuous growth, persistence and self-sustaining impetus, which proved incurable by orthodox fiscal and monetary measures and later resulted in extensive and prolonged unemployment. It was also believed that if monetary and fiscal policies were used to curb inflation, the cost would be discouragingly high (Hall, 1982).

The experiences of emerging and transitioning countries have not been the same regarding monetary policy though. Asian and Latin American countries faced monetary instability, high inflation and incessant capital flight. In this regard, emerging countries opted for exchange-rate regimes before they were hit with high inflation in the 1990s. Eventually, emerging countries scrapped pegged exchange rates for floating exchange rate regimes. Inflation-targeting approaches initiated by the countries brought the inflation rate down from 400 percent at the start of 1990s to below 10 percent in the space of 10 years (Mishkin & Savastano, 2002). Developing countries are faced with a lack of institutional capacity for monetary stability. Shifts from one monetary regime to another are thus problematic. The choice between inflation-targeting and growth-stimulating policies is a particularly difficult one. This chapter provides the theoretical foundation for different policy regimes.

In terms of policy response, although the Keynesian policy was criticised for producing both high and persistent inflation along with similar trends in unemployment in that period, the resulting change of monetary policy along the lines of Milton Friedman not only proved to be frustrating but also brought greater frustrations, high interest rates and debt problems for developed

DOI: 10.4324/9781003201847-7

countries, which made developing countries more vulnerable in an environment of a balance-of-payment crisis and volatile capital flows. To counter the situation, the IMF, using monetarist narratives, promoted two additional vital components—a tight fiscal policy and a flexible exchange-rate regime. Neoliberal hegemony for developing countries has made it imperative that macroeconomic policy acts to provide a policy conducive for foreign investment (Gabor, 2011). Again, by the 1980s, such a policy had already proven to be a failure, and the global recession of 1981–1982 was attributed directly to monetarist policies (Stanford, 2008). Still, inflation targeting (IT) dominates monetary policy management in a number of countries as "the new orthodoxy of mainstream macroeconomic thought" (Epstein & Yeldan, 2009).

In general, thus there are two exact opposite views regarding the causes of and response to inflation—one highlighting the possible effect of money supply on price levels and allowing limited scope in terms of fiscal and monetary policy, the other underlining the wider structural issues of the economy as a potential source of inflation and providing greater scope in terms of economic policies. As has been observed, they however have not always been successful, neither in explaining inflationary experiences of various countries nor suggesting suitable policy measures to counter them. As the persistence of inflation remains more or less a regular phenomenon in countries like Bangladesh, such a lack of understanding on appropriate policy options makes fighting inflation even more difficult for these countries.

Under these circumstances, the present chapter first demonstrates that the dominant theories have major theoretical shortcomings and that these theories fail to clarify the inflation experience of the developing world. It then explains the sources of inflation in these countries and identifies the conditions to be fulfilled to contain such a persistent rise in prices. For this purpose, the section shows how structural and institutional factors are linked to the inflationary process of the country and how different objectives and instruments for monetary policies affect the situation. In particular, it discusses the possible cost of following a single-minded inflation-targeting objective and the consequences of a lack of policy instruments in the context of weak institutional structure. The chapter finally links fiscal policy to monetary policy and discusses what kind of fiscal rules are required to complement the monetary policy to achieve the desired purposes.

Monetary policy and inflation: A critique

Different theories of inflation can broadly be classified into two groups: money supply–based explanations of inflation and economic structure–based explanations of inflation. The first group can further be identified as mainly being divided into classical, monetarist and neoclassical schools, all of which mainly accuse government actions for the creation of inflation and rely on the market for its prevention. Alternatively, there remains some understanding about inflation, consisting mainly of the arguments of Keynes and his followers, that takes a different view of the role of government and market regarding the matter. In addition to suffering from theoretical criticisms, both views are found to be insufficient when applied to the inflationary experience of Bangladesh.

Money supply–based explanations of inflation

The classical theory of inflation originates from the quantity theory of money. The origin of the quantity theory of money traces its roots at least to the mid-sixteenth century writing of the Salamanca School (Looney, 2001). There are, however, two quantity theories—the Cambridge version (Marshall, 1926; Pigou, 1917; Keynes, 1930) and the Fisher (Fisher, 1911) version. Although these theories follow two different approaches, both of them are devised to understand the purchasing power of money and both investigate how the price level reacts to changes in the money supply (Sheehan, 2009). Of these two approaches, Fisher's version is widely represented in academic textbooks as well as in research work. In his book, what Fisher presented is a transactions version of the theory, which starts from the equation of exchange:

$$MV = PT$$

where M is the quantity of money in circulation, T is the volume of trade, V is the velocity of circulation, and P is the average price level. Fisher defined the velocity of circulation as the ratio of the total money paid for goods in a year to the average amount of circulated money which is used to make those payments (Fisher, 1911). According to Fisher, "The velocities of circulation of money and of deposits depend … on technical conditions and bear no discoverable relation to the quantity of money in circulation" (Fisher, 1911). Fisher also argued that velocities and trade often change in the real world. Fisher concluded that if the money supply were doubled, the price level would also double.

Fisher's equation was later generally interpreted as more of a surety. As argued by Mishkin (2004), short-run velocity can reasonably be taken to be constant since Fisher assumed the institutional and technological features of an economy to be affecting velocity only slowly. Therefore, the classical economists reached the conclusion that movements in the price level result only from changes in the quantity of money (Mishkin, 2004).

Like the classical quantity theory, monetarist explanations of inflation rely on strict assumptions. Various scholars have contributed to monetarist view, among whom Milton Friedman (1980) occupies the central position. Regarding what causes inflation, Friedman considers government as the sole source of persistent inflation. He admits that psychological, structural or environmental reasons can raise the price of individual goods or can cause temporary rises in the general price level. However, he believes that none of these factors can be identified as the cause of continued inflation. The reason is simple: only an excess quantity of money supply causes inflation, and it is only the government that has control over money supply. He argued that inflation arises when the quantity of money increases faster than the output. The speed of inflation moves with the speed of the rise in quantity of money per unit of output. However, Friedman (1980) ignored the role of output in theorising inflation and the quantity of money.

There also seems a debate regarding whether this influence of the money supply is a short-term or long-term phenomenon. The concept of the Phillips curve comes in at this point. Friedman is of the opinion that "there is always a temporary trade-off between inflation and unemployment; there is no permanent trade-off" (Friedman, 1968). Here the idea is that there is a trade-off between inflation and unemployment in the short term, at least up to a certain rate of unemployment. Therefore, until that point, the money supply may produce more employment without causing any inflationary pressure (Frisch, 1983).

Friedman also makes an attempt to explain what causes excessive monetary growth. He argues that higher government spending caused by increasing the quantity of money is often the reason for inflation. If additional government spending is financed through taxes or internal borrowing, then this new government spending is matched by the equal fall in private spending. This way of raising money, however, is unpopular with the public and hence with politicians. Rather the preferred way is to finance it by increasing the quantity of money. In this way, nobody has to pay any new amount, yet the required project is carried out (Friedman, 1980).

The neoclassical school, in contrast, replaced the previous belief in adaptive expectation with the view of rational expectation, and therefore adopted a more pessimistic view of economic policy regarding inflation. The concept of adaptive expectation assumes that economic agents use the history of a particular variable to form an idea about its possible future value. A major shortcoming of this model is that it leads to a waste of any additional information, such as possession of past observations about any other economic variable. Contrary to this assumption of the adaptive expectation model, it is normal to expect that an economic agent would use that additional information to form expectations about the future values of the variable under consideration (Frisch, 1983). In contrast to the adaptive expectation model, the rational expectation view believes that agents base their decisions on much more than the past behaviour of the variable of interest. It is also assumed that economic agents possess an understanding of the structure of the economic system and have the ability to use that information properly.

One consequence of accepting the rational expectation hypothesis along with the assumption that markets always clear is the rejection of the belief that monetary policy can be used to increase output and employment even in the short term, and thus any possibility of successfully using the Phillips curve for any period of time for pursuing a counter-cyclical policy is zero (Frisch, 1983; Sargent & Wallace, 1976). The rational expectation model is criticised because of its unrealistic assumptions.

Overall, the consequence of accepting any of the above explanations is to limit the instrument's monetary policy for fighting inflation only within the money supply. One problem with the quantity theory is that the other factors involved in the equation rarely remain the same, even in the long run. They are also difficult to predict. As pointed out by Bindseil (2004):

> This equation is always verified ex post, and is thus more a description than a theory. It may form the foundation of a theory if assumptions are made about the behaviour of one or more of the variables involved. In particular, if v is assumed to be stable (or at least predictable), then any change of M will be reflected either in changes of p or of Y. Wherever it is reflected, this makes M a key policy variable. In practice, the crucial question is whether v is really stable or predictable and, related to that, which definition of M makes most sense because it implies it is stable or predictable.
>
> (Bindseil, 2004)

Moreover, prices can rise faster than the growth rate of the money supply as individuals could become more and more willing to spend money because of its falling value, as was observed in China during 1949–1950 (Burdekin, 2008). Thus, there is a causality issue as well.

Another problem with the above views is that they consider money as exogenous. However, it can also be argued that inflation is the product of what can be called "real factors" of the economy, and money supply often increases to cope with these developments. Moreover, money is created by the banking system through loan creation. Therefore, the amount of money supply depends on two factors: the demand for loans and the willingness of banks to fulfil that demand. A situation of rising prices is seen to be broadly accompanied by rising demand for loans from the producers as they move to cover the cost of production from bank loans, and the direction of causation is seen to have run from prices to money, and not vice versa (Arestis & Sawyer, 2004). The endogeneity of money comes from nominal interest rate smoothing by the central bank. However, money supply can become exogenous as central banks decide to change the money supply independently, which also happens occasionally (Yoshikawa, 1993).

Structural explanations of inflation

Originally, Keynes's view of inflation is argued to be present in his earlier writings, and not in his famous work *The General Theory of Employment Interest and Money*. For example, as opined by Humphrey (1981), "Keynes' own views on inflation … are contained chiefly in the following works … Except for the *General Theory*, which deals mainly with unemployment and will not be examined here, these works are largely concerned with the problem of inflation" (Humphrey, 1981).

Keynes considered that the price level is determined in the same way as individual prices are determined in a market economy—through the power of supply and demand. Supply in the market is determined by technical conditions, the level of wages, the state of markets and competition. On the other side, demand conditions are determined by the decisions of entrepreneurs, influencing the "incomes of individual producers", and the "disposition of such incomes" plays the pivotal role on the demand side. According to Keynes, money supply does have an influence on the price level, but only through its influence on investment:

> Money, and the quantity of money, are not direct influences at this stage of the proceedings. They have done their work at an earlier stage of the analysis. The quantity of money determines the supply of liquid resources, and hence the rate of interest, and in conjunction with other factors (particularly that of confidence) the inducement to invest, which in turn fixes the equilibrium level of incomes, output and employment and (at each stage in conjunction with other factors) the price level as a whole through the influences of supply and demand thus established.
>
> (Keynes, 1937)

Keynes then argues that the general price level is not just dependent on the rate of remuneration of the factors of production but also on the volume of output. The costs of production depend on the outputs produced by other industries. Hence, one has to take both the costs of input and volume of output in consideration when determining the change in demand (Keynes, 1937). Keynes also linked the concept of inflation and unemployment with prices. An increase in money supply will subsequently increase effective demand. When effective demand increases, according to Keynes, some part of it will be spent on increasing employment (Keynes, 1937).

However, when an increase in the money supply increases effective demand, and in turn the quantity of output, "the point of full employment" may not be reached for all of the products in the economy at the same time. For some products, the supply could be already completely inelastic, and hence the change in effective demand would only affect the price level. For others, however, there could be unused resources and an unemployed labour force, and therefore, an increase in effective demand would increase the output, leaving the price level unaffected.

Keynes therefore concludes that in terms of unemployment existing in the economy:

> When a further increase in the quantity of effective demand produces no further increase in output and entirely spends itself on an increase in the cost-unit fully proportionate to the increase in effective demand, we have reached a condition which might be appropriately designated as one of true inflation. Up to this point the effect of monetary expansion is entirely

> a question of degree, and there is no previous point at which we can draw a definite line and declare that conditions of inflation have set in. Every previous increase in the quantity of money is likely, in so far as it increases effective demand, to spend itself partly in increasing the cost-unit and partly in increasing output.
>
> (Keynes, 1937)

Two types of inflation have been synthesised by Keynes: true inflation and semi-inflation. Semi-inflation happens when an increase in nominal demand partly increases output and employment and thus raises the price level. The economy in this case operates below full employment. When the economy operates at full employment, an increase in nominal effective demand increases price with no impact on output and employment. This is known as true inflation. The classical theory of money is a special case which seeks to explain true inflation (Sheehan, 2009).

This is not inconsistent with the monetarists' NAIRU argument. A major difference between the Keynesian view and the monetarist view remains that where the latter considers that an increasing money supply is sure to raise the price level, the implication of Keynes's theory is that this need not be the case.

The new-Keynesian approach follows the Keynesian tradition in terms of the micro-economic foundations of wages and price stickiness (Gordon, 1990). Rather than believing that economic ups and downs in a market economy are aberrations from the path of equilibrium and are self-correcting over time, new-Keynesian economists assume that such deviations are not quickly restored even if economic agents behave rationally (Gordon, 1990). According to new-Keynesians, individuals have some influence over market prices, as competition is imperfect and information is either elusive or asymmetrically distributed. Markets therefore do not adjust immediately to clear in the short term. Thus, new-Keynesian economists mostly accept the idea of sufficient wage and price flexibility in the long run that nominal shocks arising from exogenous factors result in nominal change in the economy, but not any real change (Rotheim, 1998).

Now, turning from the general framework to inflation theory, new-Keynesians use what can be called the New-Keynesian Phillips curve. According to Sill (2011):

> The New Keynesian Phillips curve is derived from a structural model of the economy that features two key elements. First, firms have some pricing power. That is, they can choose to sell more of their product by setting a lower price, or they can choose to sell a little less but at a higher price. (This is known as imperfect competition.) Second, firms choose to, or are only able to, adjust prices infrequently (sticky prices). They do not adjust their prices fully and immediately to every unexpected event that affects the economy. These two features of the model allow monetary policy to affect more than just prices and inflation in the short run.
>
> (Sill, 2011)

The emphasis on imperfect competition means that firms set the prices of goods and inputs over the marginal cost to maximise profit, which stands in sharp contrast to market-clearing (competitive) prices. The concept of sticky prices arises from the fact that there are some constraints and costs involved for firms in adjusting the prices of the goods and services they sell (Galí, 2008). For example, in the short term, firms may perceive price changes on published menus to be costly even if the margin is small, which could discourage them from reducing prices when nominal demand shifts (Rotheim, 1998). Therefore, rational firms recognise the fact that today's price will prevail in the near future as well. Subsequently, they attempt to set an optimal price for the products that takes into consideration the marginal cost of production that is likely to prevail in the future along with today's marginal cost of production (Sill, 2011).

A question may arise then about the difference between the New-Keynesian Phillips curve and the traditional Phillips curve, as both deal with the determination of inflation. The main difference between the two Phillips curves involves how expected inflation and non-monetary economic variables act as drivers or determinants of current inflation. As opposed to the traditional Phillips curve, in which it is the unemployment rate that determines short-term inflation, the New-Keynesian Phillips curve suggests that short-term movements in inflation are defined by the expected path of marginal cost. Moreover, contrary to the expectation that marginal cost and unemployment rate are correlated, empirical evidence suggests that such a correlation does not appear to be high. Finally, the New-Keynesian Phillips curve implies that expansionary monetary policy is supposed to increase today's inflation. This occurs because stimulating demand makes firms hire more labour to meet the additional demand. This leads to paying higher real wages and a greater marginal cost of production. As firms respond immediately to the increasing cost by re-optimising their prices, inflation ensues (Sill, 2011). Thus, imperfect competition, sticky prices, the consideration of future expectations and the rational behaviour of firms ensures that firms respond today to any possible increase in future marginal cost of production. Altogether, expansionary monetary policy results in greater inflation.

There is also debate among new-Keynesians about whether money supply is endogenous or exogenous. For example, "credit view" models of new-Keynesian economics embrace the endogeneity of money supply as an assumption (Mazzoli, 1998). Similarly, the "new consensus" model of new-Keynesian economics adopts the belief that central banks are unable to control money supply (Rochon & Rossi, 2011). However, mostly the school does well in explaining inflation without resorting to the nature of money supply:

> the new Keynesian model, the basis of quantitative analysis in the modern theory and practice of monetary economics, does not assign money a special role for the control of inflation. This model, although it implies

> the basic monetarist principle of the neutrality of money, determines the equilibrium price level without any reference to the money supply.
>
> (Reichlin, 2008)

According to Gnos and Rochon (2007), the new consensus has two features: interest rate rule and inflation-targeting policy. Interest rate rule emphasises the exogenous nature of short-term interest rates. The inflation-targeting policy feature means keeping inflation within a specific range determined and carried out by the central bank.

Post-Keynesians believe in the basis that money supply is endogenously determined (Lavoie, 2006; Nayan et al., 2013). Post-Keynesians reject the idea that money supply depends arbitrarily on the decision of central banks. Rather, in the post-Keynesian analysis, money supply normally increases via credit creation. Thus the causality runs from loans to deposits in response to the need to accommodate increasing costs (Lavoie, 2006; Smithin, 2003). Therefore, inflation is no longer the result of excessive growth in the money supply, but rather is the consequence of a complex process.

According to Moore (1978):

> For modern post-Keynesians, in contrast, the rate of inflation is determined primarily by the rate of increase of nominal money wages relative to labour productivity. Over wide sectors of the economy, prices are largely cost-determined, based on a mark-up over unit labour costs. (The main exceptions are the agricultural and raw materials sectors where prices are still jointly determined by supply and demand.) This mark-up of prices over unit labour costs will be constant over time for the economy as a whole so long as the capital and labour shares of national income are constant, irrespective of the assumptions governing price-setting behaviour.

Then:

> As stated above, once wage contracts have been negotiated, the price level or the rate of inflation is largely a predetermined variable. To the extent labour is able to build the expected rate of inflation into its wage settlements, the ensuing rate of inflation will be governed by the extent to which money wage rates have risen more rapidly than average labour productivity.
>
> (Moore, 1978)

Alternative framework

An alternative framework can be devised from the literature review. A monetary policy from a central bank has an impact on the economy, as money creation can lead to inflation. Different actors are involved in the process of maintaining a stable cycle of money creation and flows.

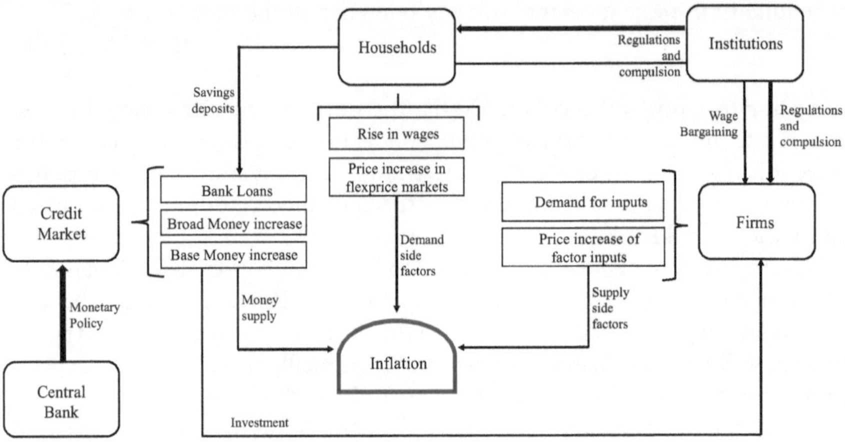

Figure 7.1 An alternative framework for inflation. Source: Prepared by the author

A central bank has the authority to print money in the economy to increase the liquidity and credit flow required by firms in production. Central banks cannot direct the flow themselves and usually rely on credit markets, banks and non-banking financial institutions. An increase in the money supply and broad money will add pressure through inflation. Households do their fair share in raising inflation through rising wages and consumption expenditure. Demand for inputs and price increases of inputs will mean that firms create inflation. This cycle can be broken by having another actor institution in place. Regulations and compulsion may direct the flow of credit to the desired sector in the economy. In the absence of institutions, credit may flow only to the clientelist network and political elites; thus credit results in primitive accumulation.

Employment creation through productive expansion can limit inflation and ensure price stability in the economy. Higher employment will result in higher real wages, which can offset the inflation arising from additional money injected into the economy. The price contraction caused by primitive accumulation will decrease demand. Institutions both formal and informal dictate prices in the market. Informal institutions like norms and behaviours can prevent excessive hoarding by consumers that creates scarcity in the market. External sectors can offset this price contraction. The rent-seeking nature of the clientelist network has to establish checks through regulations in order to limit rent and primitive accumulation (Figure 7.1).

On the basis of the above-mentioned alternative framework, the interactions between each economic entity and the vicious and virtuous cycles formed among them have led to four propositions being devised. The following sections will discuss each proposition in turn and attempt to prove the key relationships using empirical evidence.

Table 7.1 Money supply and inflation

	Political elite and primitive accumulation	*Investment in health, education, social security and infrastructure etc.*
Money supply	Inflation due to hoarding	Inflation offset by increase in real wage and productive expansion of the economy
Monetary restraint	Low level of inflation	Low level of investment and productive expansion

Source: Prepared by the author

Money supply, primitive accumulation and inflation

Money supply is exogenous, and it therefore contributes to inflation since loans are often created to meet the demands of the political elites and mainly go to support primitive accumulation. The hypothesis is that increased money supply must be used for the productive expansion of the economy, not for meeting the demands of the political elites. An increased money supply does not raise inflation; however, primitive accumulation by the elite does. Money supply leads to inflation when it goes to pockets of the political elite in the form of loans instead of being invested in productive expansion (Table 7.1). If the increased money supply is absorbed by the social sector and infrastructure sector, then the investments offset inflation.

The application of monetary restraints, however, represses public spending in productive expansion despite maintaining low level of inflation. Monetary restraining measures result in lower investment in social sectors and hence produces lower return. Primitive accumulation in times of monetary restraint results in lower level of inflation.

Price stability, productive expansion and real wages

In the growing stage of an economy, price stability and further acceleration of the economy may be ensured through an increase in real wages resulting from the productive expansion of the economy and employment. The hypothesis implies that new employment opportunities and an increase in real wages of labour can check price level instability. The productive expansion of the economy leads to the creation of new employment opportunities in the economy. New employment opportunity results in increase in real wage of labour, which offset the instability of price due to increased money supply in the economy. There is positive relation between price stability and productive expansion of the economy (Figure 7.2). The more productive expansion and employment creation, the more price stability in the economy. Hence, the trend of the real wages of labour shows an upward slope. An increase in both price stability and productive expansion results in higher real wages of labour.

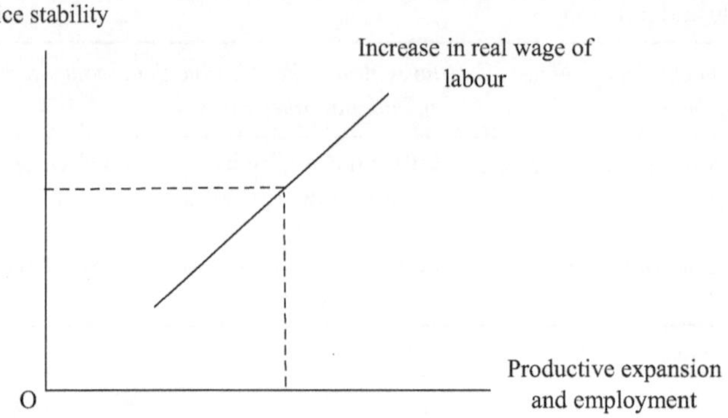

Figure 7.2 Price stability resulted from employment and increase in real wage. Source: Prepared by the author

Primitive accumulation, falling demand and role of remittances

The contraction in the price level resulting from a fall in demand because of the prevalence of primitive accumulation is offset by remittances sent from outside of the country. The hypothesis demonstrates that remittances play a crucial part in growth by raising demand and consumption and significantly offset the negative consequence of primitive accumulation in the economy. There is a positive relationship between primitive accumulation and contraction in the price level due to falling demand (Figure 7.3). Wealth and resources end up in the pockets of few at the expense of many through the widespread prevalence of rent seeking, primitive accumulation and illegal grabbing of wealth and power. As a result, inequality, poverty and deprivation increase and the public faces contraction in their ability to pay, which induces a general fall in demand. The inflow of remittances from abroad can significantly check contraction in the price level. Remittances increase the cash flow in the economy, particularly in rural areas, which raises demand and offsets the price contraction resulting from primitive accumulation.

Rent seeking, political settlement and institutions

Structural and institutional weaknesses provide widespread opportunities for rent seeking in the production and distribution process, leading to higher prices for consumers. The hypothesis implies that the distribution of power, strong and effective institutions and the enforcement of rules and regulations can significantly check rent-seeking behaviour in the economy. In the absence of stronger institutions, hoarding and subsequent price hikes increase in the economy. At the same time, increased rent seeking also increases hoarding and price hikes.

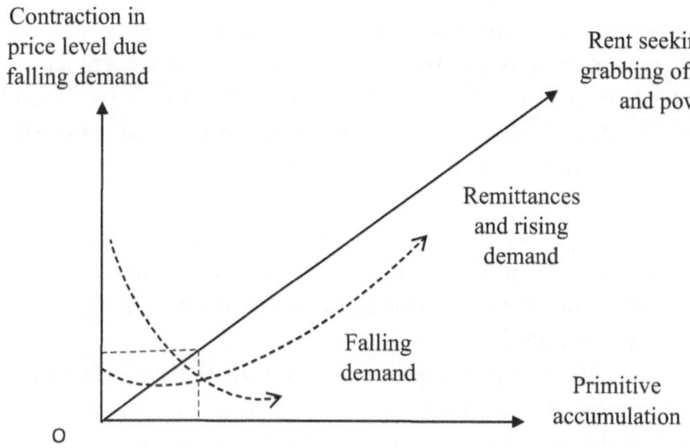

Figure 7.3 Remittances offsetting contraction in price level due to falling demand. Source: Prepared by the author

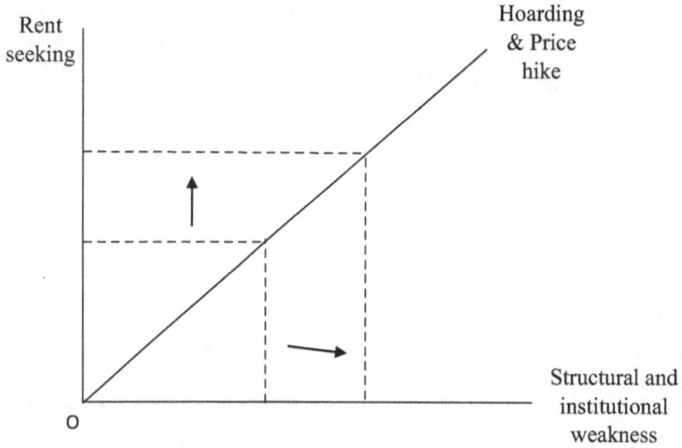

Figure 7.4 Structural and institutional weakness prompting rent seeking. Source: Prepared by the author

The association between rent seeking and structural and institutional weakness implies that a weak institutional and structural settings is responsible for rent seeking and primitive accumulation (Figure 7.4). Great institutional and structural weakness means that rent seeking will be more prevalent. The clientelist groups grab wealth and resources through the illegal hoarding of goods and services, inducing price hikes in the economy. Hoarding and price hikes therefore occur as a result of structural and institutional weakness.

Sources of inflation

This section applies the Granger causality technique to test the direction of causality between money supply and inflation in Bangladesh. We use the causality test of Toda and Yamamoto (1995) for this purpose. The test is based on a similar vector autoregression (VAR) representation of the original Granger causality tests. However, it is still applicable in the case of non-stationary time series, where the processes are integrated or cointegrated in an arbitrary order (Andersson, Burzynska & Opper, 2016; Toda & Yamamoto, 1995). The data from the Consumer Price Index for Bangladesh and remittance data are collected from monthly economic trends of the Bangladesh Bank. The sample period runs from July 2010 to October 2018.

The unit root tests used for the purpose include the augmented Dickey–Fuller (ADF) test. The results of these unit root tests for each of the variables are presented in Table 7.2. In one of the cases, the null of unit root is rejected at all levels. When the first difference is used, for the variable *broadmoney*, the null hypothesis is rejected and accepted at the second differences. The variables yield a stationary process, with maximum order of integration being 2.

At the next stage, the selection of the order of the vector autoregression is tested. The results are presented in Table 7.3. While the likelihood-ratio test suggests that p = 1, the final prediction-error criteria, the Akaike information criterion and the Hannan–Quinn information criterion and the Schwarz–Bayesian information criterion suggest that p = 2.

Table 7.2 Unit root test on inflation, money supply and remittance

Variable	*t-statistic at levels*	*t-statistic at first differences*	*t-statistic at second differences*
Cpibd	−4.770004***		
broadmoney	−0.838174	−2.516711	−9.149746***
remittance	−0.980520	−13.10009***	

Source: Author's calculation
***, ** and * denote statistical significance at the 1 percent, 5 percent and 10 percent levels, respectively.
Note: Lag length is selected based on Schwarz information criterion (SIC). Both trend and intercept are included in the equation.

Table 7.3 Selection of the order of the VAR

Lag	*LL*	*LR*	*df*	*p*	*FPE*	*AIC*	*HQIC*	*SBIC*
0	−4,100.8				7.20E+26	76.0333	76.0836	76.1574
1	−3,399.58	1402.4	25	0	2.60E+21	63.5107	63.8128	64.2558
2	−3,311.96	175.23	25	0	8.3e+20*	62.3512*	62.905*	63.7171*
3	−3,290.62	42.684*	25	0.015	8.90E+20	62.4189	63.2245	64.4057
4	−3,273.55	34.144	25	0.105	1.00E+21	62.5658	63.6231	65.1734

Source: Author's calculation

Table 7.4 Autocorrelation test

Lag	*chi2*	*Df*	*Prob> chi2*
1	22.3576	25	0.61502
2	33.8376	25	0.11143
3	19.5868	25	0.76815
4	29.284	25	0.25222
5	28.0989	25	0.30332

Source: Author's calculation

The results of the Lagrange multiplier test are presented in Table 7.4, which reveals no autocorrelation problem for the specified VAR up to lag 5.

For the causality test, VAR is augmented by the maximum order of integration of the variables, which in this case is 2. The results from the non-causality multivariate tests are shown in Table 7.3. The results summarised in Table 7.5 indicate that there exists causality between money supply and inflation as the null hypothesis is rejected. Moreover, the causality is bidirectional between money supply and inflation. This implies that money supply is endogenous in Bangladesh, meaning that the money supply is determined by the economy, and in this case it is inflation. On the other hand, it is also found that remittances do not affect the domestic price level. Hence, the money supply is not exogenous or determined by forces outside the economy.

The results summarised in Table 7.5 suggest the existence of bidirectional causality between money supply and Consumer Price Index (CPI), which are consistent with endogenous money theory. Apart from the influence of import cost on inflation, other supply-side phenomena such as production shocks can also act as a source of inflation. Such a cost-side origin of inflation in fact is not rare and is found in historical times in other places, such as in Britain and the United States (Hicks, 1977). Sometimes, it is also argued that domestic demand gets a boost in the Bangladesh economy from foreign remittance inflows (Bangladesh Bank, 2010).

Unemployment and inflation

Keynesian theory does not fully explain the inflation experience of countries like Bangladesh. It is true that the country's unemployment rate is not that high, although unemployment rate in the country worsened from 3.6 percent in 1991 to 4.5 percent in 2012. It is also true that the NAIRU rate varies from time to time and from country to country. For example, NAIRU is generally found to be within the limit of between 5.5 percent and 6.5 percent in the United States for the most part (Blanchard & Katz, 1996; Gordon, 1996; Weiner, 1993). It is also reasonable to assume that persons employed in Bangladesh are actually involved in disguised employment. Time-related

Table 7.5 Causality test

Direction of causality	*chi2*	*Prob> chi2*
broadmoney does not cause granger *cpibd*	8.1023	0.017
remittance does not cause granger *cpibd*	0.09523	0.953
cpibd does not granger cause *broadmoney*	42.806	0

Source: Author's calculation

underemployment in Bangladesh is 4.9 percent. This rate measures the number of people who are either willing to or available for additional work or worked less than a threshold relating to working time. The underemployment rate is 1.2 and 1.5 for Thailand and Vietnam respectively (ILO, 2020). Thus, the actual unemployment scenario is much worse than official statistics depict.

Furthermore, globalisation is supposed to work against inflation even if the unemployment rate is low. This has been the cause of disinflation in developed countries. Globalisation has a positive relation with disinflation as the import of cheaper manufacturing goods reduces the price of domestic goods (Pehnelt, 2007). In the age of globalisation, if the price of any domestic product rises, consumers enjoy the opportunity to switch to the foreign substitutes. This results in a fall in the NAIRU rate (Ball & Mankiw, 2002). A lower NAIRU would mean that even a low unemployment rate may often not result in higher inflation. There is thus underemployment in the Bangladesh economy; nonetheless, the inflation rate is generally showing an upward trend.

Historically, the inflation rate in Bangladesh has seen frequent ups and downs. The unemployment rate, however, has been rising steadily over the years. Hence, employment in Bangladesh does not work as a good indicator of inflation.

Wage and price stickiness

The new-Keynesian explanation also proves to be inadequate for developing countries. The reasons for increasing the money wage in any country are mainly attributed to three sets of factors. The first is the people's expectations about the movement of the general price level. The second one consists of the desire of workers to move the current real wage towards some target real wage. The third set involves the relative power of labour relative to that of management, and hence the ability of workers to secure wage increases. This relative power, in turn, depends on factors as diverse as the general political climate, the nature of industrial relations and labour laws. The macroeconomic factors in this regard are those related to unemployment, including the rate of unemployment and the rate of change in unemployment (Arestis & Sawyer, 2004).

Due to the dominance of the growing informal sector, the costs of changing prices do not seem high. This has become possible because Bangladesh has promoted a model where wages are not determined in a competitive labour market. The labour law of the country is extremely weak and have an anti-labour bias. In this regard, it is important to compare the wage rate with the cost of living to observe whether wage increases have been able to revise the trend of inflation or not.

The idea of a living wage is still far-fetched in developing countries like Bangladesh. A living wage ensures the needs of the people are met and totals to an amount that fulfils the standard of the community one lives in (Stabile, 2008; Werner & Lim, 2016). The minimum wage set by the government is far removed from the living wage. A living wage pays the amount needed for a worker to live a dignified and healthy life. It is calculated by taking account of the number of dependents, housing costs, food and other costs. The Asian Floor Wage, for example calculates the living wage by compiling food and non-food costs. Workers reserve 50 percent of the living wage for food to meet a need of 3,000 calories per day. This is calculated through a food basket calculation. Hence, double the cost of food represents the actual living wage of a country. They also take into account the number of dependents per worker. The living wage in Bangladesh stood at BDT 37661 and INR 23588 in India. However, workers in the readymade garments sector earn much less than the living wage. The minimum wage is a quarter of the living wage.

Another issue is garment-sector wages and civil service salaries and what happens to expectations and prices. It can be argued that setting minimum wages or increasing the salaries of civil service workers on the basis of what can be called pressure from parties such as trade unions could have contributed to the inflationary trend in the country. It has, however, been seen in places like Britain that general workers as well as public servants come together to protect their living standards against inflation, so it is inflation that has produced trade unions there (Robinson, 1978). Not only are trade unions formed to protect against growing inflation, but also such unions become more assertive in terms of influencing the wage rate when a rise is observed in the rate of inflation (Hicks, 1977). Much of the wage inequality in developed countries has been linked to a reduced number of trade unions. It is seen from the United States and the United Kingdom that wage inequality rose as the number of unions reduced (Card, Lemieux & Riddell, 2004). Trade unions fail to protect those working in low-paying jobs, particularly in service sectors. Such jobs also employ a higher number of women and children. This type of job has been traditionally left out of unions (Dølvik & Waddington, 2004).

Finally, labour productivity does not affect inflation in developing countries, as can be seen from the case of Bangladesh. The Wage Rate Index (WRI), which measures the change in nominal wages in low-paid skilled and unskilled work, has remained relatively stagnant. When compared with the average CPI growth rate for the period, it is only 0.19 of a percentage point higher than the average WRI growth rate (8.09 percent versus 8.28 percent). Since 2009–2010, it is actually the growth rate of WRI that has been lower than the growth rate of CPI. Moreover, since 2007–2008, nominal GDP has grown by an average of 13.61 percent (Table 7.6). Hence, wages have not

Table 7.6 Growth rate of CPI, WRI and nominal GDP since 2007–2008

Fiscal year	*CPI*	*WRI*	*Nominal GDP*
2007–08	12.30	11.86	14.35
2008–09	7.60	18.88	12.15
2009–10	6.81	8.28	13.11
2010–11	10.92	6.27	14.83
2011–12	8.69	6.24	15.22
2012–13	6.78	6.01	13.62
2013–14	7.35	5.51	12.07
2014–15	6.41	4.94	12.81
2015–16	5.92	6.51	14.32

Source: BBS, 2017

Note: * Base: 2005–2006 = 100, **up to 2010–2011, base: 1969–2070 = 100, from 2011 to 2012, base: 2010–2011 = 100, *** base: 2005–2006 = 100

changed in the same way that inflation has done in Bangladesh. Therefore, a rise in wage rate compared to labour productivity can be ruled out as a source of inflation in recent years.

Sources of inflation: An alternative explanation

The notion put forward by Keynes is that the price level is determined by the function of real forces in the economy, i.e., forces that affect both the demand for and supply of goods in the economy. Bangladesh is taken as an example to illustrate this. The source of inflationary pressure in Bangladesh can be explained through the following four propositions. First, money supply could be exogenous in the country, and it therefore contributes to inflation as loans are created to meet the demands of the political elites and mainly go to support primitive accumulation. Second, the contraction in the price level resulting from the fall of demand because of the prevalence of primitive accumulation is offset to some extent by remittances sent from outside of the country. Third, the higher cost of production from international price pass-through significantly affects the price level. Fourth, structural and institutional weaknesses provide widespread opportunities for rent seeking in the production and distribution process, leading to higher prices for consumers. The markets in the country are not competitive due to the influence of class, institutional weakness and structural limitations. The flow of information is frequently limited, and the cost of transportation is prohibitively high.

Power and money supply

From the econometric analysis above, it seems that money supply in Bangladesh is endogenous. This is due to the influence of influential classes on the loan-supply process of the banks, contributing to inflation. Money supply can be endogenous or exogenous; theoretically, both are possible. The endogenous money story asserts that it is the increase in the money supply that results in inflation. Moreover, the process price and wage determination may not have any significant effect on the inflationary process. On the other hand, money treated as endogenous means that the changes in the money supply arise from the inflationary process itself, and hence the importance of price and wage determination processes cannot be overlooked when examining the causes of inflation (Arestis & Sawyer, 2004).

To understand the influence of the money supply on inflation in Bangladesh, it is important to consider whether loan supply is market based or class based. There is a tendency among high-up bank officials to allow loans for various personal rent-seeking activities. Lower management also has to prove their efficacy by providing loans to their own contacts. These loans especially end as bad loans. The monetary policy, even if contractionary, then fails at two stages. At one stage, loan flow increases to relatively unproductive sources. At the other stage, the flow of resources to productive and important areas decrease, making the supply fall short of the demand.

Money from the banks has often been used to support these fellow classes. To win elections, the ruling elite needs to appease its supporters as well as to raise enough resources to win the next election. Money from the banks provides them with an easy option. Such loans have been extensively used in the past to garner political support by creating a new subordinate class during certain regimes in Bangladesh (Khondker, 2004). This practice however is still continuing, and political connections as well as class influence makes loan sanctions easier.

Power and costs of production

As found in the causality test, the international price level seems to have influence on the consumer price level. Supply-side phenomena such as import costs, oil price hikes and exchange rates are considered to have an important contributory effect on consumer price inflation in Bangladesh. Wage inflation, in comparison, has been found to be weakly related to inflation (Majumder, 2006). Similarly, inflation in Bangladesh is mainly dominated by food inflation, and the prices of rice, wheat, and edible oil significantly have the biggest effect on food inflation (Mortaza & Rahman, 2008). The ratio of import to consumption of rice is very low, but it is significantly higher for wheat and edible oil. The empirical results of their study suggest that the pass-through elasticity of international prices lies between 0.19 and 0.33 for rice, between 0.14 and 0.31 for wheat and between 0.15 and 0.55 for edible oil. The pass-through of international prices to domestic prices is supposed to be higher for those goods that have a higher import–consumption ratio. Therefore, the empirical finding of the study is consistent with a higher import–consumption ratio for edible oil, followed by that of wheat and rice.

For the years the data has been available, the difference between inflation in wholesale price index (WPI) for agricultural and industrial products and that in CPI is large in Bangladesh, indicating a larger price increase at the consumer level. Considering the dominance of the intermediate class, it is not very unreasonable to assume that members of that class influence the distribution channel of products, thwarting any regulatory attempts. Small and marginal farmers, being the largest producer groups, have to sell their produce to intermediaries. The price they receive is very low due to the absence of bargaining power (Mondol, 2010). Wholesale price indices have fared lower than the inflation measured by CPI (Table 7.7). The difference between wholesale price and consumer price goes to middlemen at various stages of the supply chain, giving rise to rent accumulation. This also proves that inflation is not just a phenomenon that can be explained by money supply.

The state policy of Bangladesh regarding its economy has been extractive. Additionally, the state has promoted primitive accumulation. A lack of institutional and policy checks on the economy creates an environment that leaves many of the economic units carry out rent-seeking behaviour. The implication of widespread economic opportunism is that the demand side of the economy arises from exploitative acts by a great majority of the masses. One major consequence is that an increase in rent-seeking activity by some does not leave others in trouble, and those others respond by increasing their rent-seeking activity as well. Furthermore, foreign remittance plays a significant role by boosting the demand side of the phenomena. Therefore, a fall in demand arising from a continuous increase in price is not a problem.

Table 7.7 Trend in WPI and CPI between 1994–1995 and 2005–2006

Year	*Percent increase in wholesale price indices of agricultural and industrial products (Base year: 1969–1970 = 100)*	*Inflation 12-month average (Base year: 1995–1996 = 100)*	*Inflation 12-month average (Base year: 1985–1986 = 100)*
1994–1995	4.7		8.87
1995–1996	5.4		6.65
1996–1997	0.6	3.96	2.52
1997–1998	5.1	8.66	6.99
1998–1999	6.8	7.06	8.91
1999–2000	−0.4	2.79	3.41
2000–2001	−1.5	1.94	
2001–2002	0.23	2.79	
2002–2003	5.31	4.38	
2003–2004	3.68	5.83	
2004–2005	3.43	6.48	
2005–2006	8.90	7.17	

Source: Ministry of Finance, 2019; BBS, 2017

Power and scarcity

Scarcity in economic terms means limited resources for unlimited human wants. Even in a world full of modern technology, there is always a limit to resources, and hence there is a trade-off for individuals. Within the limited resource spectrum, an individual has to choose one good over the other (Heyne, Boettke & Prychitko, 2014). Scarcity can be both demand-induced and supply-induced. Increased demand for a particular good may cause scarcity in the market. In a market economy with limited resources, increasing demand increases scarcity. On the other hand, when suppliers produce on the basis of limited resources, an increase in supply may soon deplete those resources. Scarcity has the ability to increase the price of a good. However, in reality, scarcity may arise due to primitive accumulation as well as an inefficient market. Monopolies, oligopolies or cartels can create an artificial scarcity. This is more evident in the developing world, where political power results in cartels and middlemen, which may increase the price of a good. For example, the price at the consumers' level has been on the rise for agricultural goods even when the production of those goods has increased. This is due to middlemen in the transaction process as well as political groups who seek rent. Meanwhile, producers see little price rise. The difference between the producers' price and the consumers' price is basically going to these cartels. At the same time, the hoarding of goods also increases scarcity in the market. In times of crisis, suppliers tend to hoard goods to get a better price. Lack of oversight, norms and values allow groups to use their power to raise the prices of goods.

Alternative monetary policy strategy

Since the first adoption of inflation targeting in New Zealand in 1989, many countries in Europe, Asia and Latin America have switched to inflation targeting, especially since the early 1990s, due to the poor results of monetary targeting due to such things as the exchange rate crisis and financial crisis (Roger, 2010). This especially occurred with the emergence of the new consensus view of macroeconomics, which stressed the use of inflation targeting as a monetary policy strategy instead of monetary targeting (Gnos & Rochon, 2011).

Inflation-targeting strategy, nevertheless, is not without problems. However, several criticisms remain about inflation targeting. First, the focus on numerical inflation puts constraint on central bank policies in an inflation-targeting regime. It reduces the ability of the bank to implement other monetary measures (Rudebusch & Walsh, 2002). Second, inflation targeting suffers from practical implementation issues. Implementing agencies would have to depend on future inflation. This becomes extremely difficult in the face of economic uncertainties. This opens up the opportunity to overestimate or underestimate future inflation. (Rudebusch & Walsh, 2002).

About the applicability of inflation targeting in Bangladesh, Hossain (2015) remained sceptical. He rightly argued:

> A follow-up policy question is whether the Bangladesh Bank should switch from monetary targeting to inflation targeting in order to improve its monetary policy. The monetary policy literature suggests that inflation targeting itself does not achieve credibility in an uncertain inflationary environment when a central bank claims bad luck, adverse shocks and extenuating circumstances in missing its inflation target. Over-rationalisation undermines the credibility of a central bank. A possible solution for recovering policy credibility is to sustain steady money growth and to avoid adopting the strategy of monetary activism, including the monetary accommodation of supply shocks.

Inflation targeting is often interpreted as an "encompassing case of monetary targeting or exchange rate targeting" (Bain & Howells, 2003). In pure monetary targeting, non-monetary variables are weighed as zero while monetary variables are weighed as unity. In contrast, inflation targeting uses "an eclectic mix of information variables, with non-zero weights assigned to both real and monetary magnitudes when forming an inflationary assessment" (Haldane, 1998). Inflation targeting thus draws on information from a wide range of variables, including "money and credit growth, the exchange rate, wage trends, asset prices, employment figures, the 'output-gap', surveys of 'confidence' etc." (Bain & Howells, 2003). "In particular, an inflation targeting central bank need not care only about inflation. Indeed, most inflation targeting central banks continue to recognise multiple goals for monetary policy with no single primary one" (Rudebusch & Walsh, 2002).

The problem of inflexibility could be resolved if multiple bands to cater for other needs of the economy apart from the inflation objective are decided or set.

> Anticipating potential problems, policymakers generally build certain flexibilities into inflation-targeting regimes. Many nations adopt a price index that not only excludes such volatile components as energy and food prices, but also eliminates indirect government taxes and mortgage interest payments. In New Zealand, attempts are made to eliminate price-level movements due to supply shocks. The rationale is that supply shocks can shift the price level without altering the underlying inflation rate, and the central bank is not to be held responsible for such supply shocks. One also supposes that supply shocks are expected to be both positive and negative over time, so that the price level itself will not drift away from its intended long-run path as a result of such shocks alone.
>
> (Sniderman, 2002)

COVID-19 and role of monetary policies in SMEs and employment

The COVID-19 crisis requires significant monetary intervention in the economy, as the lockdown to curb the spread of the virus has resulted in the shutdown of businesses and the loss of jobs. Income erosion from these job losses will substantially reduce consumption expenditure. Restarting and restoring the economy will depend on the ability of businesses to bounce back to the pre-COVID-19 level. Central banks and financial institutions in developing countries will need to step in as the prime financers. Developing countries have been facing a lack of financing options because of minimal secondary bond market and limited stock market capacity.

Hence, the pressure on banks to provide funds in developing countries will multiply many times and will result in a credit crunch. Central banks will again have to make a choice between inflation targeting and growth-stimulating policies. Undoubtedly, central banks will need to print money for reopening businesses and new investments. Aggregate demand needs to be raised as well. Inflation comes into the discussion automatically when talking about money creation. The chances of runaway inflation happening is very low because of the lower consumption expenditure and production resulting from the shutdown. Price inflates when nominal expenditure exceeds the real capacity of reducing goods and services in an economy. Interest rates can be adjusted on a measured basis without having to worry about inflation (Figure 7.5).

Central banks have been injecting liquidity through various measures. From developed countries to developing ones, every country has opted for money creation. Public debt may increase through money creation, but it is needed to revive the economy. Central banks and financial banks have been given the job of disbursing economic relief packages or stimulus packages. As a result, banks will see a liquidity crunch. Central banks come forward at such a time with various instruments. Money creation does not occur physically or by governments physically printing money. Various measures taken by the central banks will be discussed.

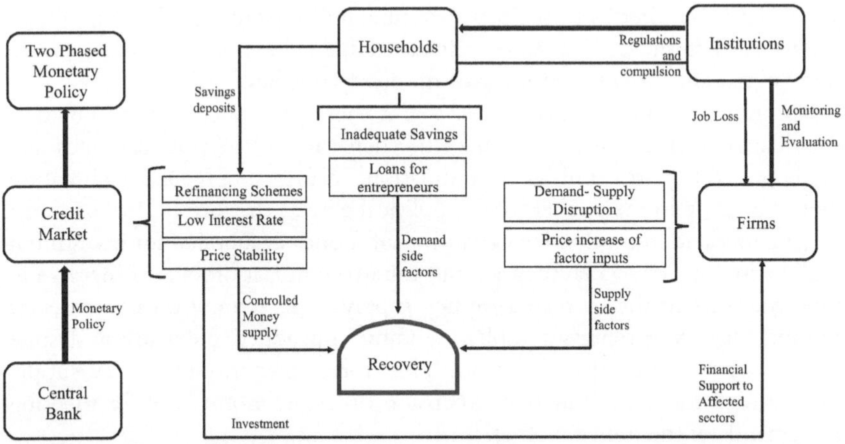

Figure 7.5 Monetary policy framework as a recovery plan from the pandemic. Source: Prepared by the author

Central banks have taken steps to generate employment in the economy in the face of unprecedented job loss. Bangladesh Bank, the central bank of Bangladesh, cut the interest rate to increase its Export Development Fund from 3.2 billion USD to 5 billion USD. At the same time, the bank has created refinancing schemes and credit guarantee schemes for exporters, farmers and small and medium enterprises (SMEs) worth 4.6 billion USD. These financing schemes have been taken up by the central bank to facilitate the government stimulus package. The package also includes a subsidy programme for farmers that will be coordinated by the central bank (IMF, 2021). Governments elsewhere have also taken initiatives to facilitate employment creation through funding small and micro industries. In India, the Reserve Bank of India implemented regulations to divert funds to SMEs. Similarly, Thailand approved low-interest rate loans to informal workers and SMEs linked to the tourism sector, as the country relies heavily on the tourism-related service sector (IMF, 2021).

Conclusion

This chapter argues that money-supply explanations for inflation do not hold in a developing country such as Bangladesh. Additionally, Keynesian and new-Keynesian views of inflation do not provide a full explanation for the country's inflationary process. Here, supply is less responsive to price because of poor infrastructural facilities. As a result, the Keynesian notion of excess capacity does not work here to reduce the rate of inflation. Additionally, class has a role to play in determining both supply and demand, thus becoming a significant determiner of wage stickiness, which the neoclassical school failed to mention. Because of class, markets are not competitive. Also for the same reason, rising wages are again less of a reason for inflation. Finally, structural issues are also present because of poor policies. In a developing country like Bangladesh, where the informal sector is quite large, price stickiness is seldom a problem. What is required is to include structural and institutional factors, which, because of class and accumulation, affect the behaviour of the market, create inflation and affect the functioning of monetary policies.

The money supply is exogenous, and it therefore contributes to inflation since loans are often created to meet the demands of the political elites and mainly go to support primitive accumulation. Money supply leads to inflation when it ends up in the pockets of the political elite in the form of loans instead of being invested in productive expansion. If money is supplied for investment in education, health, social security and infrastructure, it offsets the increase in price level due to the increased money supply. The application of monetary restraints, however, represses public spending in productive expansion despite maintaining a low level of inflation. Therefore, an increased money supply must be used for the productive expansion of the economy, not for meeting the demands of the political elites.

At a growing stage of the economy, price stability and the further acceleration of the economy could be ensured through an increase in real wages resulting from the productive expansion of the economy and employment. Productive expansion of the economy leads to the creation of new employment opportunities in the economy. New employment opportunities result in an increase in the real wages of labour, which offset the instability of prices due to the increased money supply in the economy. There is a positive relation between price stability and the productive expansion of the economy. The more productive expansion and employment creation there is, the more price stability in the economy. Hence, new employment opportunities and increases in real wages of labour can check price-level instability.

The contraction in the price level resulting from the fall of demand because of the prevalence of primitive accumulation is offset by remittances sent from outside of the country. There is a positive relation between primitive accumulation and a contraction in price level due to falling demand. Wealth and resources end up in the pockets of few at the expense of many through the widespread prevalence of rent seeking, primitive accumulation and illegal grabbing of wealth and power. As a result, inequality, poverty and deprivation increase and the general populace face a contraction in their ability to pay, which induces a general fall in demand. The inflow of remittances from abroad can significantly check the contraction in price level. Remittances increase the cash flow in the economy, particularly in rural areas, which raises demand and offsets the price contraction resulting from primitive accumulation. Moreover, remittances play a crucial part in growth through raising demand and consumption and significantly offset the negative consequences of primitive accumulation in the economy.

Structural and institutional weaknesses provide widespread opportunities for rent seeking in the production and distribution process, leading to higher prices for consumers. The positive relation between rent seeking and structural and institutional weakness implies that a weak institutional and structural setting is responsible for rent seeking and primitive accumulation. The more institutional and structural weakness there is, the more prevalence of rent seeking. Clientelist groups grab wealth and resources through the illegal hoarding of goods and services, inducing price hikes in the economy. Hoarding and price hikes therefore occur as a result of structural and institutional weakness. Finally, the distribution of power, strong and effective institutions and the enforcement of rules and regulations can significantly check rent-seeking behaviour in the economy.

The unprecedented fallout from the COVID-19 virus has bought the economic sector to a standstill, as economic activities have closed amidst justifiable quarantine and social distancing measures. This has occurred differently across the world. The emerging markets followed suit, as the scale of economic harm spanned continents, clogged supply chains and increased the risks of contagion. In developing economies, central banks have equally resorted to monetary accommodation in an attempt to lessen the spill-over from advanced economies, mitigate funding pressures via money market operations and lessen the impact of the virus on the real economy.

Monetary policy achieves its mandate of an explicit inflation target, or one with a variation band. The transmission from monetary policy and reserve management approaches to inflation operates via monetary and non-monetary targets. Monetary targets are driven by changes in the level of policy rates, which increase or reduce money supply. While lower interest rates cause banks to pay less for their deposits held at the central bank, they can transmit the perceived benefits of lower interest rates via the credit channel. Lending from businesses and corporations triggers investments in fixed assets and machinery, with additional employment created to utilise the infrastructure and transform inputs into outputs.

The presence of primitive accumulation, a growing informal economy, supply-side deficiencies and demand-side influences means that inflation in developing countries such as Bangladesh do not occur in accordance with any of the theories commonly preferred. Rather, inflation is a result of a combination of structural and institutional failures, aggravated by policy failures. Thus, the Keynesian explanation of inflation slightly holds in Bangladesh, especially as movement in individual prices collectively moves the price level. Moreover, as opposed to the mainstream emphasis that inflation is primarily caused by excess money growth, inflation mainly occurs because of structural and institutional failures. Moreover, such failures are the results of faulty policies as well as of the prevalence of a particular form of accumulation and power relations, which is more or less a regular characteristic of a free-market economy in a developing country, thus also opposing the Keynesian understanding of inflation.

References

Andersson, F. N. G., Burzynska, K., & Opper, S. (2016). Lending for growth? A Granger causality analysis of China's finance–growth nexus. *Empirical Economics*, 51, 897–920.

Arestis, P., & Sawyer, M. (2004). *Re-examining Monetary and Fiscal Policy for the 21st Century*. Cheltenham, UK: Edward Elgar.

Bain, K., & Howells, P. (2003). *Monetary Economics: Policy and its Theoretical Basis*. New York: Palgrave Macmillan.

Ball, L., & Mankiw, N. G. (2002). *The NAIRU in Theory and Practice Working Paper*. Cambridge, MA: National Bureau of Economic Research.

Bangladesh Bank. (2010). *Monetary Policy Statement* (January 2010) Dhaka: Bangladesh Bank.

BBS. (2017). *Consumer Price Index (CPI), Inflation Rate and Wage Rate Index (WRI) in Bangladesh*. Dhaka: Bangladesh Bureau of Statistics (BBS).

Bindseil, U. (2004). *Monetary Policy Implementation Theory, Past, and Present*. New York: Oxford University Press.

Blanchard, O., & Katz, L. F. (1996). *What We Know and Do Not Know about the Natural Rate of Unemployment Working Paper*. National Bureau of Economic Research, Cambridge, MA.

Burdekin, R. C. K. (2008). *China's Monetary Challenges: Past Experiences and Future Prospects*. New York: Cambridge University Press.

Card, D., Lemieux, T., & Riddell, W. C. (2004). Unions and wage inequality. *Journal of Labor Research*, 25(4), 519–559.

Dølvik, J. E., & Waddington, J. (2004). Organizing marketized services: Are trade unions up to the job? *Economic and Industrial Democracy*, 25(1), 9–40.

Epstein, G., & Yeldan, A. E. (2009). Beyond inflation targeting: Assessing the impacts and policy alternatives. In G. Epstein & A. E. Yeldan (Eds.), *Beyond Inflation Targeting: Assessing the Impacts and Policy Alternatives*. Cheltenham, UK: Edward Elgar.

Fisher, I. (1911). *The Purchasing Power of Money*. New York: MacMillan Company.
Friedman, M. (1968). The role of monetary policy. *The American Economic Review*, 58(1), 1–17.
Friedman, M. (1980). *Free to Choose: A Personal Statement*. New York: Harcourt Brace Jovanovich.
Frisch, H. (1983). *Theories of Inflation*. New York: Cambridge University Press.
Gabor, D. (2011). *Central Banking and Financialization A Romanian Account of How Eastern Europe Became Subprime*. New York: Palgrave Macmillan.
Galí, J. (2008). *Monetary Policy, Inflation, and the Business Cycle: An Introduction to the New Keynesian Framework*. Princeton, NJ: Princeton University Press.
Gnos, C., & Rochon, L.-P. (2007). The new consensus and post-Keynesian interest rate policy. *Review of Political Economy*, 19(3), 369–386.
Gnos, C., & Rochon, L.-P. (2011). *Credit, Money and Macroeconomic Policy: A Post-Keynesian Approach*. Cheltenham, UK: Edward Elgar Publishing.
Gordon, R. J. (1990). What is New-Keynesian economics? *Journal of Economic Literature*, 28(3), 1115–1171.
Gordon, R. J. (1996). *The Time-Varying NAIRU and Its Implications for Economic Policy Working Paper*. National Bureau of Economic Research, Cambridge, MA.
Haldane, A. G. (1998). On inflation targeting in the United Kingdom. *Scottish Journal of Political Economy*, 45(1), 1–32.
Hall, R. E. (1982). *Inflation: Causes and Effects*. Chicago: The University of Chicago Press.
Heyne, P., Boettke, P. J., & Prychitko, D. L. (2014). *The Economic Way of Thinking* (13th ed.). New Jersey: Pearson. ISBN 978-0-13-299129-2.
Hicks, J. (1977). *Economic Perspectives: Further Essays on Money and Growth*. Oxford: Clarendon Press.
Hossain, A. A. (2015). Inflation volatility, economic growth and monetary policy in Bangladesh. *Applied Economics*, 47, 5667–5688.
Humphrey, T. M. (1981). Keynes on inflation. *Economic Review*, January/February, 1–13.
ILO. (2020). *ILOStat*. International Labour Organisation
IMF. (2021). *Policy Responses to Covid-19*. International Monetary Fund.
Keynes, J. M. (1930). *Treatise on Money*. London: Macmillan.
Keynes, J. M. (1937). The general theory of employment. *The Quarterly Journal of Economics*, 51(2), 209–223.
Khondker, H. H. (2004). Class and state in Bangladesh: Political economy of authoritarian democracy. *Journal of Bangladesh Studies*, 6(1), 20–34.
Lavoie, M. (2006). *Introduction to Post-Keynesian Economics*. New York: Palgrave Macmillan.
Looney, R. (2001). Quantity Theory of Money (QTM). In R. J. B. Jones (Ed.), *Routledge Encyclopedia of International Political Economy* (Vol. 3). New York: Routledge.
Majumder, M. A. (2006). *Inflation in Bangladesh: Supply Side Perspectives Policy Note Series (PN 0705)*. Dhaka, Bangladesh.
Marshall, A. (1926). Official Papers by Alfred Marshall.
Mazzoli, M. (1998). *Credit, Investments, and the Macroeconomy*. New York: Cambridge University Press.
Ministry of Finance. (2019). *Bangladesh Economic Review 2019*. Government of People's Republic of Bangladesh.
Mishkin, F. S. (2004). *The Economics of Money, Banking, and Financial Markets*. Pearson and ddison-Wesley, Boston.
Mishkin, F. S., & Savastano, M. A. (2002). Monetary policy strategies for emerging market countries: Lessons from Latin America. *Comparative Economic Studies*, 44(2), 45–82.

Mondol, M.H. (2010). Crop agriculture of Bangladesh: Challenges and opportunities. *Bangladesh Journal of Agricultural Research*, 35(2), 235–245.

Moore, B. J. (1978). A Post-Keynesian approach to monetary theory. *Challenge*, 21(4), 44–52.

Mortaza, M. G., & Rahman, H. (2008). *Transmission of International Commodity Prices to Domestic Prices in Bangladesh Working Paper Series*. Bangladesh Bank, Dhaka.

Nayan, S., Kadir, N., Abdullah, M. S., & Ahmad, M. (2013). Post Keynesian endogeneity of money supply: Panel evidence. *Procedia Economics and Finance*, 7, 48–54.

Pehnelt, G. (2007). *Globalisation and Inflation in OECD Countries*. Jena Economic Research Paper (2007–055).

Pigou, A. C. (1917). The value of money. *The Quarterly Journal of Economics*, 32(1), 38–65.

Reichlin, L. (2008). *Introduction*. Paper presented at the Fourth ECB Central Banking Conference 9–10 November 2016, Frankfurt, Germany.

Robinson, J. (1978). *Contributions to Modern Economics*. New York: Academic Press.

Rochon, L.-P., & Rossi, S. (2011). Monetary policy without reserve requirements: Central bank money as means of final payment on the interbank market. In C. Gnos & L.-P. Rochon (Eds.), *Credit, Money and Macroeconomic Policy: A Post-Keynesian Approach* (pp. 98–115). Cheltenham, UK: Edward Elgar Publishing.

Roger, S. (2010). Inflation targeting at twenty: Achievements and challenges. In D. Cobham, Ø. Eitrheim, S. Gerlach, & J. F. Qvigstad (Eds.), *Twenty Years of Inflation Targeting: Lessons Learned and Future Prospects* (pp. 25–56). New York: Cambridge University Press.

Rotheim, R. J. (1998). New Keynesian macroeconomics and markets. In R. J. Rotheim (Ed.), *New Keynesian Economics/Post Keynesian Alternatives*. New York: Routledge.

Rudebusch, G. D., & Walsh, C. E. (2002). U.S. inflation targeting: Pro and Con. In J. Rabin & G. L. Stevens (Eds.), *Handbook of Monetary Policy* (pp. 715–719). New York: Marcel Dekker.

Sargent, T. J., & Wallace, N. (1976). Rational expectations and the theory of economic policy. *Journal of Monetary Economics*, 2, 169–183.

Sheehan, B. (2009). *Understanding Keynes' General Theory*. New York: Palgrave MacMillan.

Sill, K. (2011). Inflation Dynamics and the New Keynesian Phillips Curve. *Business Review*: Federal Reserve Bank of Philadelphia, issue Q1, 1–9.

Smithin, J. (2003). Inflation. In J. E. King (Ed.), *The Elgar Companion to Post Keynesian Economics*. Cheltenham, UK: Edward Elgar Publishing.

Sniderman, M. S. (2002). Inflation targets: The next step for monetary policy. *Public Administration and Public Policy*, 97, 253–260.

Stabile, D. (2008). *The Living Wage: Lessons from the History of Economic Thought*. Cheltenham: Edward Elgar Publishing.

Stanford, J. (2008). *Economics for Everyone: A Short Guide to the Economics of Capitalism*. London: Pluto Press.

Toda, H. Y., & Yamamoto, T. (1995). Statistical inferences in vector autoregressions with possibly integrated processes. *Journal of Econometrics*, 66, 225–250.

Weiner, S. E. (1993). New estimates of the natural rate of unemployment. *Economic Review (Vol. Fourth Quarter): Federal Reserve Bank of Kansas City* ,78(Q IV), 53–69.

Werner, A., & Lim, M. (2016). The ethics of the living wage: A review and research agenda. *Journal of Business Ethics*, 137(3), 433–447.

Yoshikawa, H. (1993). Monetary policy and the real economy in Japan. In K. J. Singleton (Ed.), *Japanese Monetary Policy*. London: University of Chicago Press.

8 An agenda for transformation

This book primarily aims to provide a roadmap to transformative and sustainable fiscal and monetary policies for creating a citizen-state. In order to be accessible to the policymaker, the contents comprise a summary of the intricate idiosyncrasies of developing countries in terms of state-building, the state–citizen relationship, productive capacity, equality and welfare, growth and employment, price and inflation, formal and informal institutions and political settlement. A thorough analysis of the incongruences between the necessary and sufficient conditions for transformation and growth is likely to aid the policymaker in devising economic policies that cater to the problems facing the economy using a comprehensive understanding of the institutions and political settlement required for an equalising citizen-state.

The colonial regimes in most developing countries gave rise to a political elite class that is extractive in nature. These extractive classes have dominated economic policymaking in developing countries and have often directed the machines of policymaking to their own benefit. Over the years, the continuation of such extraction has led to weaker institutions, both formal and informal. State formation in developing countries in terms of pre-colonial, colonial and post-colonial experiences has been demonstrated and analysed for these countries by highlighting the experiences of Bangladesh as a case study, coupled with a cross-country assessment of the experiences of East Asian, Latin American, African and some developed countries.

The chapters investigate the dynamics of economic policies, states and institutions and suggest necessary, sufficient and sustainability conditions for transformation in developing countries, particularly post-colonial states in Africa and Asia. The pandemic has fractured the pre-existing structural rigidities in these economies more than ever, necessitating a rethinking of fiscal and monetary policies—the main vehicles for relief, recovery and reconstruction. The economic downturn warrants the need for deliberately targeted interventions in the form of fiscal and monetary stimulus to resuscitate a withering economy. Broken and incoherent parts of the broader system have been left exposed—the fractures have revealed the pre- and post-COVID-19 fault lines by exhibiting the efficacy of the state in combating a crisis and the role of citizenship in tending to shortcomings in sociality. The situation is particularly dismal for

DOI: 10.4324/9781003201847-8

developing countries that are already marred by pre-existing deficiencies in policymaking and governance prior to the COVID-19 crisis, which have led to alienation between state and citizens over decades due to inherent failings in state formation and nation-building.

The discussions have attempted to unearth the structural rigidities and institutional fragilities thwarting the transformation of developing countries in the wake of the COVID-19 crisis. It has juxtaposed fiscal and monetary policies and state-building from pre- and post-colonial periods to the present-day pandemic context. The book addresses the neglect in the literature of the politico-economic experience of developing economies, from the standpoint of functioning institutions, state and citizenship, in a manner that meshes together political and economic elements. It proposed new frameworks, buttressed by strengthening state and citizen relationships in lieu of the extractive nature of political settlement, focusing on two conditions: necessary and sufficient conditions for transformation. Thus, the book arrives at a range of innovative economic policy options to meet the requirements of a transformative state, factoring in the exposed fundamental fragilities of institutions during the COVID-19 pandemic. Concurrently, the evidence and empirical findings presented the chapters necessitate the greater availability and credibility of data in forms that can be compared and extrapolated between countries—particularly monthly and quarterly data—which will aid in measuring indicators of public welfare over time.

State formation

The introductory chapter pinpoints the relationship between the nature of the state and consequential economic policies in developing countries, laying a suitable groundwork for the chapters to follow. The historical institutional analysis of pre- and post-colonial epochs, including the COVID-19 period, grids the transmission mechanisms of the realities between economic policymaking and the concentration of wealth and power and differential access to markets and resources. State formation in developing economies inherently has led to the creation of rentier classes whose primary goal is the accumulation of capital.

Policies, citizen and state

The second chapter makes an attempt to understand the cause-and-effect relations as well as transformational conditions of economic policies and the alienated citizen–state relationship. The discussion posits that transformational institutions are key to a functioning market and state. Against the backdrop of different schools of thought, the chapter comes up with an alternative diagnostic framework, which has intrinsic properties necessary to act as a theory of change. The framework introduced is concerned with state-building and economic policymaking, taking a historical institutionalism approach. It also questions the so-called apolitical approach of new-consensus, neoclassical/monetarists and public choice theorists and establishes that fiscal policy is an overtly political process by demonstrating how the decisions of state–citizens–firms are shaped by formal institutions, contingent upon the informal institutions of norms (informal codes) and values (reproduced by society).

State–citizen relationship

The third chapter ascertains the importance of fiscal policy in under-developed countries, delineating a different objective than that of advanced countries. Since fiscal policy involves a political process, the process of state-building in developing countries needs to be critically understood. The process of state-building largely depends on the capacity of the government to raise sufficient amounts of revenue and then to utilise them in an efficient manner. However, how taxation can be used to promote state-building has remained an under-studied area in the academic arena. For transformation, it suggests, the fiscal policy has to accelerate the rate of physical and human capital formation by expanding investment in public and private enterprises and by diverting resources from socially less desirable sectors to achieve full employment and equitable distribution of income and wealth. Amidst the COVID-19 crisis, the state–citizen relationship has been analysed on the basis of following state directives and the distribution of fiscal stimulus to the productive sectors in the economy.

Productive capacity

The fourth chapter demonstrates how productivity can be influenced by existing power relations, the role political settlement plays in this regard and how the endogeneity of politics affects the advancement of the whole process. Much of the literature predominantly falls within the realm of either the neoclassical growth theory or the new growth theory, and thus researchers have neglected to examine how the state, underwritten by appropriate political settlement, plays an active role in ensuring and maintaining high rates of investment and the shift to higher productivity-inducing technology acquisition, catching up and deepening. This chapter contributes to the debate and exhibits that productivity in factors of production—labour, capital and technology—are brought about through the endogeneity of political settlement or social property relationships and informal institutions, as understood in terms of the nature and distribution of power in a given society. It utilises instruments such as technology acquisition and organisational capabilities to determine the level of productivity contributed by the role of fiscal policy. In the time of COVID-19, developing countries may choose to use these instruments to boost productive economic sectors and induce an effective policy response to improve productivity.

Equalising policies

The fifth chapter provides a new framework for understanding inequality while being mindful of systemic escalating inequality arising out of low returns on labour vis-à-vis capital (permanent systemic inequality). Here, an elaborate theoretical distinction has been made between demand, want and need in support of each according to his ability to each according to his need, as opposed to the neoclassical theory of demand—the relationship between consumer demand for goods and services and their prices (being willing and able to buy at a given price in a given time period)—which is intrinsically inequalising. This chapter also demonstrates the factors needed for a welfare state in the trajectories of debates on the necessary and sufficient conditions for sustained and rapid improvement in living standards, exacerbated by the COVID-19 crisis. It looks into people's struggles and aspirations for equality, human dignity and social justice, and proposes a wide range of redistributive fiscal tools for translating those normative principles as a part of developmental needs and state-building.

Money and employment

The sixth chapter challenges the mainstream consensus of the money–inflation trade-off and the neutrality of money to present ways through which monetary policy exerts real effects on growth and employment in the long term. It then establishes additional channels through which monetary policy augurs credit to sectors that are crucial for long-term growth, employment creation and productivity augmentation. The chapter also analyses monetary policy in the context of developing countries during the economic downturn, which put the financial sector under major strain. Finally, it discusses the particular fiscal–monetary policy combinations (known as fiscal–monetary policy mixes) that can reinforce long-term stability. In order to recover from the economic slowdown due to the COVID-19 crisis, the chapter determines monetary policy aiming to ensure financial conditions are sufficiently accommodative to incentivise high-capital investments and deficit-financed spending. The transmissions under such a context are driven by variations in wage and employment outcomes in the real economy.

Price and inflation

The seventh chapter focuses primarily on the transmission mechanism of a sound monetary policy. The policy of central banks changed significantly in favour of solely focusing on price stability rather than taking a policy perspective centring on employment. The chapter argues that the dominant theories have major theoretical shortcomings and that these theories fail to clarify the inflation experience of developing states. It points out that structural and institutional weaknesses provide widespread opportunities for rent-seeking in the production and distribution process, leading to higher prices for consumers.

For this purpose, it exhibits how structural and institutional factors, both formal and informal, are linked to the inflationary process and how different objectives and instruments for monetary policies affect the situation. It discusses the possible cost of following a single-minded inflation-targeting objective and the consequences of a lack of multiple instruments and a weak institutional structure. The arguments are buttressed by an assessment of the use of monetary policy instruments in stabilising the money market and the subsequent effects on inflation during the COVID-19 crisis in developing countries. The chapter finally links fiscal policy to monetary policy and discusses what kind of fiscal rules are required to complement the monetary policy to achieve its purpose.

All the chapters, therefore, strive to offer an original conceptualisation in understanding the historical and current politico-economic scenarios, and suggest new transformational pathways, advancing virtuous cycles between households, firms and other intervening variables, for economic policymaking in developing countries. For the transformational pathway, the discussion in the chapters highlights the interrelationships between the necessary conditions for transformation (factors of production such as land, labour and capital, and their returns) and the sufficient conditions of state formation and citizenship, interjected with institutions, power and political settlement. It also undertakes dynamic analysis to study changes beyond the traditional comparative statics of two different outcomes. The book takes a new approach to studying economic policymaking through the use of institutions—formal and informal, past and present—to theorise the politico-economic structures in developing countries in order to comprehend the problems. These sufficient conditions are, then, linked with the circular flow in the economy—stocks and flows of households and firms. The cause-and-effect relationships and directionalities between the variables will allow for determining the drivers and triggers for transformational pathways.

The book demonstrates current debates on development, and to do so investigates the most rapidly growing countries of the world, the transitional states and the so-called "failed states" to find out determinants of acceleration or deceleration of the transition from low- to middle-income and to high-income status. State formation in developing countries inherently creates a rentier class that accumulates capital. This results in non-economic factors such as power structures influencing the economic outcomes of policies. Therefore, the new framework of state-building and economic policymaking in developing countries is based on the premise that transformational institutions are key to creating a functioning state and market that produce economic outcomes that are equitable and sustainable. It assesses the distributive effects of fiscal and monetary policies through the effectiveness of both formal and informal (norms and values) institutions. In addition, the discussion also entails an analysis of the resilience of developing countries before and during the COVID-19 crisis, highlighting the shock-absorption capacity of these economies.

In this final chapter, the discussion lays out the various aspects of monetary and fiscal policies in developing countries by conflating the outcomes of each chapter. The chapter integrates the propositions laid out in each chapter and summarises the relevant implications in constructing fiscal and monetary policies suited to the context of developing countries for their transformation, including those required for recovery and reconstruction after the COVID-19 pandemic–induced downturns, serving as a roadmap for the post-pandemic world.

State, citizen and fiscal policy

While studying the post-colonial states, major schools of thought have focused very little on the political economy aspect. The proposition of classical economics that "supply creates demand" does not work, and this is true not only for post-colonial developing economies but also for developed capitalist economies. The debt crisis faced by Africa largely pertains to its colonial legacies. Western countries have kept their ideology intact by electing rentier and powerful classes to the government. Colonial business corporations flourished in Africa by exploiting the low cost of labour and clientelist groups in power. A lack of property rights and the extractive nature of the government plunged the region into a deep financial crisis. Inept policymaking coupled with a global crisis resulted in huge debt accumulation by the poorest region of the world.

The main purpose of fiscal policy in a developing country is to accelerate the rate of capital formation and investment by expanding investments in public and private enterprises and by diverting resources from socially less desirable to more desirable sectors in the forms of full employment, price stability, equitable distribution of income and wealth, economic stability, capital formation and growth and investment generation. Since fiscal policy involves a political process, the process of state-building in developing countries needs to be critically understood. The process of state-building largely depends on the capacity of the government to raise sufficient revenue and then to utilise it in an efficient manner. The ability of governments to interact with society by means of fiscal policy to provide public goods and meet basic and other development needs are important components of state-building.

There exists a consensus that sustaining growth in poor countries is a challenge not only because the right economic policies have to be identified but also because those policies have to be buttressed by suitable governance capabilities for aggressive technological acquisition and productive expansion to take place. This book thus contributes to this debate and demonstrates that productivity in factors of production—labour and capital (technology induced)—are brought about through the endogeneity of political settlement or social property relationships as understood in terms of the nature and distribution of power in a given society.

Despite growing concerns about inequality, there is little consensus about how to fight it. Moreover, although almost all countries have embraced the welfare state concept in the post-war period, the objectives they have adopted remain non-uniform. This book argues for a new kind of welfare state in developing countries such as Bangladesh, one that has inequality at its core and a wide range of redistributive fiscal tools under policy options to meet the state-building as well as the developmental needs of a developing country. It is demonstrated that the welfare state as it is traditionally defined cannot solve the issue of inequality and welfare issues in a developing country like Bangladesh.

State, citizen and monetary policy

The dominant strand of literature follows the conception of the neutrality of money in terms of monetary policy in influencing long-term growth, employment and investment in the economy. The debate mainly involves whether an expansionary monetary policy does have an effect on growth or not. Existing theories about monetary policy mostly believe that monetary policy only has a limited impact on economic growth, especially in the long term. Moreover, it is supposed that such an impact can only be delivered through achieving a low-inflation economy. This book argues that as opposed to monetarist and those beliefs, monetary policy can be effectively used to shape the type and path of economic activity in the long term. It can initiate diversification and structural change in the economy, especially through the credit channel. Additionally, the policy of capital management increases the state-building ability of the government.

The book demonstrates that money-supply explanations for inflation do not hold in developing countries. Keynesian and new-Keynesian views of inflation do not provide a full explanation for the country's inflationary process. Additionally, class has a role to play in determining both supply and demand, thereby becoming a significant determiner of wage stickiness, which the neoclassical school fails to mention. Because of class, markets are not competitive. Also, for the same reason, rising wages are again less of a reason for inflation. Finally, structural issues are also present because of poor policies. In developing countries such as Bangladesh, where the informal sector is quite large, price stickiness is another problem. What is required is to include structural and institutional factors which, because of class and accumulation, affect the behaviour of the market, create inflation and impact the functioning of monetary policies. The presence of primitive accumulation, a growing informal economy, supply-side deficiencies and demand-side influences means that inflation in the country does not occur in accordance with any of the theories commonly preferred. Rather, inflation is a result of a combination of structural and institutional failures, aggravated by policy failures.

To be exact, some long-term measures are necessary to make economic improvement sustainable. In the developed and developing world, several countries have considered such aspects of strategic planning and policy implementation and have established social security schemes. The evidence indicates that these have played an essential role in keeping people out of extreme poverty and helping them to sustain themselves in the long run. The institutional mechanisms of these countries can be contextualised to enact laws, create organisations, devise policies and design an operational system for social security schemes. Such exercises are not a far-fetched task, given that the leadership is visionary and considers both short-term and long-term economic solutions.

The fundamental fragilities of institutions in the face of systemic shocks in turn have further compelled a search for appropriate fiscal and monetary policies, which can not only chart the course of recovery but also lead to a transformational pathway. Much of the literature on monetary and fiscal policies in the developing world have focused on policy directions and effectiveness in achieving the neoliberal agenda, largely rooted in neoclassical economics, public choice theories and the new public administration paradigm. The assumptions of such theories, including the current dominant modern monetary theory (MMT) in practice for the recovery in advanced economies from the pandemic-induced recession, have little relevance for developing countries. First, they mischaracterise the essence of the economic development challenge for low- and middle-income countries, which concerns structural transformation, i.e., the transition to an industrial economy, rather than general aggregate demand insufficiency in the developed world during the pandemic, which the MMT espouses to address. Second, there is a need not only to restore the economy to a post-COVID scenario but also to develop a sustained development pathway, which will require a concerted effort and a mix of both monetary and fiscal policy measures.

Institutions, policies and the agenda for transformation

The book questions the aptness of policies in the contexts of developing countries and proposes new frameworks by contextualising and rethinking economic policy dynamics to make them more suitable for the contexts of developing countries. It transcends the sphere of neoliberal approaches, which originated to cater to the needs of developed economies, to adopt a heterodox interdisciplinary dialogue along with a historical institutional analysis of state formation during the pre-colonial, colonial and post-colonial periods. Simultaneously, the discussion throughout the book highlights that economic policymaking is not solely an economic phenomenon—the process of formulating policies has a significant political element, which makes analyses based only on the aspect of economic variables insufficient. This is because non-economic factors such as power structures or informal codes of conduct have implications for economic outcomes.

The key concept of political settlement here is concerned with the process of harmonising the state and citizenship, and it is not limited to clientelism. Transformative institutions act as the countervailing power against the extractive process of the rentier state and the non-inclusive political settlement of dominant resource-dependent networks. As a result, these institutions transfer power from the intermediate classes, driven by capital accumulation, to the median-income citizen, thereby harmonising the state–citizen relationship. The circular flow between households and firms is composed of the factors of production and returns to capital and labour, along with the intervening variables of state and institutions. Therefore, empowering the position of the median-income citizen in this regard will integrate the circular flow between the households and firms as a virtuous cycle supported by the sufficient conditions of strong formal and informal institutions. Throughout the chapters, the frameworks for necessary and sufficient conditions highlight the key intervening variables in the circular flow between households and firms.

The role of fiscal policy in the state should be directed at expanding productive capacity. This is achievable through a strong industrial policy, targeted productive rents, aggressive technology acquisition and institutional capabilities to oversee and ensure a transformative trajectory. Firms will be responsible for aggressive technology acquisition that leads to capital formation in such a way that it contributes to the enhancement of the skill formation of the workforce, and is not accumulated by resource-dependent networks. Moreover, diversification in production is likely to lead to investments in new industries or sectors. Investment in these sectors will require initial large-scale technology acquisition, which will significantly increase capital formation in the economy. New capital formation or accumulation, along with the expansion of new sectors, will subsequently demand the formation of new skills, thus increasing the productive capacity in the economy. This triggers the other necessary conditions, as skill formation will enhance human capital, and adoption of new technologies is likely to improve competitiveness. The state should devise a strong industrial policy geared towards specific sectors and designed to catalyse the process of active technology acquisition. Institutions safeguard productive rents for firms to undertake expansion of productive capacity, and accordingly, the institutional capability or strength will determine the efficacy of these rents. This is particularly important if a demographic dividend exists in the economy, in order to harness the maximum productive capacity of the economy. A demographic dividend refers to a shift in the age structure such that the proportion of working people in the population is high, thereby denoting higher productive capacity if utilised. Simultaneously, technology acquisition and productive rents should be more geared towards cottage, micro, small and medium enterprises, primarily in the manufacturing industry, in order to facilitate diversification in production and the faster generation of employment. Small enterprises are also generally more adept in undertaking digital transformation owing to more flexible decision-making and implementation processes.

Equalising policies consist of the interaction between household and government in a market system. Institutions, both formal and informal, influence this interaction. The state, with the help of formal institutions, internalises the externalities created by the market system. The distribution of power within the government determines the level of public goods provision. A citizen-state is directed by the idea of providing public goods to its citizens. In order to achieve greater equality, the state should therefore focus on the provision of goods such as skill formation, innovation, employment, healthcare and universal social security for all. Instead of a direct cash transfer from the rich to the poor, redistribution can be achieved through public provisioning of these goods in a manner that ensures the capability enhancement of citizens. The provision of education for all serves as an example of the means to enhance the capability of citizens, particularly through skill formation, citizenship education and agency for all. Such policies may also include protection of workers; rights, human dignity and social justice, along with determining norms such as the need to respect all types of work equally. Equalising policies are indispensable to cater to the needs of the sections of the population that are disproportionately affected by politico-economic setbacks—women, children, youth, the elderly and persons with disabilities—which has been made more evident by the consequences of COVID-19.

The transmission of monetary policy to create employment and growth is dependent on the virtuous cycle leading from lowering interest rates to productive expansion and capacity utilisation, which eventually results in a rise in effective demand, creating new employment opportunities. Apart from the inflation-targeting strategy, the employment-targeting strategy for monetary policy addresses the links between institutions in the money market and the central bank that governs the transmission mechanism of money, leading to a virtuous or vicious cycle. Monetary policy induces growth through capital formation and productive expansion of the economy by technology financing. The increased amount of capital formation results in more investment in technological acquisition and productivity growth, which leads to higher growth performance of the economy. Regulations limit loan defaulting and the outflow of capital abroad and thus lead to higher private investment in the economy. The strict enforcement of rules and regulations reduces the possibility of risk in the financial sector. Checking capital flight and loan defaulting leads to more investment in the economy, which results in productive expansion and new employment creation.

In the growing stage of an economy, price stability and further acceleration of the economy may be ensured through an increase in real wages resulting from the productive expansion of the economy and employment. New employment opportunities and increases in the real wage of labour can limit the instability in the price level that is determined largely by the political settlement for primitive accumulation in developing countries, instead of free market forces. Productive expansion of the economy, on the other hand, leads to creation of new employment, resulting in an increase in the real wage of labour. Increasing returns for labour are thus more likely to aid the equalising policies of redistribution, and thereby decrease the price instability caused by mismatched power relations. In terms of a higher real wage, remittances may also play a crucial role in expanding growth through raising demand and consumption, and could significantly offset the negative consequences of primitive accumulation. Structural and institutional weaknesses provide widespread opportunities for rent-seeking in the production and distribution process, leading to higher prices for consumers. The association between rent-seeking and structural and institutional weakness implies that a weak institutional and structural setting is responsible for rent-seeking and primitive accumulation. The distribution of power, strong and effective institutions and the enforcement of rules and regulations can significantly check rent-seeking behaviour in the economy.

Finally, fiscal and monetary policymaking in developing countries will serve to be transformative once it recognises the vitality of living in harmony with nature and promotes human–nature sociality. For countries with climate risk, policies must address the vulnerabilities of populations to climate shocks and embolden the shock-absorption capacity to build resilience for these populations. Beyond climate vulnerabilities, prudent management of coastal and marine ecosystems and water resources will account for future productive capacity, welfare and human sociality with nature, leading to a sustainable, transformative trajectory of development. In addition, policies addressing biodiversity will lead to protection of indigenous livelihoods of farmers, fishermen and other resource users; a reduction in climate migration, thereby improving the sustainability of urban cities and livelihoods; and the improvement of health by curbing the use of harmful chemicals and other pollutants in agriculture as well as promoting clean and green energy, nature-based solutions and sustainable production and consumption. Therefore, by living in harmony with nature along with upholding human dignity and social justice for all, while ensuring productive expansion and creation of employment for the citizenry, a developing country will be likely to embark on a trajectory of development that reaches the individual at the last mile and enriches the state–citizen relationship looking forward.

Index

Note: Page locators in italics refer to figures.